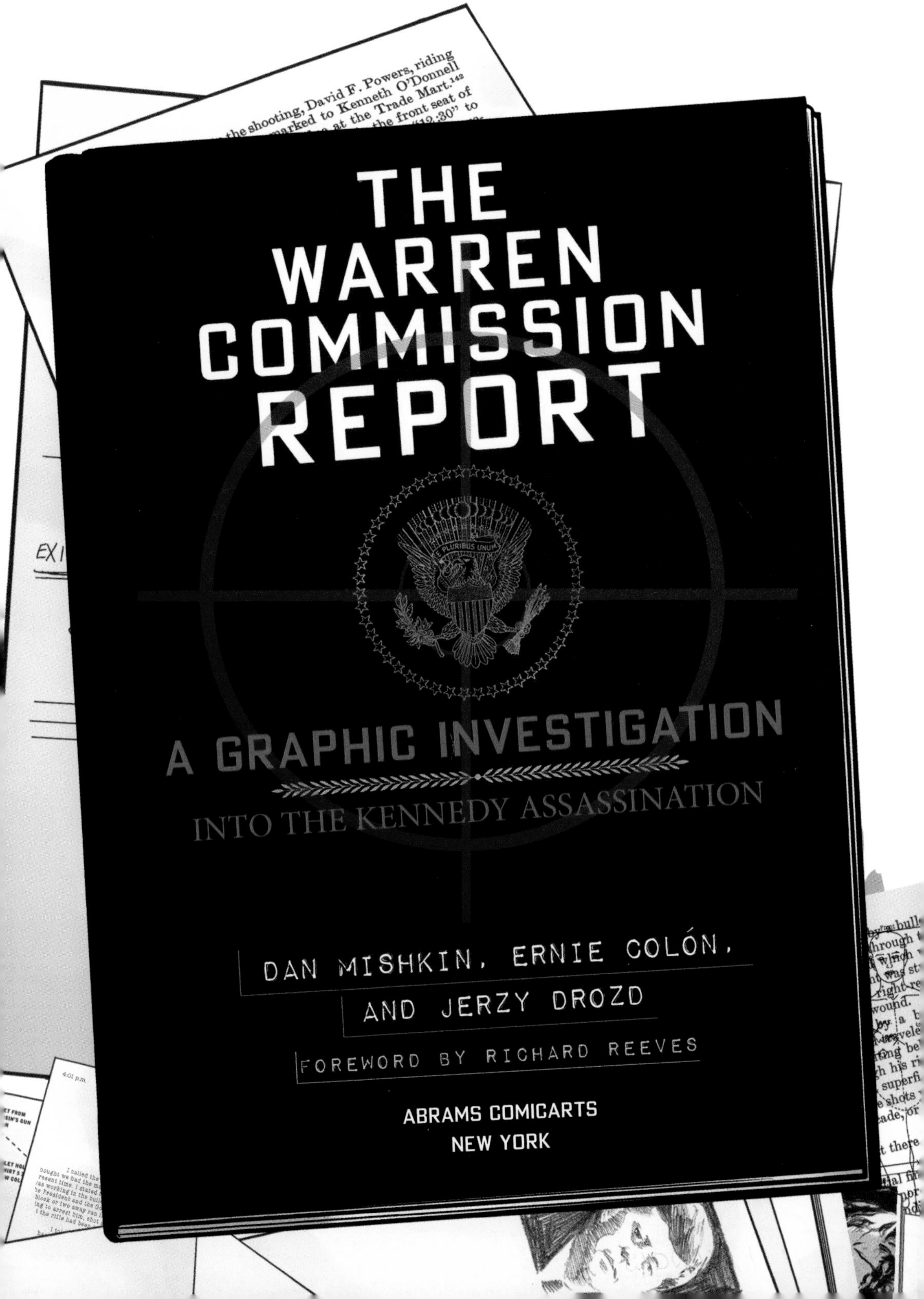

THE WARREN COMMISSION REPORT

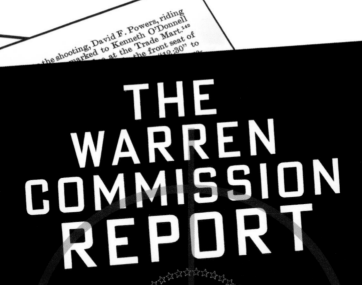

A GRAPHIC INVESTIGATION

INTO THE KENNEDY ASSASSINATION

DAN MISHKIN, ERNIE COLÓN,
AND JERZY DROZD

FOREWORD BY RICHARD REEVES

ABRAMS COMICARTS
NEW YORK

DIRECT QUOTES FROM THE *REPORT OF THE PRESIDENT'S COMMISSION ON THE ASSASSINATION OF PRESIDENT JOHN F. KENNEDY* ARE PRESENTED IN YELLOW CAPTION BOXES. IN SOME CASES TEXT HAS BEEN CONDENSED FOR BREVITY.

EDITOR: CAROL M. BURRELL
DESIGNERS: KATE FITCH AND MEAGAN BENNETT
MANAGING EDITOR: JEN GRAHAM
PRODUCTION MANAGER: ALISON GERVAIS

LIBRARY OF CONGRESS CATALOGING-IN-PUBLICATION DATA
MISHKIN, DANIEL.
THE WARREN COMMISSION REPORT : A GRAPHIC INVESTIGATION INTO THE KENNEDY ASSASSINATION / BY DAN MISHKIN, ERNIE COLÓN, AND JERZY DROZD.
PAGES CM.
ISBN 978-1-4197-1230-2 (HARDCOVER) — ISBN 978-1-4197-1231-9 (PBK.)
1. KENNEDY, JOHN F. (JOHN FITZGERALD), 1917-1963—ASSASSINATION—JUVENILE LITERATURE. 2. KENNEDY, JOHN F. (JOHN FITZGERALD), 1917-1963—ASSASSINATION—COMIC BOOKS, STRIPS, ETC. 3. UNITED STATES. WARREN COMMISSION—JUVENILE LITERATURE. 4. UNITED STATES. WARREN COMMISSION—COMIC BOOKS, STRIPS, ETC. 5. GRAPHIC NOVELS. I. COLÓN, ERNIE. II. DROZD, JERZY. III. TITLE.
E842.9.M55 2014
364.15'240973—DC23
2014011915

HARDCOVER ISBN: 978-1-4197-1230-2
PAPERBACK ISBN: 978-1-4197-1231-9

PRINTED AND BOUND IN U.S.A.
10 9 8 7 6 5 4 3 2 1

ABRAMS COMICARTS BOOKS ARE AVAILABLE AT SPECIAL DISCOUNTS WHEN PURCHASED IN QUANTITY FOR PREMIUMS AND PROMOTIONS AS WELL AS FUNDRAISING OR EDUCATIONAL USE. SPECIAL EDITIONS CAN ALSO BE CREATED TO SPECIFICATION. FOR DETAILS, CONTACT SPECIALSALES@ABRAMSBOOKS.COM OR THE ADDRESS BELOW.

ABRAMS
THE ART OF BOOKS SINCE 1949
115 WEST 18TH STREET
NEW YORK, NY 10011
WWW.ABRAMSBOOKS.COM

All this will not be finished in the first one hundred days. Nor will it be finished in the first one thousand days, nor in the life of this Administration, nor even perhaps in our lifetime on this planet. But let us begin.

—John F. Kennedy, Inaugural Address, January 20, 1961

CONTENTS

>>>>>>>>>>>>>>>>>>>>>>>>>•<<<<<<<<<<<<<<<<<<<<<

FOREWORD

⇢⇢⇢⇢⇢⇢⇢⇢⇢⇢⇢⇢ ⬗ ⬖ ⬖⬖⬖⬖⬖⬖⬖⬖⬖⬖⬖⬖

I have written thousands of pages on the presidency of John F. Kennedy and read hundreds of thousands of pages by others on our thirty-fifth president, but I never expected to read a comic book about the man, his tragic assassination, and the controversy that has engulfed that murder most foul.

The Warren Commission Report: A Graphic Investigation into the Kennedy Assassination, by Dan Mishkin, Ernie Colón, and Jerzy Drozd, is not comic at all. The writer and two artists have produced an intelligent, fair, and provocative—and very accessible—study of the government investigation of the death of a president.

I ended my book *President Kennedy: Profile of Power* at that sad day in Dallas, November 22, 1963. I did that for a reason: I did not know much about the mystery of the assassination and the many debates, serious and foolish, that have followed over the past fifty years. I know more after reading this book. This book did not, however, change my opinion that the Warren Commission—political, rushed, flawed, and sometimes incorporating official dishonesty—was right on its main point: that a lone gunman named Lee Harvey Oswald killed John F. Kennedy, and if there was a conspiracy, it was in Oswald's own sick head.

Mishkin and his co-creators, in fact, do a very good, compressed job of showing why conspiracy theories were inevitable. Like any journalist, I have spent hours, days, and weeks questioning witnesses to traumatic events and then listening to them contradict one another, and common sense, in courtrooms around the country. There may be such a thing as a perfect murder, but I have never encountered a perfect witness or trial. We are all the same under such stress, and our eyes and minds often trick us. I never thought the Kennedy assassination, except in scale, sowed any more confusion than other murders—although obviously, every move and thought was heightened by the importance of the victim of this one.

Then there were the many, many people who had their own ideological agendas and tried to fit the murder into their geopolitical thinking. Others were trying to make a buck in a society that was becoming more and more suspicious of "official versions." One point well made in this book is that the official report itself became part of a pattern or a symbol of government secrecy and lying in a nation that was becoming more polarized, perhaps more paranoid.

My own feeling, then and now, is that, in a way, Kennedy was responsible for his own death. With his brother, attorney general Robert Kennedy, and the Central Intelligence Agency, President Kennedy created a culture of assassination, particularly in attempts to kill Fidel Castro of Cuba. In our arrogance, we thought such a thing could never happen to a modern American leader. Sooner or later, though, some very marginal people were going to be pulled into that vortex—and Oswald was one of them.

Am I right about that? I don't know, but this "comic book" has me thinking about all that again. It is a worthwhile piece of work, and it ends with a sure conclusion—embodied in its final page in the response given by senator Richard Russell of Georgia, a member of the Warren Commission, when asked by a reporter, "Are you glad it's over?" Read on to discover the perceptiveness of his reply.

—Richard Reeves

Richard Reeves is the senior lecturer at the Annenberg School for Communication and Journalism at the University of Southern California and the author of *President Kennedy: Profile of Power, The Kennedy Years: From the Pages of the New York Times,* and *Portrait of Camelot: A Thousand Days in the Kennedy White House.*

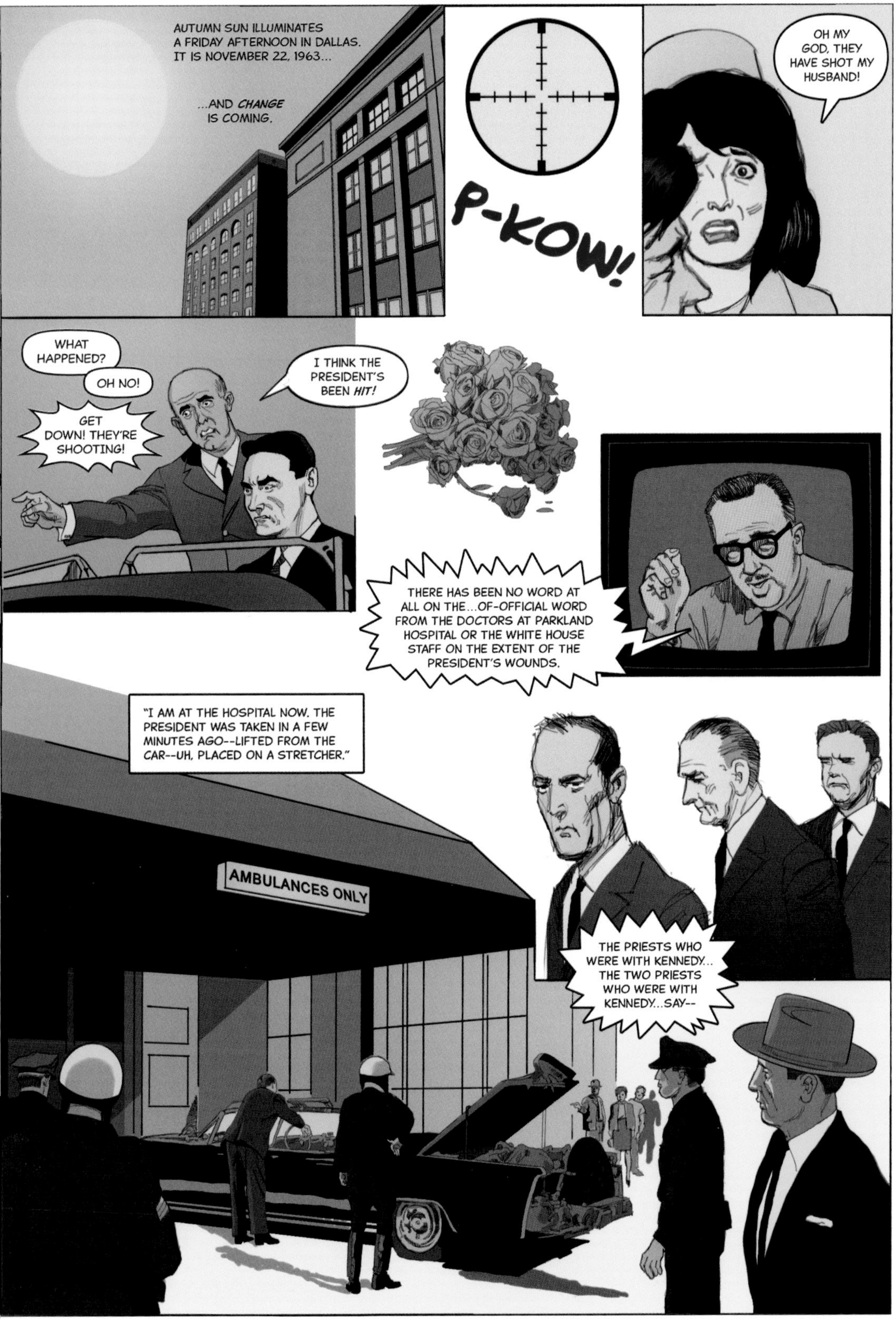
AUTUMN SUN ILLUMINATES A FRIDAY AFTERNOON IN DALLAS. IT IS NOVEMBER 22, 1963...
...AND CHANGE IS COMING.
P-KOW!
OH MY GOD, THEY HAVE SHOT MY HUSBAND!
WHAT HAPPENED?
OH NO!
GET DOWN! THEY'RE SHOOTING!
I THINK THE PRESIDENT'S BEEN HIT!
THERE HAS BEEN NO WORD AT ALL ON THE...OF-OFFICIAL WORD FROM THE DOCTORS AT PARKLAND HOSPITAL OR THE WHITE HOUSE STAFF ON THE EXTENT OF THE PRESIDENT'S WOUNDS.
"I AM AT THE HOSPITAL NOW. THE PRESIDENT WAS TAKEN IN A FEW MINUTES AGO--LIFTED FROM THE CAR--UH, PLACED ON A STRETCHER."
AMBULANCES ONLY
THE PRIESTS WHO WERE WITH KENNEDY... THE TWO PRIESTS WHO WERE WITH KENNEDY...SAY--

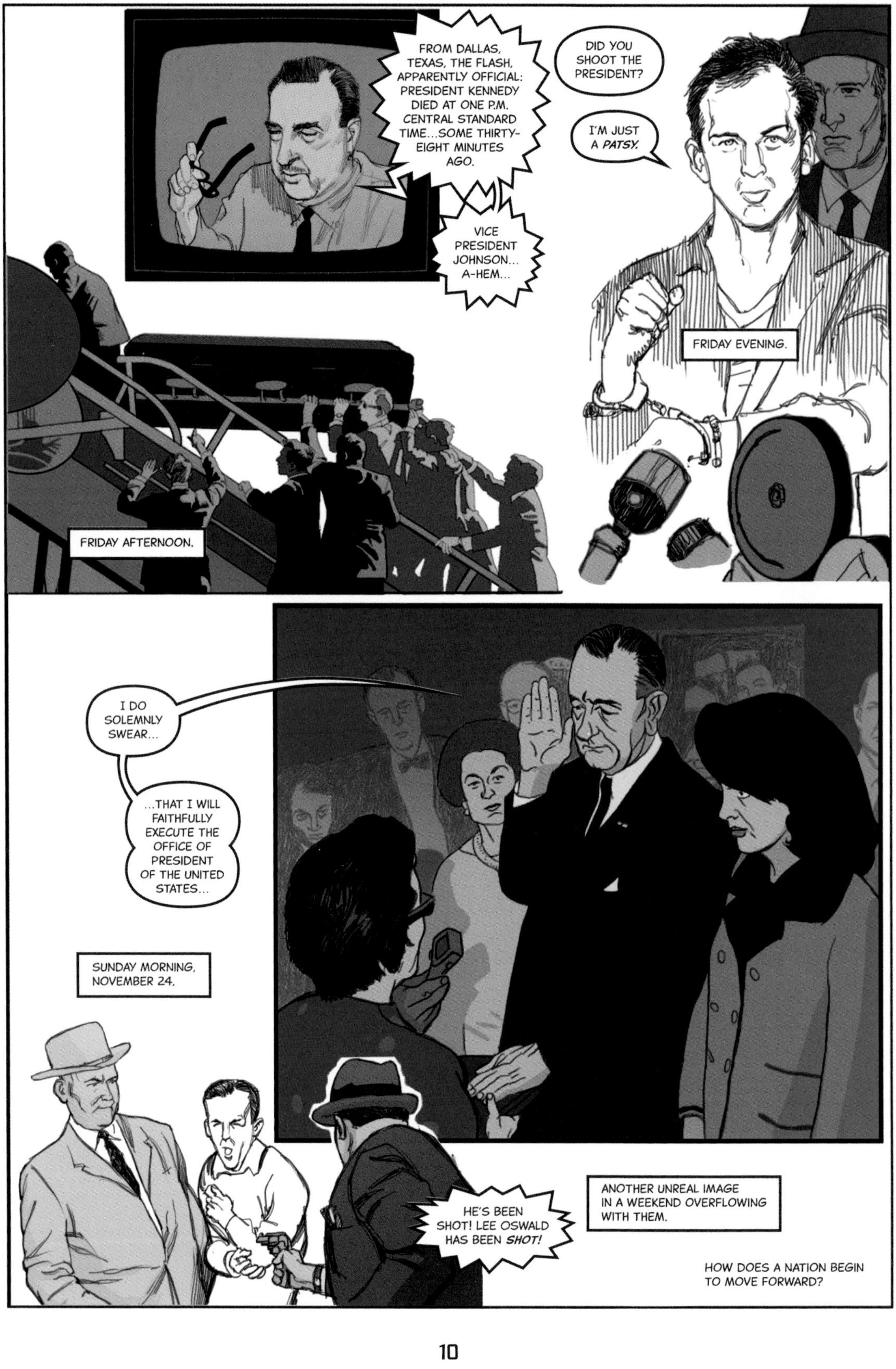
FROM DALLAS, TEXAS, THE FLASH, APPARENTLY OFFICIAL: PRESIDENT KENNEDY DIED AT ONE P.M. CENTRAL STANDARD TIME...SOME THIRTY-EIGHT MINUTES AGO.
VICE PRESIDENT JOHNSON... A-HEM...
FRIDAY AFTERNOON.
DID YOU SHOOT THE PRESIDENT?
I'M JUST A PATSY.
FRIDAY EVENING.
I DO SOLEMNLY SWEAR...
...THAT I WILL FAITHFULLY EXECUTE THE OFFICE OF PRESIDENT OF THE UNITED STATES...
SUNDAY MORNING, NOVEMBER 24.
HE'S BEEN SHOT! LEE OSWALD HAS BEEN SHOT!
ANOTHER UNREAL IMAGE IN A WEEKEND OVERFLOWING WITH THEM.
HOW DOES A NATION BEGIN TO MOVE FORWARD?

FRIDAY. ANDREWS AIR FORCE BASE IN MARYLAND. THE NEW PRESIDENT MAKES HIS FIRST PUBLIC STATEMENT.

I WILL DO MY BEST. THAT IS ALL I *CAN* DO.

I ASK FOR YOUR HELP. AND GOD'S.

FOLLOWING THE FUNERAL ON MONDAY, THE WHITE HOUSE ANNOUNCES THAT "THE PEOPLE OF THE NATION MAY BE SURE THAT ALL THE FACTS WILL BE MADE PUBLIC."

AND ONE WEEK AFTER THE ASSASSINATION...

EXECUTIVE ORDER 11130 OF NOVEMBER 29, 1963

APPOINTING A COMMISSION TO REPORT UPON THE ASSASSINATION OF PRESIDENT JOHN F. KENNEDY

...TO EVALUATE ALL THE FACTS AND CIRCUMSTANCES SURROUNDING SUCH ASSASSINATION, INCLUDING THE SUBSEQUENT VIOLENT DEATH OF THE MAN CHARGED WITH THE ASSASSINATION--

--AND TO REPORT TO ME ITS FINDINGS AND CONCLUSIONS.

THE COMMISSION SHALL CONSIST OF--

EARL WARREN

THE CHIEF JUSTICE OF THE UNITED STATES, CHAIRMAN

CONGRESSMAN GERALD R. FORD

SENATOR RICHARD B. RUSSELL

SENATOR JOHN COOPER

THE HONORABLE JOHN J. McCLOY

CONGRESSMAN HALE BOGGS

THE HONORABLE ALLEN W. DULLES

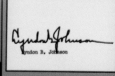

Lyndon B. Johnson

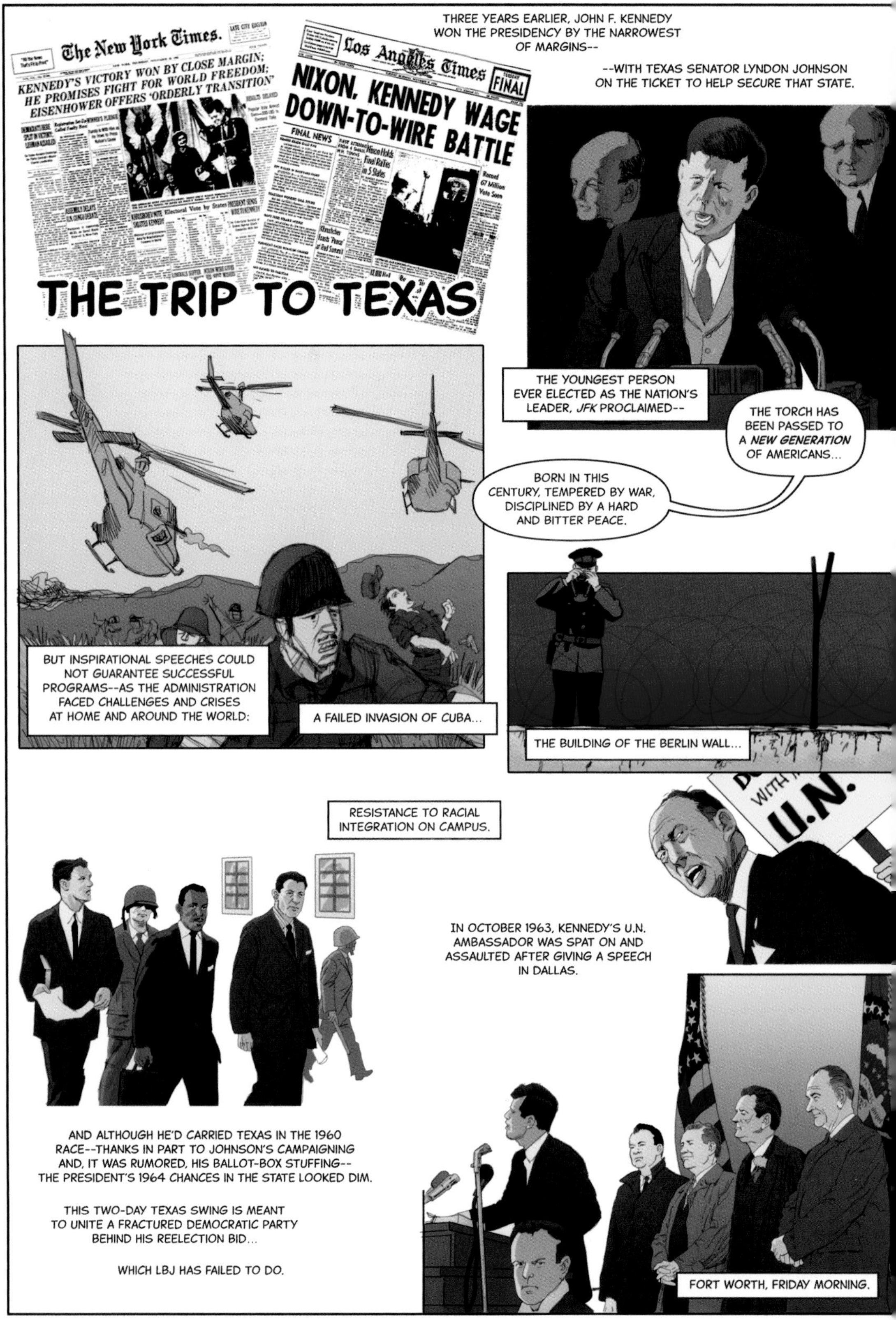
The New York Times.
KENNEDY'S VICTORY WON BY CLOSE MARGIN; HE PROMISES FIGHT FOR WORLD FREEDOM; EISENHOWER OFFERS 'ORDERLY TRANSITION'
Los Angeles Times
FINAL
NIXON, KENNEDY WAGE DOWN-TO-WIRE BATTLE
THE TRIP TO TEXAS
THREE YEARS EARLIER, JOHN F. KENNEDY WON THE PRESIDENCY BY THE NARROWEST OF MARGINS--
--WITH TEXAS SENATOR LYNDON JOHNSON ON THE TICKET TO HELP SECURE THAT STATE.
THE YOUNGEST PERSON EVER ELECTED AS THE NATION'S LEADER, *JFK* PROCLAIMED--
THE TORCH HAS BEEN PASSED TO A ***NEW GENERATION*** OF AMERICANS...
BORN IN THIS CENTURY, TEMPERED BY WAR, DISCIPLINED BY A HARD AND BITTER PEACE.
BUT INSPIRATIONAL SPEECHES COULD NOT GUARANTEE SUCCESSFUL PROGRAMS--AS THE ADMINISTRATION FACED CHALLENGES AND CRISES AT HOME AND AROUND THE WORLD:
A FAILED INVASION OF CUBA...
THE BUILDING OF THE BERLIN WALL...
RESISTANCE TO RACIAL INTEGRATION ON CAMPUS.
U.N.
IN OCTOBER 1963, KENNEDY'S U.N. AMBASSADOR WAS SPAT ON AND ASSAULTED AFTER GIVING A SPEECH IN DALLAS.
AND ALTHOUGH HE'D CARRIED TEXAS IN THE 1960 RACE--THANKS IN PART TO JOHNSON'S CAMPAIGNING AND, IT WAS RUMORED, HIS BALLOT-BOX STUFFING--THE PRESIDENT'S 1964 CHANCES IN THE STATE LOOKED DIM.
THIS TWO-DAY TEXAS SWING IS MEANT TO UNITE A FRACTURED DEMOCRATIC PARTY BEHIND HIS REELECTION BID...
WHICH LBJ HAS FAILED TO DO.
FORT WORTH, FRIDAY MORNING.

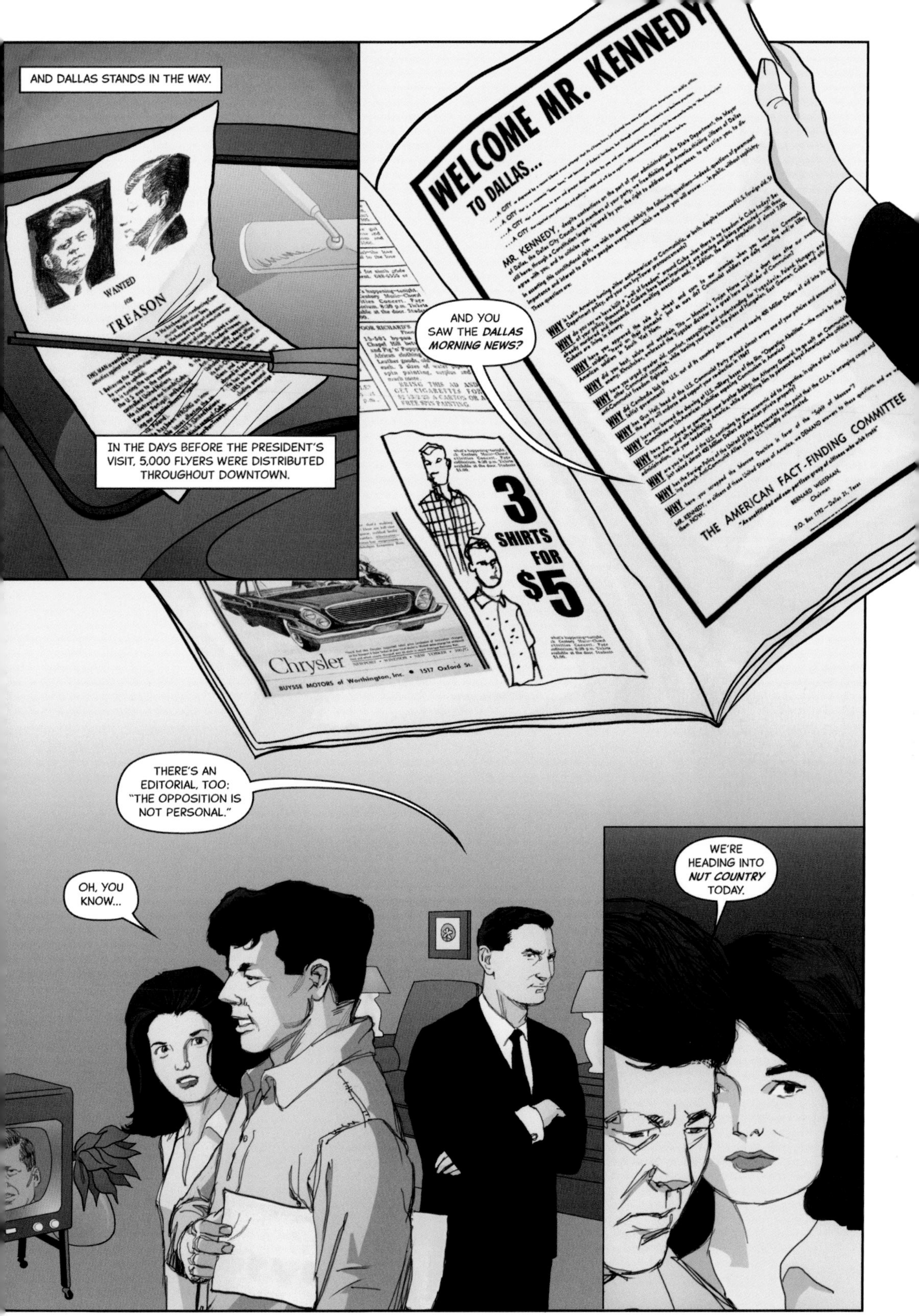

AND DALLAS STANDS IN THE WAY.
WANTED FOR TREASON
IN THE DAYS BEFORE THE PRESIDENT'S VISIT, 5,000 FLYERS WERE DISTRIBUTED THROUGHOUT DOWNTOWN.
WELCOME MR. KENNEDY TO DALLAS...
AND YOU SAW THE *DALLAS MORNING NEWS?*
THE AMERICAN FACT-FINDING COMMITTEE
3 SHIRTS FOR $5
Chrysler
BUYSSE MOTORS of Worthington, Inc. • 1517 Oxford St.
THERE'S AN EDITORIAL, TOO: "THE OPPOSITION IS NOT PERSONAL."
OH, YOU KNOW...
WE'RE HEADING INTO *NUT COUNTRY* TODAY.

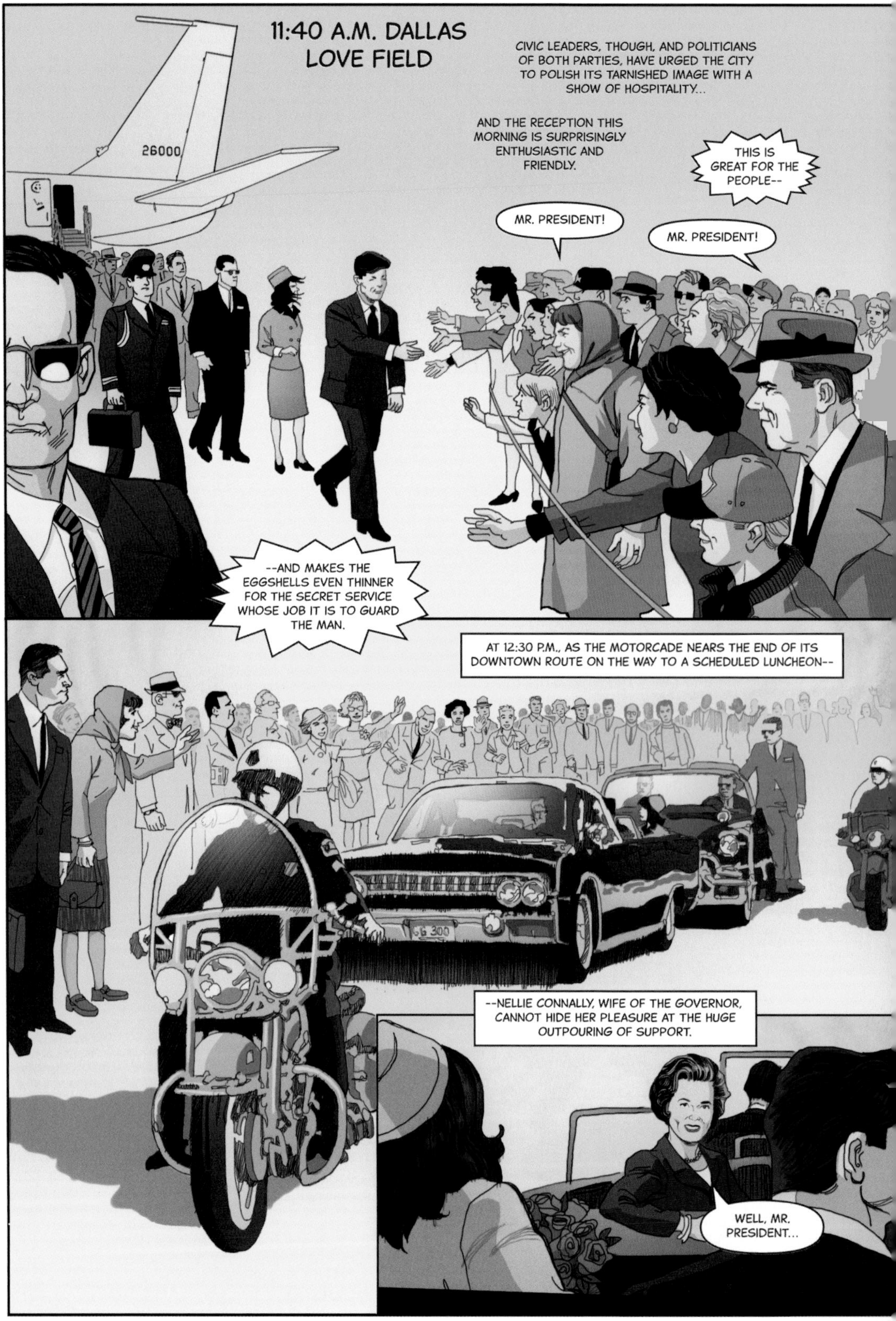
11:40 A.M. DALLAS LOVE FIELD
CIVIC LEADERS, THOUGH, AND POLITICIANS OF BOTH PARTIES, HAVE URGED THE CITY TO POLISH ITS TARNISHED IMAGE WITH A SHOW OF HOSPITALITY...
AND THE RECEPTION THIS MORNING IS SURPRISINGLY ENTHUSIASTIC AND FRIENDLY.
THIS IS GREAT FOR THE PEOPLE--
MR. PRESIDENT!
MR. PRESIDENT!
26000
--AND MAKES THE EGGSHELLS EVEN THINNER FOR THE SECRET SERVICE WHOSE JOB IT IS TO GUARD THE MAN.
AT 12:30 P.M., AS THE MOTORCADE NEARS THE END OF ITS DOWNTOWN ROUTE ON THE WAY TO A SCHEDULED LUNCHEON--
--NELLIE CONNALLY, WIFE OF THE GOVERNOR, CANNOT HIDE HER PLEASURE AT THE HUGE OUTPOURING OF SUPPORT.
WELL, MR. PRESIDENT...

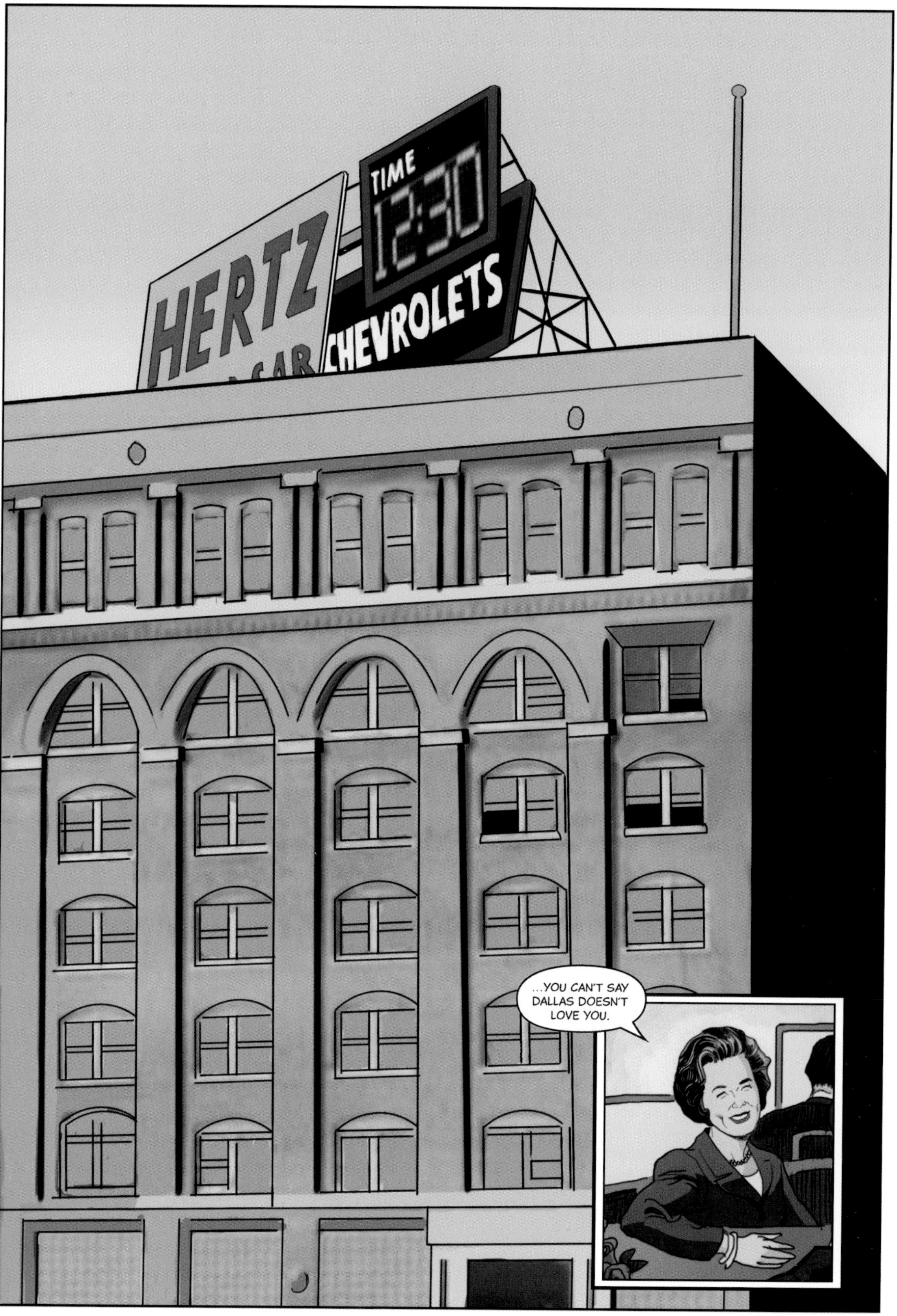
HERTZ
TIME
12:30
CHEVROLETS
...YOU CAN'T SAY DALLAS DOESN'T LOVE YOU.

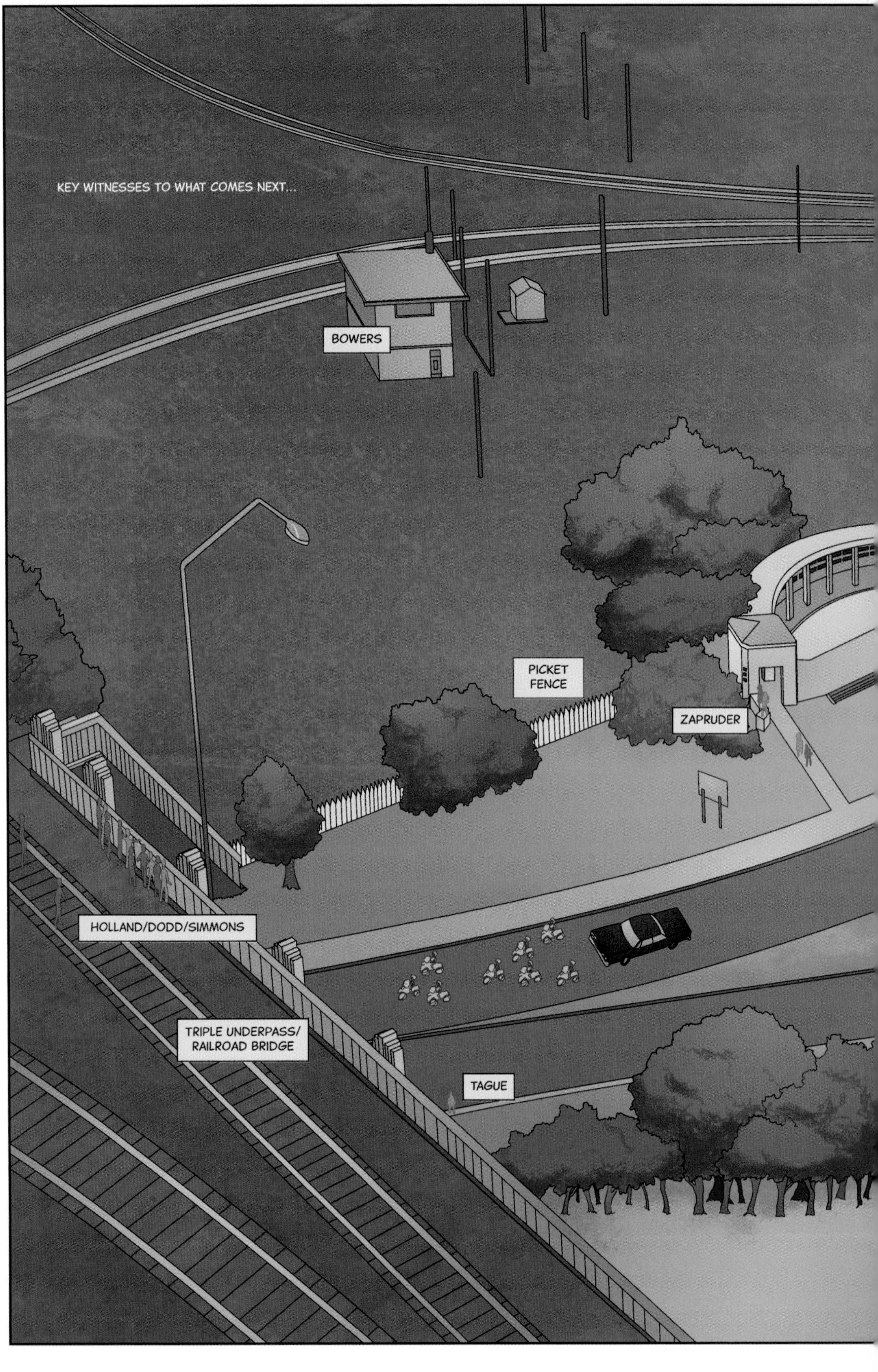
KEY WITNESSES TO WHAT COMES NEXT...
BOWERS
PICKET FENCE
ZAPRUDER
HOLLAND/DODD/SIMMONS
TRIPLE UNDERPASS/
RAILROAD BRIDGE
TAGUE

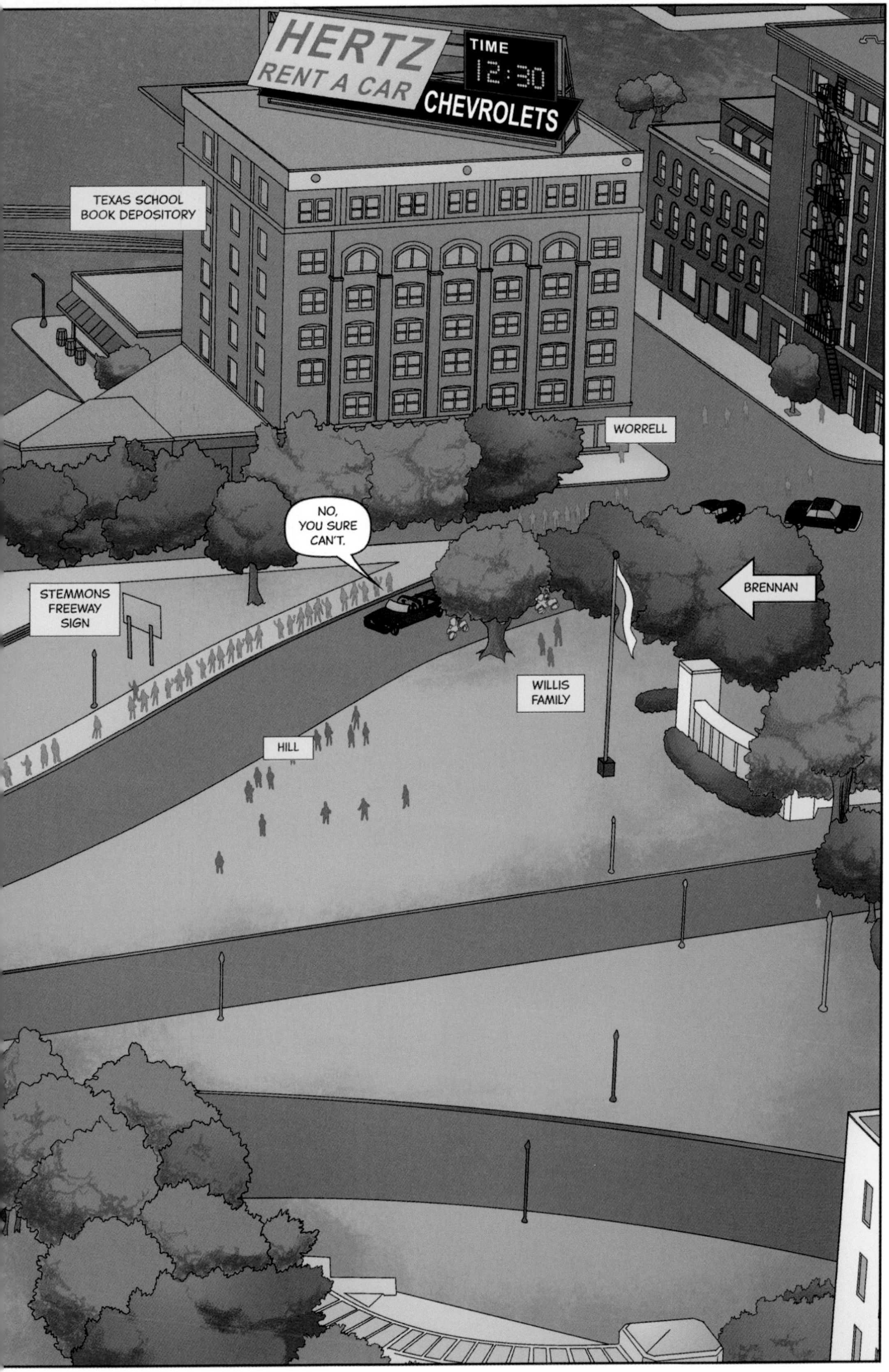
HERTZ
RENT A CAR
TIME
12:30
CHEVROLETS
TEXAS SCHOOL BOOK DEPOSITORY
WORRELL
NO, YOU SURE CAN'T.
STEMMONS FREEWAY SIGN
BRENNAN
WILLIS FAMILY
HILL

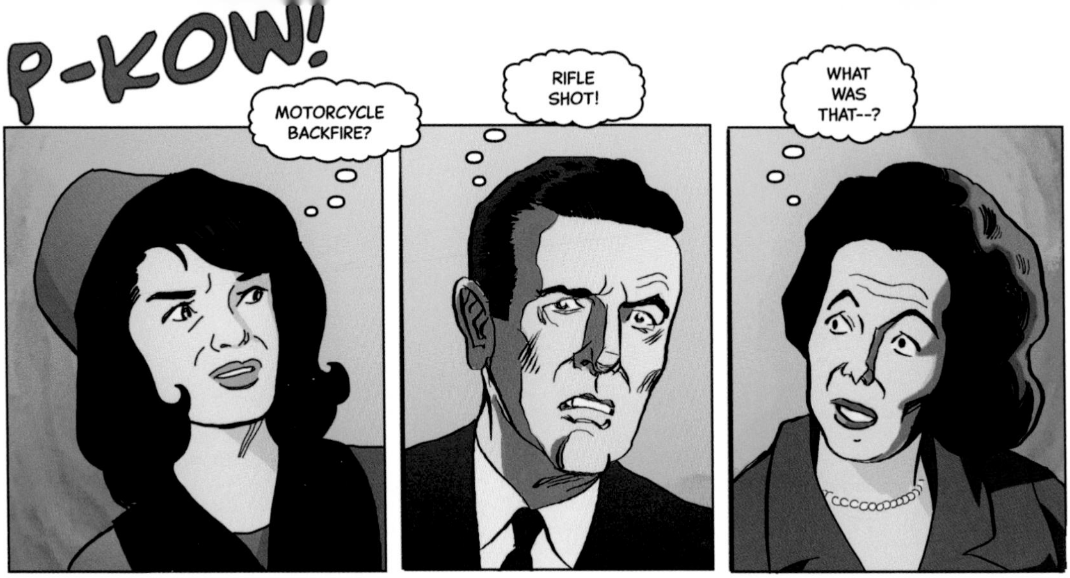
P-KOW!
MOTORCYCLE BACKFIRE?
RIFLE SHOT!
WHAT WAS THAT--?

THE *WARREN COMMISSION REPORT* DESCRIBES MUCH OF WHAT COMES NEXT IN MINUTE DETAIL...

THE EXACT TIME OF THE ASSASSINATION WAS FIXED BY THE TESTIMONY OF FOUR WITNESSES.

WILLIAM GREER, OPERATOR OF THE PRESIDENTIAL LIMOUSINE, ESTIMATED THE CAR'S SPEED AT THE TIME OF THE FIRST SHOT AS 12 TO 15 MILES PER HOUR.

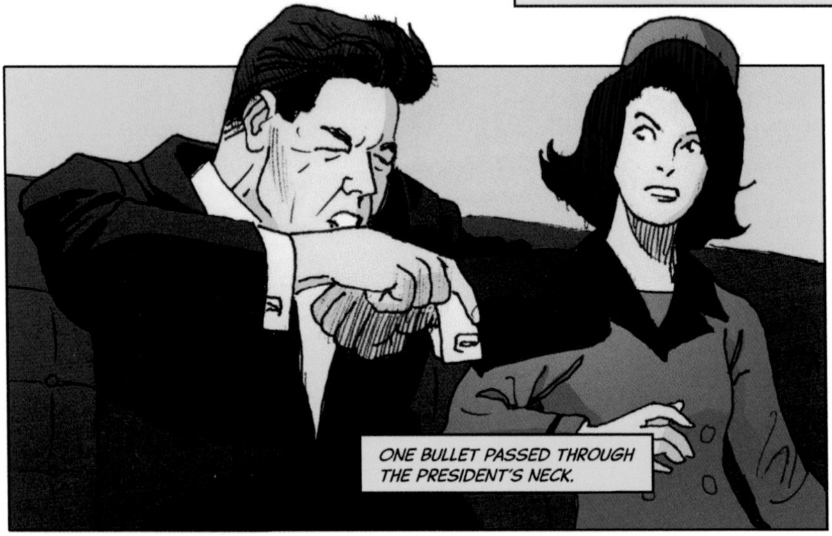
ONE BULLET PASSED THROUGH THE PRESIDENT'S NECK.

THE BULLET TRAVELED THROUGH [THE GOVERNOR'S] *CHEST IN A DOWNWARD AND FORWARD DIRECTION*

EXITED BELOW HIS RIGHT NIPPLE

PASSED THROUGH HIS RIGHT WRIST WHICH HAD BEEN IN HIS LAP

AND THEN CAUSED A WOUND TO HIS LEFT THIGH.

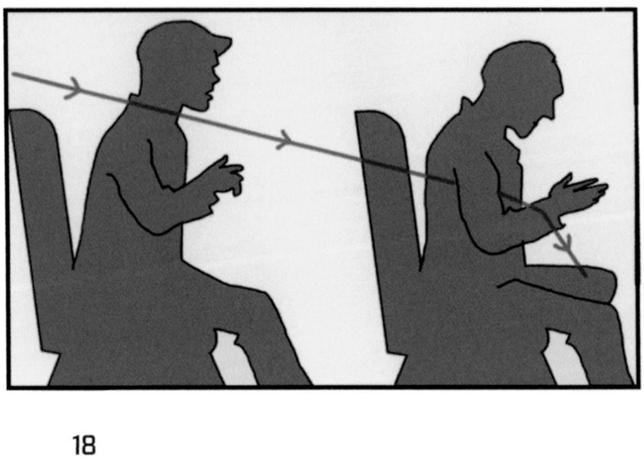

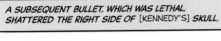

P-KOW!

A SUBSEQUENT BULLET, WHICH WAS LETHAL, SHATTERED THE RIGHT SIDE OF [KENNEDY'S] SKULL.

GET US OUT OF HERE *FAST!*

WHAT ARE THEY DOING TO YOU!

MRS. KENNEDY WOULD PROBABLY HAVE FALLEN OFF THE REAR END OF THE CAR AND BEEN KILLED IF [AGENT CLINT] HILL HAD NOT PUSHED HER BACK INTO THE PRESIDENTIAL AUTOMOBILE.

MRS. KENNEDY HAD JUMPED UP FROM THE SEAT AND WAS, IT APPEARED TO ME, REACHING FOR SOMETHING.

LIKELY A FRAGMENT OF HER HUSBAND'S SKULL.

SHE TURNED TOWARD ME AND I *GRABBED* HER AND PUT HER BACK IN THE BACKSEAT.

APPROXIMATELY TWELVE SECONDS HAVE PASSED SINCE THE FIRST SHOT RANG OUT.

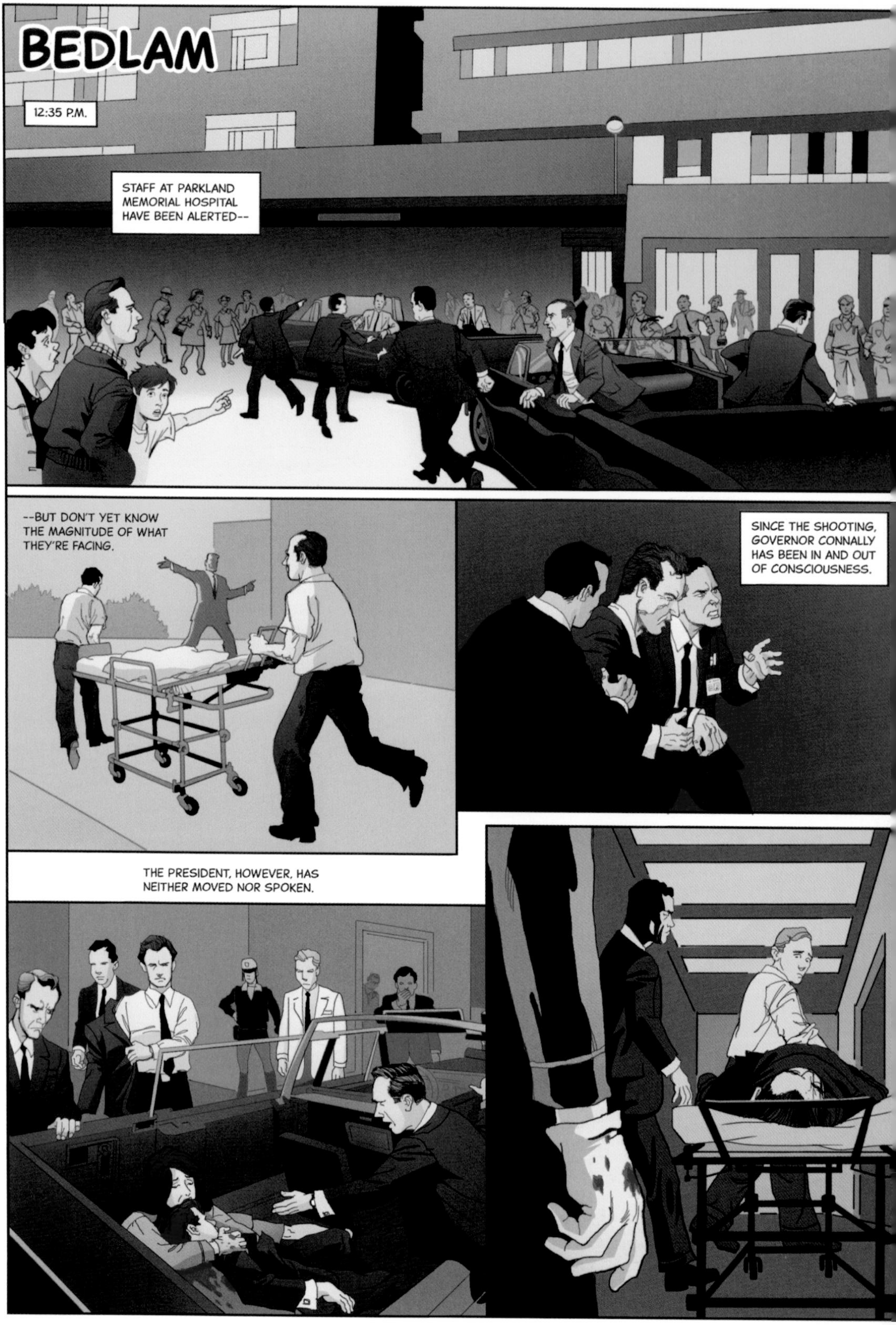
BEDLAM
12:35 P.M.
STAFF AT PARKLAND MEMORIAL HOSPITAL HAVE BEEN ALERTED--
--BUT DON'T YET KNOW THE MAGNITUDE OF WHAT THEY'RE FACING.
SINCE THE SHOOTING, GOVERNOR CONNALLY HAS BEEN IN AND OUT OF CONSCIOUSNESS.
THE PRESIDENT, HOWEVER, HAS NEITHER MOVED NOR SPOKEN.

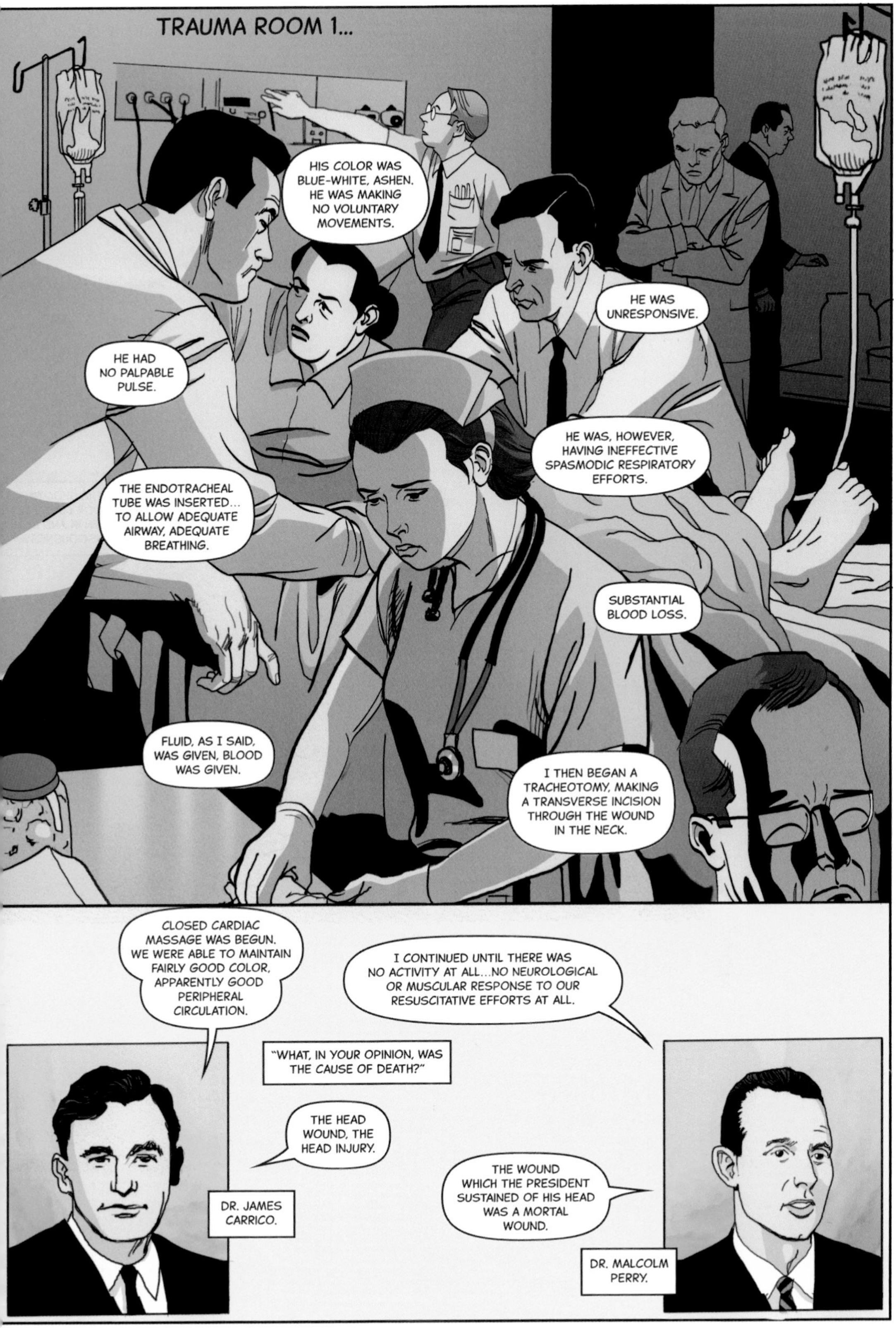
TRAUMA ROOM 1...
HIS COLOR WAS BLUE-WHITE, ASHEN. HE WAS MAKING NO VOLUNTARY MOVEMENTS.
HE WAS UNRESPONSIVE.
HE HAD NO PALPABLE PULSE.
HE WAS, HOWEVER, HAVING INEFFECTIVE SPASMODIC RESPIRATORY EFFORTS.
THE ENDOTRACHEAL TUBE WAS INSERTED... TO ALLOW ADEQUATE AIRWAY, ADEQUATE BREATHING.
SUBSTANTIAL BLOOD LOSS.
FLUID, AS I SAID, WAS GIVEN, BLOOD WAS GIVEN.
I THEN BEGAN A TRACHEOTOMY, MAKING A TRANSVERSE INCISION THROUGH THE WOUND IN THE NECK.
CLOSED CARDIAC MASSAGE WAS BEGUN. WE WERE ABLE TO MAINTAIN FAIRLY GOOD COLOR, APPARENTLY GOOD PERIPHERAL CIRCULATION.
I CONTINUED UNTIL THERE WAS NO ACTIVITY AT ALL...NO NEUROLOGICAL OR MUSCULAR RESPONSE TO OUR RESUSCITATIVE EFFORTS AT ALL.
"WHAT, IN YOUR OPINION, WAS THE CAUSE OF DEATH?"
THE HEAD WOUND, THE HEAD INJURY.
DR. JAMES CARRICO.
THE WOUND WHICH THE PRESIDENT SUSTAINED OF HIS HEAD WAS A MORTAL WOUND.
DR. MALCOLM PERRY.

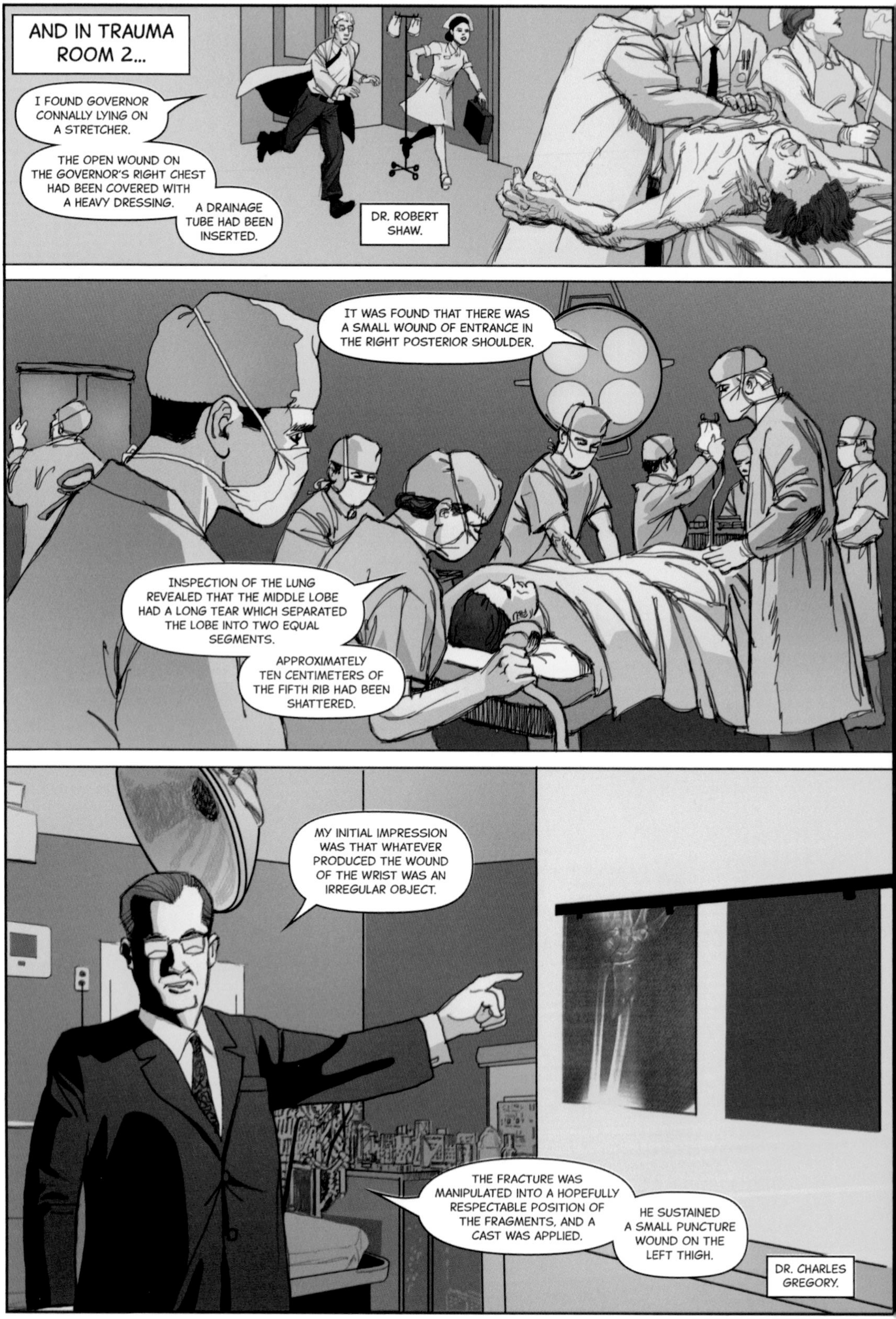
AND IN TRAUMA ROOM 2...
I FOUND GOVERNOR CONNALLY LYING ON A STRETCHER.
THE OPEN WOUND ON THE GOVERNOR'S RIGHT CHEST HAD BEEN COVERED WITH A HEAVY DRESSING.
A DRAINAGE TUBE HAD BEEN INSERTED.
DR. ROBERT SHAW.
IT WAS FOUND THAT THERE WAS A SMALL WOUND OF ENTRANCE IN THE RIGHT POSTERIOR SHOULDER.
INSPECTION OF THE LUNG REVEALED THAT THE MIDDLE LOBE HAD A LONG TEAR WHICH SEPARATED THE LOBE INTO TWO EQUAL SEGMENTS.
APPROXIMATELY TEN CENTIMETERS OF THE FIFTH RIB HAD BEEN SHATTERED.
MY INITIAL IMPRESSION WAS THAT WHATEVER PRODUCED THE WOUND OF THE WRIST WAS AN IRREGULAR OBJECT.
THE FRACTURE WAS MANIPULATED INTO A HOPEFULLY RESPECTABLE POSITION OF THE FRAGMENTS, AND A CAST WAS APPLIED.
HE SUSTAINED A SMALL PUNCTURE WOUND ON THE LEFT THIGH.
DR. CHARLES GREGORY.

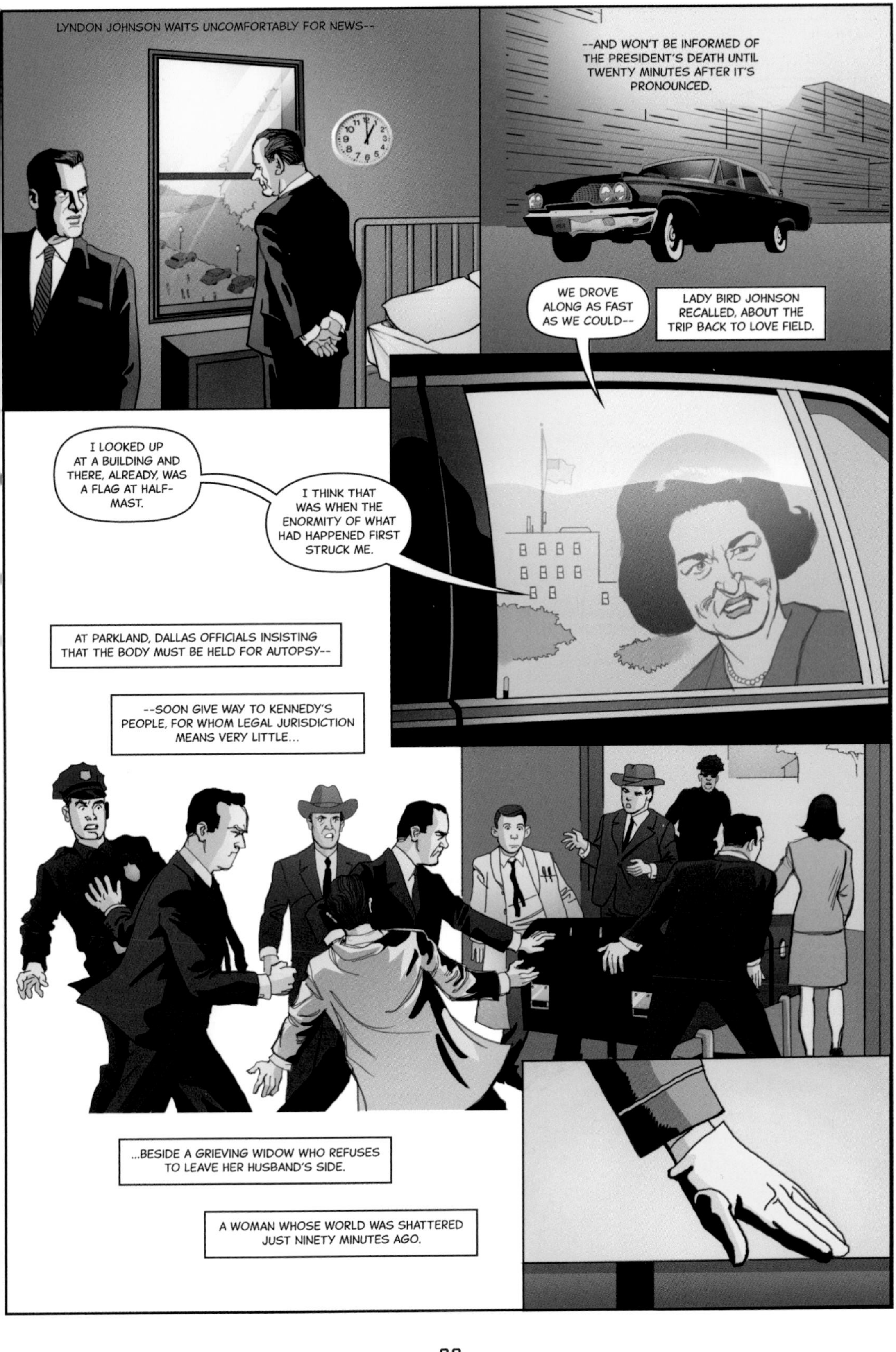
LYNDON JOHNSON WAITS UNCOMFORTABLY FOR NEWS--
--AND WON'T BE INFORMED OF THE PRESIDENT'S DEATH UNTIL TWENTY MINUTES AFTER IT'S PRONOUNCED.
LADY BIRD JOHNSON RECALLED, ABOUT THE TRIP BACK TO LOVE FIELD.
WE DROVE ALONG AS FAST AS WE COULD--
I LOOKED UP AT A BUILDING AND THERE, ALREADY, WAS A FLAG AT HALF-MAST.
I THINK THAT WAS WHEN THE ENORMITY OF WHAT HAD HAPPENED FIRST STRUCK ME.
AT PARKLAND, DALLAS OFFICIALS INSISTING THAT THE BODY MUST BE HELD FOR AUTOPSY--
--SOON GIVE WAY TO KENNEDY'S PEOPLE, FOR WHOM LEGAL JURISDICTION MEANS VERY LITTLE...
...BESIDE A GRIEVING WIDOW WHO REFUSES TO LEAVE HER HUSBAND'S SIDE.
A WOMAN WHOSE WORLD WAS SHATTERED JUST NINETY MINUTES AGO.

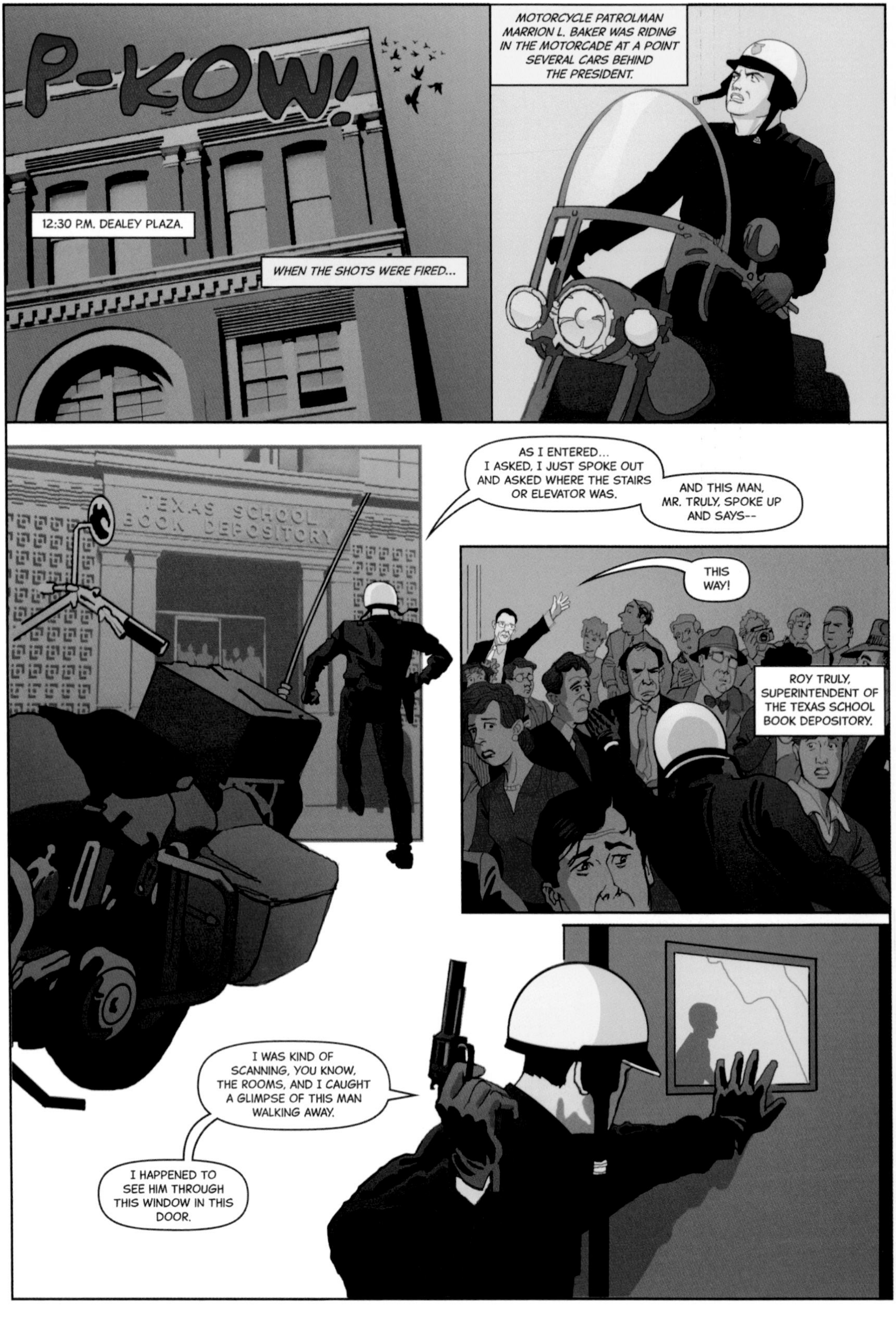
P-KOW!
12:30 P.M. DEALEY PLAZA.
WHEN THE SHOTS WERE FIRED...
MOTORCYCLE PATROLMAN MARRION L. BAKER WAS RIDING IN THE MOTORCADE AT A POINT SEVERAL CARS BEHIND THE PRESIDENT.
TEXAS SCHOOL BOOK DEPOSITORY
AS I ENTERED... I ASKED, I JUST SPOKE OUT AND ASKED WHERE THE STAIRS OR ELEVATOR WAS.
AND THIS MAN, MR. TRULY, SPOKE UP AND SAYS--
THIS WAY!
ROY TRULY, SUPERINTENDENT OF THE TEXAS SCHOOL BOOK DEPOSITORY.
I WAS KIND OF SCANNING, YOU KNOW, THE ROOMS, AND I CAUGHT A GLIMPSE OF THIS MAN WALKING AWAY.
I HAPPENED TO SEE HIM THROUGH THIS WINDOW IN THIS DOOR.

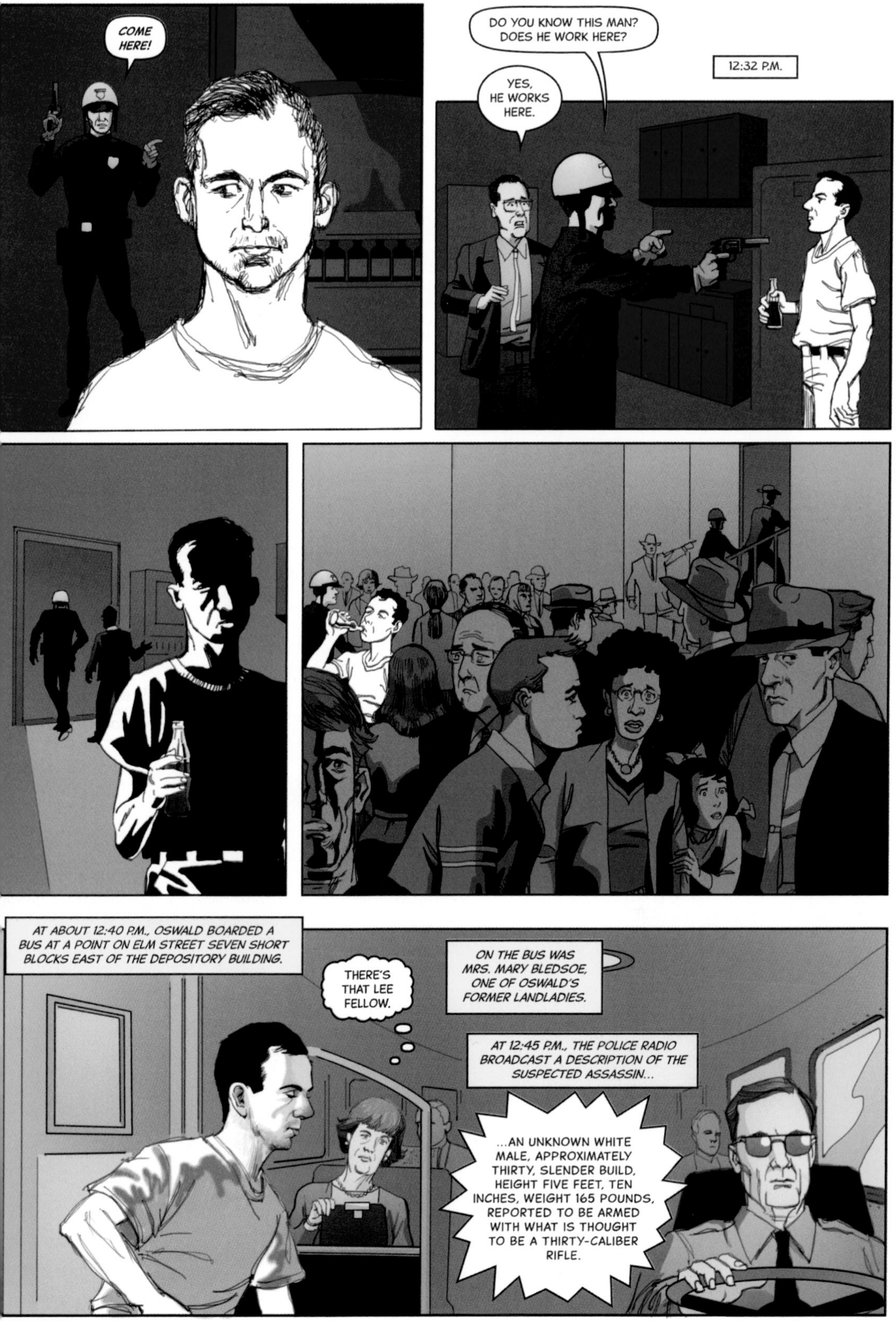
COME HERE!
DO YOU KNOW THIS MAN? DOES HE WORK HERE?
12:32 P.M.
YES, HE WORKS HERE.
AT ABOUT 12:40 P.M., OSWALD BOARDED A BUS AT A POINT ON ELM STREET SEVEN SHORT BLOCKS EAST OF THE DEPOSITORY BUILDING.
THERE'S THAT LEE FELLOW.
ON THE BUS WAS MRS. MARY BLEDSOE, ONE OF OSWALD'S FORMER LANDLADIES.
AT 12:45 P.M., THE POLICE RADIO BROADCAST A DESCRIPTION OF THE SUSPECTED ASSASSIN...
...AN UNKNOWN WHITE MALE, APPROXIMATELY THIRTY, SLENDER BUILD, HEIGHT FIVE FEET, TEN INCHES, WEIGHT 165 POUNDS, REPORTED TO BE ARMED WITH WHAT IS THOUGHT TO BE A THIRTY-CALIBER RIFLE.

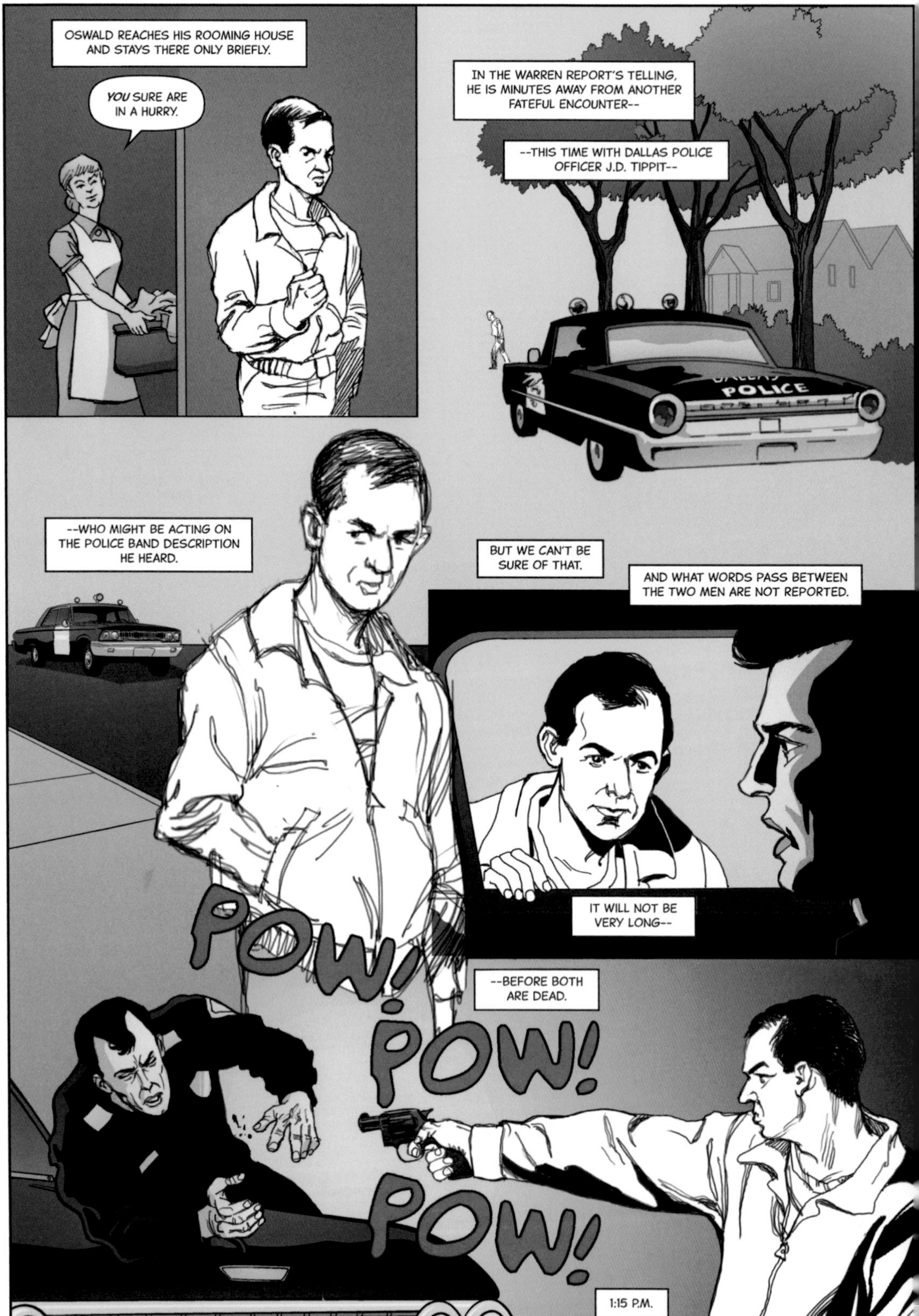
OSWALD REACHES HIS ROOMING HOUSE AND STAYS THERE ONLY BRIEFLY.
YOU SURE ARE IN A HURRY.
IN THE WARREN REPORT'S TELLING, HE IS MINUTES AWAY FROM ANOTHER FATEFUL ENCOUNTER--
--THIS TIME WITH DALLAS POLICE OFFICER J.D. TIPPIT--
POLICE
--WHO MIGHT BE ACTING ON THE POLICE BAND DESCRIPTION HE HEARD.
BUT WE CAN'T BE SURE OF THAT.
AND WHAT WORDS PASS BETWEEN THE TWO MEN ARE NOT REPORTED.
IT WILL NOT BE VERY LONG--
POW!
--BEFORE BOTH ARE DEAD.
POW!
POW!
1:15 P.M.

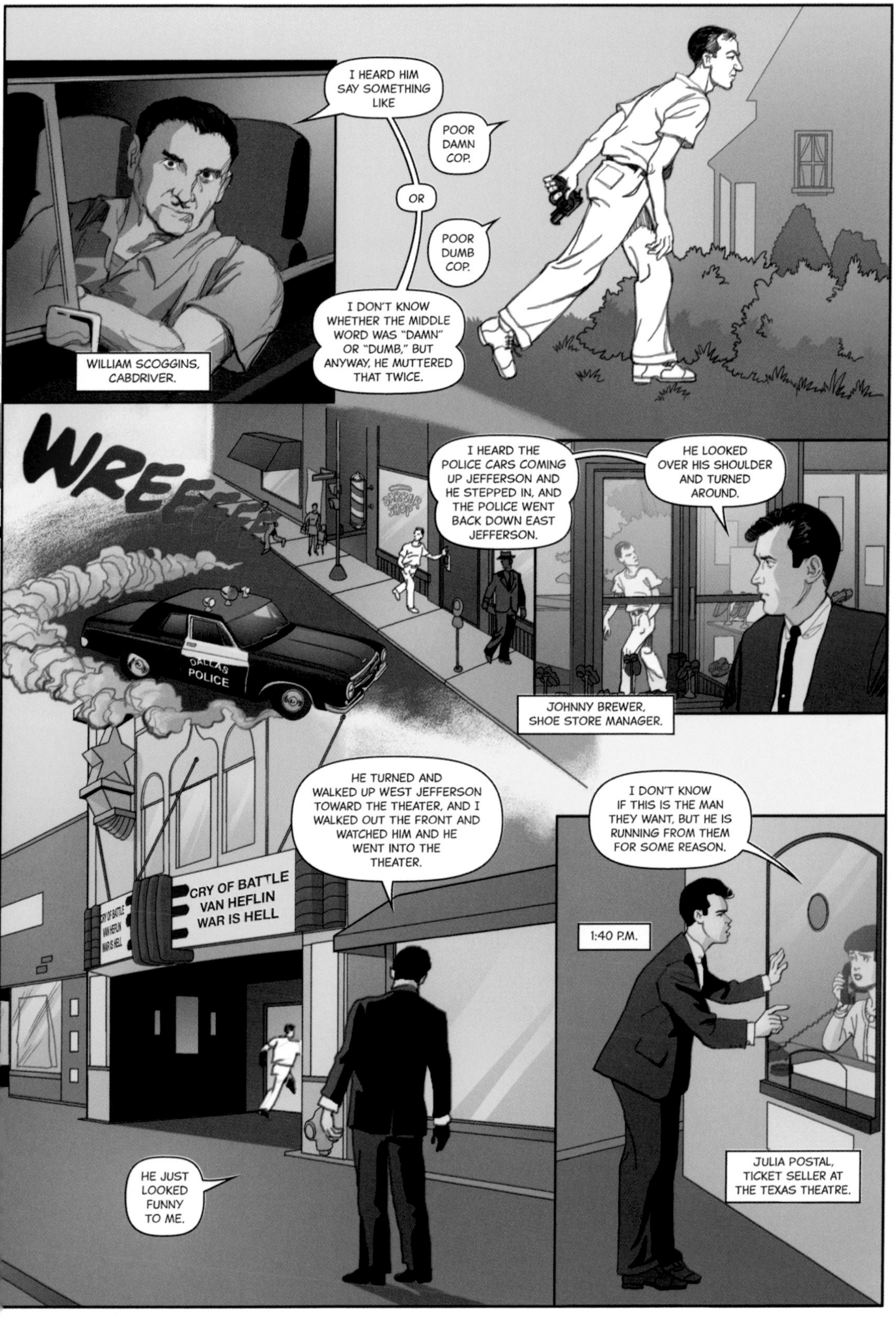
I HEARD HIM SAY SOMETHING LIKE
POOR DAMN COP.
OR
POOR DUMB COP.
I DON'T KNOW WHETHER THE MIDDLE WORD WAS "DAMN" OR "DUMB," BUT ANYWAY, HE MUTTERED THAT TWICE.
WILLIAM SCOGGINS, CABDRIVER.
WREEEEE
DALLAS POLICE
BARBER SHOP
I HEARD THE POLICE CARS COMING UP JEFFERSON AND HE STEPPED IN, AND THE POLICE WENT BACK DOWN EAST JEFFERSON.
HE LOOKED OVER HIS SHOULDER AND TURNED AROUND.
JOHNNY BREWER, SHOE STORE MANAGER.
HE TURNED AND WALKED UP WEST JEFFERSON TOWARD THE THEATER, AND I WALKED OUT THE FRONT AND WATCHED HIM AND HE WENT INTO THE THEATER.
CRY OF BATTLE
VAN HEFLIN
WAR IS HELL
HE JUST LOOKED FUNNY TO ME.
I DON'T KNOW IF THIS IS THE MAN THEY WANT, BUT HE IS RUNNING FROM THEM FOR SOME REASON.
1:40 P.M.
JULIA POSTAL, TICKET SELLER AT THE TEXAS THEATRE.

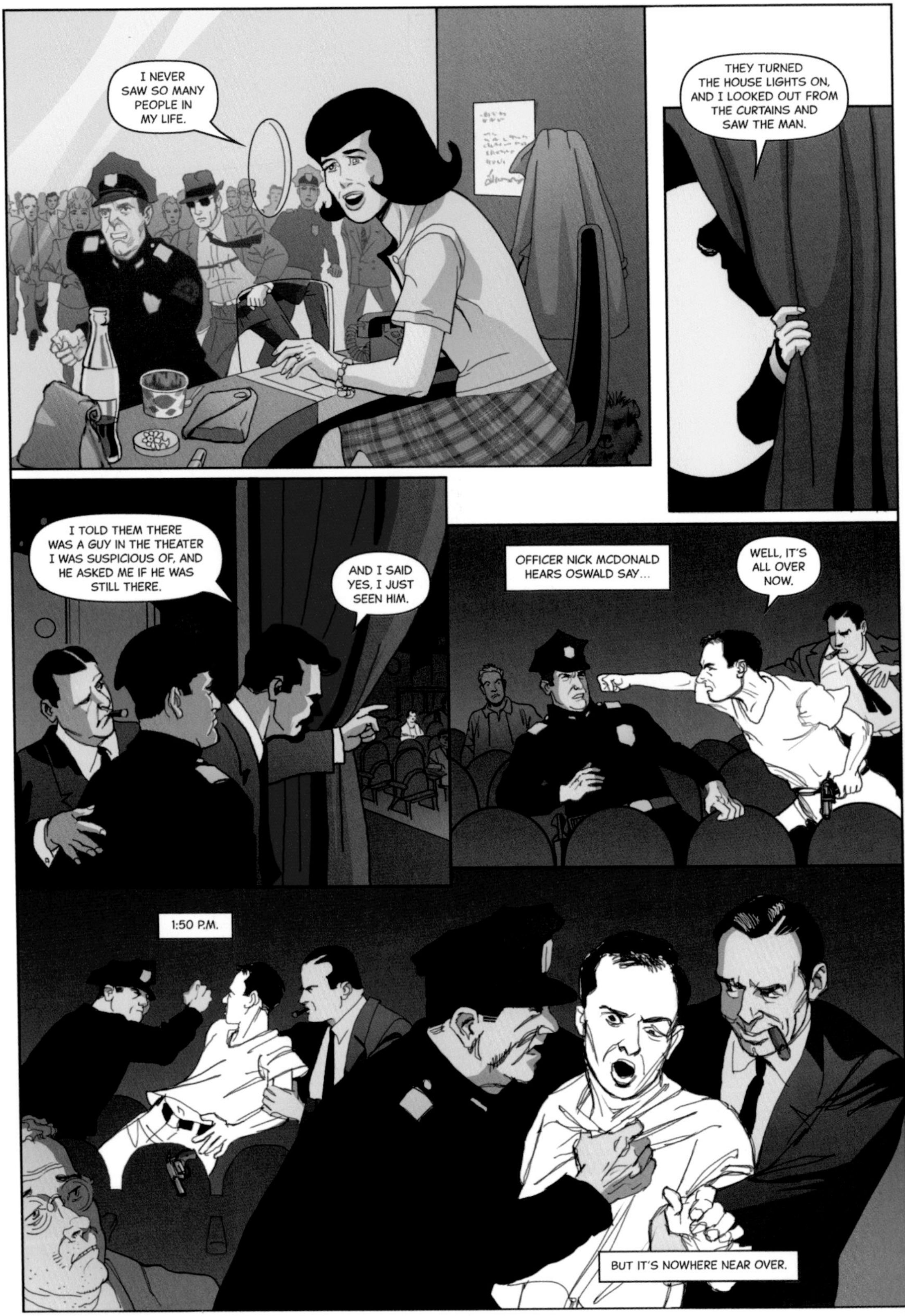
I NEVER SAW SO MANY PEOPLE IN MY LIFE.
THEY TURNED THE HOUSE LIGHTS ON, AND I LOOKED OUT FROM THE CURTAINS AND SAW THE MAN.
I TOLD THEM THERE WAS A GUY IN THE THEATER I WAS SUSPICIOUS OF, AND HE ASKED ME IF HE WAS STILL THERE.
AND I SAID YES, I JUST SEEN HIM.
OFFICER NICK MCDONALD HEARS OSWALD SAY...
WELL, IT'S ALL OVER NOW.
1:50 P.M.
BUT IT'S NOWHERE NEAR OVER.

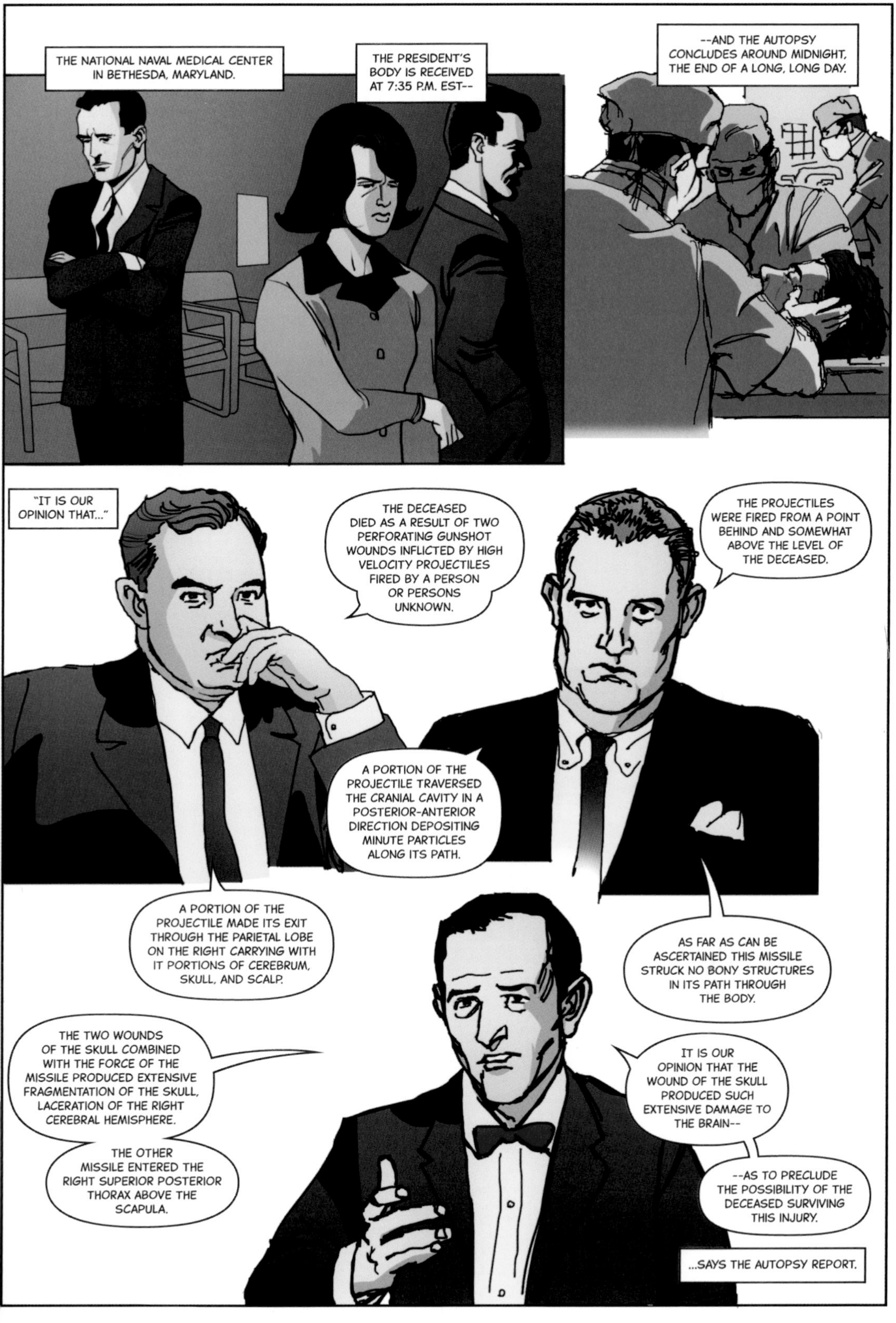
THE NATIONAL NAVAL MEDICAL CENTER IN BETHESDA, MARYLAND.
THE PRESIDENT'S BODY IS RECEIVED AT 7:35 P.M. EST--
--AND THE AUTOPSY CONCLUDES AROUND MIDNIGHT, THE END OF A LONG, LONG DAY.
"IT IS OUR OPINION THAT..."
THE DECEASED DIED AS A RESULT OF TWO PERFORATING GUNSHOT WOUNDS INFLICTED BY HIGH VELOCITY PROJECTILES FIRED BY A PERSON OR PERSONS UNKNOWN.
THE PROJECTILES WERE FIRED FROM A POINT BEHIND AND SOMEWHAT ABOVE THE LEVEL OF THE DECEASED.
A PORTION OF THE PROJECTILE TRAVERSED THE CRANIAL CAVITY IN A POSTERIOR-ANTERIOR DIRECTION DEPOSITING MINUTE PARTICLES ALONG ITS PATH.
A PORTION OF THE PROJECTILE MADE ITS EXIT THROUGH THE PARIETAL LOBE ON THE RIGHT CARRYING WITH IT PORTIONS OF CEREBRUM, SKULL, AND SCALP.
AS FAR AS CAN BE ASCERTAINED THIS MISSILE STRUCK NO BONY STRUCTURES IN ITS PATH THROUGH THE BODY.
THE TWO WOUNDS OF THE SKULL COMBINED WITH THE FORCE OF THE MISSILE PRODUCED EXTENSIVE FRAGMENTATION OF THE SKULL, LACERATION OF THE RIGHT CEREBRAL HEMISPHERE.
THE OTHER MISSILE ENTERED THE RIGHT SUPERIOR POSTERIOR THORAX ABOVE THE SCAPULA.
IT IS OUR OPINION THAT THE WOUND OF THE SKULL PRODUCED SUCH EXTENSIVE DAMAGE TO THE BRAIN--
--AS TO PRECLUDE THE POSSIBILITY OF THE DECEASED SURVIVING THIS INJURY.
...SAYS THE AUTOPSY REPORT.

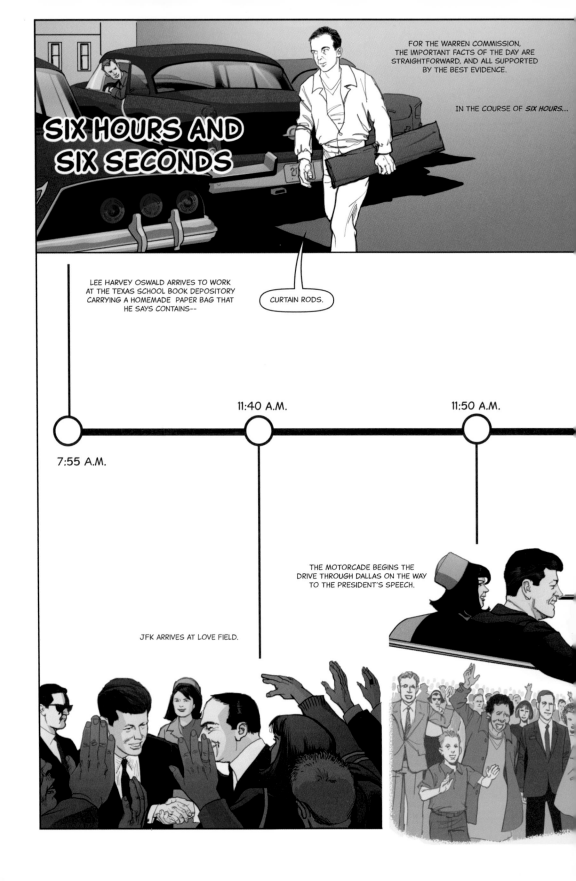

SIX HOURS AND SIX SECONDS

FOR THE WARREN COMMISSION, THE IMPORTANT FACTS OF THE DAY ARE STRAIGHTFORWARD, AND ALL SUPPORTED BY THE BEST EVIDENCE.

IN THE COURSE OF *SIX HOURS*...

LEE HARVEY OSWALD ARRIVES TO WORK AT THE TEXAS SCHOOL BOOK DEPOSITORY CARRYING A HOMEMADE PAPER BAG THAT HE SAYS CONTAINS--

CURTAIN RODS.

11:40 A.M.

11:50 A.M.

7:55 A.M.

THE MOTORCADE BEGINS THE DRIVE THROUGH DALLAS ON THE WAY TO THE PRESIDENT'S SPEECH.

JFK ARRIVES AT LOVE FIELD.

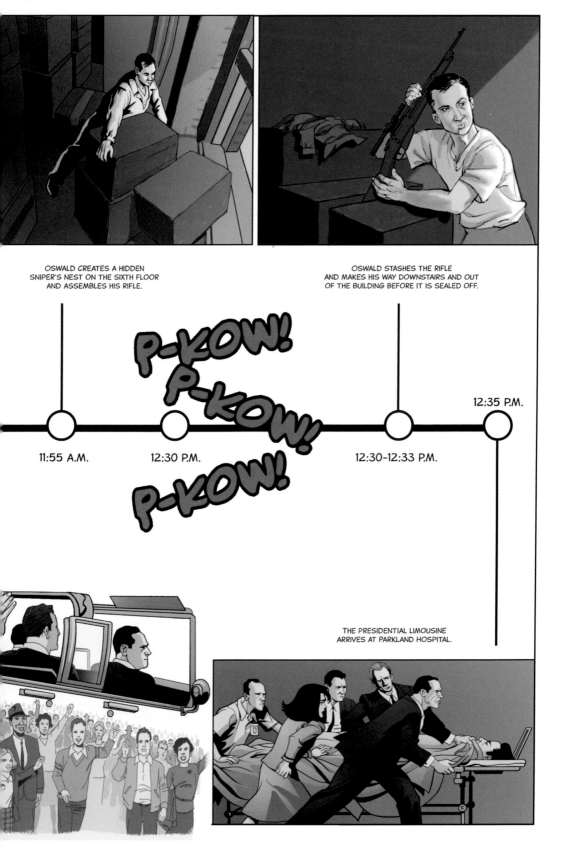

OSWALD CREATES A HIDDEN
SNIPER'S NEST ON THE SIXTH FLOOR
AND ASSEMBLES HIS RIFLE.

OSWALD STASHES THE RIFLE
AND MAKES HIS WAY DOWNSTAIRS AND OUT
OF THE BUILDING BEFORE IT IS SEALED OFF.

P-KOW!

P-KOW!

P-KOW!

12:35 P.M.

11:55 A.M.

12:30 P.M.

12:30–12:33 P.M.

THE PRESIDENTIAL LIMOUSINE
ARRIVES AT PARKLAND HOSPITAL.

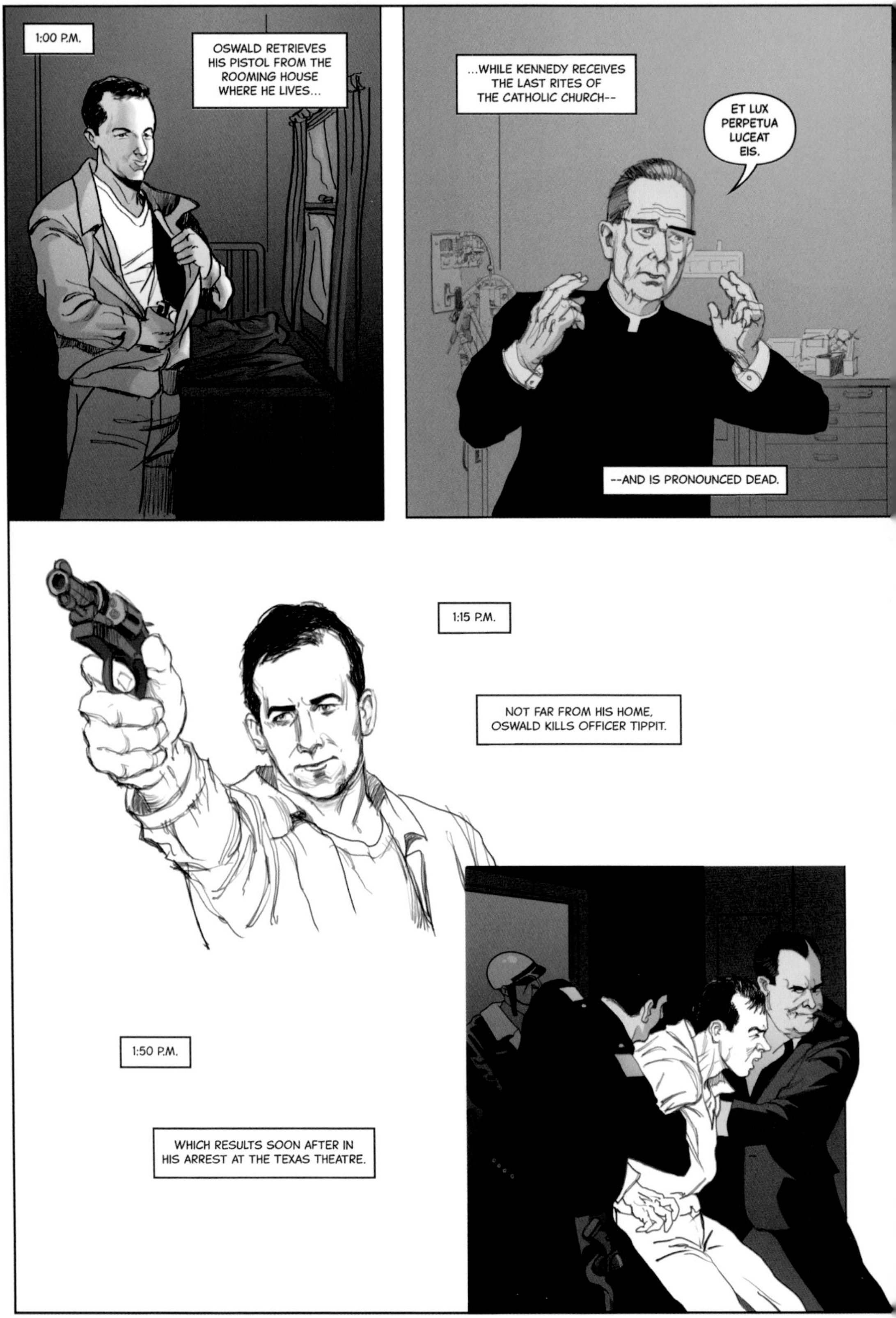
1:00 P.M.
OSWALD RETRIEVES HIS PISTOL FROM THE ROOMING HOUSE WHERE HE LIVES...
...WHILE KENNEDY RECEIVES THE LAST RITES OF THE CATHOLIC CHURCH--
ET LUX PERPETUA LUCEAT EIS.
--AND IS PRONOUNCED DEAD.
1:15 P.M.
NOT FAR FROM HIS HOME, OSWALD KILLS OFFICER TIPPIT.
1:50 P.M.
WHICH RESULTS SOON AFTER IN HIS ARREST AT THE TEXAS THEATRE.

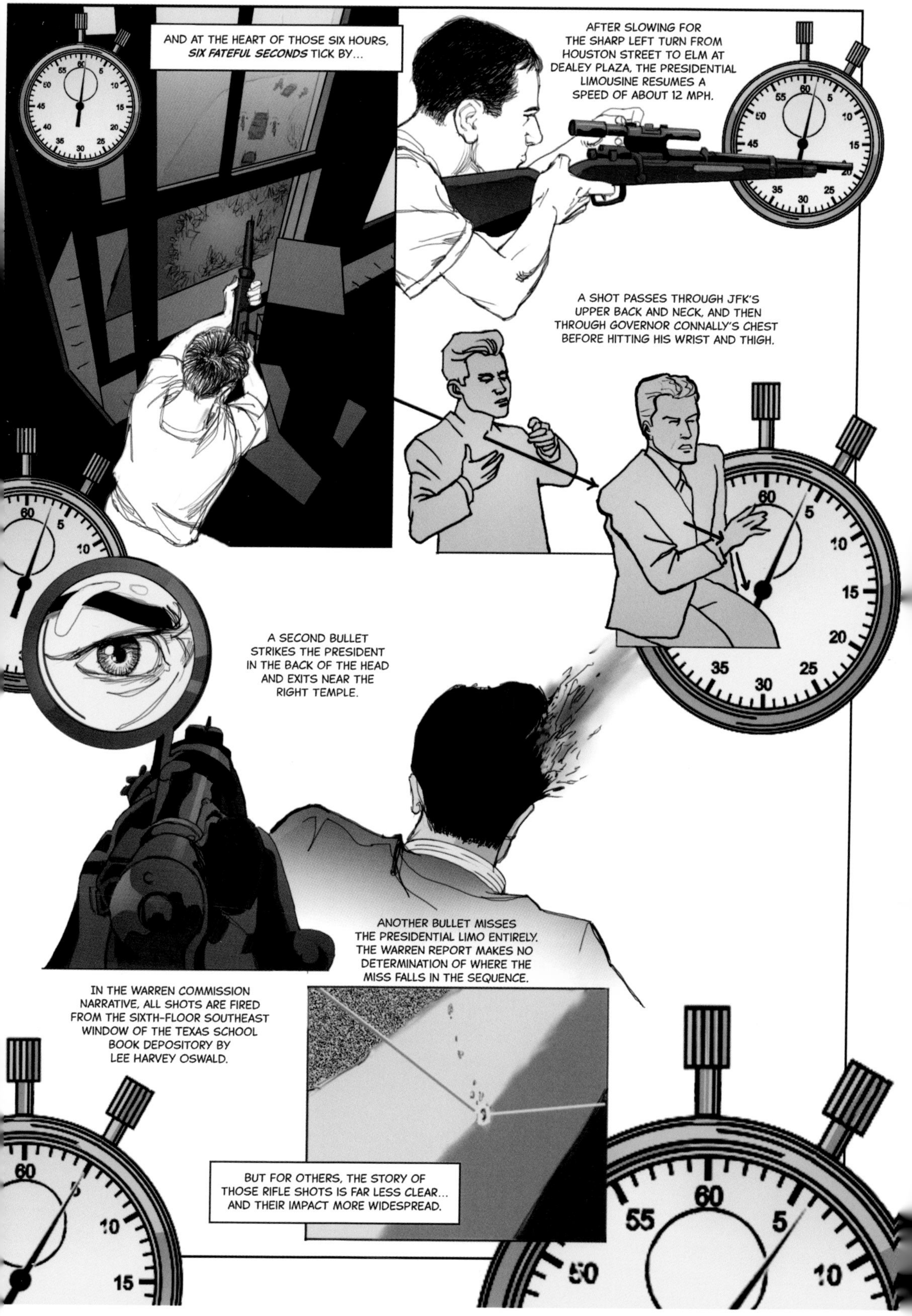
AND AT THE HEART OF THOSE SIX HOURS, *SIX FATEFUL SECONDS* TICK BY...
AFTER SLOWING FOR THE SHARP LEFT TURN FROM HOUSTON STREET TO ELM AT DEALEY PLAZA, THE PRESIDENTIAL LIMOUSINE RESUMES A SPEED OF ABOUT 12 MPH.
A SHOT PASSES THROUGH JFK'S UPPER BACK AND NECK, AND THEN THROUGH GOVERNOR CONNALLY'S CHEST BEFORE HITTING HIS WRIST AND THIGH.
A SECOND BULLET STRIKES THE PRESIDENT IN THE BACK OF THE HEAD AND EXITS NEAR THE RIGHT TEMPLE.
ANOTHER BULLET MISSES THE PRESIDENTIAL LIMO ENTIRELY. THE WARREN REPORT MAKES NO DETERMINATION OF WHERE THE MISS FALLS IN THE SEQUENCE.
IN THE WARREN COMMISSION NARRATIVE, ALL SHOTS ARE FIRED FROM THE SIXTH-FLOOR SOUTHEAST WINDOW OF THE TEXAS SCHOOL BOOK DEPOSITORY BY LEE HARVEY OSWALD.
BUT FOR OTHERS, THE STORY OF THOSE RIFLE SHOTS IS FAR LESS CLEAR... AND THEIR IMPACT MORE WIDESPREAD.

ON A NEW FRONTIER

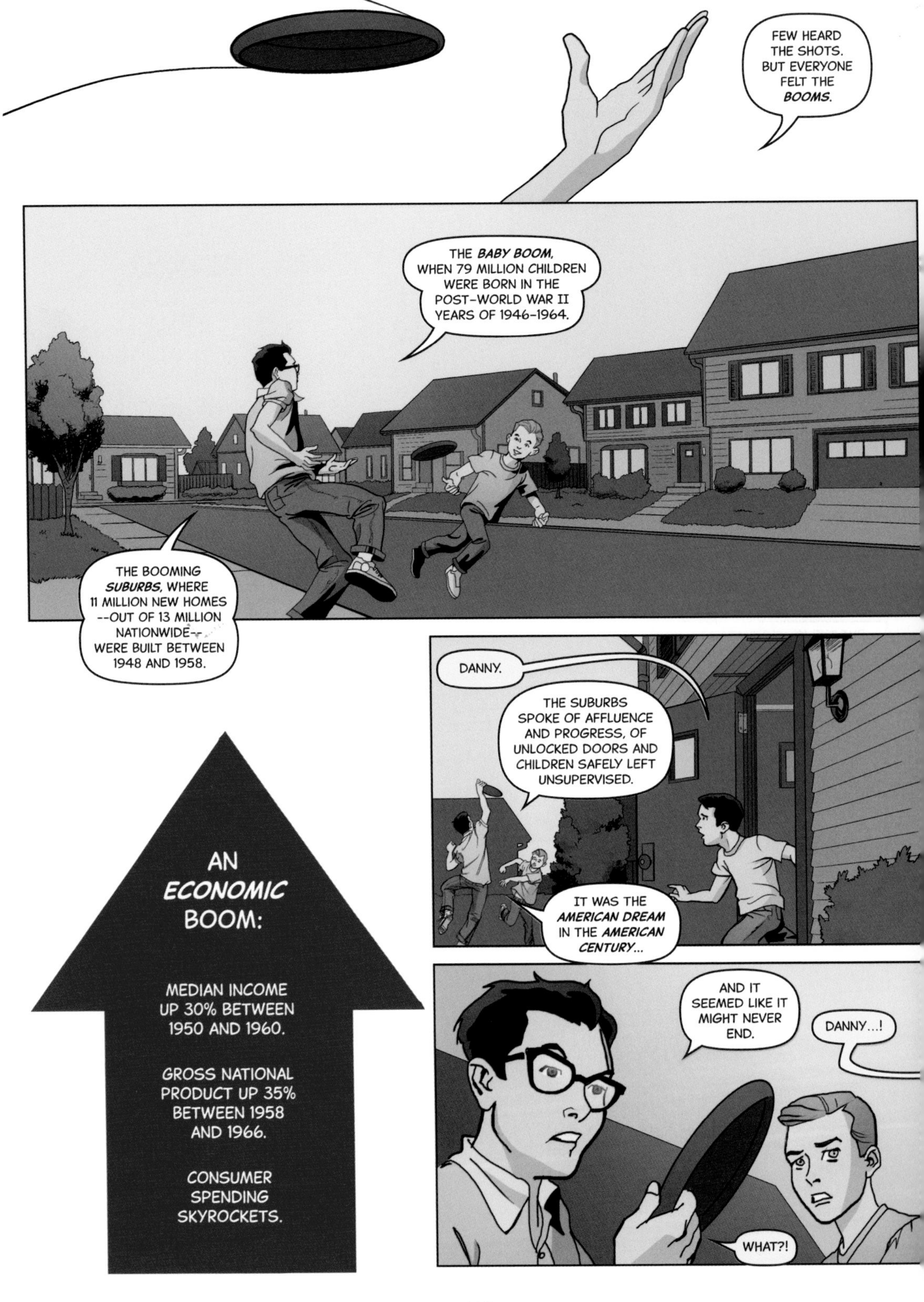

FEW HEARD THE SHOTS. BUT EVERYONE FELT THE *BOOMS*.
THE *BABY BOOM*, WHEN 79 MILLION CHILDREN WERE BORN IN THE POST-WORLD WAR II YEARS OF 1946-1964.
THE BOOMING *SUBURBS*, WHERE 11 MILLION NEW HOMES --OUT OF 13 MILLION NATIONWIDE-- WERE BUILT BETWEEN 1948 AND 1958.
DANNY.
THE SUBURBS SPOKE OF AFFLUENCE AND PROGRESS, OF UNLOCKED DOORS AND CHILDREN SAFELY LEFT UNSUPERVISED.
IT WAS THE *AMERICAN DREAM* IN THE *AMERICAN CENTURY*...
AN *ECONOMIC* BOOM:
MEDIAN INCOME UP 30% BETWEEN 1950 AND 1960.
GROSS NATIONAL PRODUCT UP 35% BETWEEN 1958 AND 1966.
CONSUMER SPENDING SKYROCKETS.
AND IT SEEMED LIKE IT MIGHT NEVER END.
DANNY...!
WHAT?!

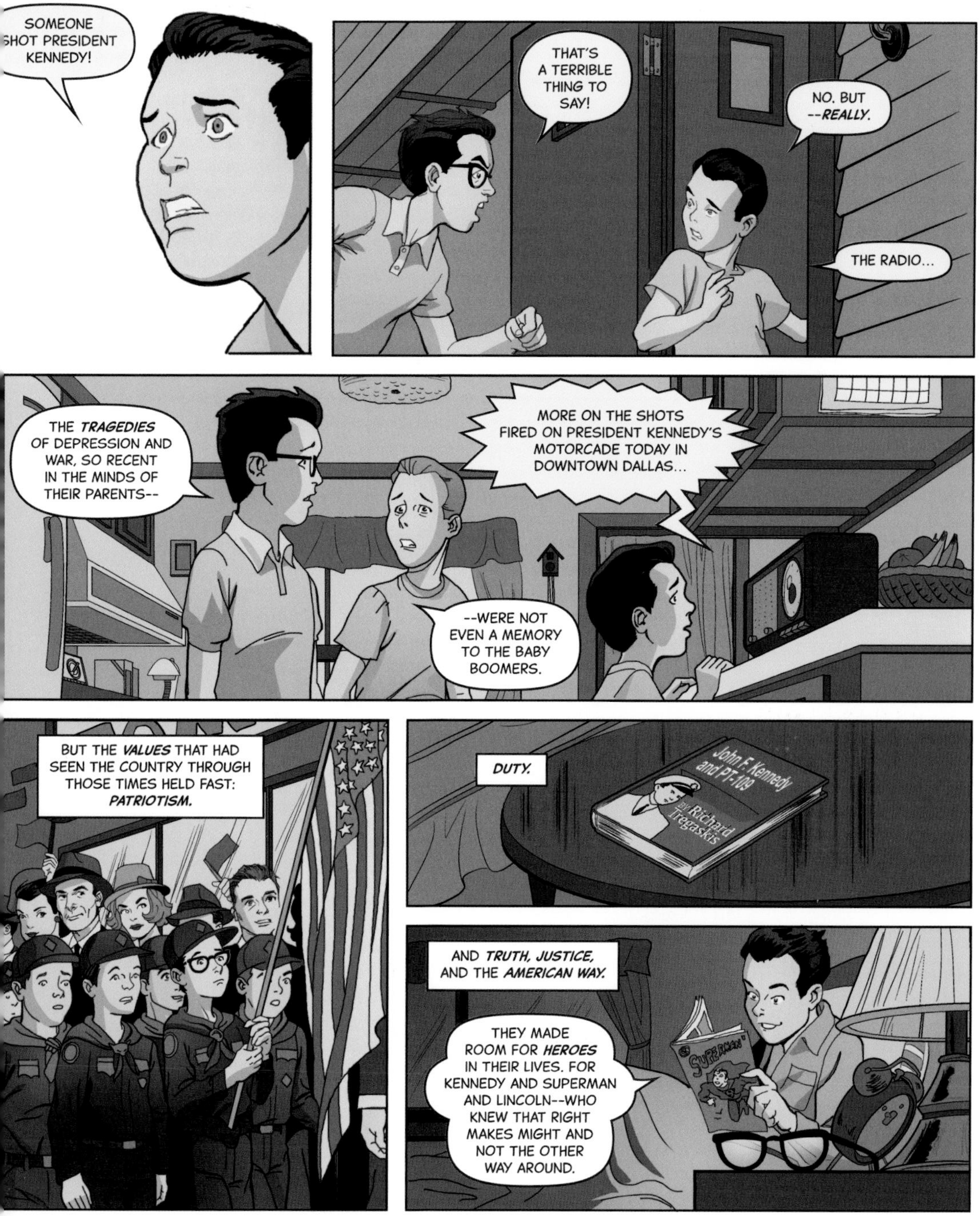
SOMEONE SHOT PRESIDENT KENNEDY!
THAT'S A TERRIBLE THING TO SAY!
NO. BUT --*REALLY.*
THE RADIO...
THE *TRAGEDIES* OF DEPRESSION AND WAR, SO RECENT IN THE MINDS OF THEIR PARENTS--
MORE ON THE SHOTS FIRED ON PRESIDENT KENNEDY'S MOTORCADE TODAY IN DOWNTOWN DALLAS...
--WERE NOT EVEN A MEMORY TO THE BABY BOOMERS.
BUT THE *VALUES* THAT HAD SEEN THE COUNTRY THROUGH THOSE TIMES HELD FAST: *PATRIOTISM.*
DUTY.
John F. Kennedy and PT-109
by Richard Tregaskis
AND *TRUTH, JUSTICE,* AND THE *AMERICAN WAY.*
THEY MADE ROOM FOR *HEROES* IN THEIR LIVES. FOR KENNEDY AND SUPERMAN AND LINCOLN--WHO KNEW THAT RIGHT MAKES MIGHT AND NOT THE OTHER WAY AROUND.

THE PRESENT WAS IMPERFECT.
SOMEWHERE IN THE LAND WERE ***CIVIL RIGHTS STRUGGLES***
AND THE STIRRINGS OF A ***FEMINIST MOVEMENT***.

BUT IF PROBLEMS EXISTED,
AMERICA WOULD FIND A WAY TO SOLVE THEM.
THAT WAS WHAT AMERICA DID.

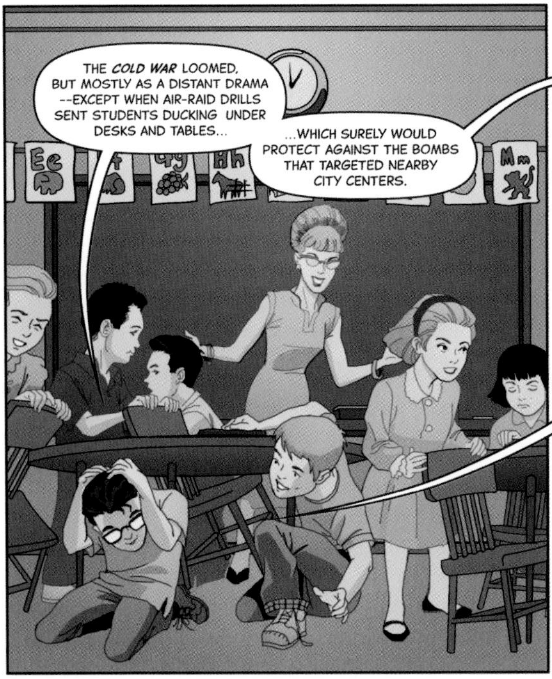
THE *COLD WAR* LOOMED, BUT MOSTLY AS A DISTANT DRAMA --EXCEPT WHEN AIR-RAID DRILLS SENT STUDENTS DUCKING UNDER DESKS AND TABLES...
...WHICH SURELY WOULD PROTECT AGAINST THE BOMBS THAT TARGETED NEARBY CITY CENTERS.

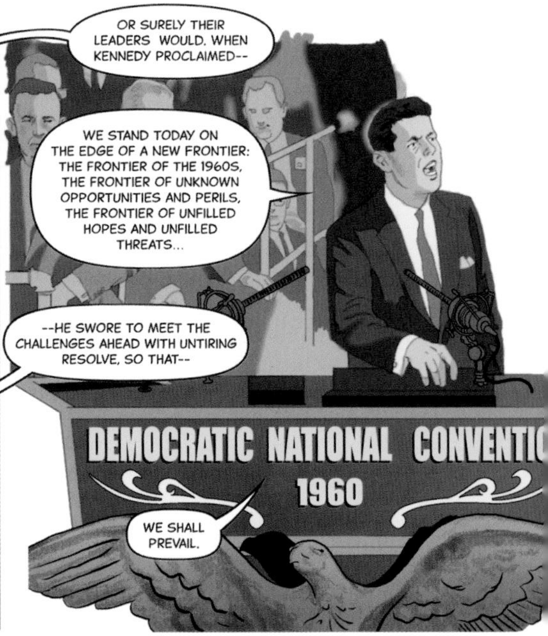
OR SURELY THEIR LEADERS WOULD. WHEN KENNEDY PROCLAIMED--
WE STAND TODAY ON THE EDGE OF A NEW FRONTIER: THE FRONTIER OF THE 1960S, THE FRONTIER OF UNKNOWN OPPORTUNITIES AND PERILS, THE FRONTIER OF UNFILLED HOPES AND UNFILLED THREATS...
--HE SWORE TO MEET THE CHALLENGES AHEAD WITH UNTIRING RESOLVE, SO THAT--
DEMOCRATIC NATIONAL CONVENTIO
1960
WE SHALL PREVAIL.

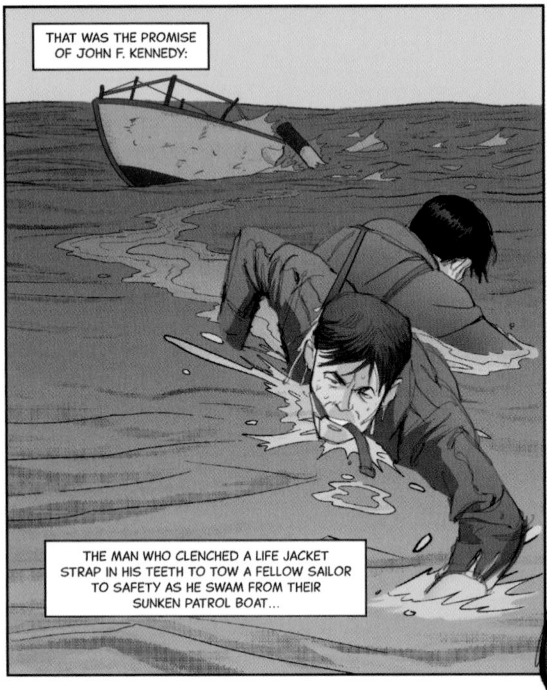
THAT WAS THE PROMISE OF JOHN F. KENNEDY:
THE MAN WHO CLENCHED A LIFE JACKET STRAP IN HIS TEETH TO TOW A FELLOW SAILOR TO SAFETY AS HE SWAM FROM THEIR SUNKEN PATROL BOAT...

...WHO WOULD FACE DOWN THE RUSSIANS OVER MISSILES IN CUBA IN THE FALL OF 1962.

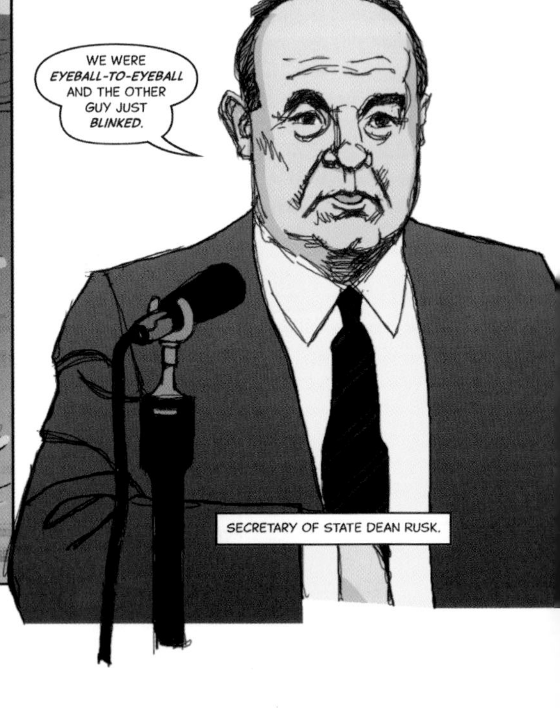
WE WERE *EYEBALL-TO-EYEBALL* AND THE OTHER GUY JUST *BLINKED*.
SECRETARY OF STATE DEAN RUSK.

FOR ALL THE DANGERS THAT MIGHT LURK IN 1963,
TOMORROW SEEMS SECURE. AND AS THE POSTWAR BOOMS RESOUND--

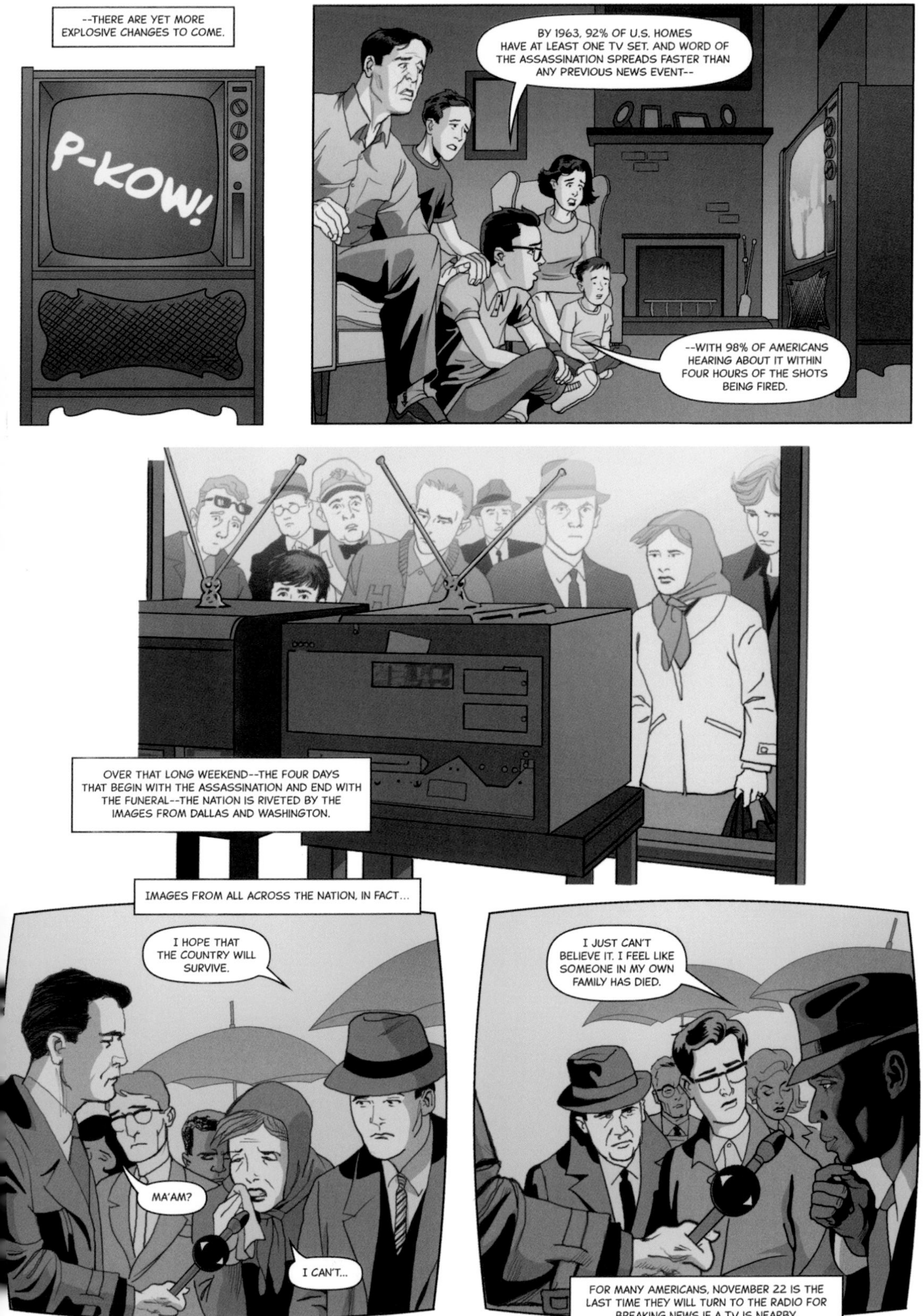
--THERE ARE YET MORE EXPLOSIVE CHANGES TO COME.
P-KOW!
BY 1963, 92% OF U.S. HOMES HAVE AT LEAST ONE TV SET. AND WORD OF THE ASSASSINATION SPREADS FASTER THAN ANY PREVIOUS NEWS EVENT--
--WITH 98% OF AMERICANS HEARING ABOUT IT WITHIN FOUR HOURS OF THE SHOTS BEING FIRED.
OVER THAT LONG WEEKEND--THE FOUR DAYS THAT BEGIN WITH THE ASSASSINATION AND END WITH THE FUNERAL--THE NATION IS RIVETED BY THE IMAGES FROM DALLAS AND WASHINGTON.
IMAGES FROM ALL ACROSS THE NATION, IN FACT...
I HOPE THAT THE COUNTRY WILL SURVIVE.
MA'AM?
I CAN'T...
I JUST CAN'T BELIEVE IT. I FEEL LIKE SOMEONE IN MY OWN FAMILY HAS DIED.
FOR MANY AMERICANS, NOVEMBER 22 IS THE LAST TIME THEY WILL TURN TO THE RADIO FOR BREAKING NEWS IF A TV IS NEARBY.

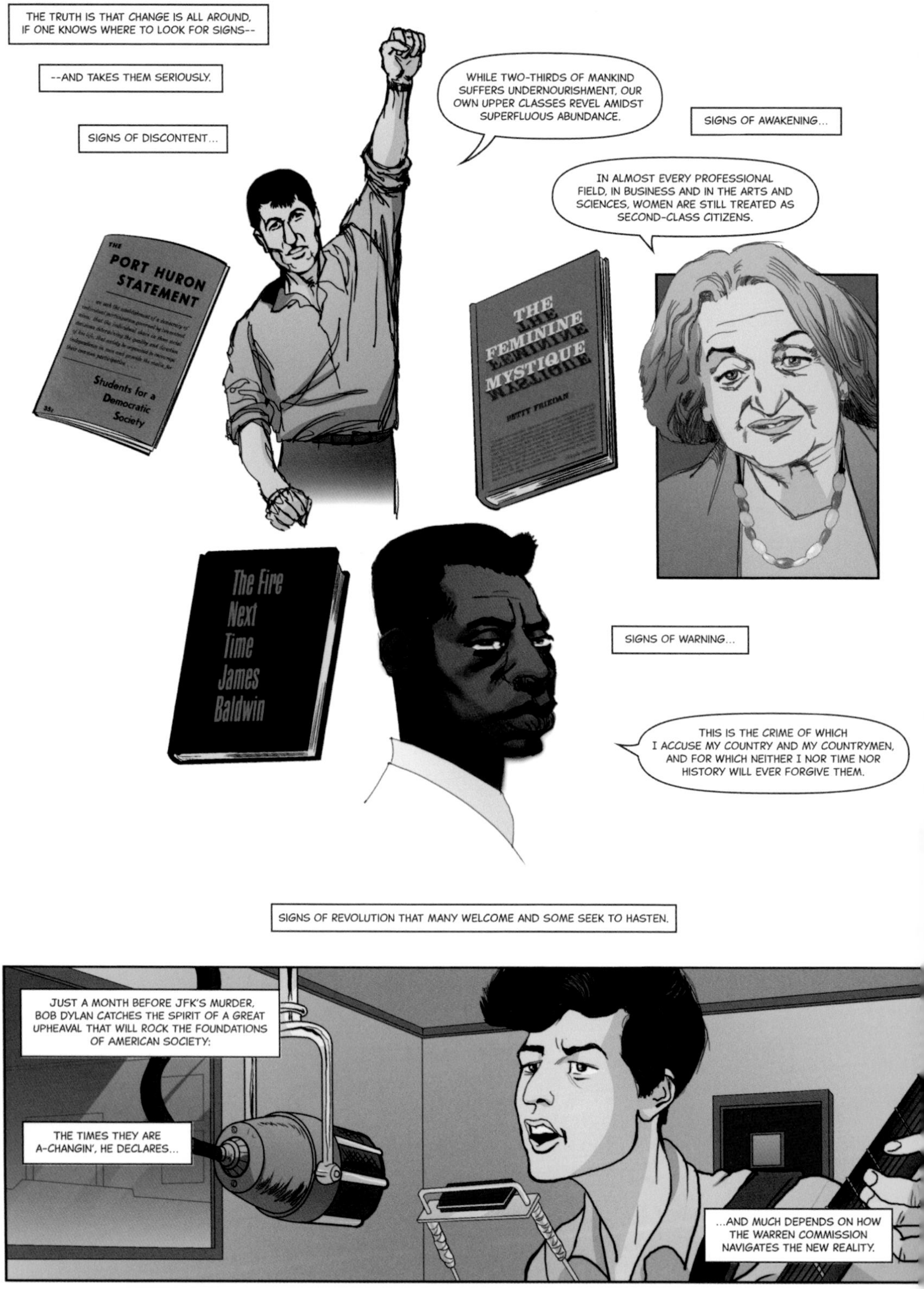

THE TRUTH IS THAT CHANGE IS ALL AROUND, IF ONE KNOWS WHERE TO LOOK FOR SIGNS--
--AND TAKES THEM SERIOUSLY.
SIGNS OF DISCONTENT...
WHILE TWO-THIRDS OF MANKIND SUFFERS UNDERNOURISHMENT, OUR OWN UPPER CLASSES REVEL AMIDST SUPERFLUOUS ABUNDANCE.
THE PORT HURON STATEMENT
Students for a Democratic Society
SIGNS OF AWAKENING...
IN ALMOST EVERY PROFESSIONAL FIELD, IN BUSINESS AND IN THE ARTS AND SCIENCES, WOMEN ARE STILL TREATED AS SECOND-CLASS CITIZENS.
THE FEMININE MYSTIQUE
BETTY FRIEDAN
The Fire Next Time James Baldwin
SIGNS OF WARNING...
THIS IS THE CRIME OF WHICH I ACCUSE MY COUNTRY AND MY COUNTRYMEN, AND FOR WHICH NEITHER I NOR TIME NOR HISTORY WILL EVER FORGIVE THEM.
SIGNS OF REVOLUTION THAT MANY WELCOME AND SOME SEEK TO HASTEN.
JUST A MONTH BEFORE JFK'S MURDER, BOB DYLAN CATCHES THE SPIRIT OF A GREAT UPHEAVAL THAT WILL ROCK THE FOUNDATIONS OF AMERICAN SOCIETY:
THE TIMES THEY ARE A-CHANGIN', HE DECLARES...
...AND MUCH DEPENDS ON HOW THE WARREN COMMISSION NAVIGATES THE NEW REALITY.

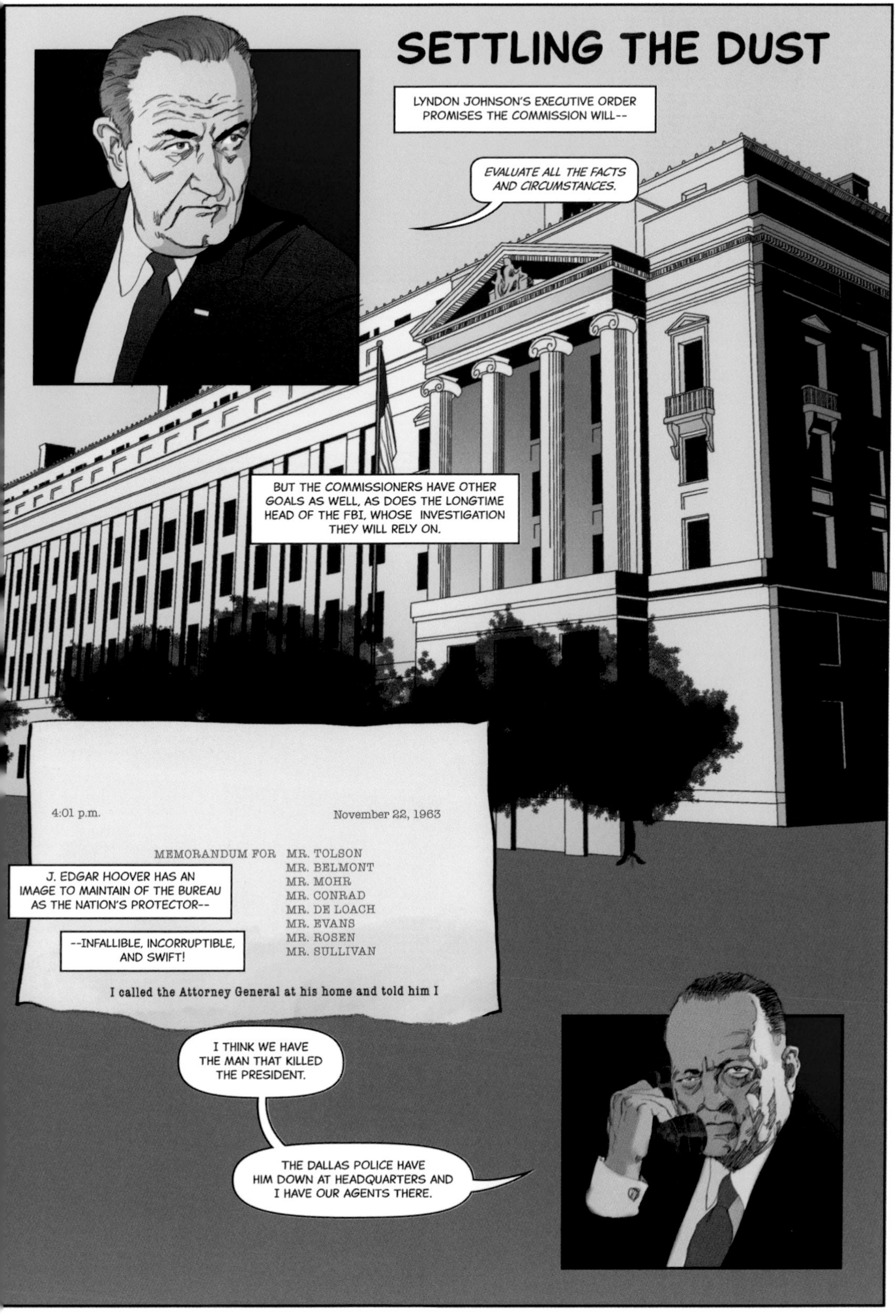

SETTLING THE DUST
LYNDON JOHNSON'S EXECUTIVE ORDER PROMISES THE COMMISSION WILL--
EVALUATE ALL THE FACTS AND CIRCUMSTANCES.
BUT THE COMMISSIONERS HAVE OTHER GOALS AS WELL, AS DOES THE LONGTIME HEAD OF THE FBI, WHOSE INVESTIGATION THEY WILL RELY ON.
4:01 p.m.
November 22, 1963
MEMORANDUM FOR MR. TOLSON
MR. BELMONT
MR. MOHR
MR. CONRAD
MR. DE LOACH
MR. EVANS
MR. ROSEN
MR. SULLIVAN
I called the Attorney General at his home and told him I
J. EDGAR HOOVER HAS AN IMAGE TO MAINTAIN OF THE BUREAU AS THE NATION'S PROTECTOR--
--INFALLIBLE, INCORRUPTIBLE, AND SWIFT!
I THINK WE HAVE THE MAN THAT KILLED THE PRESIDENT.
THE DALLAS POLICE HAVE HIM DOWN AT HEADQUARTERS AND I HAVE OUR AGENTS THERE.

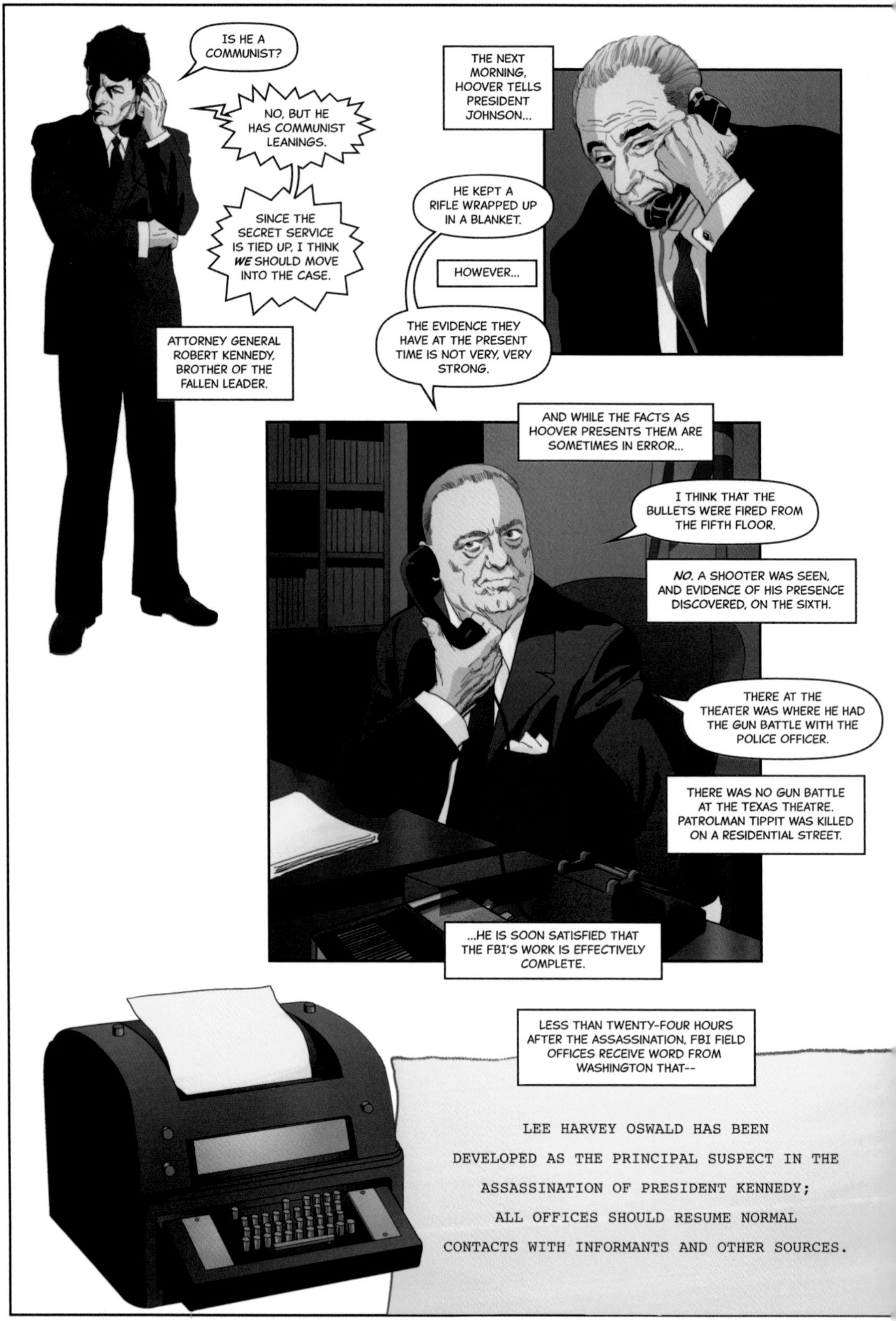
IS HE A COMMUNIST?
NO, BUT HE HAS COMMUNIST LEANINGS.
SINCE THE SECRET SERVICE IS TIED UP, I THINK *WE* SHOULD MOVE INTO THE CASE.
ATTORNEY GENERAL ROBERT KENNEDY, BROTHER OF THE FALLEN LEADER.
THE NEXT MORNING, HOOVER TELLS PRESIDENT JOHNSON...
HE KEPT A RIFLE WRAPPED UP IN A BLANKET.
HOWEVER...
THE EVIDENCE THEY HAVE AT THE PRESENT TIME IS NOT VERY, VERY STRONG.
AND WHILE THE FACTS AS HOOVER PRESENTS THEM ARE SOMETIMES IN ERROR...
I THINK THAT THE BULLETS WERE FIRED FROM THE FIFTH FLOOR.
NO. A SHOOTER WAS SEEN, AND EVIDENCE OF HIS PRESENCE DISCOVERED, ON THE SIXTH.
THERE AT THE THEATER WAS WHERE HE HAD THE GUN BATTLE WITH THE POLICE OFFICER.
THERE WAS NO GUN BATTLE AT THE TEXAS THEATRE. PATROLMAN TIPPIT WAS KILLED ON A RESIDENTIAL STREET.
...HE IS SOON SATISFIED THAT THE FBI'S WORK IS EFFECTIVELY COMPLETE.
LESS THAN TWENTY-FOUR HOURS AFTER THE ASSASSINATION, FBI FIELD OFFICES RECEIVE WORD FROM WASHINGTON THAT--
LEE HARVEY OSWALD HAS BEEN DEVELOPED AS THE PRINCIPAL SUSPECT IN THE ASSASSINATION OF PRESIDENT KENNEDY; ALL OFFICES SHOULD RESUME NORMAL CONTACTS WITH INFORMANTS AND OTHER SOURCES.

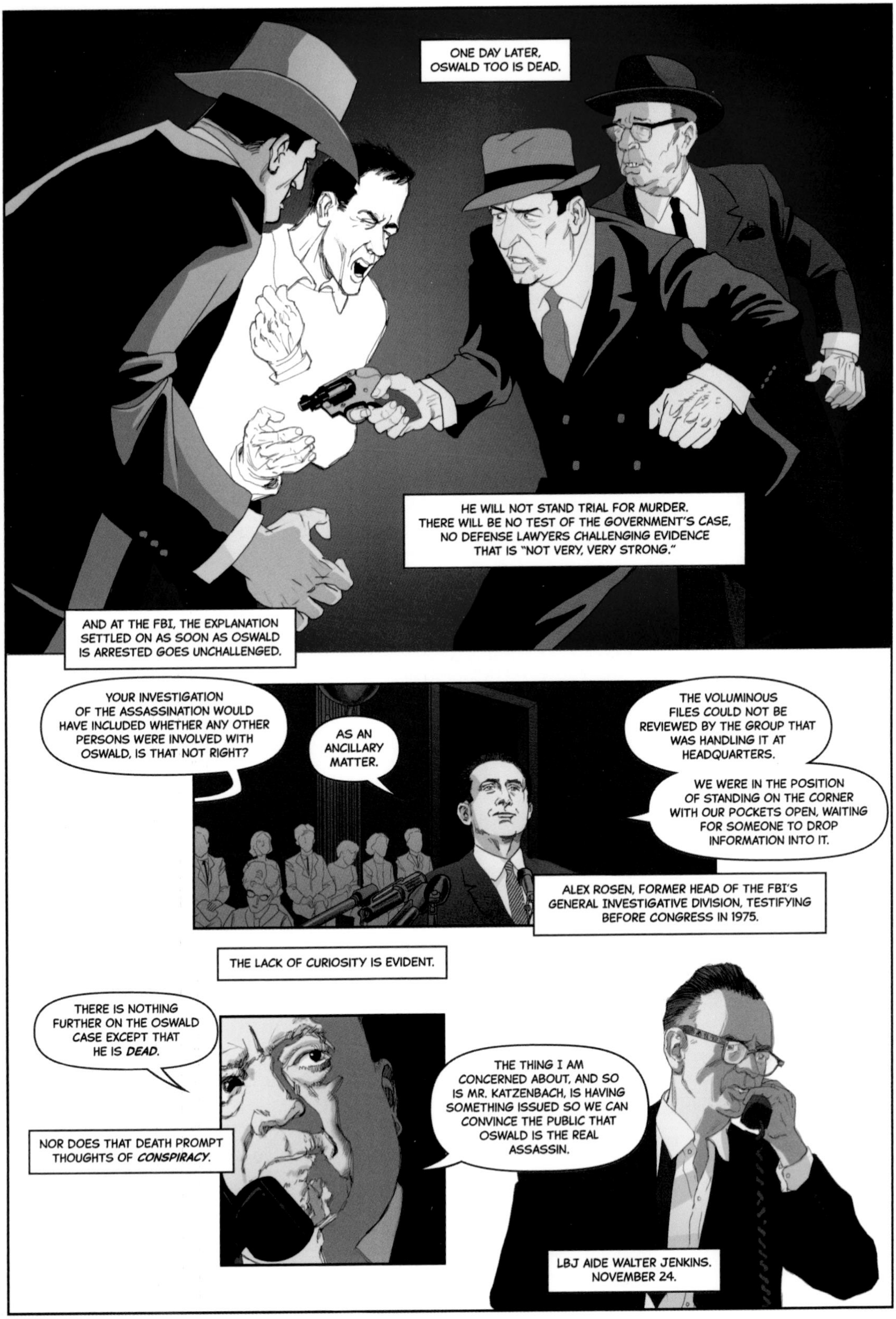
ONE DAY LATER, OSWALD TOO IS DEAD.
HE WILL NOT STAND TRIAL FOR MURDER. THERE WILL BE NO TEST OF THE GOVERNMENT'S CASE, NO DEFENSE LAWYERS CHALLENGING EVIDENCE THAT IS "NOT VERY, VERY STRONG."
AND AT THE FBI, THE EXPLANATION SETTLED ON AS SOON AS OSWALD IS ARRESTED GOES UNCHALLENGED.
YOUR INVESTIGATION OF THE ASSASSINATION WOULD HAVE INCLUDED WHETHER ANY OTHER PERSONS WERE INVOLVED WITH OSWALD, IS THAT NOT RIGHT?
AS AN ANCILLARY MATTER.
THE VOLUMINOUS FILES COULD NOT BE REVIEWED BY THE GROUP THAT WAS HANDLING IT AT HEADQUARTERS.
WE WERE IN THE POSITION OF STANDING ON THE CORNER WITH OUR POCKETS OPEN, WAITING FOR SOMEONE TO DROP INFORMATION INTO IT.
ALEX ROSEN, FORMER HEAD OF THE FBI'S GENERAL INVESTIGATIVE DIVISION, TESTIFYING BEFORE CONGRESS IN 1975.
THE LACK OF CURIOSITY IS EVIDENT.
THERE IS NOTHING FURTHER ON THE OSWALD CASE EXCEPT THAT HE IS *DEAD*.
NOR DOES THAT DEATH PROMPT THOUGHTS OF *CONSPIRACY*.
THE THING I AM CONCERNED ABOUT, AND SO IS MR. KATZENBACH, IS HAVING SOMETHING ISSUED SO WE CAN CONVINCE THE PUBLIC THAT OSWALD IS THE REAL ASSASSIN.
LBJ AIDE WALTER JENKINS. NOVEMBER 24.

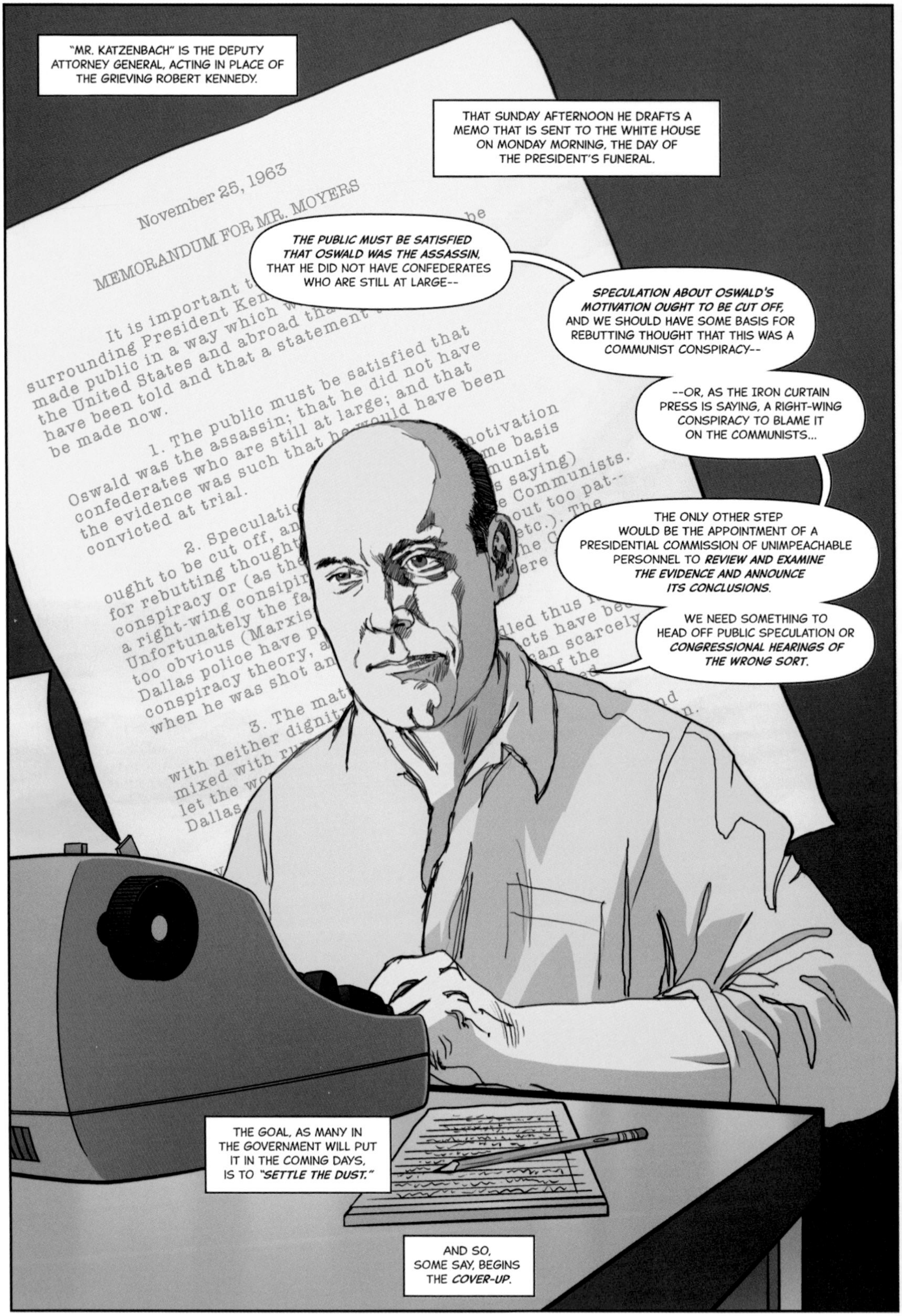
"MR. KATZENBACH" IS THE DEPUTY ATTORNEY GENERAL, ACTING IN PLACE OF THE GRIEVING ROBERT KENNEDY.
THAT SUNDAY AFTERNOON HE DRAFTS A MEMO THAT IS SENT TO THE WHITE HOUSE ON MONDAY MORNING, THE DAY OF THE PRESIDENT'S FUNERAL.
November 25, 1963
MEMORANDUM FOR MR. MOYERS
THE PUBLIC MUST BE SATISFIED THAT OSWALD WAS THE ASSASSIN, THAT HE DID NOT HAVE CONFEDERATES WHO ARE STILL AT LARGE--
SPECULATION ABOUT OSWALD'S MOTIVATION OUGHT TO BE CUT OFF, AND WE SHOULD HAVE SOME BASIS FOR REBUTTING THOUGHT THAT THIS WAS A COMMUNIST CONSPIRACY--
--OR, AS THE IRON CURTAIN PRESS IS SAYING, A RIGHT-WING CONSPIRACY TO BLAME IT ON THE COMMUNISTS...
THE ONLY OTHER STEP WOULD BE THE APPOINTMENT OF A PRESIDENTIAL COMMISSION OF UNIMPEACHABLE PERSONNEL TO *REVIEW AND EXAMINE THE EVIDENCE AND ANNOUNCE ITS CONCLUSIONS*.
WE NEED SOMETHING TO HEAD OFF PUBLIC SPECULATION OR *CONGRESSIONAL HEARINGS OF THE WRONG SORT*.
THE GOAL, AS MANY IN THE GOVERNMENT WILL PUT IT IN THE COMING DAYS, IS TO *"SETTLE THE DUST."*
AND SO, SOME SAY, BEGINS THE *COVER-UP*.

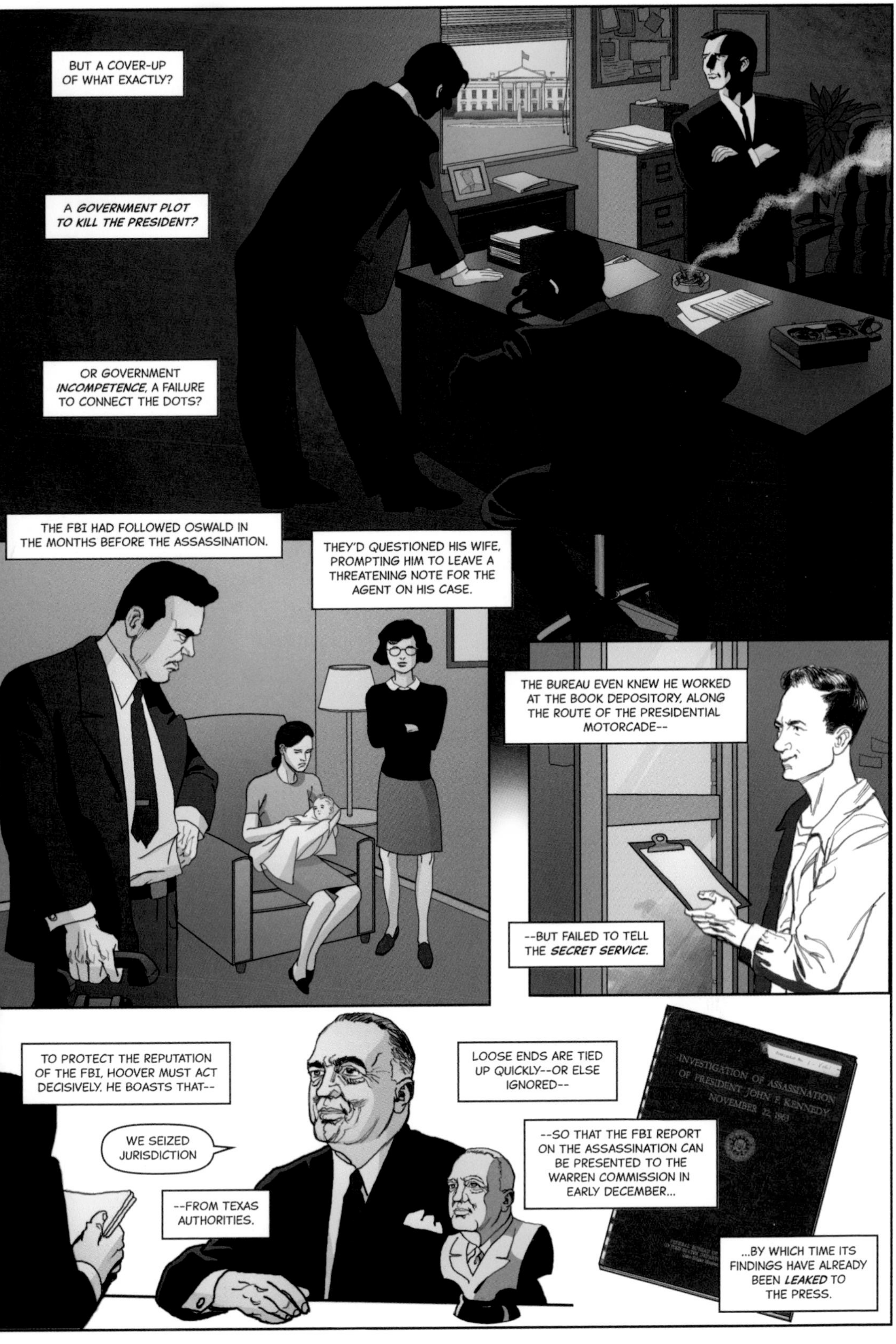
BUT A COVER-UP OF WHAT EXACTLY?
A *GOVERNMENT PLOT* TO KILL THE PRESIDENT?
OR GOVERNMENT *INCOMPETENCE*, A FAILURE TO CONNECT THE DOTS?
THE FBI HAD FOLLOWED OSWALD IN THE MONTHS BEFORE THE ASSASSINATION.
THEY'D QUESTIONED HIS WIFE, PROMPTING HIM TO LEAVE A THREATENING NOTE FOR THE AGENT ON HIS CASE.
THE BUREAU EVEN KNEW HE WORKED AT THE BOOK DEPOSITORY, ALONG THE ROUTE OF THE PRESIDENTIAL MOTORCADE--
--BUT FAILED TO TELL THE *SECRET SERVICE*.
TO PROTECT THE REPUTATION OF THE FBI, HOOVER MUST ACT DECISIVELY. HE BOASTS THAT--
WE SEIZED JURISDICTION
--FROM TEXAS AUTHORITIES.
LOOSE ENDS ARE TIED UP QUICKLY--OR ELSE IGNORED--
INVESTIGATION OF ASSASSINATION OF PRESIDENT JOHN F. KENNEDY NOVEMBER 22, 1963
--SO THAT THE FBI REPORT ON THE ASSASSINATION CAN BE PRESENTED TO THE WARREN COMMISSION IN EARLY DECEMBER...
...BY WHICH TIME ITS FINDINGS HAVE ALREADY BEEN *LEAKED* TO THE PRESS.

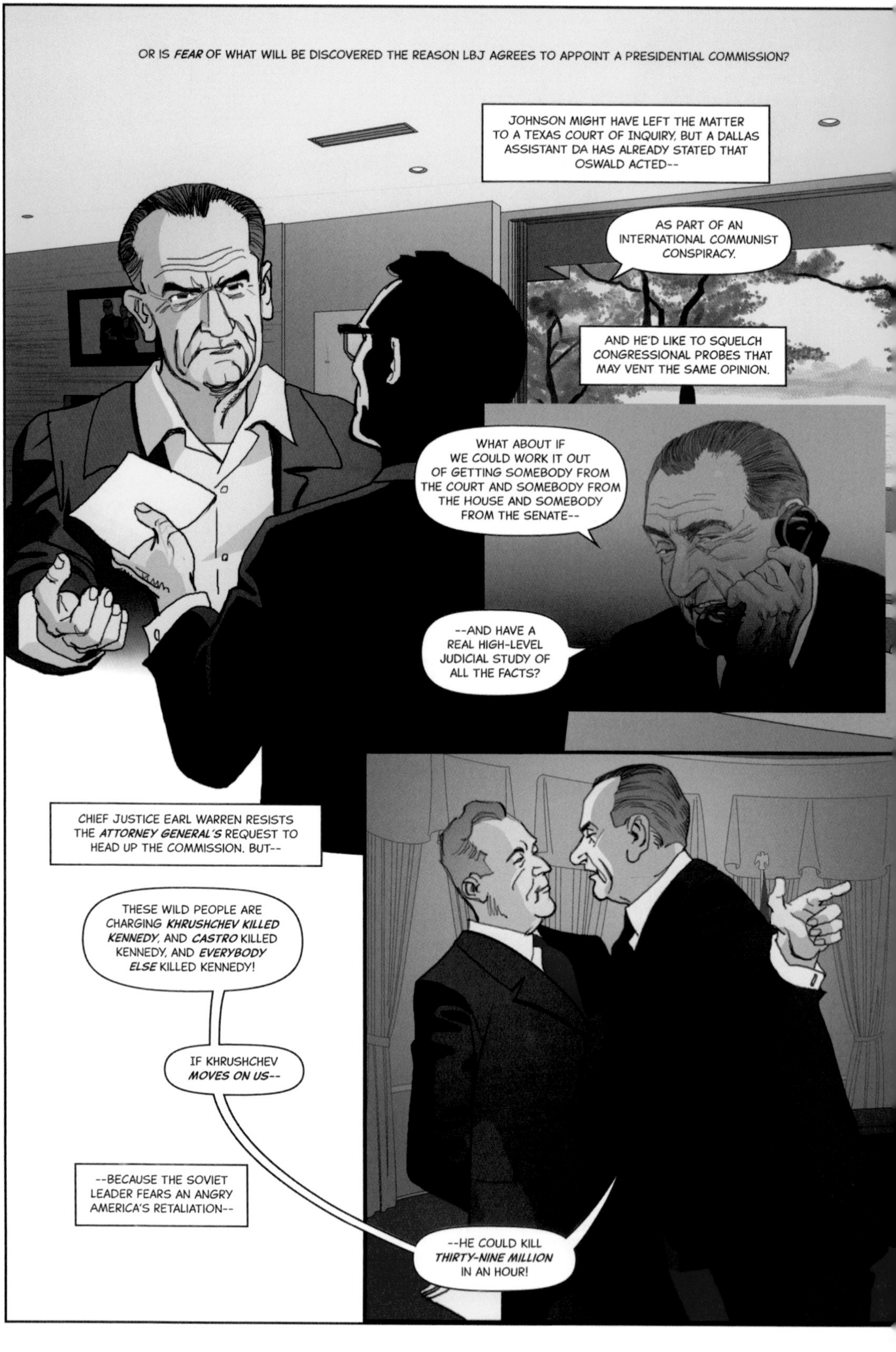
OR IS *FEAR* OF WHAT WILL BE DISCOVERED THE REASON LBJ AGREES TO APPOINT A PRESIDENTIAL COMMISSION?
JOHNSON MIGHT HAVE LEFT THE MATTER TO A TEXAS COURT OF INQUIRY, BUT A DALLAS ASSISTANT DA HAS ALREADY STATED THAT OSWALD ACTED--
AS PART OF AN INTERNATIONAL COMMUNIST CONSPIRACY.
AND HE'D LIKE TO SQUELCH CONGRESSIONAL PROBES THAT MAY VENT THE SAME OPINION.
WHAT ABOUT IF WE COULD WORK IT OUT OF GETTING SOMEBODY FROM THE COURT AND SOMEBODY FROM THE HOUSE AND SOMEBODY FROM THE SENATE--
--AND HAVE A REAL HIGH-LEVEL JUDICIAL STUDY OF ALL THE FACTS?
CHIEF JUSTICE EARL WARREN RESISTS THE *ATTORNEY GENERAL'S* REQUEST TO HEAD UP THE COMMISSION. BUT--
THESE WILD PEOPLE ARE CHARGING ***KHRUSHCHEV KILLED KENNEDY***, AND ***CASTRO*** KILLED KENNEDY, AND ***EVERYBODY ELSE*** KILLED KENNEDY!
IF KHRUSHCHEV ***MOVES ON US--***
--BECAUSE THE SOVIET LEADER FEARS AN ANGRY AMERICA'S RETALIATION--
--HE COULD KILL ***THIRTY-NINE MILLION*** IN AN HOUR!

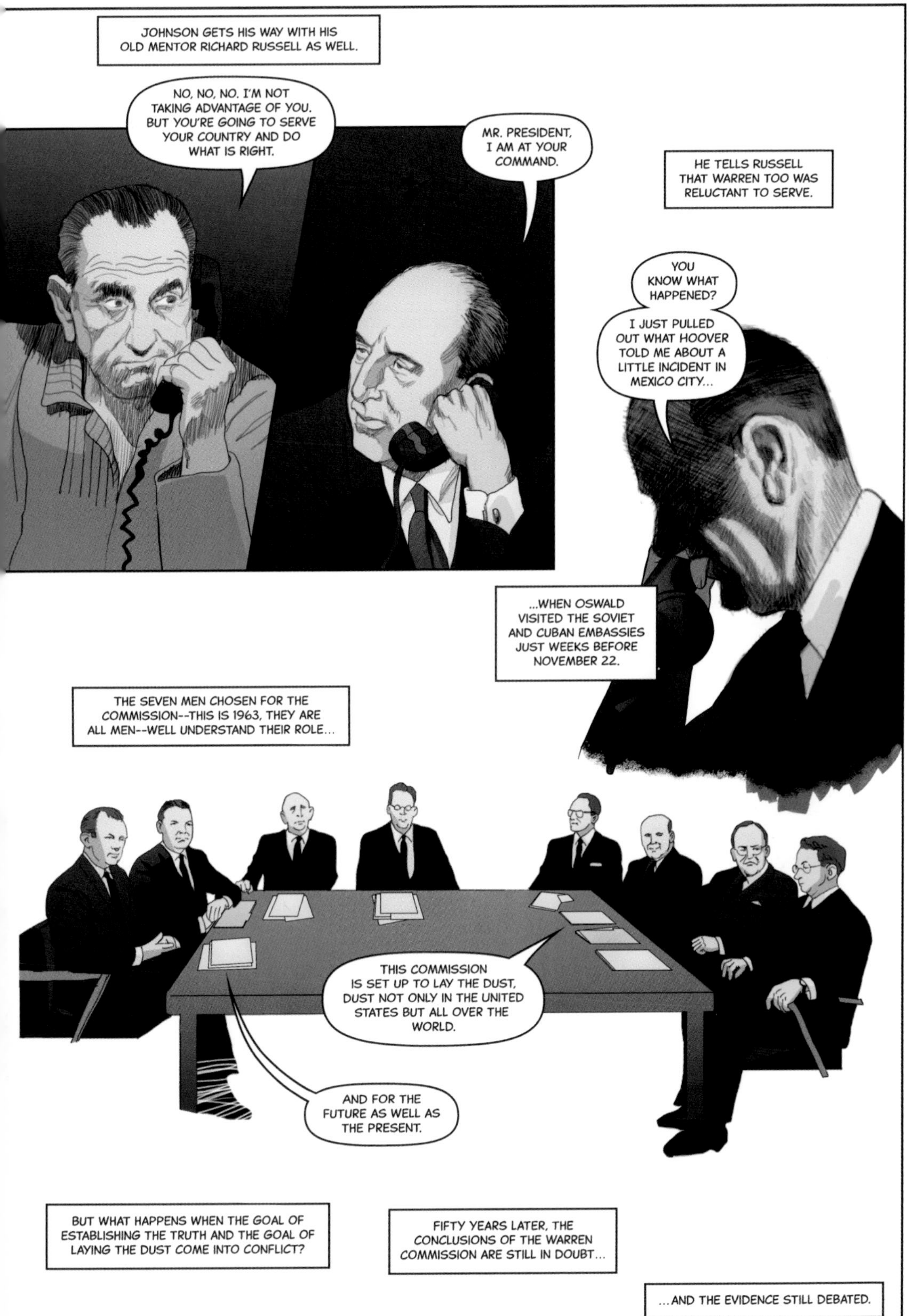
JOHNSON GETS HIS WAY WITH HIS OLD MENTOR RICHARD RUSSELL AS WELL.
NO, NO, NO. I'M NOT TAKING ADVANTAGE OF YOU. BUT YOU'RE GOING TO SERVE YOUR COUNTRY AND DO WHAT IS RIGHT.
MR. PRESIDENT, I AM AT YOUR COMMAND.
HE TELLS RUSSELL THAT WARREN TOO WAS RELUCTANT TO SERVE.
YOU KNOW WHAT HAPPENED?
I JUST PULLED OUT WHAT HOOVER TOLD ME ABOUT A LITTLE INCIDENT IN MEXICO CITY...
...WHEN OSWALD VISITED THE SOVIET AND CUBAN EMBASSIES JUST WEEKS BEFORE NOVEMBER 22.
THE SEVEN MEN CHOSEN FOR THE COMMISSION--THIS IS 1963, THEY ARE ALL MEN--WELL UNDERSTAND THEIR ROLE...
THIS COMMISSION IS SET UP TO LAY THE DUST, DUST NOT ONLY IN THE UNITED STATES BUT ALL OVER THE WORLD.
AND FOR THE FUTURE AS WELL AS THE PRESENT.
BUT WHAT HAPPENS WHEN THE GOAL OF ESTABLISHING THE TRUTH AND THE GOAL OF LAYING THE DUST COME INTO CONFLICT?
FIFTY YEARS LATER, THE CONCLUSIONS OF THE WARREN COMMISSION ARE STILL IN DOUBT...
...AND THE EVIDENCE STILL DEBATED.

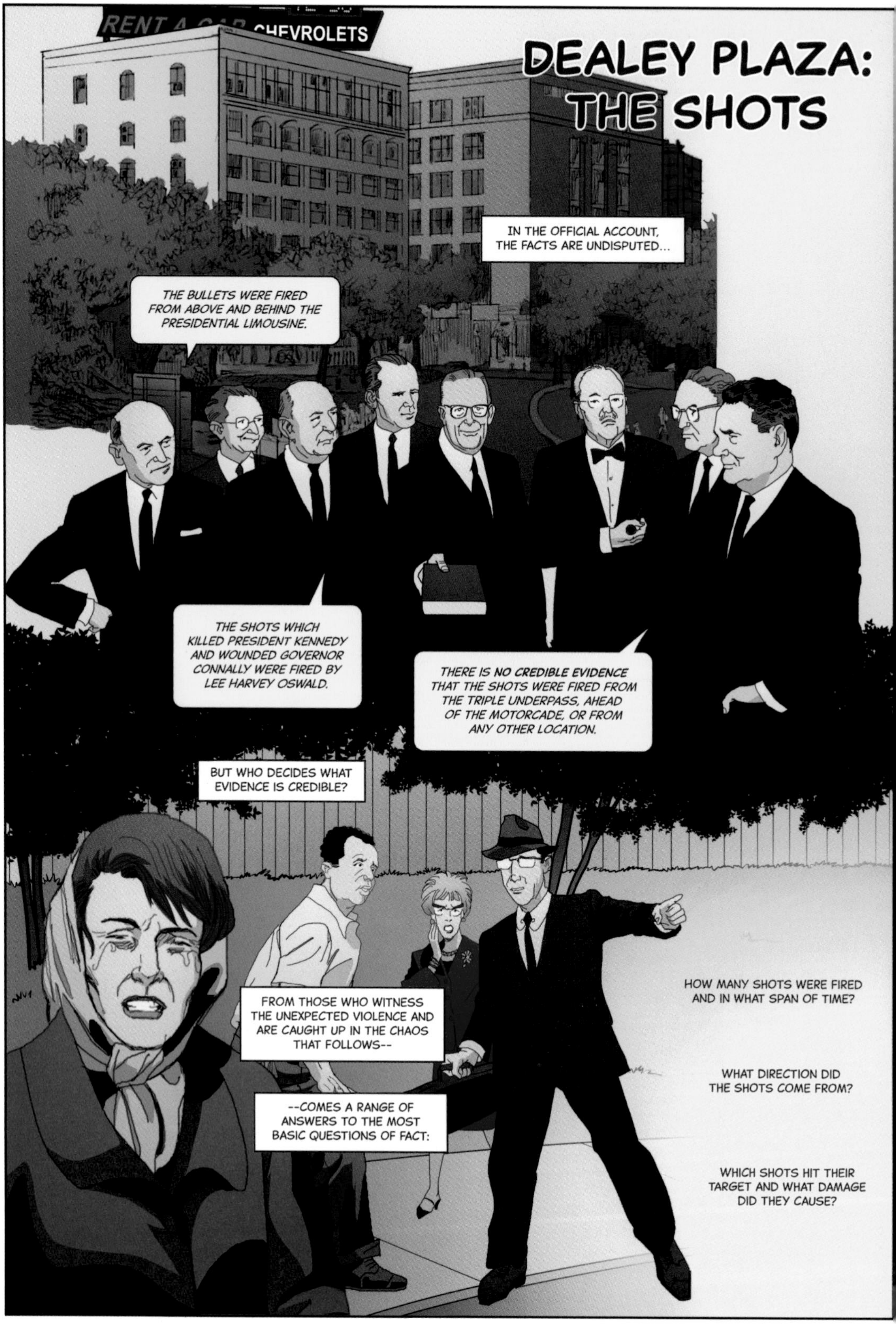
RENT A CAR CHEVROLETS
DEALEY PLAZA: THE SHOTS
IN THE OFFICIAL ACCOUNT, THE FACTS ARE UNDISPUTED...
THE BULLETS WERE FIRED FROM ABOVE AND BEHIND THE PRESIDENTIAL LIMOUSINE.
THE SHOTS WHICH KILLED PRESIDENT KENNEDY AND WOUNDED GOVERNOR CONNALLY WERE FIRED BY LEE HARVEY OSWALD.
THERE IS NO CREDIBLE EVIDENCE THAT THE SHOTS WERE FIRED FROM THE TRIPLE UNDERPASS, AHEAD OF THE MOTORCADE, OR FROM ANY OTHER LOCATION.
BUT WHO DECIDES WHAT EVIDENCE IS CREDIBLE?
FROM THOSE WHO WITNESS THE UNEXPECTED VIOLENCE AND ARE CAUGHT UP IN THE CHAOS THAT FOLLOWS--
--COMES A RANGE OF ANSWERS TO THE MOST BASIC QUESTIONS OF FACT:
HOW MANY SHOTS WERE FIRED AND IN WHAT SPAN OF TIME?
WHAT DIRECTION DID THE SHOTS COME FROM?
WHICH SHOTS HIT THEIR TARGET AND WHAT DAMAGE DID THEY CAUSE?

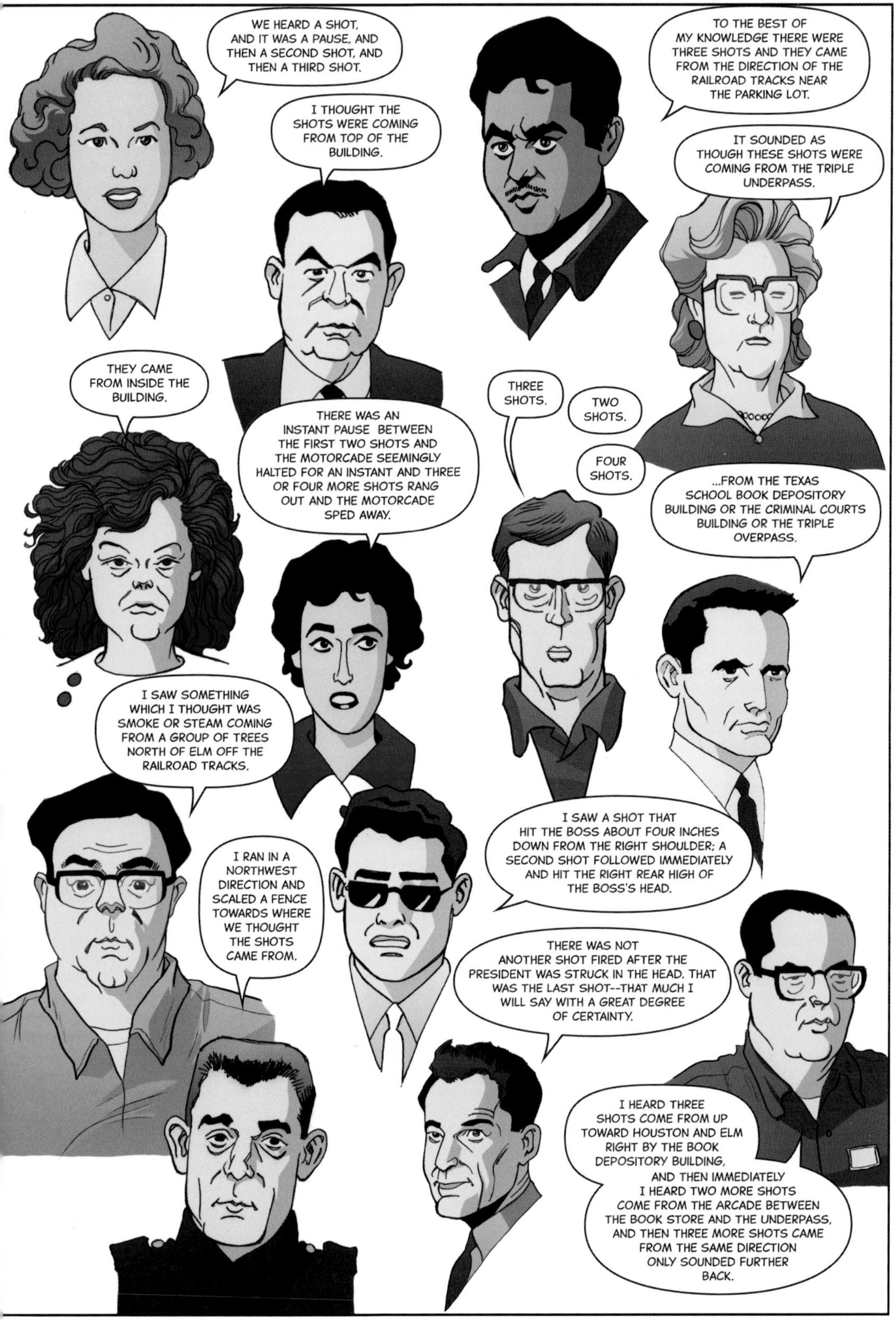
WE HEARD A SHOT, AND IT WAS A PAUSE, AND THEN A SECOND SHOT, AND THEN A THIRD SHOT.
I THOUGHT THE SHOTS WERE COMING FROM TOP OF THE BUILDING.
TO THE BEST OF MY KNOWLEDGE THERE WERE THREE SHOTS AND THEY CAME FROM THE DIRECTION OF THE RAILROAD TRACKS NEAR THE PARKING LOT.
IT SOUNDED AS THOUGH THESE SHOTS WERE COMING FROM THE TRIPLE UNDERPASS.
THEY CAME FROM INSIDE THE BUILDING.
THERE WAS AN INSTANT PAUSE BETWEEN THE FIRST TWO SHOTS AND THE MOTORCADE SEEMINGLY HALTED FOR AN INSTANT AND THREE OR FOUR MORE SHOTS RANG OUT AND THE MOTORCADE SPED AWAY.
THREE SHOTS.
TWO SHOTS.
FOUR SHOTS.
...FROM THE TEXAS SCHOOL BOOK DEPOSITORY BUILDING OR THE CRIMINAL COURTS BUILDING OR THE TRIPLE OVERPASS.
I SAW SOMETHING WHICH I THOUGHT WAS SMOKE OR STEAM COMING FROM A GROUP OF TREES NORTH OF ELM OFF THE RAILROAD TRACKS.
I SAW A SHOT THAT HIT THE BOSS ABOUT FOUR INCHES DOWN FROM THE RIGHT SHOULDER; A SECOND SHOT FOLLOWED IMMEDIATELY AND HIT THE RIGHT REAR HIGH OF THE BOSS'S HEAD.
I RAN IN A NORTHWEST DIRECTION AND SCALED A FENCE TOWARDS WHERE WE THOUGHT THE SHOTS CAME FROM.
THERE WAS NOT ANOTHER SHOT FIRED AFTER THE PRESIDENT WAS STRUCK IN THE HEAD. THAT WAS THE LAST SHOT--THAT MUCH I WILL SAY WITH A GREAT DEGREE OF CERTAINTY.
I HEARD THREE SHOTS COME FROM UP TOWARD HOUSTON AND ELM RIGHT BY THE BOOK DEPOSITORY BUILDING, AND THEN IMMEDIATELY I HEARD TWO MORE SHOTS COME FROM THE ARCADE BETWEEN THE BOOK STORE AND THE UNDERPASS, AND THEN THREE MORE SHOTS CAME FROM THE SAME DIRECTION ONLY SOUNDED FURTHER BACK.

THERE ARE WITNESSES WHO PLACE THE SHOOTER EXACTLY WHERE THE WARREN COMMISSION PUTS LEE HARVEY OSWALD...

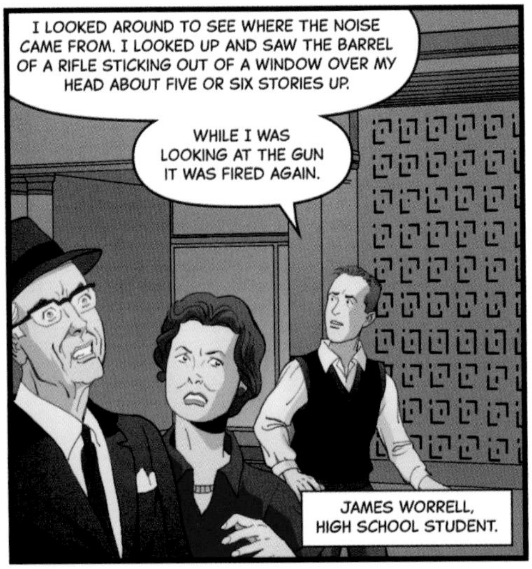
I LOOKED AROUND TO SEE WHERE THE NOISE CAME FROM. I LOOKED UP AND SAW THE BARREL OF A RIFLE STICKING OUT OF A WINDOW OVER MY HEAD ABOUT FIVE OR SIX STORIES UP.
WHILE I WAS LOOKING AT THE GUN IT WAS FIRED AGAIN.
JAMES WORRELL, HIGH SCHOOL STUDENT.

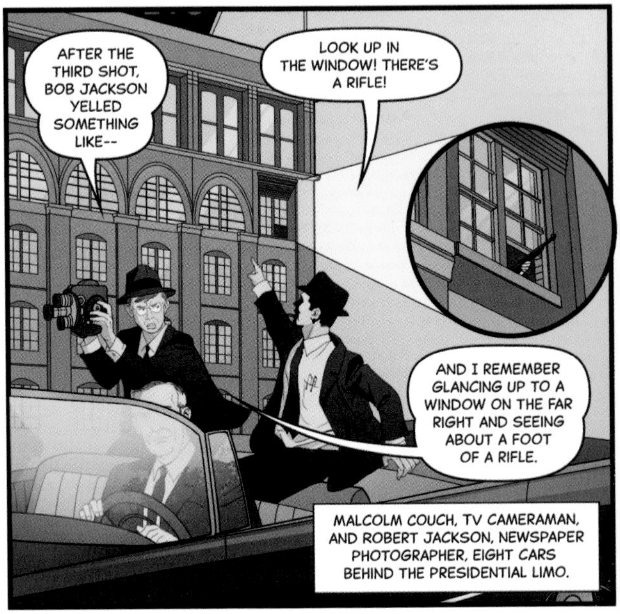
AFTER THE THIRD SHOT, BOB JACKSON YELLED SOMETHING LIKE--
LOOK UP IN THE WINDOW! THERE'S A RIFLE!
AND I REMEMBER GLANCING UP TO A WINDOW ON THE FAR RIGHT AND SEEING ABOUT A FOOT OF A RIFLE.
MALCOLM COUCH, TV CAMERAMAN, AND ROBERT JACKSON, NEWSPAPER PHOTOGRAPHER, EIGHT CARS BEHIND THE PRESIDENTIAL LIMO.

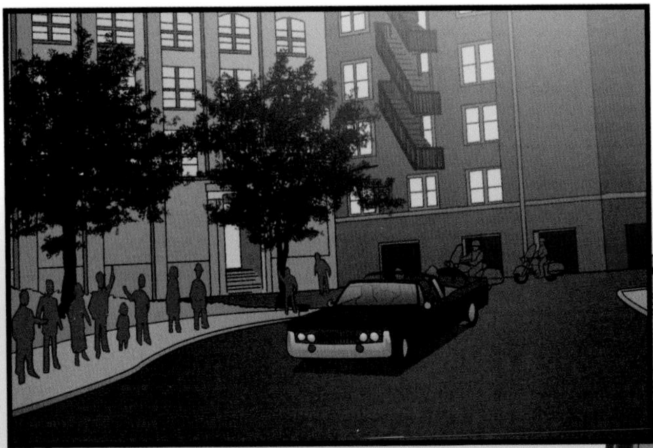

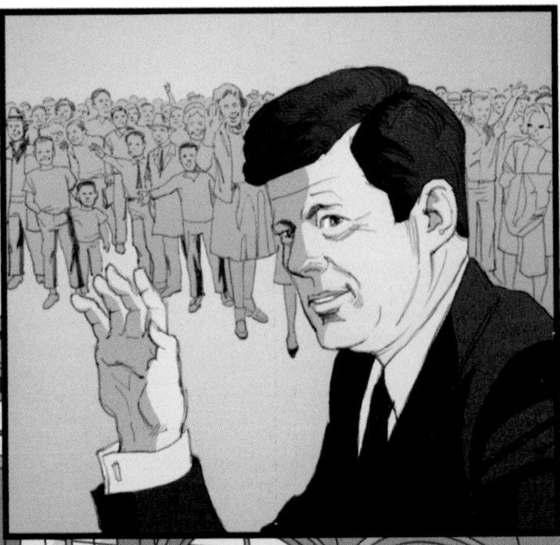

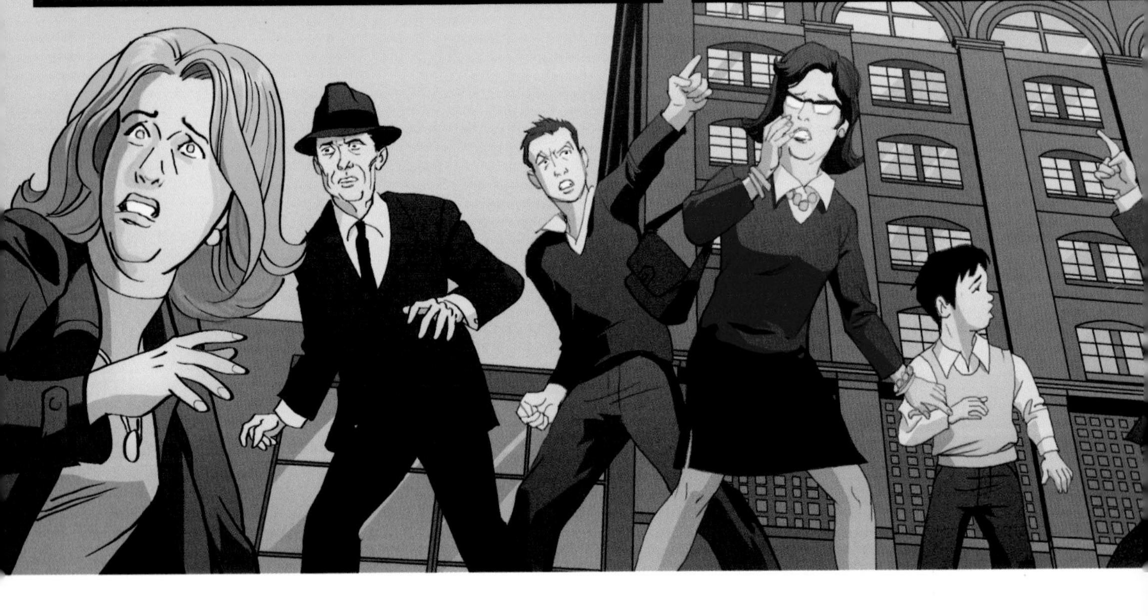

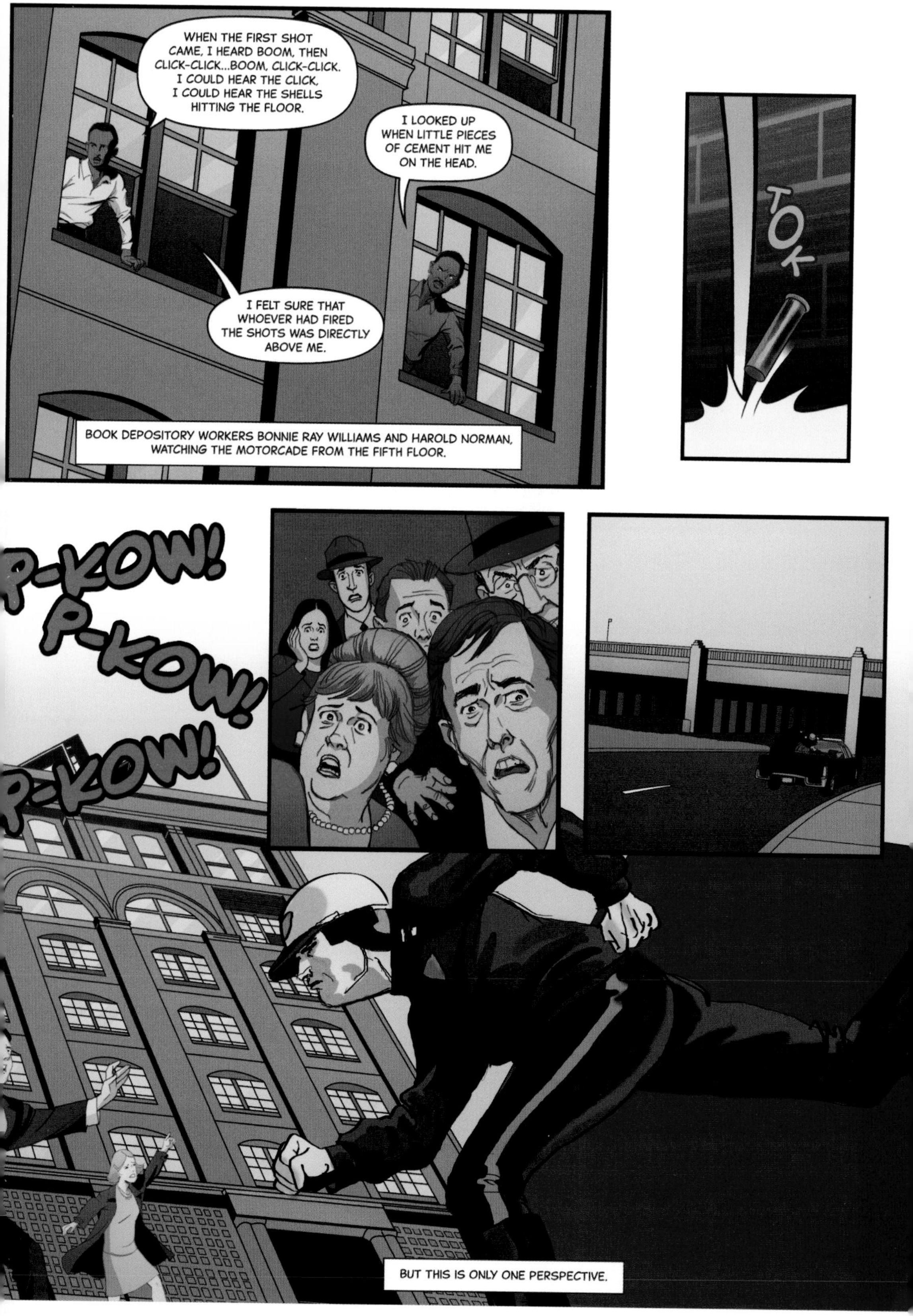

WHEN THE FIRST SHOT CAME, I HEARD BOOM, THEN CLICK-CLICK...BOOM, CLICK-CLICK. I COULD HEAR THE CLICK, I COULD HEAR THE SHELLS HITTING THE FLOOR.
I LOOKED UP WHEN LITTLE PIECES OF CEMENT HIT ME ON THE HEAD.
I FELT SURE THAT WHOEVER HAD FIRED THE SHOTS WAS DIRECTLY ABOVE ME.
BOOK DEPOSITORY WORKERS BONNIE RAY WILLIAMS AND HAROLD NORMAN, WATCHING THE MOTORCADE FROM THE FIFTH FLOOR.
TOK
P-KOW!
P-KOW!
P-KOW!
BUT THIS IS ONLY ONE PERSPECTIVE.

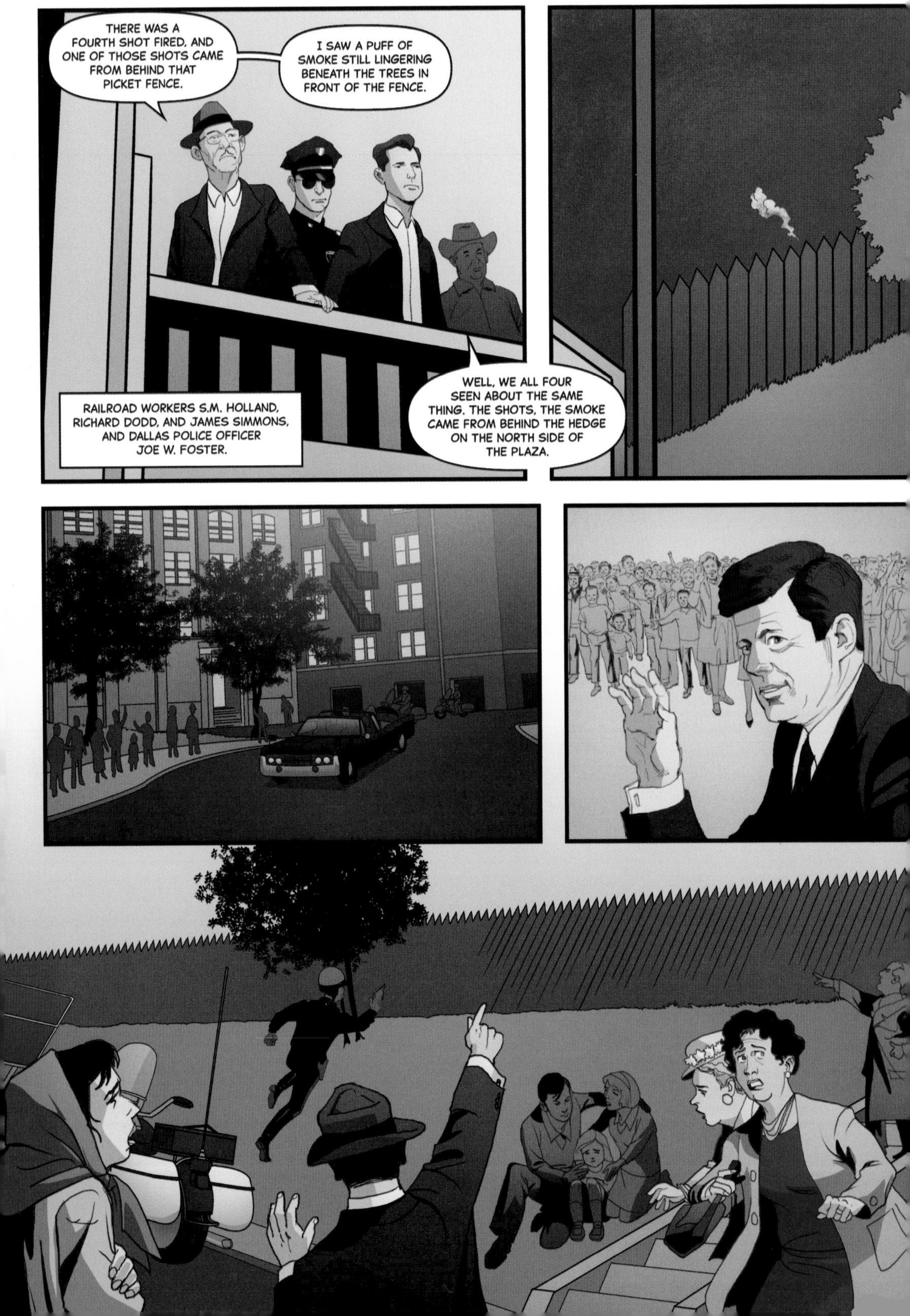
THERE WAS A FOURTH SHOT FIRED, AND ONE OF THOSE SHOTS CAME FROM BEHIND THAT PICKET FENCE.
I SAW A PUFF OF SMOKE STILL LINGERING BENEATH THE TREES IN FRONT OF THE FENCE.
RAILROAD WORKERS S.M. HOLLAND, RICHARD DODD, AND JAMES SIMMONS, AND DALLAS POLICE OFFICER JOE W. FOSTER.
WELL, WE ALL FOUR SEEN ABOUT THE SAME THING. THE SHOTS, THE SMOKE CAME FROM BEHIND THE HEDGE ON THE NORTH SIDE OF THE PLAZA.

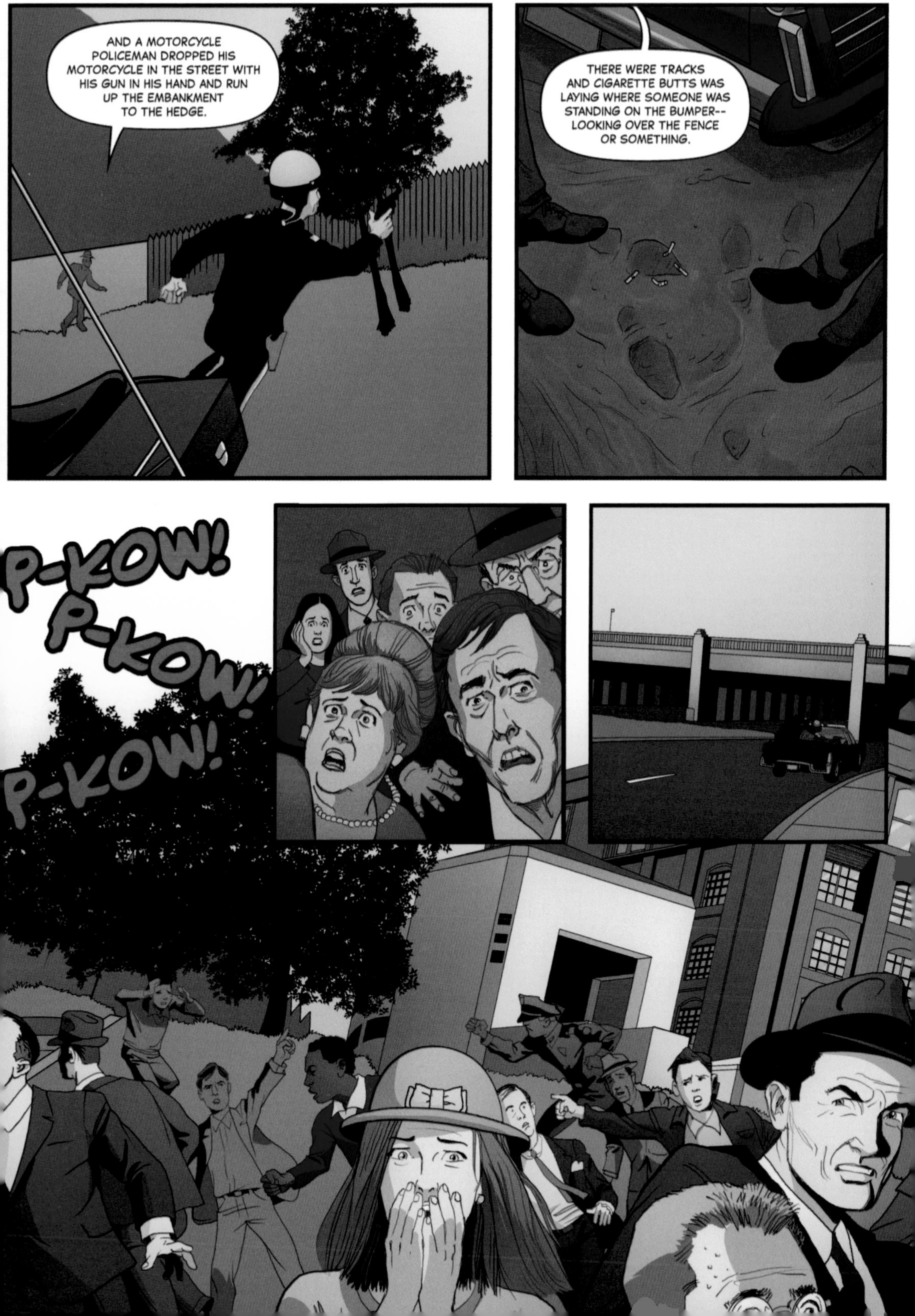
AND A MOTORCYCLE POLICEMAN DROPPED HIS MOTORCYCLE IN THE STREET WITH HIS GUN IN HIS HAND AND RUN UP THE EMBANKMENT TO THE HEDGE.
THERE WERE TRACKS AND CIGARETTE BUTTS WAS LAYING WHERE SOMEONE WAS STANDING ON THE BUMPER-- LOOKING OVER THE FENCE OR SOMETHING.
P-KOW!
P-KOW!
P-KOW!

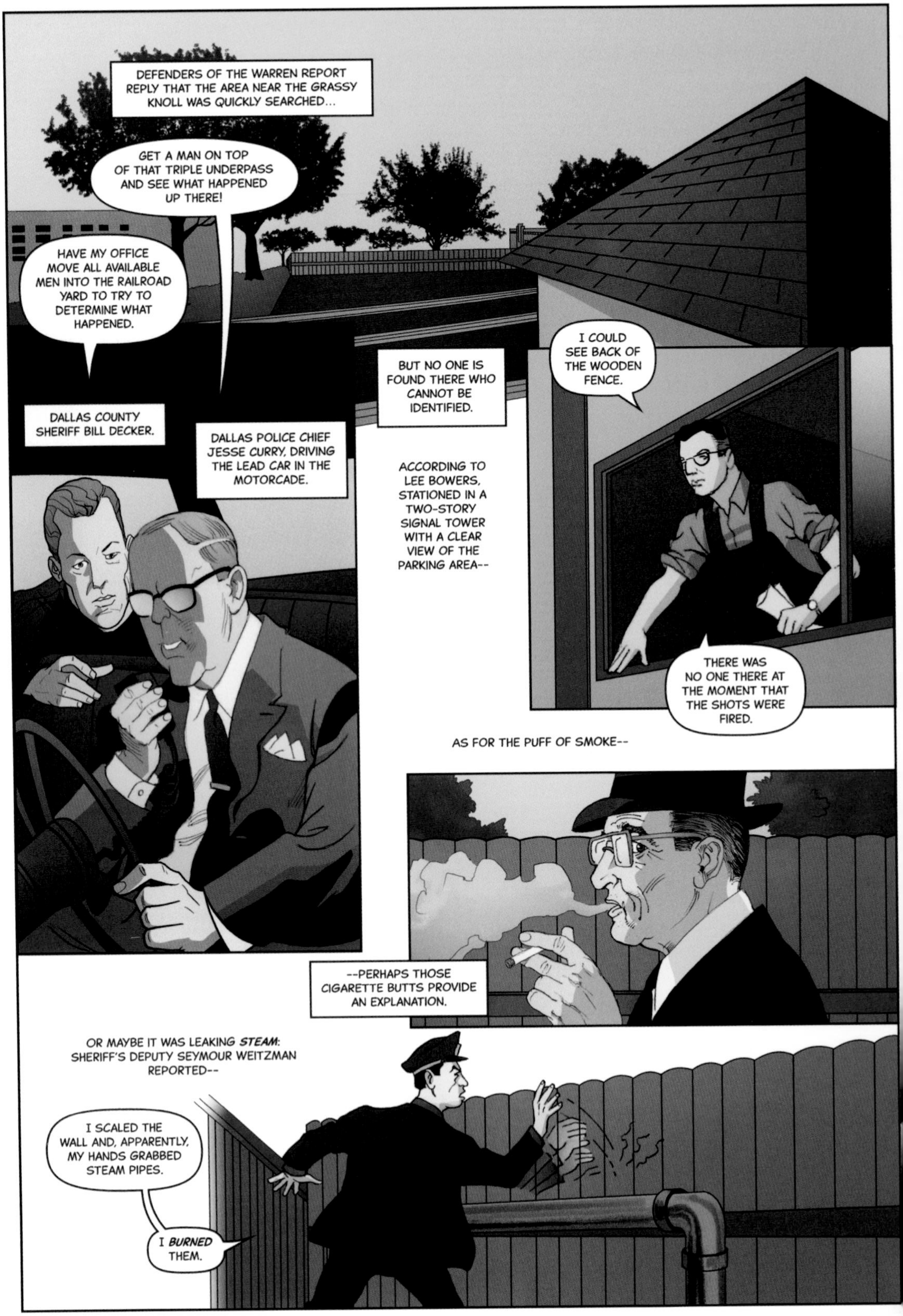
DEFENDERS OF THE WARREN REPORT REPLY THAT THE AREA NEAR THE GRASSY KNOLL WAS QUICKLY SEARCHED...
GET A MAN ON TOP OF THAT TRIPLE UNDERPASS AND SEE WHAT HAPPENED UP THERE!
HAVE MY OFFICE MOVE ALL AVAILABLE MEN INTO THE RAILROAD YARD TO TRY TO DETERMINE WHAT HAPPENED.
DALLAS COUNTY SHERIFF BILL DECKER.
DALLAS POLICE CHIEF JESSE CURRY, DRIVING THE LEAD CAR IN THE MOTORCADE.
BUT NO ONE IS FOUND THERE WHO CANNOT BE IDENTIFIED.
ACCORDING TO LEE BOWERS, STATIONED IN A TWO-STORY SIGNAL TOWER WITH A CLEAR VIEW OF THE PARKING AREA--
I COULD SEE BACK OF THE WOODEN FENCE.
THERE WAS NO ONE THERE AT THE MOMENT THAT THE SHOTS WERE FIRED.
AS FOR THE PUFF OF SMOKE--
--PERHAPS THOSE CIGARETTE BUTTS PROVIDE AN EXPLANATION.
OR MAYBE IT WAS LEAKING *STEAM*: SHERIFF'S DEPUTY SEYMOUR WEITZMAN REPORTED--
I SCALED THE WALL AND, APPARENTLY, MY HANDS GRABBED STEAM PIPES.
I *BURNED* THEM.

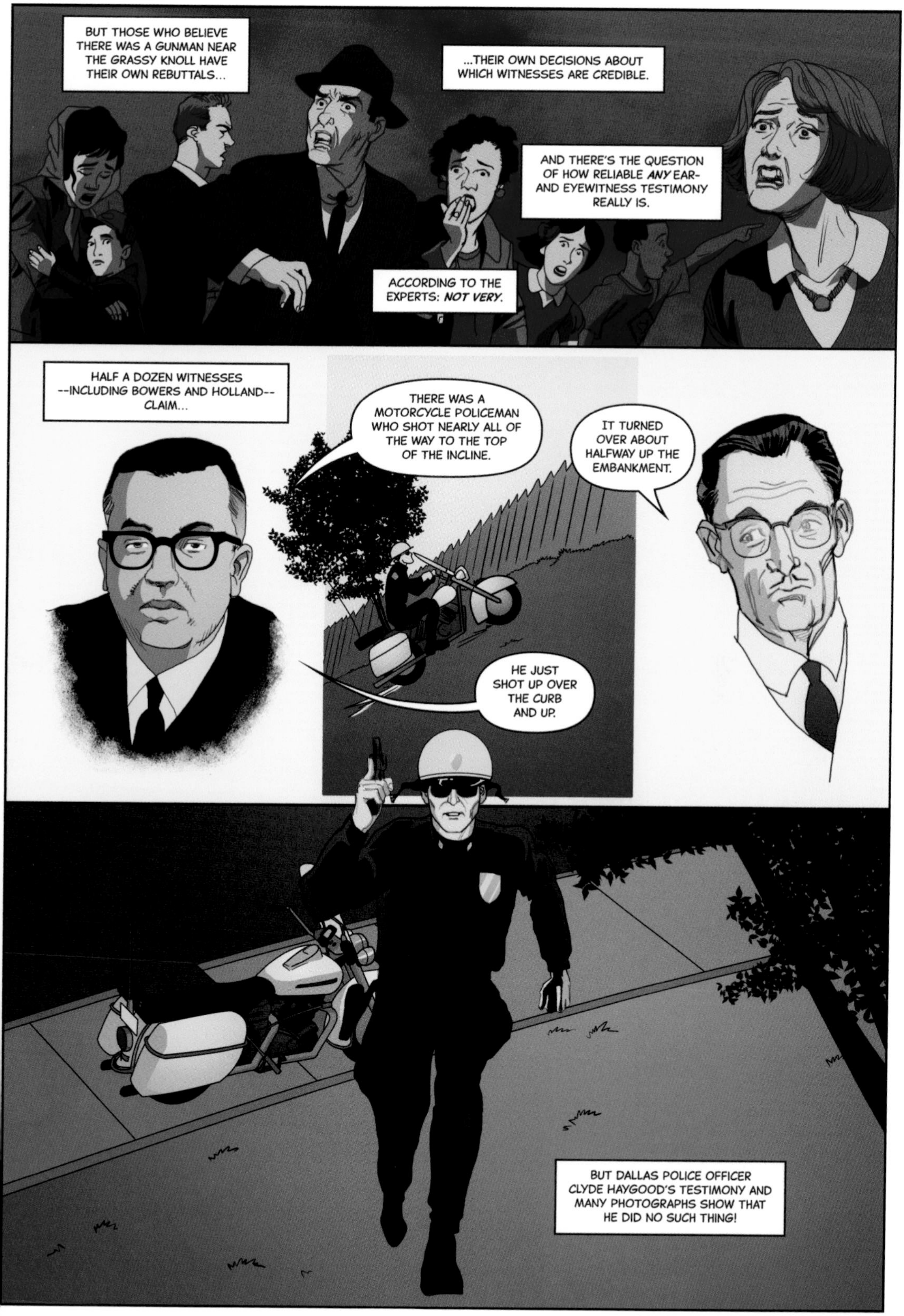
BUT THOSE WHO BELIEVE THERE WAS A GUNMAN NEAR THE GRASSY KNOLL HAVE THEIR OWN REBUTTALS...
...THEIR OWN DECISIONS ABOUT WHICH WITNESSES ARE CREDIBLE.
AND THERE'S THE QUESTION OF HOW RELIABLE *ANY* EAR- AND EYEWITNESS TESTIMONY REALLY IS.
ACCORDING TO THE EXPERTS: ***NOT VERY.***
HALF A DOZEN WITNESSES --INCLUDING BOWERS AND HOLLAND-- CLAIM...
THERE WAS A MOTORCYCLE POLICEMAN WHO SHOT NEARLY ALL OF THE WAY TO THE TOP OF THE INCLINE.
IT TURNED OVER ABOUT HALFWAY UP THE EMBANKMENT.
HE JUST SHOT UP OVER THE CURB AND UP.
BUT DALLAS POLICE OFFICER CLYDE HAYGOOD'S TESTIMONY AND MANY PHOTOGRAPHS SHOW THAT HE DID NO SUCH THING!

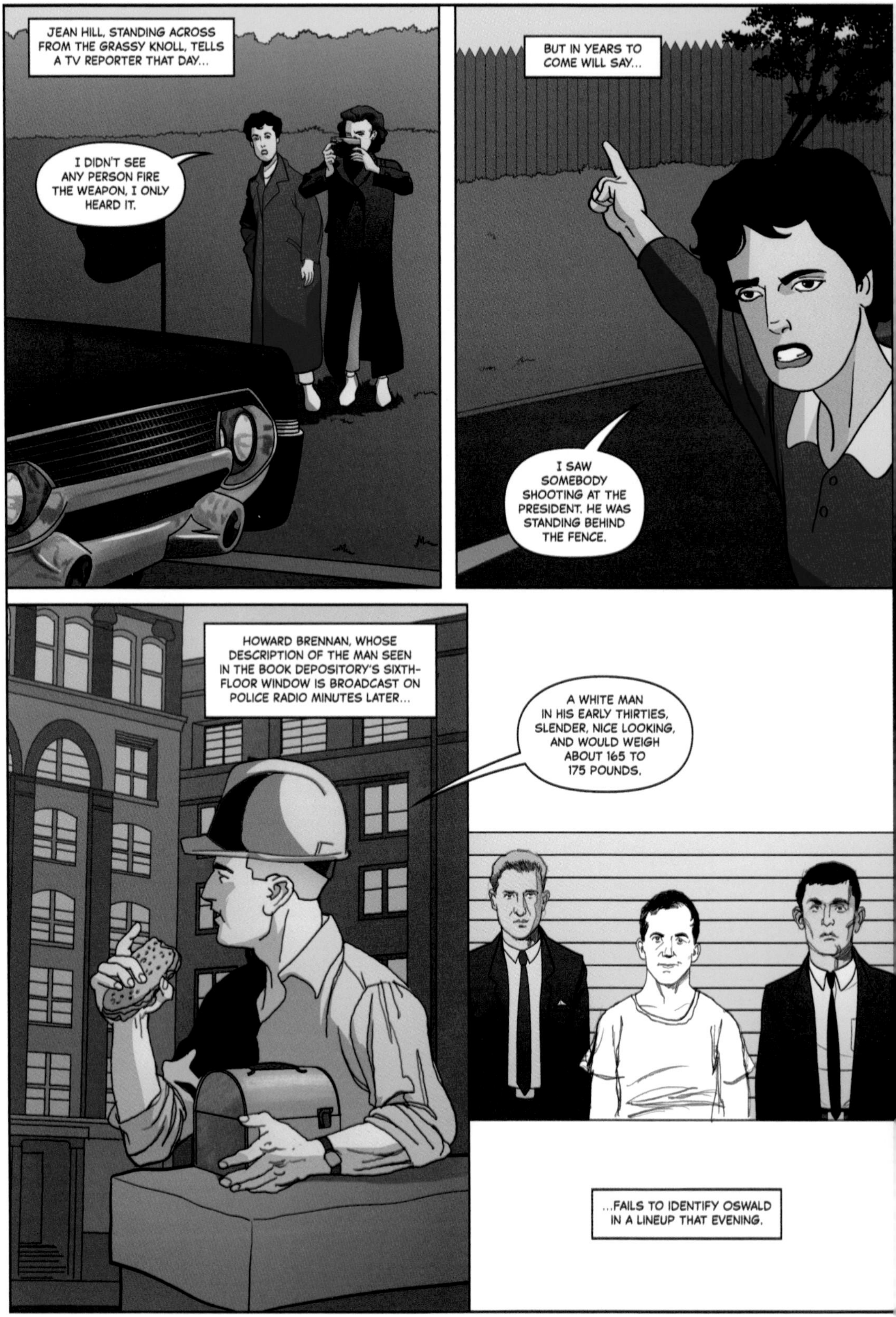
JEAN HILL, STANDING ACROSS FROM THE GRASSY KNOLL, TELLS A TV REPORTER THAT DAY...
I DIDN'T SEE ANY PERSON FIRE THE WEAPON, I ONLY HEARD IT.
BUT IN YEARS TO COME WILL SAY...
I SAW SOMEBODY SHOOTING AT THE PRESIDENT. HE WAS STANDING BEHIND THE FENCE.
HOWARD BRENNAN, WHOSE DESCRIPTION OF THE MAN SEEN IN THE BOOK DEPOSITORY'S SIXTH-FLOOR WINDOW IS BROADCAST ON POLICE RADIO MINUTES LATER...
A WHITE MAN IN HIS EARLY THIRTIES, SLENDER, NICE LOOKING, AND WOULD WEIGH ABOUT 165 TO 175 POUNDS.
...FAILS TO IDENTIFY OSWALD IN A LINEUP THAT EVENING.

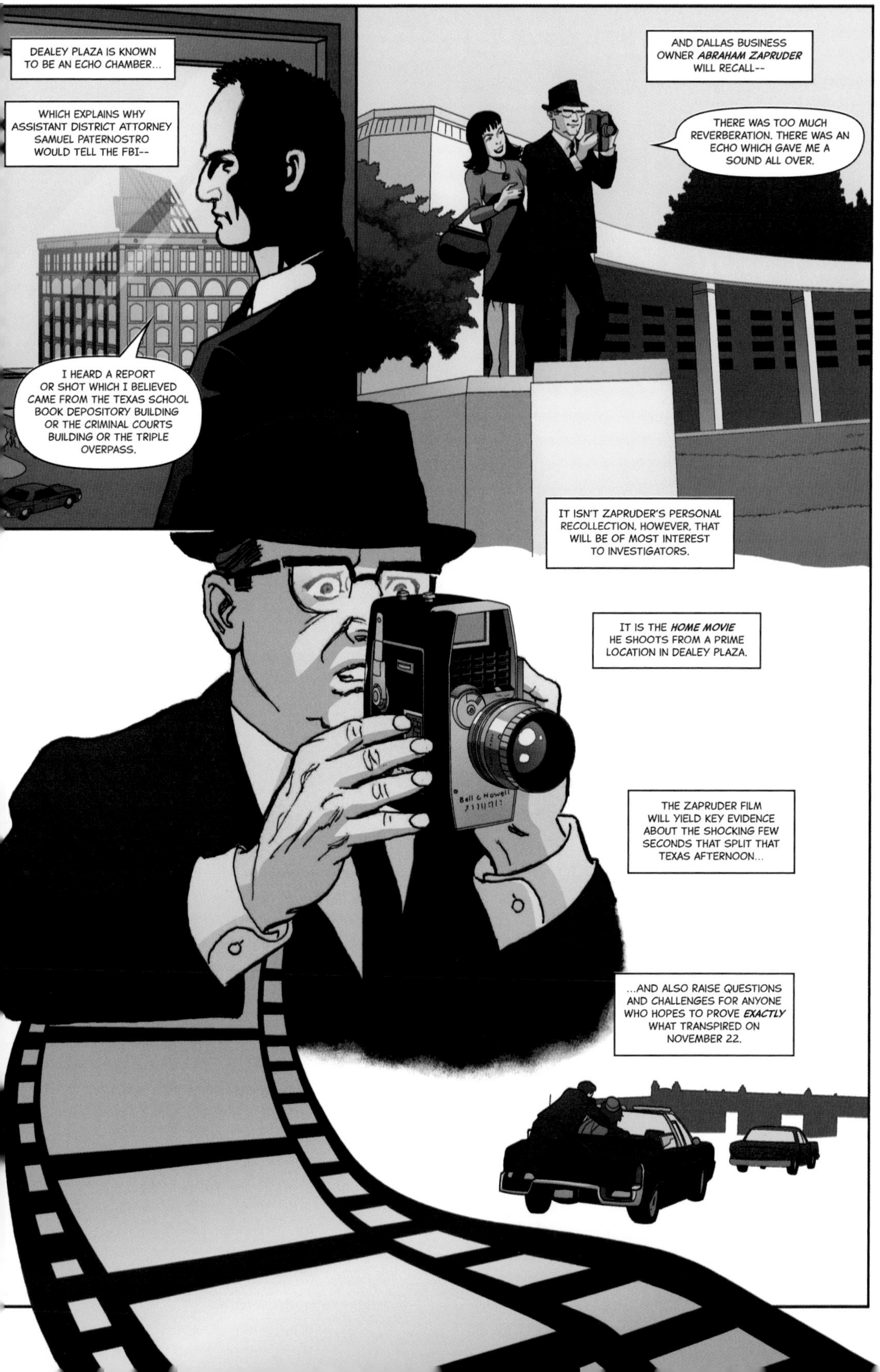
DEALEY PLAZA IS KNOWN TO BE AN ECHO CHAMBER...
WHICH EXPLAINS WHY ASSISTANT DISTRICT ATTORNEY SAMUEL PATERNOSTRO WOULD TELL THE FBI--
I HEARD A REPORT OR SHOT WHICH I BELIEVED CAME FROM THE TEXAS SCHOOL BOOK DEPOSITORY BUILDING OR THE CRIMINAL COURTS BUILDING OR THE TRIPLE OVERPASS.
AND DALLAS BUSINESS OWNER ABRAHAM ZAPRUDER WILL RECALL--
THERE WAS TOO MUCH REVERBERATION. THERE WAS AN ECHO WHICH GAVE ME A SOUND ALL OVER.
IT ISN'T ZAPRUDER'S PERSONAL RECOLLECTION, HOWEVER, THAT WILL BE OF MOST INTEREST TO INVESTIGATORS.
IT IS THE HOME MOVIE HE SHOOTS FROM A PRIME LOCATION IN DEALEY PLAZA.
Bell & Howell
THE ZAPRUDER FILM WILL YIELD KEY EVIDENCE ABOUT THE SHOCKING FEW SECONDS THAT SPLIT THAT TEXAS AFTERNOON...
...AND ALSO RAISE QUESTIONS AND CHALLENGES FOR ANYONE WHO HOPES TO PROVE EXACTLY WHAT TRANSPIRED ON NOVEMBER 22.

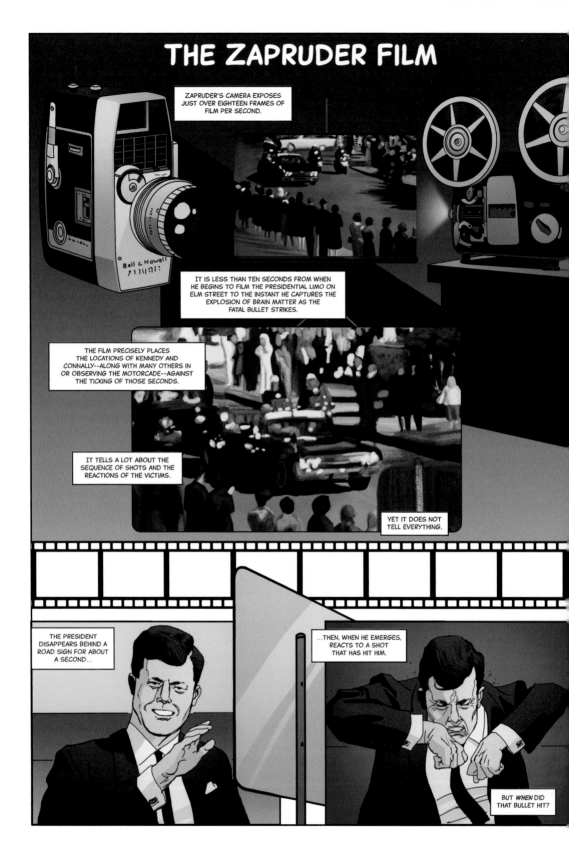

THE ZAPRUDER FILM

ZAPRUDER'S CAMERA EXPOSES JUST OVER EIGHTEEN FRAMES OF FILM PER SECOND.

IT IS LESS THAN TEN SECONDS FROM WHEN HE BEGINS TO FILM THE PRESIDENTIAL LIMO ON ELM STREET TO THE INSTANT HE CAPTURES THE EXPLOSION OF BRAIN MATTER AS THE FATAL BULLET STRIKES.

THE FILM PRECISELY PLACES THE LOCATIONS OF KENNEDY AND CONNALLY--ALONG WITH MANY OTHERS IN OR OBSERVING THE MOTORCADE--AGAINST THE TICKING OF THOSE SECONDS.

IT TELLS A LOT ABOUT THE SEQUENCE OF SHOTS AND THE REACTIONS OF THE VICTIMS.

YET IT DOES NOT TELL EVERYTHING.

THE PRESIDENT DISAPPEARS BEHIND A ROAD SIGN FOR ABOUT A SECOND...

...THEN, WHEN HE EMERGES, REACTS TO A SHOT THAT HAS HIT HIM.

BUT *WHEN* DID THAT BULLET HIT?

AND WHAT *CAN* THE LOW-RESOLUTION IMAGES TELL US ABOUT *GOVERNOR JOHN CONNALLY'S* WOUNDS?

DOES THIS ONE SHOW THE GOVERNOR'S LAPEL FLYING OUTWARD AS A BULLET EXITS HIS CHEST?

OR DOES THIS *LATER* IMAGE SHOW HIS SHOULDER DROPPING AND HIS CHEEKS PUFFING OUT AT THE INSTANT OF THE BULLET'S IMPACT?

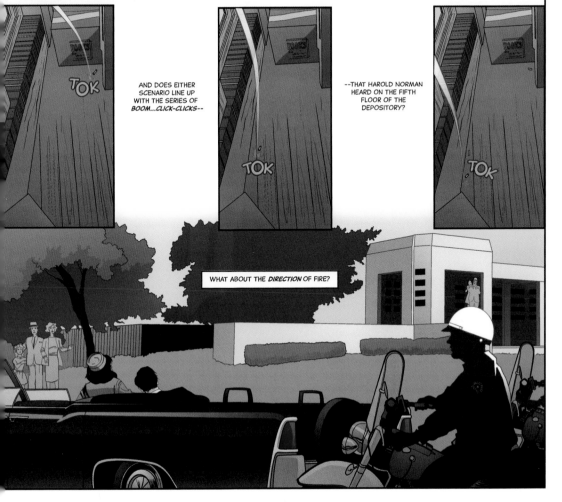

AND DOES EITHER SCENARIO LINE UP WITH THE SERIES OF *BOOM...CLICK-CLICKS--*

--THAT HAROLD NORMAN HEARD ON THE FIFTH FLOOR OF THE DEPOSITORY?

TOK

TOK

TOK

WHAT ABOUT THE *DIRECTION* OF FIRE?

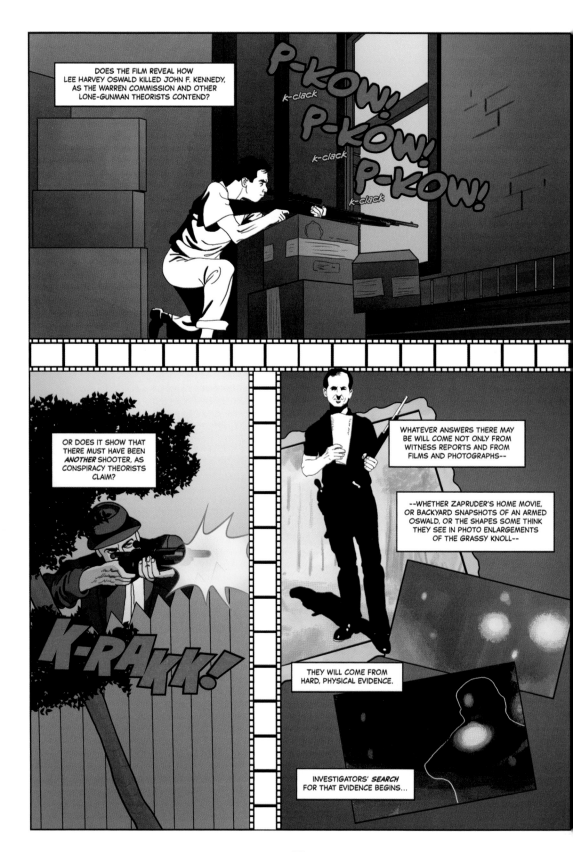

DOES THE FILM REVEAL HOW LEE HARVEY OSWALD KILLED JOHN F. KENNEDY, AS THE WARREN COMMISSION AND OTHER LONE-GUNMAN THEORISTS CONTEND?

P-KOW!
k-clack
P-KOW!
k-clack
P-KOW!
k-clack

OR DOES IT SHOW THAT THERE MUST HAVE BEEN *ANOTHER* SHOOTER, AS CONSPIRACY THEORISTS CLAIM?

K-RAKK!

WHATEVER ANSWERS THERE MAY BE WILL COME NOT ONLY FROM WITNESS REPORTS AND FROM FILMS AND PHOTOGRAPHS--

--WHETHER ZAPRUDER'S HOME MOVIE, OR BACKYARD SNAPSHOTS OF AN ARMED OSWALD, OR THE SHAPES SOME THINK THEY SEE IN PHOTO ENLARGEMENTS OF THE GRASSY KNOLL--

THEY WILL COME FROM HARD, PHYSICAL EVIDENCE.

INVESTIGATORS' *SEARCH* FOR THAT EVIDENCE BEGINS...

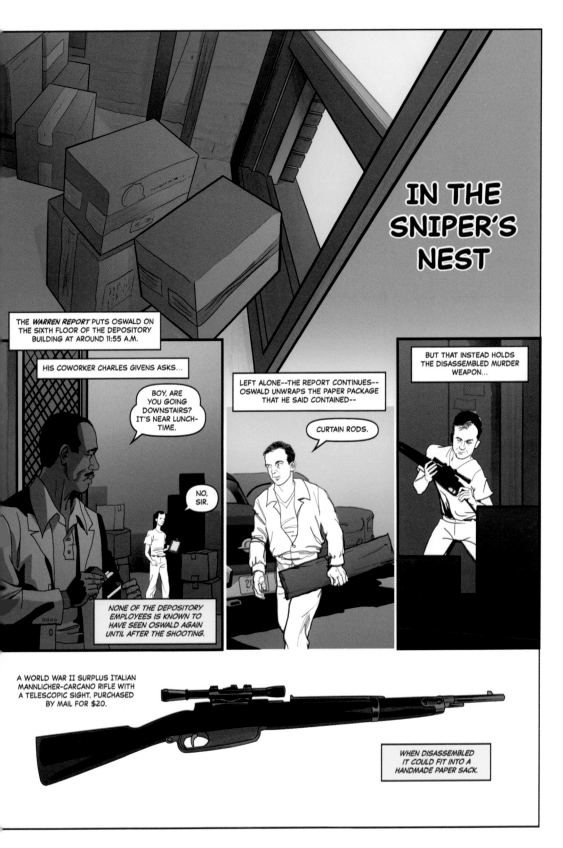

IN THE SNIPER'S NEST

THE *WARREN REPORT* PUTS OSWALD ON THE SIXTH FLOOR OF THE DEPOSITORY BUILDING AT AROUND 11:55 A.M.

HIS COWORKER CHARLES GIVENS ASKS...

BOY, ARE YOU GOING DOWNSTAIRS? IT'S NEAR LUNCH-TIME.

NO, SIR.

NONE OF THE DEPOSITORY EMPLOYEES IS KNOWN TO HAVE SEEN OSWALD AGAIN UNTIL AFTER THE SHOOTING.

LEFT ALONE--THE REPORT CONTINUES--OSWALD UNWRAPS THE PAPER PACKAGE THAT HE SAID CONTAINED--

CURTAIN RODS.

BUT THAT INSTEAD HOLDS THE DISASSEMBLED MURDER WEAPON...

A WORLD WAR II SURPLUS ITALIAN MANNLICHER-CARCANO RIFLE WITH A TELESCOPIC SIGHT, PURCHASED BY MAIL FOR $20.

WHEN DISASSEMBLED IT COULD FIT INTO A HANDMADE PAPER SACK.

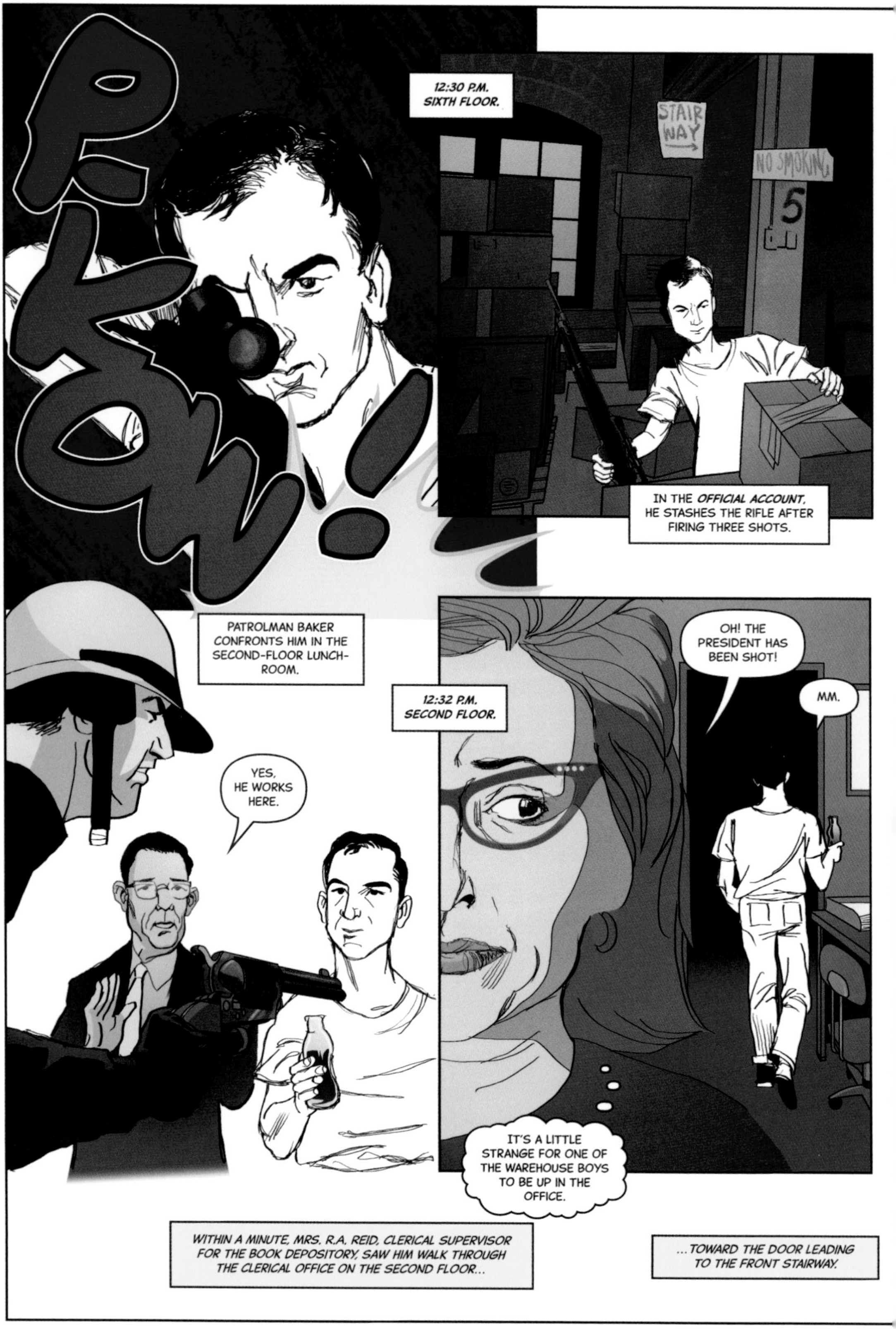
P-KOW!
12:30 P.M. SIXTH FLOOR.
STAIR WAY
NO SMOKING
5
IN THE OFFICIAL ACCOUNT, HE STASHES THE RIFLE AFTER FIRING THREE SHOTS.
PATROLMAN BAKER CONFRONTS HIM IN THE SECOND-FLOOR LUNCH-ROOM.
YES, HE WORKS HERE.
12:32 P.M. SECOND FLOOR.
OH! THE PRESIDENT HAS BEEN SHOT!
MM.
IT'S A LITTLE STRANGE FOR ONE OF THE WAREHOUSE BOYS TO BE UP IN THE OFFICE.
WITHIN A MINUTE, MRS. R.A. REID, CLERICAL SUPERVISOR FOR THE BOOK DEPOSITORY, SAW HIM WALK THROUGH THE CLERICAL OFFICE ON THE SECOND FLOOR...
...TOWARD THE DOOR LEADING TO THE FRONT STAIRWAY.

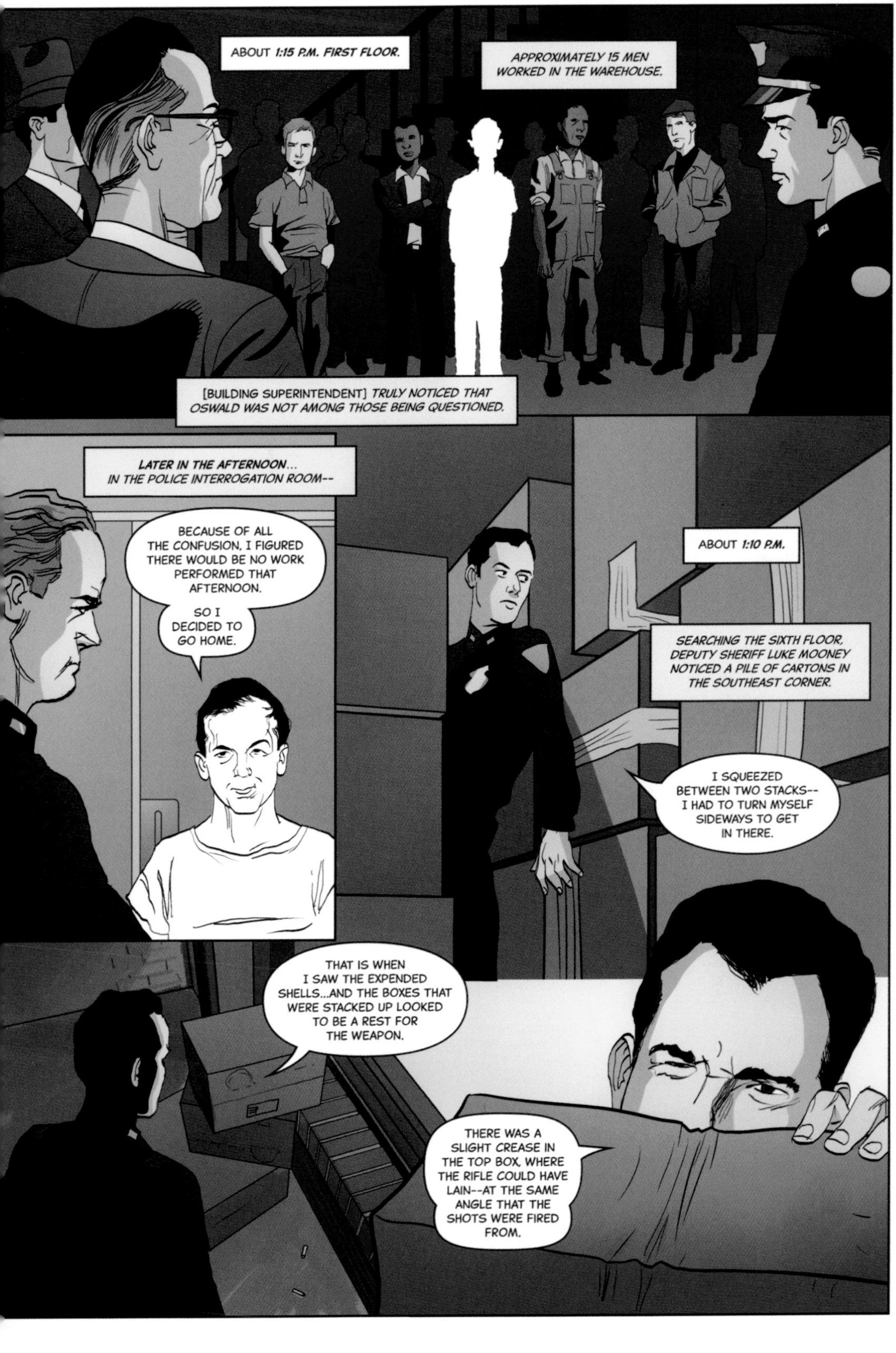
ABOUT 1:15 P.M. FIRST FLOOR.
APPROXIMATELY 15 MEN WORKED IN THE WAREHOUSE.
[BUILDING SUPERINTENDENT] TRULY NOTICED THAT OSWALD WAS NOT AMONG THOSE BEING QUESTIONED.
LATER IN THE AFTERNOON... IN THE POLICE INTERROGATION ROOM--
BECAUSE OF ALL THE CONFUSION, I FIGURED THERE WOULD BE NO WORK PERFORMED THAT AFTERNOON.
SO I DECIDED TO GO HOME.
ABOUT 1:10 P.M.
SEARCHING THE SIXTH FLOOR, DEPUTY SHERIFF LUKE MOONEY NOTICED A PILE OF CARTONS IN THE SOUTHEAST CORNER.
I SQUEEZED BETWEEN TWO STACKS-- I HAD TO TURN MYSELF SIDEWAYS TO GET IN THERE.
THAT IS WHEN I SAW THE EXPENDED SHELLS...AND THE BOXES THAT WERE STACKED UP LOOKED TO BE A REST FOR THE WEAPON.
THERE WAS A SLIGHT CREASE IN THE TOP BOX, WHERE THE RIFLE COULD HAVE LAIN--AT THE SAME ANGLE THAT THE SHOTS WERE FIRED FROM.

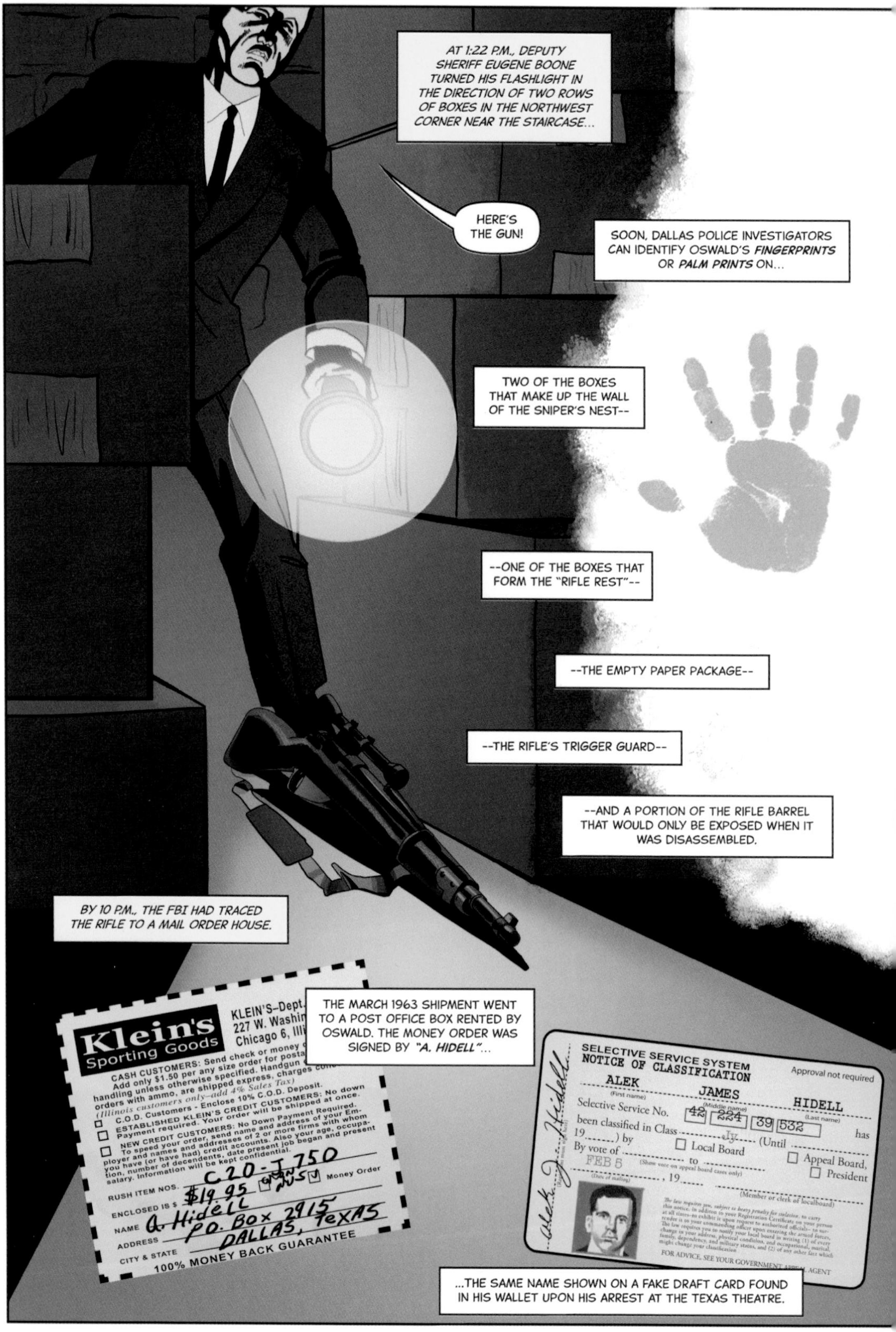
AT 1:22 P.M., DEPUTY SHERIFF EUGENE BOONE TURNED HIS FLASHLIGHT IN THE DIRECTION OF TWO ROWS OF BOXES IN THE NORTHWEST CORNER NEAR THE STAIRCASE...
HERE'S THE GUN!
SOON, DALLAS POLICE INVESTIGATORS CAN IDENTIFY OSWALD'S FINGERPRINTS OR PALM PRINTS ON...
TWO OF THE BOXES THAT MAKE UP THE WALL OF THE SNIPER'S NEST--
--ONE OF THE BOXES THAT FORM THE "RIFLE REST"--
--THE EMPTY PAPER PACKAGE--
--THE RIFLE'S TRIGGER GUARD--
--AND A PORTION OF THE RIFLE BARREL THAT WOULD ONLY BE EXPOSED WHEN IT WAS DISASSEMBLED.
BY 10 P.M., THE FBI HAD TRACED THE RIFLE TO A MAIL ORDER HOUSE.
Klein's Sporting Goods
KLEIN'S–Dept.
227 W. Washin
Chicago 6, Illi
CASH CUSTOMERS: Send check or money
Add only $1.50 per any size order for posta
handling unless otherwise specified. Handgun
orders with ammo, are shipped express, charges
(Illinois customers only–add 4% Sales Tax)
C.O.D. Customers - Enclose 10% C.O.D. Deposit.
ESTABLISHED KLEIN'S CREDIT CUSTOMERS: No down
Payment required. Your order will be shipped at once.
NEW CREDIT CUSTOMERS: No Down Payment Required.
To speed your order, send name and address of your Em-
ployer and names and addresses of 2 or more firms with whom
you have (or have had) credit accounts. Also your age, occupa-
tion, number of decendents, date present job began and present
salary. Information will be kept confidential.
RUSH ITEM NOS. C20-T750
ENCLOSED IS $ $19.95 Money Order
NAME A. Hidell
ADDRESS P.O. Box 2915
CITY & STATE DALLAS, TEXAS
100% MONEY BACK GUARANTEE
THE MARCH 1963 SHIPMENT WENT TO A POST OFFICE BOX RENTED BY OSWALD. THE MONEY ORDER WAS SIGNED BY "A. HIDELL"...
SELECTIVE SERVICE SYSTEM
NOTICE OF CLASSIFICATION
Approval not required
ALEK JAMES HIDELL
Selective Service No. 42 224 39 532 has
been classified in Class Iy (Until
19) by Local Board
By vote of to Appeal Board,
FEB 5 President
(Member or clerk of localboard)
FOR ADVICE, SEE YOUR GOVERNMENT APPEAL AGENT
...THE SAME NAME SHOWN ON A FAKE DRAFT CARD FOUND IN HIS WALLET UPON HIS ARREST AT THE TEXAS THEATRE.

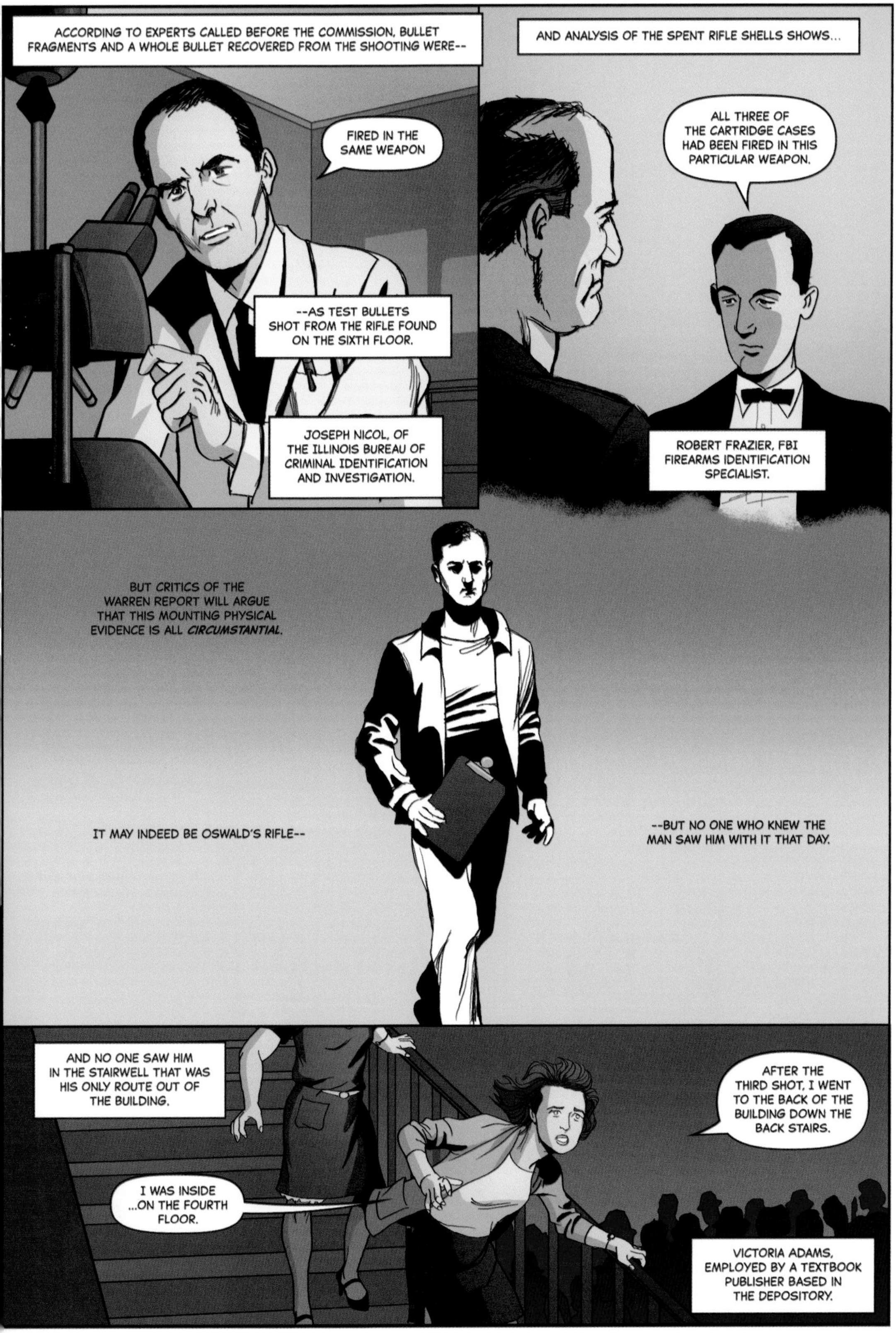

ACCORDING TO EXPERTS CALLED BEFORE THE COMMISSION, BULLET FRAGMENTS AND A WHOLE BULLET RECOVERED FROM THE SHOOTING WERE--
FIRED IN THE SAME WEAPON
--AS TEST BULLETS SHOT FROM THE RIFLE FOUND ON THE SIXTH FLOOR.
JOSEPH NICOL, OF THE ILLINOIS BUREAU OF CRIMINAL IDENTIFICATION AND INVESTIGATION.
AND ANALYSIS OF THE SPENT RIFLE SHELLS SHOWS...
ALL THREE OF THE CARTRIDGE CASES HAD BEEN FIRED IN THIS PARTICULAR WEAPON.
ROBERT FRAZIER, FBI FIREARMS IDENTIFICATION SPECIALIST.
BUT CRITICS OF THE WARREN REPORT WILL ARGUE THAT THIS MOUNTING PHYSICAL EVIDENCE IS ALL *CIRCUMSTANTIAL*.
IT MAY INDEED BE OSWALD'S RIFLE--
--BUT NO ONE WHO KNEW THE MAN SAW HIM WITH IT THAT DAY.
AND NO ONE SAW HIM IN THE STAIRWELL THAT WAS HIS ONLY ROUTE OUT OF THE BUILDING.
AFTER THE THIRD SHOT, I WENT TO THE BACK OF THE BUILDING DOWN THE BACK STAIRS.
I WAS INSIDE ...ON THE FOURTH FLOOR.
VICTORIA ADAMS, EMPLOYED BY A TEXTBOOK PUBLISHER BASED IN THE DEPOSITORY.

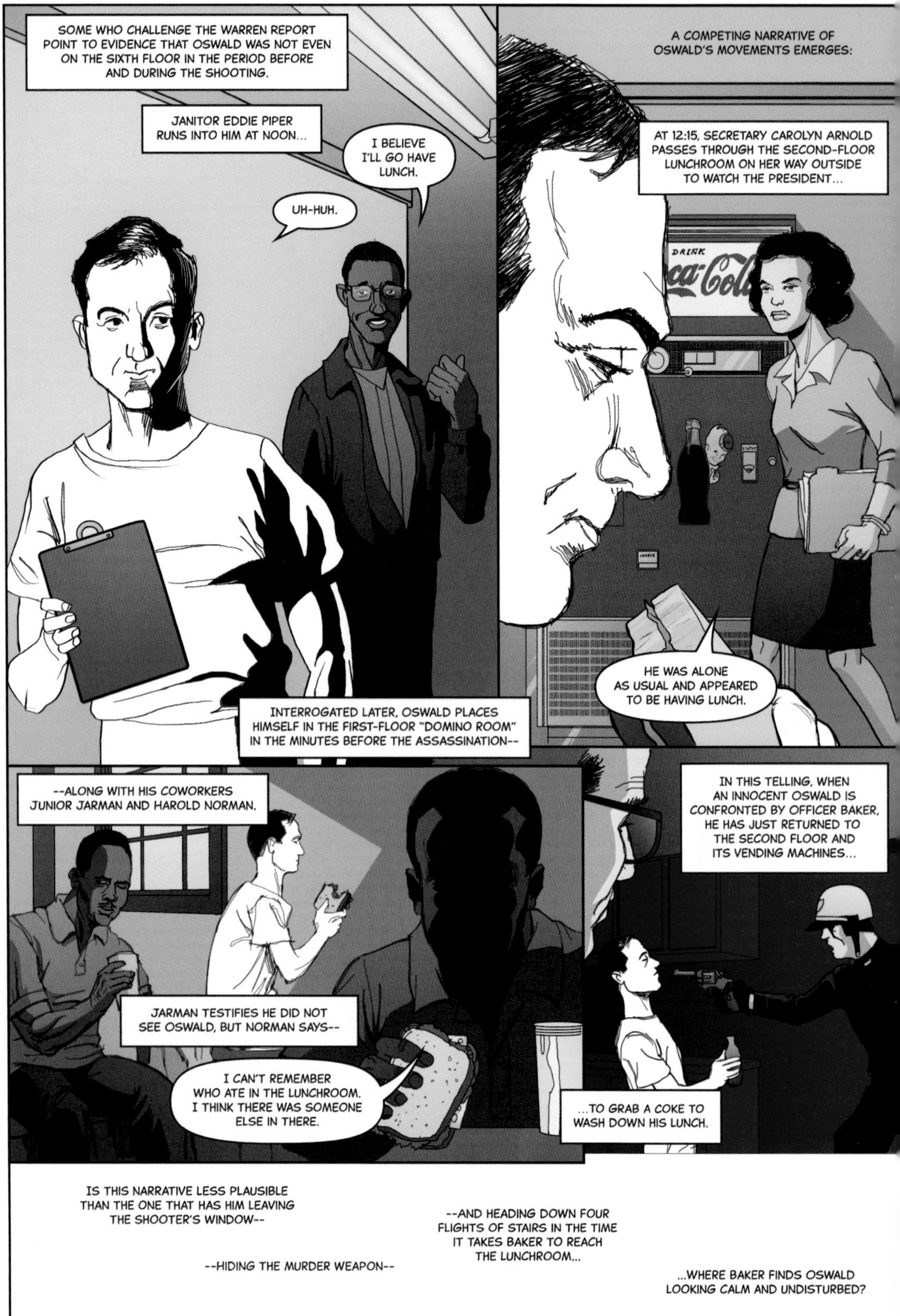
SOME WHO CHALLENGE THE WARREN REPORT POINT TO EVIDENCE THAT OSWALD WAS NOT EVEN ON THE SIXTH FLOOR IN THE PERIOD BEFORE AND DURING THE SHOOTING.
JANITOR EDDIE PIPER RUNS INTO HIM AT NOON...
I BELIEVE I'LL GO HAVE LUNCH.
UH-HUH.
INTERROGATED LATER, OSWALD PLACES HIMSELF IN THE FIRST-FLOOR "DOMINO ROOM" IN THE MINUTES BEFORE THE ASSASSINATION--
A COMPETING NARRATIVE OF OSWALD'S MOVEMENTS EMERGES:
AT 12:15, SECRETARY CAROLYN ARNOLD PASSES THROUGH THE SECOND-FLOOR LUNCHROOM ON HER WAY OUTSIDE TO WATCH THE PRESIDENT...
DRINK
Coca-Cola
HE WAS ALONE AS USUAL AND APPEARED TO BE HAVING LUNCH.
--ALONG WITH HIS COWORKERS JUNIOR JARMAN AND HAROLD NORMAN.
JARMAN TESTIFIES HE DID NOT SEE OSWALD, BUT NORMAN SAYS--
I CAN'T REMEMBER WHO ATE IN THE LUNCHROOM. I THINK THERE WAS SOMEONE ELSE IN THERE.
IN THIS TELLING, WHEN AN INNOCENT OSWALD IS CONFRONTED BY OFFICER BAKER, HE HAS JUST RETURNED TO THE SECOND FLOOR AND ITS VENDING MACHINES...
...TO GRAB A COKE TO WASH DOWN HIS LUNCH.
IS THIS NARRATIVE LESS PLAUSIBLE THAN THE ONE THAT HAS HIM LEAVING THE SHOOTER'S WINDOW--
--HIDING THE MURDER WEAPON--
--AND HEADING DOWN FOUR FLIGHTS OF STAIRS IN THE TIME IT TAKES BAKER TO REACH THE LUNCHROOM...
...WHERE BAKER FINDS OSWALD LOOKING CALM AND UNDISTURBED?

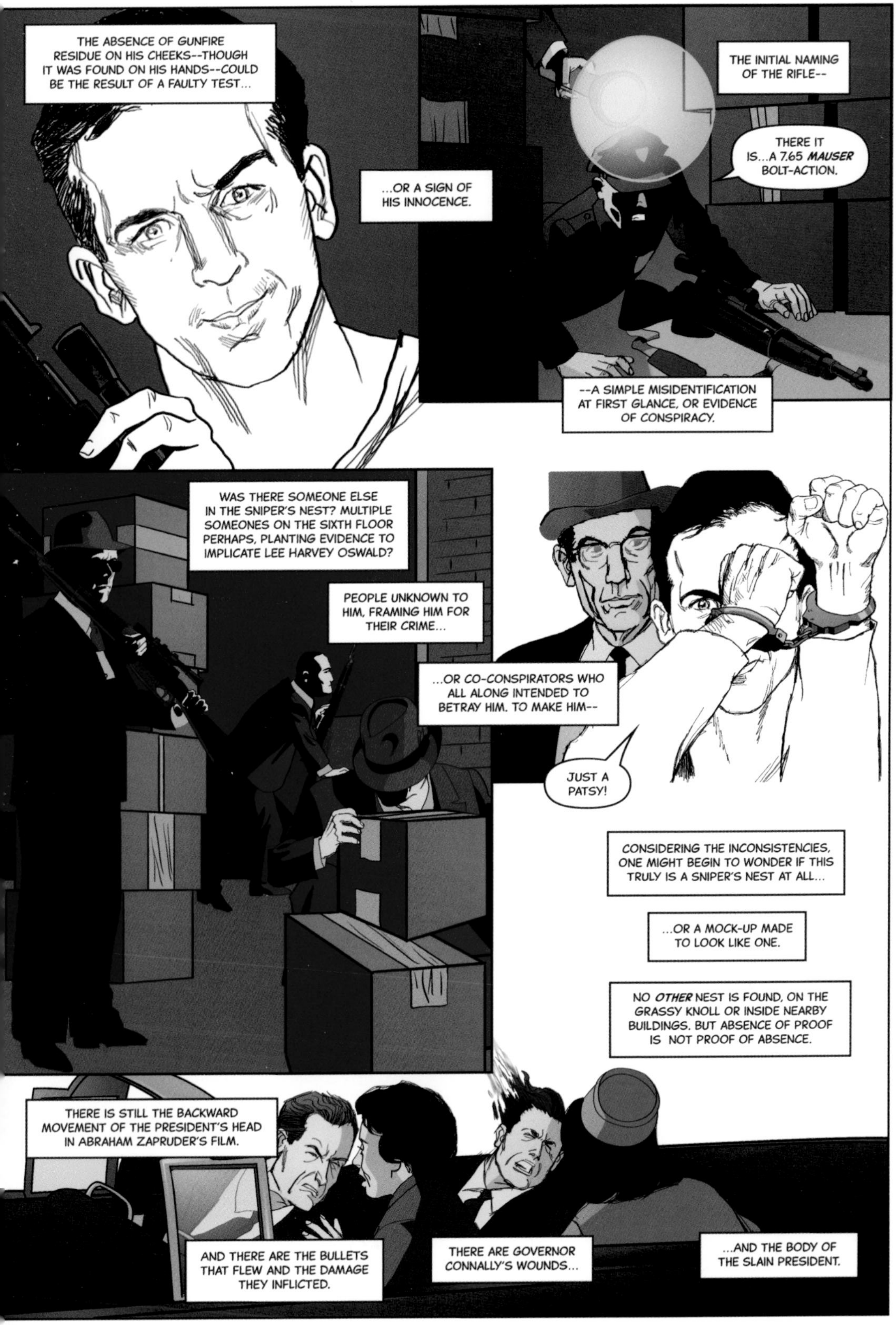
THE ABSENCE OF GUNFIRE RESIDUE ON HIS CHEEKS--THOUGH IT WAS FOUND ON HIS HANDS--COULD BE THE RESULT OF A FAULTY TEST...
...OR A SIGN OF HIS INNOCENCE.
THE INITIAL NAMING OF THE RIFLE--
THERE IT IS...A 7.65 *MAUSER* BOLT-ACTION.
--A SIMPLE MISIDENTIFICATION AT FIRST GLANCE, OR EVIDENCE OF CONSPIRACY.
WAS THERE SOMEONE ELSE IN THE SNIPER'S NEST? MULTIPLE SOMEONES ON THE SIXTH FLOOR PERHAPS, PLANTING EVIDENCE TO IMPLICATE LEE HARVEY OSWALD?
PEOPLE UNKNOWN TO HIM, FRAMING HIM FOR THEIR CRIME...
...OR CO-CONSPIRATORS WHO ALL ALONG INTENDED TO BETRAY HIM. TO MAKE HIM--
JUST A PATSY!
CONSIDERING THE INCONSISTENCIES, ONE MIGHT BEGIN TO WONDER IF THIS TRULY IS A SNIPER'S NEST AT ALL...
...OR A MOCK-UP MADE TO LOOK LIKE ONE.
NO *OTHER* NEST IS FOUND, ON THE GRASSY KNOLL OR INSIDE NEARBY BUILDINGS. BUT ABSENCE OF PROOF IS NOT PROOF OF ABSENCE.
THERE IS STILL THE BACKWARD MOVEMENT OF THE PRESIDENT'S HEAD IN ABRAHAM ZAPRUDER'S FILM.
AND THERE ARE THE BULLETS THAT FLEW AND THE DAMAGE THEY INFLICTED.
THERE ARE GOVERNOR CONNALLY'S WOUNDS...
...AND THE BODY OF THE SLAIN PRESIDENT.

THE MEDICAL EVIDENCE

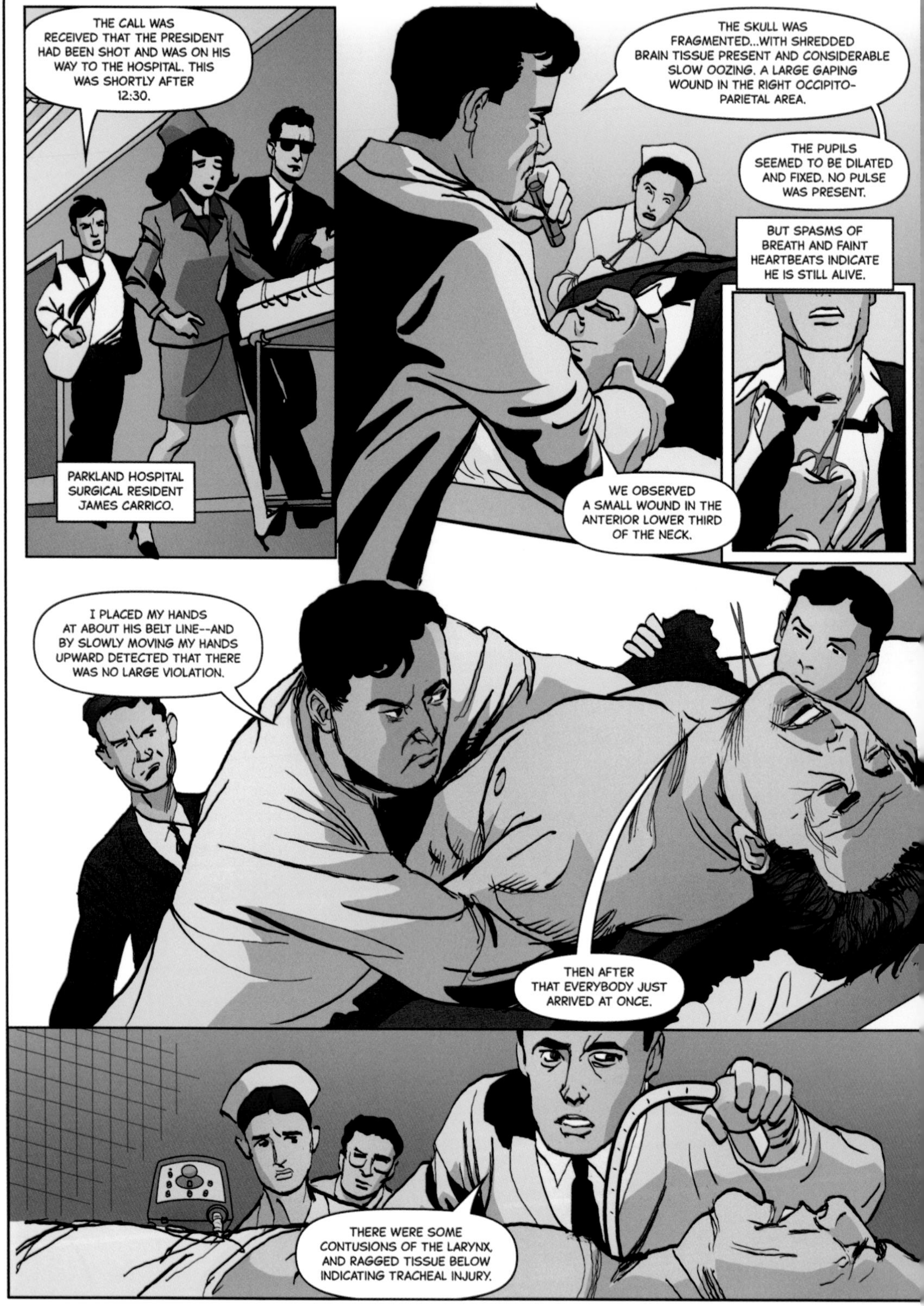
THE CALL WAS RECEIVED THAT THE PRESIDENT HAD BEEN SHOT AND WAS ON HIS WAY TO THE HOSPITAL. THIS WAS SHORTLY AFTER 12:30.
PARKLAND HOSPITAL SURGICAL RESIDENT JAMES CARRICO.
THE SKULL WAS FRAGMENTED...WITH SHREDDED BRAIN TISSUE PRESENT AND CONSIDERABLE SLOW OOZING. A LARGE GAPING WOUND IN THE RIGHT OCCIPITO-PARIETAL AREA.
THE PUPILS SEEMED TO BE DILATED AND FIXED. NO PULSE WAS PRESENT.
BUT SPASMS OF BREATH AND FAINT HEARTBEATS INDICATE HE IS STILL ALIVE.
WE OBSERVED A SMALL WOUND IN THE ANTERIOR LOWER THIRD OF THE NECK.
I PLACED MY HANDS AT ABOUT HIS BELT LINE--AND BY SLOWLY MOVING MY HANDS UPWARD DETECTED THAT THERE WAS NO LARGE VIOLATION.
THEN AFTER THAT EVERYBODY JUST ARRIVED AT ONCE.
THERE WERE SOME CONTUSIONS OF THE LARYNX, AND RAGGED TISSUE BELOW INDICATING TRACHEAL INJURY.

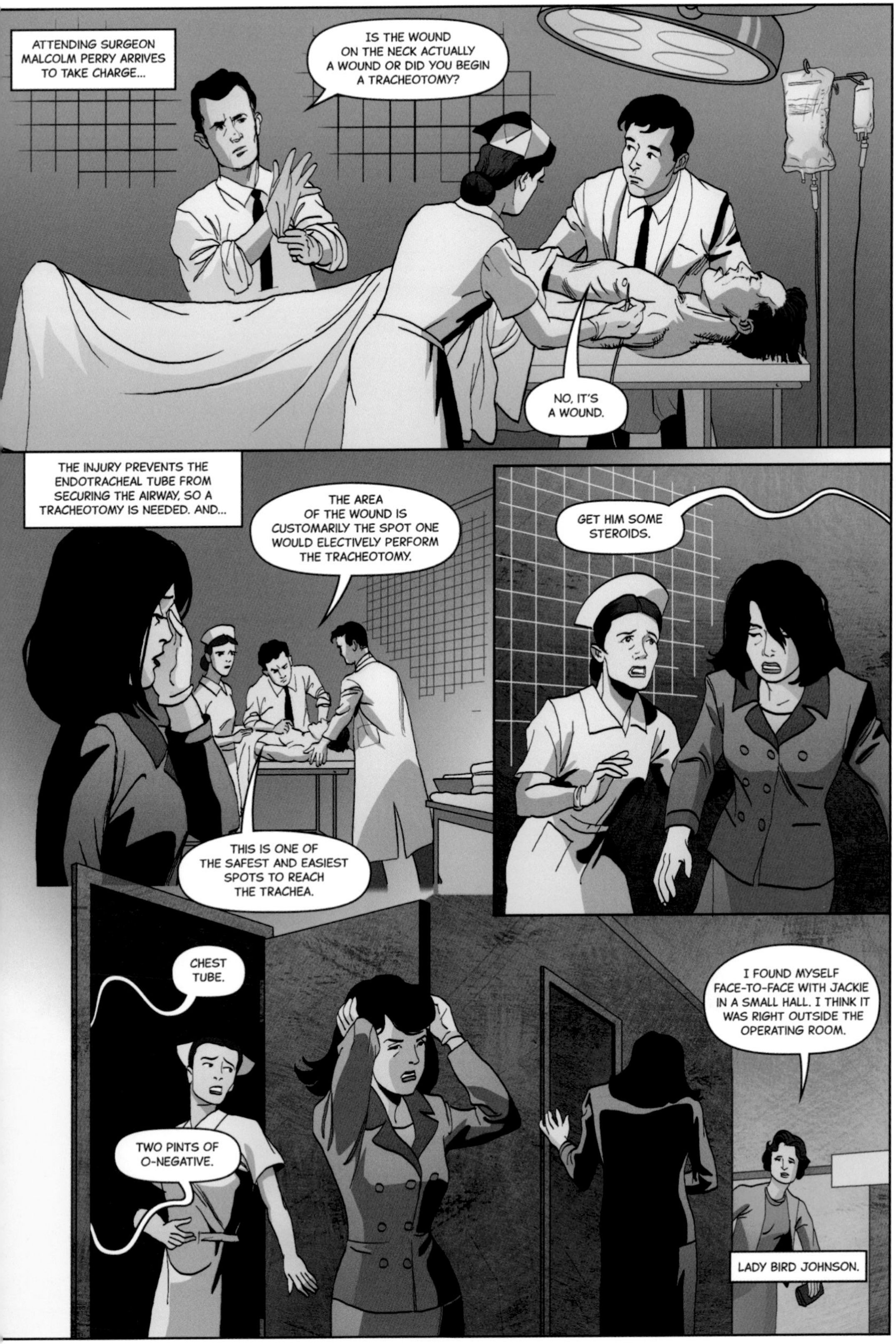
ATTENDING SURGEON MALCOLM PERRY ARRIVES TO TAKE CHARGE...
IS THE WOUND ON THE NECK ACTUALLY A WOUND OR DID YOU BEGIN A TRACHEOTOMY?
NO, IT'S A WOUND.
THE INJURY PREVENTS THE ENDOTRACHEAL TUBE FROM SECURING THE AIRWAY, SO A TRACHEOTOMY IS NEEDED. AND...
THE AREA OF THE WOUND IS CUSTOMARILY THE SPOT ONE WOULD ELECTIVELY PERFORM THE TRACHEOTOMY.
THIS IS ONE OF THE SAFEST AND EASIEST SPOTS TO REACH THE TRACHEA.
GET HIM SOME STEROIDS.
CHEST TUBE.
TWO PINTS OF O-NEGATIVE.
I FOUND MYSELF FACE-TO-FACE WITH JACKIE IN A SMALL HALL. I THINK IT WAS RIGHT OUTSIDE THE OPERATING ROOM.
LADY BIRD JOHNSON.

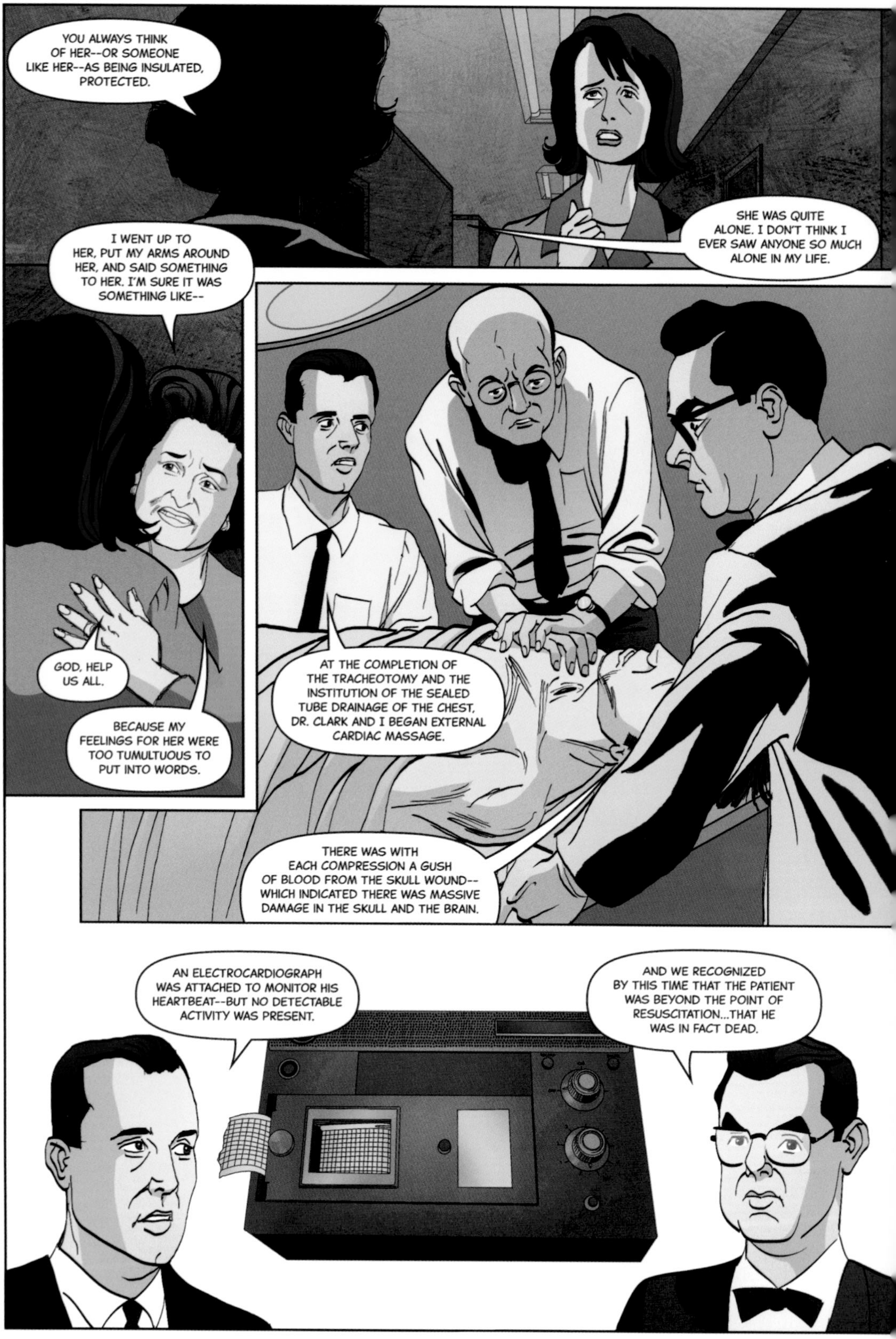
YOU ALWAYS THINK OF HER--OR SOMEONE LIKE HER--AS BEING INSULATED, PROTECTED.
SHE WAS QUITE ALONE. I DON'T THINK I EVER SAW ANYONE SO MUCH ALONE IN MY LIFE.
I WENT UP TO HER, PUT MY ARMS AROUND HER, AND SAID SOMETHING TO HER. I'M SURE IT WAS SOMETHING LIKE--
GOD, HELP US ALL.
BECAUSE MY FEELINGS FOR HER WERE TOO TUMULTUOUS TO PUT INTO WORDS.
AT THE COMPLETION OF THE TRACHEOTOMY AND THE INSTITUTION OF THE SEALED TUBE DRAINAGE OF THE CHEST, DR. CLARK AND I BEGAN EXTERNAL CARDIAC MASSAGE.
THERE WAS WITH EACH COMPRESSION A GUSH OF BLOOD FROM THE SKULL WOUND--WHICH INDICATED THERE WAS MASSIVE DAMAGE IN THE SKULL AND THE BRAIN.
AN ELECTROCARDIOGRAPH WAS ATTACHED TO MONITOR HIS HEARTBEAT--BUT NO DETECTABLE ACTIVITY WAS PRESENT.
AND WE RECOGNIZED BY THIS TIME THAT THE PATIENT WAS BEYOND THE POINT OF RESUSCITATION...THAT HE WAS IN FACT DEAD.

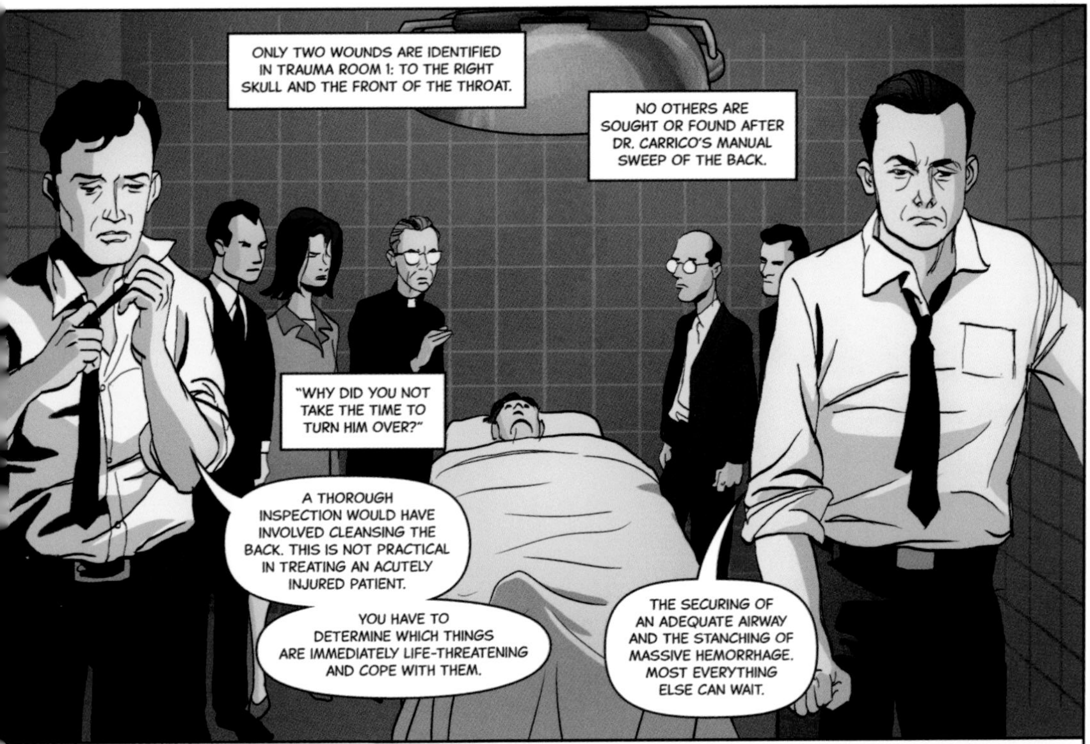
ONLY TWO WOUNDS ARE IDENTIFIED IN TRAUMA ROOM 1: TO THE RIGHT SKULL AND THE FRONT OF THE THROAT.
NO OTHERS ARE SOUGHT OR FOUND AFTER DR. CARRICO'S MANUAL SWEEP OF THE BACK.
"WHY DID YOU NOT TAKE THE TIME TO TURN HIM OVER?"
A THOROUGH INSPECTION WOULD HAVE INVOLVED CLEANSING THE BACK. THIS IS NOT PRACTICAL IN TREATING AN ACUTELY INJURED PATIENT.
YOU HAVE TO DETERMINE WHICH THINGS ARE IMMEDIATELY LIFE-THREATENING AND COPE WITH THEM.
THE SECURING OF AN ADEQUATE AIRWAY AND THE STANCHING OF MASSIVE HEMORRHAGE. MOST EVERYTHING ELSE CAN WAIT.

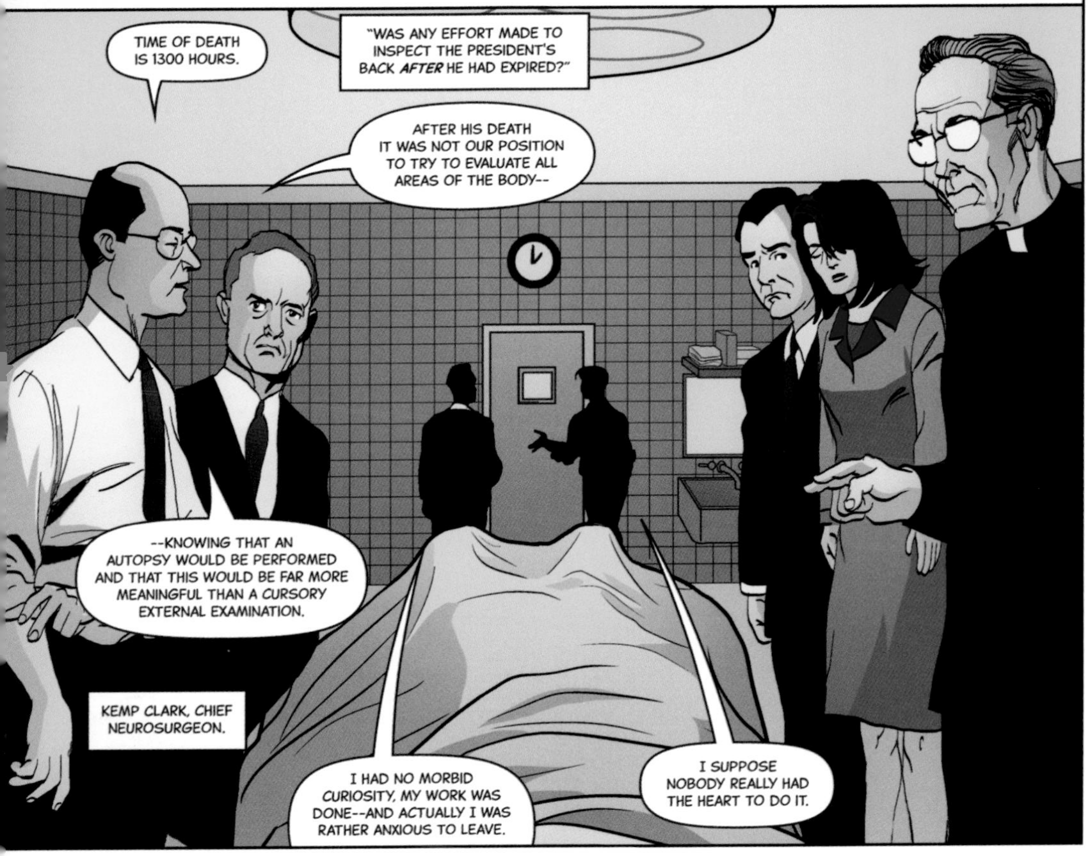
TIME OF DEATH IS 1300 HOURS.
"WAS ANY EFFORT MADE TO INSPECT THE PRESIDENT'S BACK *AFTER* HE HAD EXPIRED?"
AFTER HIS DEATH IT WAS NOT OUR POSITION TO TRY TO EVALUATE ALL AREAS OF THE BODY--
--KNOWING THAT AN AUTOPSY WOULD BE PERFORMED AND THAT THIS WOULD BE FAR MORE MEANINGFUL THAN A CURSORY EXTERNAL EXAMINATION.
KEMP CLARK, CHIEF NEUROSURGEON.
I HAD NO MORBID CURIOSITY, MY WORK WAS DONE--AND ACTUALLY I WAS RATHER ANXIOUS TO LEAVE.
I SUPPOSE NOBODY REALLY HAD THE HEART TO DO IT.

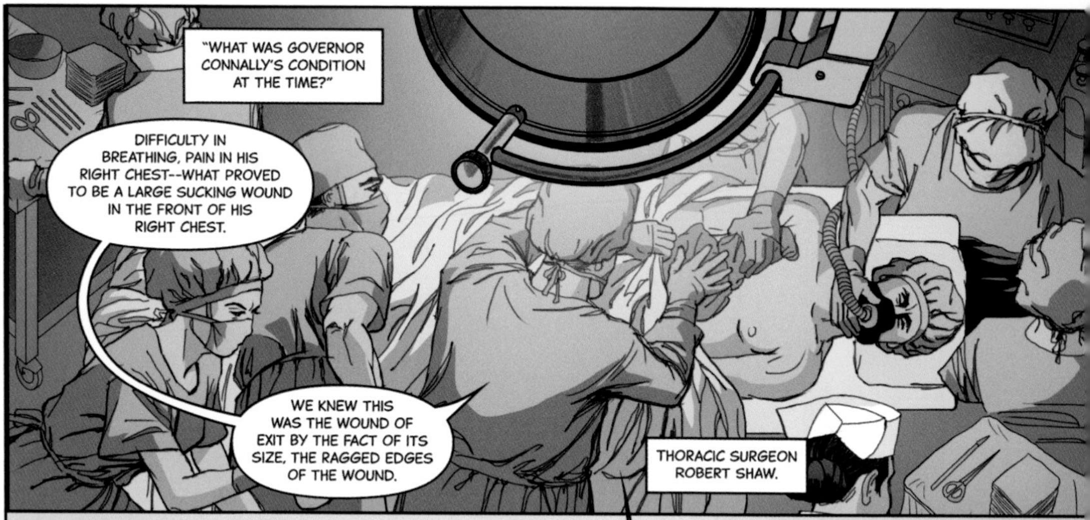
"WHAT WAS GOVERNOR CONNALLY'S CONDITION AT THE TIME?"
DIFFICULTY IN BREATHING, PAIN IN HIS RIGHT CHEST--WHAT PROVED TO BE A LARGE SUCKING WOUND IN THE FRONT OF HIS RIGHT CHEST.
WE KNEW THIS WAS THE WOUND OF EXIT BY THE FACT OF ITS SIZE, THE RAGGED EDGES OF THE WOUND.
THORACIC SURGEON ROBERT SHAW.

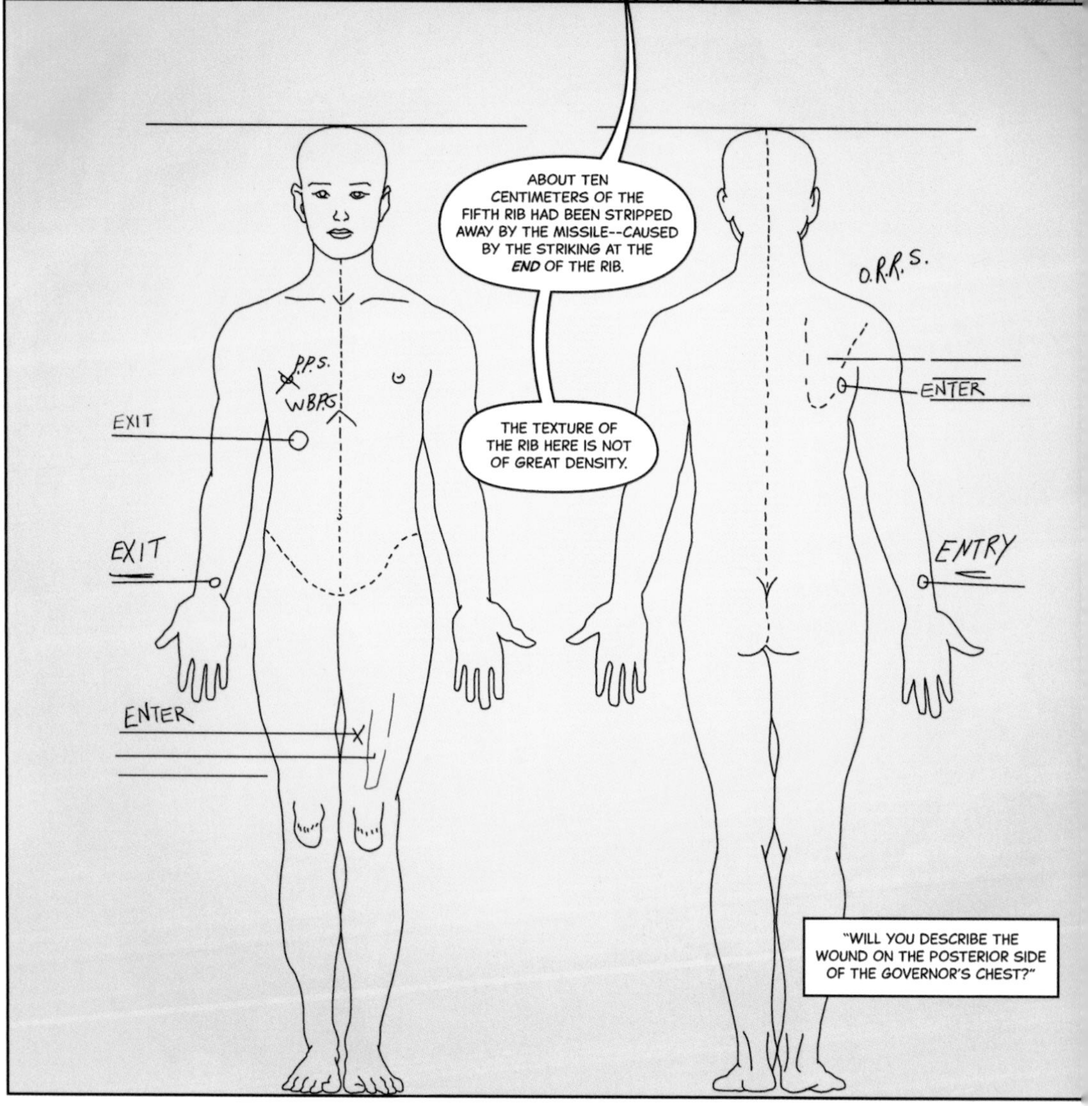
ABOUT TEN CENTIMETERS OF THE FIFTH RIB HAD BEEN STRIPPED AWAY BY THE MISSILE--CAUSED BY THE STRIKING AT THE *END* OF THE RIB.
THE TEXTURE OF THE RIB HERE IS NOT OF GREAT DENSITY.
P.P.S.
W.B.P.G.
EXIT
EXIT
ENTER
O.R.R.S.
ENTER
ENTRY
"WILL YOU DESCRIBE THE WOUND ON THE POSTERIOR SIDE OF THE GOVERNOR'S CHEST?"

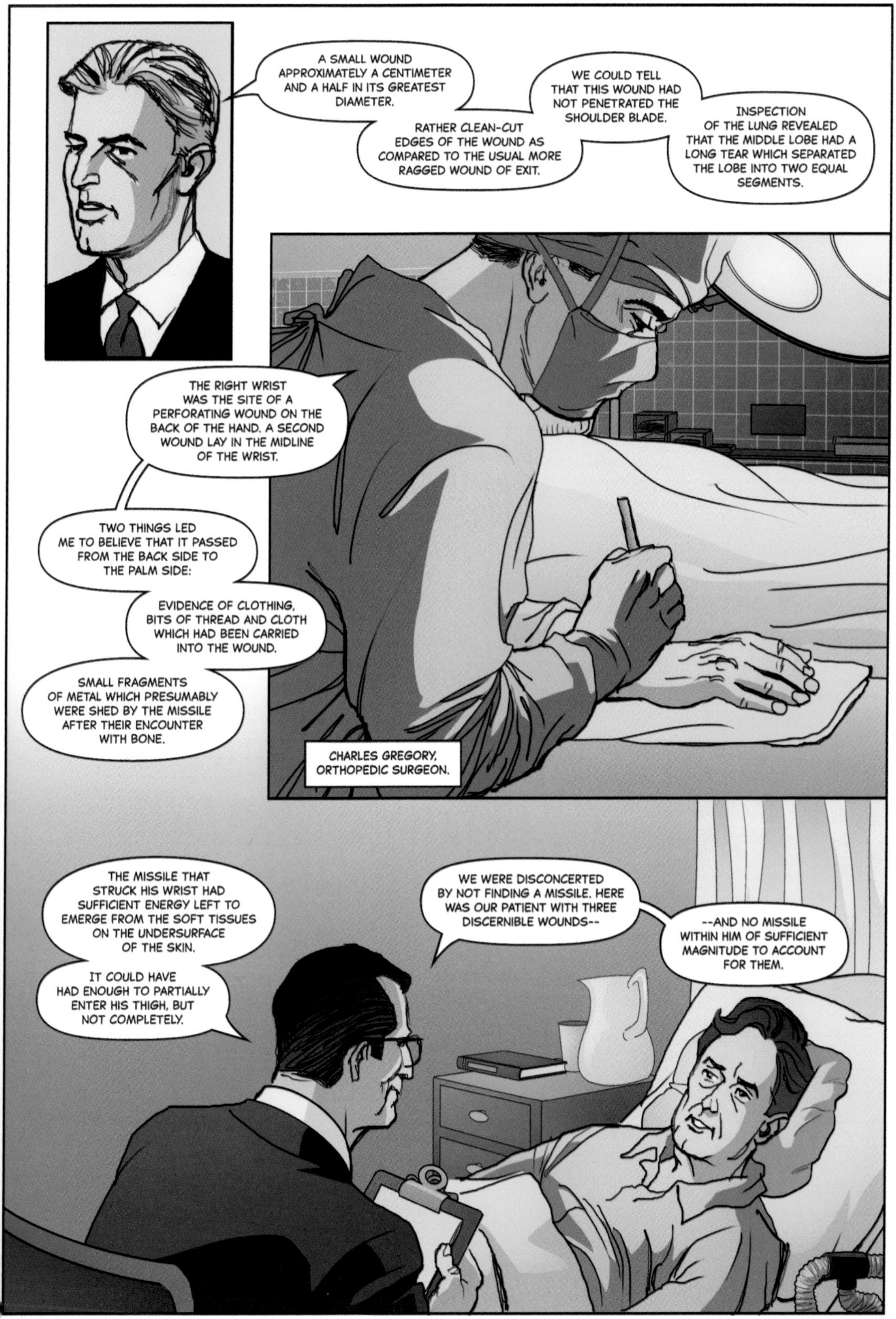
A SMALL WOUND APPROXIMATELY A CENTIMETER AND A HALF IN ITS GREATEST DIAMETER.
RATHER CLEAN-CUT EDGES OF THE WOUND AS COMPARED TO THE USUAL MORE RAGGED WOUND OF EXIT.
WE COULD TELL THAT THIS WOUND HAD NOT PENETRATED THE SHOULDER BLADE.
INSPECTION OF THE LUNG REVEALED THAT THE MIDDLE LOBE HAD A LONG TEAR WHICH SEPARATED THE LOBE INTO TWO EQUAL SEGMENTS.
THE RIGHT WRIST WAS THE SITE OF A PERFORATING WOUND ON THE BACK OF THE HAND. A SECOND WOUND LAY IN THE MIDLINE OF THE WRIST.
TWO THINGS LED ME TO BELIEVE THAT IT PASSED FROM THE BACK SIDE TO THE PALM SIDE:
EVIDENCE OF CLOTHING, BITS OF THREAD AND CLOTH WHICH HAD BEEN CARRIED INTO THE WOUND.
SMALL FRAGMENTS OF METAL WHICH PRESUMABLY WERE SHED BY THE MISSILE AFTER THEIR ENCOUNTER WITH BONE.
CHARLES GREGORY, ORTHOPEDIC SURGEON.
THE MISSILE THAT STRUCK HIS WRIST HAD SUFFICIENT ENERGY LEFT TO EMERGE FROM THE SOFT TISSUES ON THE UNDERSURFACE OF THE SKIN.
IT COULD HAVE HAD ENOUGH TO PARTIALLY ENTER HIS THIGH, BUT NOT COMPLETELY.
WE WERE DISCONCERTED BY NOT FINDING A MISSILE. HERE WAS OUR PATIENT WITH THREE DISCERNIBLE WOUNDS--
--AND NO MISSILE WITHIN HIM OF SUFFICIENT MAGNITUDE TO ACCOUNT FOR THEM.

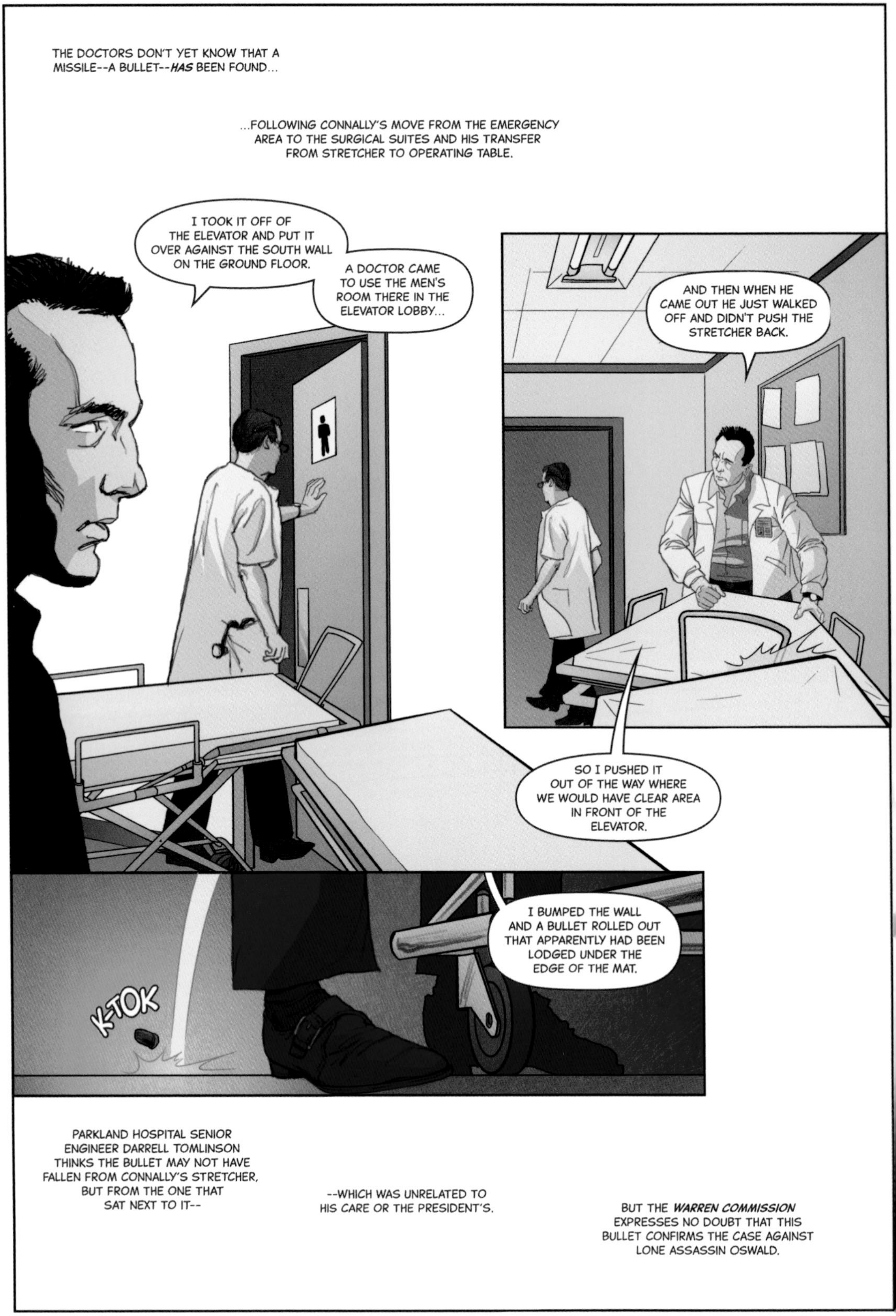
THE DOCTORS DON'T YET KNOW THAT A MISSILE--A BULLET--*HAS* BEEN FOUND...
...FOLLOWING CONNALLY'S MOVE FROM THE EMERGENCY AREA TO THE SURGICAL SUITES AND HIS TRANSFER FROM STRETCHER TO OPERATING TABLE.
I TOOK IT OFF OF THE ELEVATOR AND PUT IT OVER AGAINST THE SOUTH WALL ON THE GROUND FLOOR.
A DOCTOR CAME TO USE THE MEN'S ROOM THERE IN THE ELEVATOR LOBBY...
AND THEN WHEN HE CAME OUT HE JUST WALKED OFF AND DIDN'T PUSH THE STRETCHER BACK.
SO I PUSHED IT OUT OF THE WAY WHERE WE WOULD HAVE CLEAR AREA IN FRONT OF THE ELEVATOR.
I BUMPED THE WALL AND A BULLET ROLLED OUT THAT APPARENTLY HAD BEEN LODGED UNDER THE EDGE OF THE MAT.
K-TOK
PARKLAND HOSPITAL SENIOR ENGINEER DARRELL TOMLINSON THINKS THE BULLET MAY NOT HAVE FALLEN FROM CONNALLY'S STRETCHER, BUT FROM THE ONE THAT SAT NEXT TO IT--
--WHICH WAS UNRELATED TO HIS CARE OR THE PRESIDENT'S.
BUT THE *WARREN COMMISSION* EXPRESSES NO DOUBT THAT THIS BULLET CONFIRMS THE CASE AGAINST LONE ASSASSIN OSWALD.

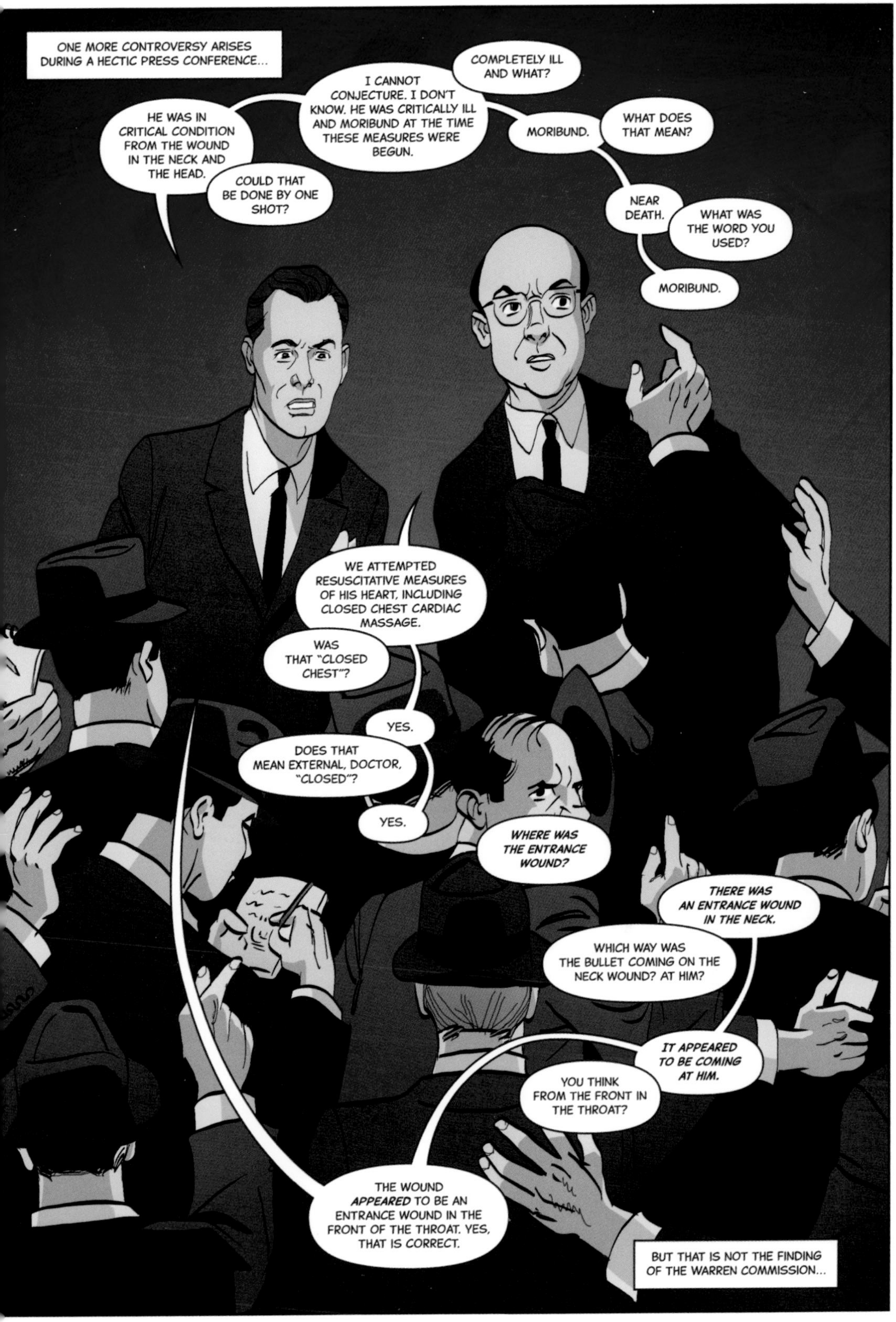
ONE MORE CONTROVERSY ARISES DURING A HECTIC PRESS CONFERENCE...
HE WAS IN CRITICAL CONDITION FROM THE WOUND IN THE NECK AND THE HEAD.
COULD THAT BE DONE BY ONE SHOT?
I CANNOT CONJECTURE. I DON'T KNOW. HE WAS CRITICALLY ILL AND MORIBUND AT THE TIME THESE MEASURES WERE BEGUN.
COMPLETELY ILL AND WHAT?
MORIBUND.
WHAT DOES THAT MEAN?
NEAR DEATH.
WHAT WAS THE WORD YOU USED?
MORIBUND.
WE ATTEMPTED RESUSCITATIVE MEASURES OF HIS HEART, INCLUDING CLOSED CHEST CARDIAC MASSAGE.
WAS THAT "CLOSED CHEST"?
YES.
DOES THAT MEAN EXTERNAL, DOCTOR, "CLOSED"?
YES.
WHERE WAS THE ENTRANCE WOUND?
THERE WAS AN ENTRANCE WOUND IN THE NECK.
WHICH WAY WAS THE BULLET COMING ON THE NECK WOUND? AT HIM?
IT APPEARED TO BE COMING AT HIM.
YOU THINK FROM THE FRONT IN THE THROAT?
THE WOUND APPEARED TO BE AN ENTRANCE WOUND IN THE FRONT OF THE THROAT. YES, THAT IS CORRECT.
BUT THAT IS NOT THE FINDING OF THE WARREN COMMISSION...

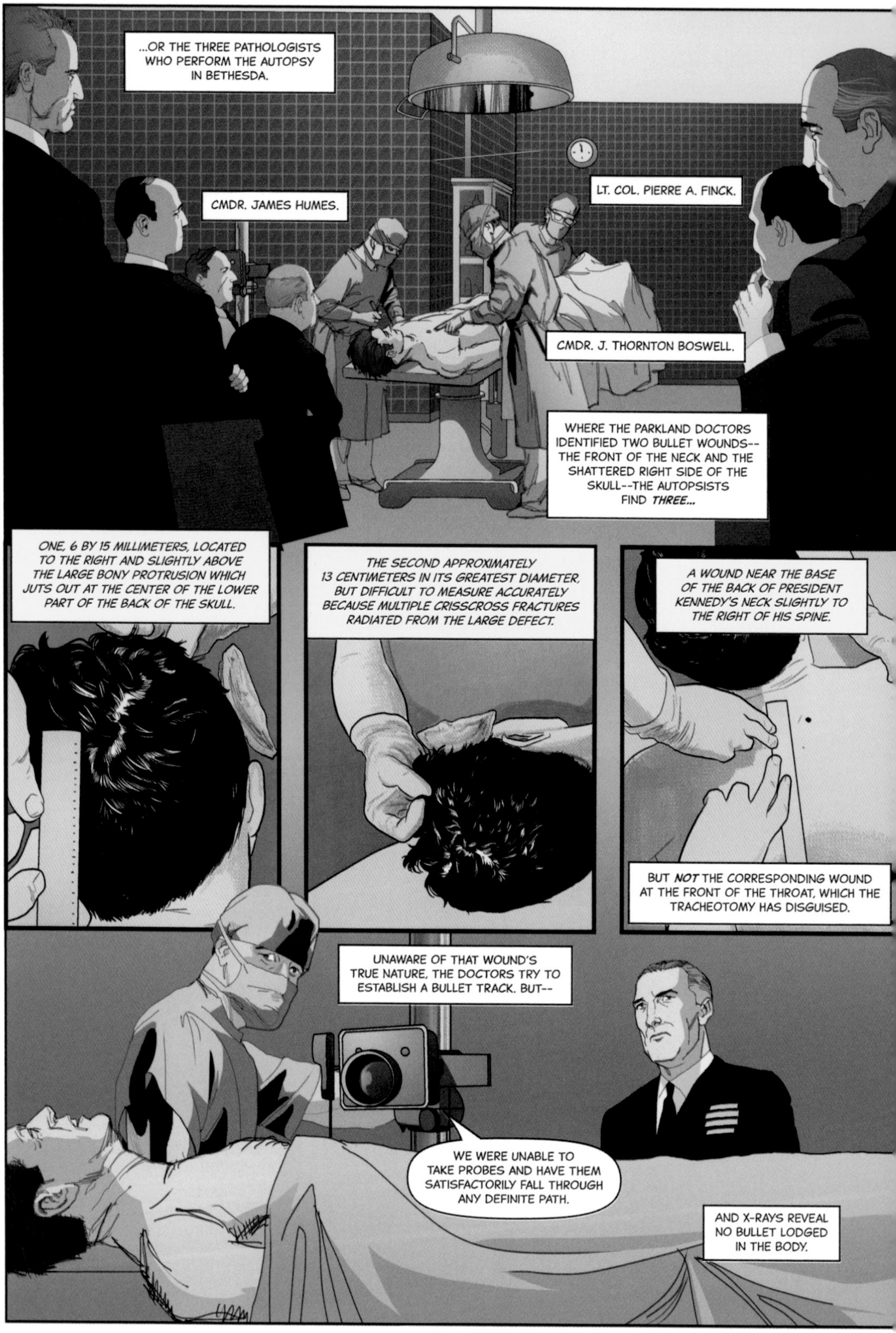
...OR THE THREE PATHOLOGISTS WHO PERFORM THE AUTOPSY IN BETHESDA.
CMDR. JAMES HUMES.
LT. COL. PIERRE A. FINCK.
CMDR. J. THORNTON BOSWELL.
WHERE THE PARKLAND DOCTORS IDENTIFIED TWO BULLET WOUNDS-- THE FRONT OF THE NECK AND THE SHATTERED RIGHT SIDE OF THE SKULL--THE AUTOPSISTS FIND *THREE...*
ONE, 6 BY 15 MILLIMETERS, LOCATED TO THE RIGHT AND SLIGHTLY ABOVE THE LARGE BONY PROTRUSION WHICH JUTS OUT AT THE CENTER OF THE LOWER PART OF THE BACK OF THE SKULL.
THE SECOND APPROXIMATELY 13 CENTIMETERS IN ITS GREATEST DIAMETER, BUT DIFFICULT TO MEASURE ACCURATELY BECAUSE MULTIPLE CRISSCROSS FRACTURES RADIATED FROM THE LARGE DEFECT.
A WOUND NEAR THE BASE OF THE BACK OF PRESIDENT KENNEDY'S NECK SLIGHTLY TO THE RIGHT OF HIS SPINE.
BUT ***NOT*** THE CORRESPONDING WOUND AT THE FRONT OF THE THROAT, WHICH THE TRACHEOTOMY HAS DISGUISED.
UNAWARE OF THAT WOUND'S TRUE NATURE, THE DOCTORS TRY TO ESTABLISH A BULLET TRACK. BUT--
WE WERE UNABLE TO TAKE PROBES AND HAVE THEM SATISFACTORILY FALL THROUGH ANY DEFINITE PATH.
AND X-RAYS REVEAL NO BULLET LODGED IN THE BODY.

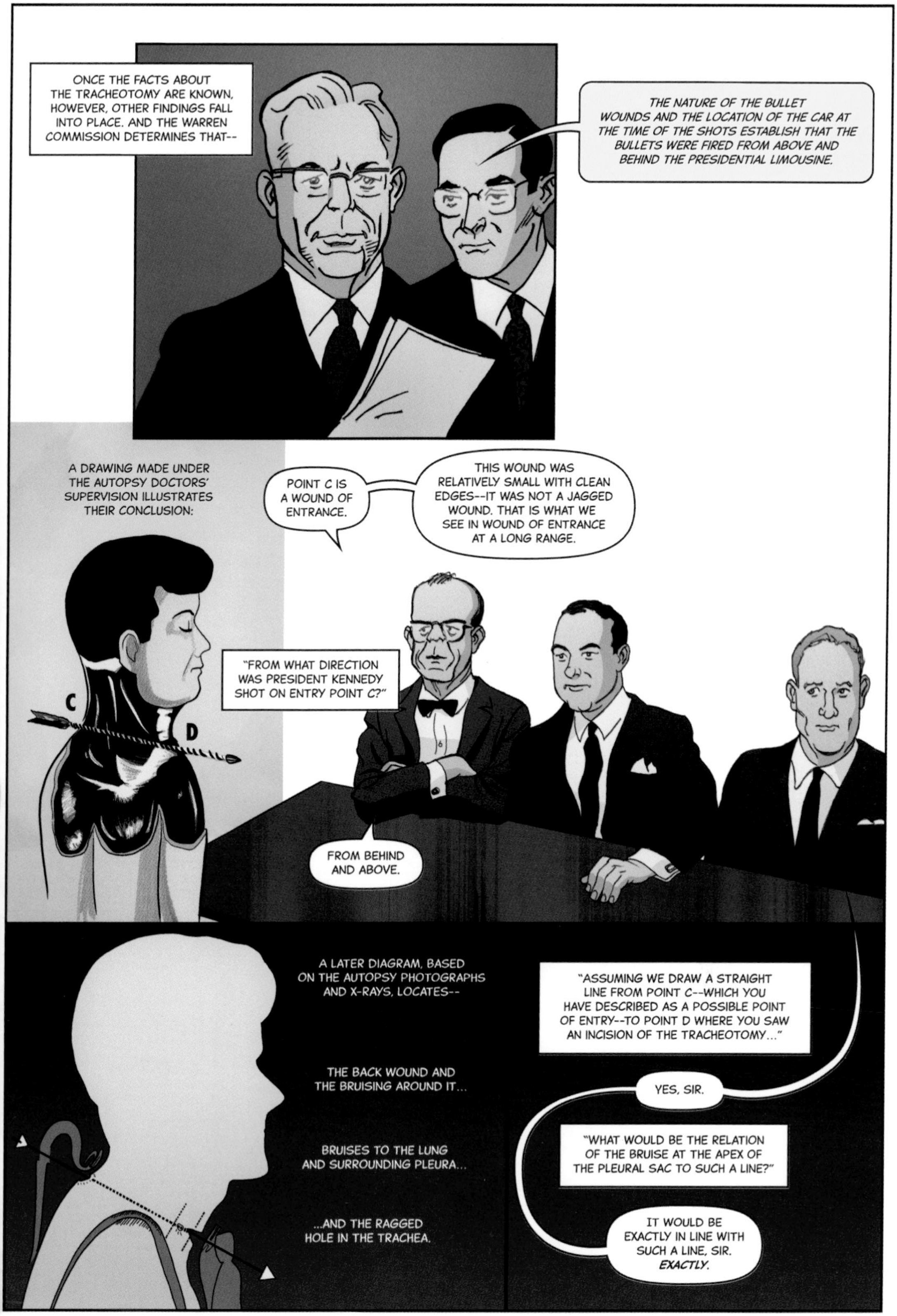
ONCE THE FACTS ABOUT THE TRACHEOTOMY ARE KNOWN, HOWEVER, OTHER FINDINGS FALL INTO PLACE. AND THE WARREN COMMISSION DETERMINES THAT--
THE NATURE OF THE BULLET WOUNDS AND THE LOCATION OF THE CAR AT THE TIME OF THE SHOTS ESTABLISH THAT THE BULLETS WERE FIRED FROM ABOVE AND BEHIND THE PRESIDENTIAL LIMOUSINE.
A DRAWING MADE UNDER THE AUTOPSY DOCTORS' SUPERVISION ILLUSTRATES THEIR CONCLUSION:
POINT C IS A WOUND OF ENTRANCE.
THIS WOUND WAS RELATIVELY SMALL WITH CLEAN EDGES--IT WAS NOT A JAGGED WOUND. THAT IS WHAT WE SEE IN WOUND OF ENTRANCE AT A LONG RANGE.
C
D
"FROM WHAT DIRECTION WAS PRESIDENT KENNEDY SHOT ON ENTRY POINT C?"
FROM BEHIND AND ABOVE.
A LATER DIAGRAM, BASED ON THE AUTOPSY PHOTOGRAPHS AND X-RAYS, LOCATES--
THE BACK WOUND AND THE BRUISING AROUND IT...
BRUISES TO THE LUNG AND SURROUNDING PLEURA...
...AND THE RAGGED HOLE IN THE TRACHEA.
"ASSUMING WE DRAW A STRAIGHT LINE FROM POINT C--WHICH YOU HAVE DESCRIBED AS A POSSIBLE POINT OF ENTRY--TO POINT D WHERE YOU SAW AN INCISION OF THE TRACHEOTOMY..."
YES, SIR.
"WHAT WOULD BE THE RELATION OF THE BRUISE AT THE APEX OF THE PLEURAL SAC TO SUCH A LINE?"
IT WOULD BE EXACTLY IN LINE WITH SUCH A LINE, SIR. *EXACTLY.*

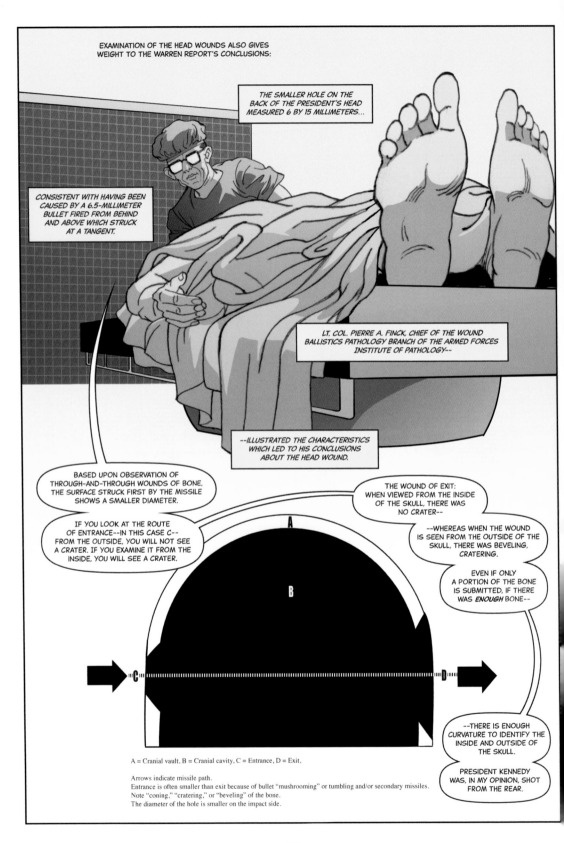

EXAMINATION OF THE HEAD WOUNDS ALSO GIVES WEIGHT TO THE WARREN REPORT'S CONCLUSIONS:

THE SMALLER HOLE ON THE BACK OF THE PRESIDENT'S HEAD MEASURED 6 BY 15 MILLIMETERS...

CONSISTENT WITH HAVING BEEN CAUSED BY A 6.5-MILLIMETER BULLET FIRED FROM BEHIND AND ABOVE WHICH STRUCK AT A TANGENT.

LT. COL. PIERRE A. FINCK, CHIEF OF THE WOUND BALLISTICS PATHOLOGY BRANCH OF THE ARMED FORCES INSTITUTE OF PATHOLOGY--

--ILLUSTRATED THE CHARACTERISTICS WHICH LED TO HIS CONCLUSIONS ABOUT THE HEAD WOUND.

BASED UPON OBSERVATION OF THROUGH-AND-THROUGH WOUNDS OF BONE, THE SURFACE STRUCK FIRST BY THE MISSILE SHOWS A SMALLER DIAMETER.

THE WOUND OF EXIT: WHEN VIEWED FROM THE INSIDE OF THE SKULL, THERE WAS NO CRATER--

IF YOU LOOK AT THE ROUTE OF ENTRANCE--IN THIS CASE C-- FROM THE OUTSIDE, YOU WILL NOT SEE A CRATER. IF YOU EXAMINE IT FROM THE INSIDE, YOU WILL SEE A CRATER.

--WHEREAS WHEN THE WOUND IS SEEN FROM THE OUTSIDE OF THE SKULL, THERE WAS BEVELING, CRATERING.

EVEN IF ONLY A PORTION OF THE BONE IS SUBMITTED, IF THERE WAS *ENOUGH* BONE--

--THERE IS ENOUGH CURVATURE TO IDENTIFY THE INSIDE AND OUTSIDE OF THE SKULL.

PRESIDENT KENNEDY WAS, IN MY OPINION, SHOT FROM THE REAR.

A = Cranial vault, B = Cranial cavity, C = Entrance, D = Exit,

Arrows indicate missile path.
Entrance is often smaller than exit because of bullet "mushrooming" or tumbling and/or secondary missiles.
Note "coning," "cratering," or "beveling" of the bone.
The diameter of the hole is smaller on the impact side.

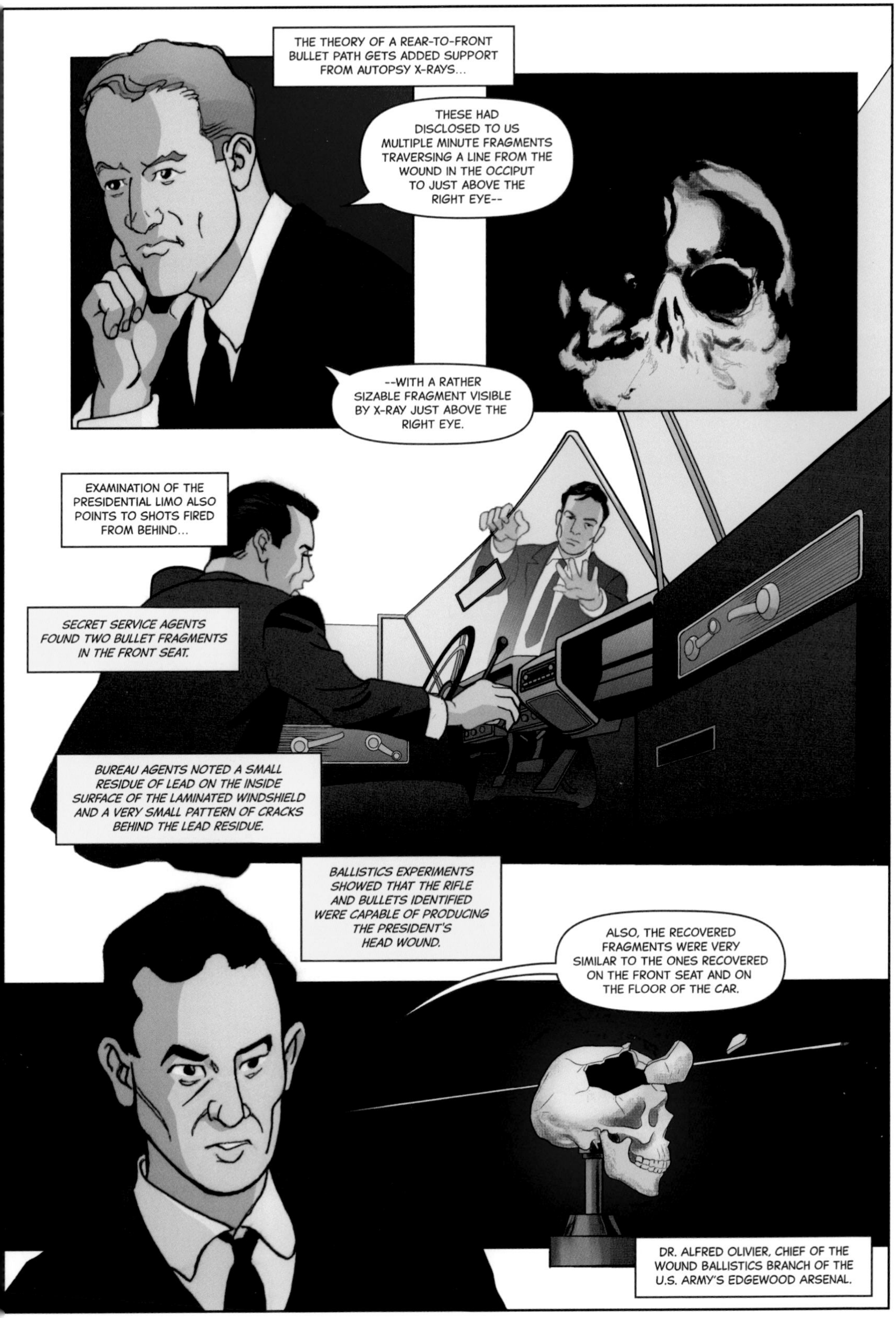

THE THEORY OF A REAR-TO-FRONT BULLET PATH GETS ADDED SUPPORT FROM AUTOPSY X-RAYS...
THESE HAD DISCLOSED TO US MULTIPLE MINUTE FRAGMENTS TRAVERSING A LINE FROM THE WOUND IN THE OCCIPUT TO JUST ABOVE THE RIGHT EYE--
--WITH A RATHER SIZABLE FRAGMENT VISIBLE BY X-RAY JUST ABOVE THE RIGHT EYE.
EXAMINATION OF THE PRESIDENTIAL LIMO ALSO POINTS TO SHOTS FIRED FROM BEHIND...
SECRET SERVICE AGENTS FOUND TWO BULLET FRAGMENTS IN THE FRONT SEAT.
BUREAU AGENTS NOTED A SMALL RESIDUE OF LEAD ON THE INSIDE SURFACE OF THE LAMINATED WINDSHIELD AND A VERY SMALL PATTERN OF CRACKS BEHIND THE LEAD RESIDUE.
BALLISTICS EXPERIMENTS SHOWED THAT THE RIFLE AND BULLETS IDENTIFIED WERE CAPABLE OF PRODUCING THE PRESIDENT'S HEAD WOUND.
ALSO, THE RECOVERED FRAGMENTS WERE VERY SIMILAR TO THE ONES RECOVERED ON THE FRONT SEAT AND ON THE FLOOR OF THE CAR.
DR. ALFRED OLIVIER, CHIEF OF THE WOUND BALLISTICS BRANCH OF THE U.S. ARMY'S EDGEWOOD ARSENAL.

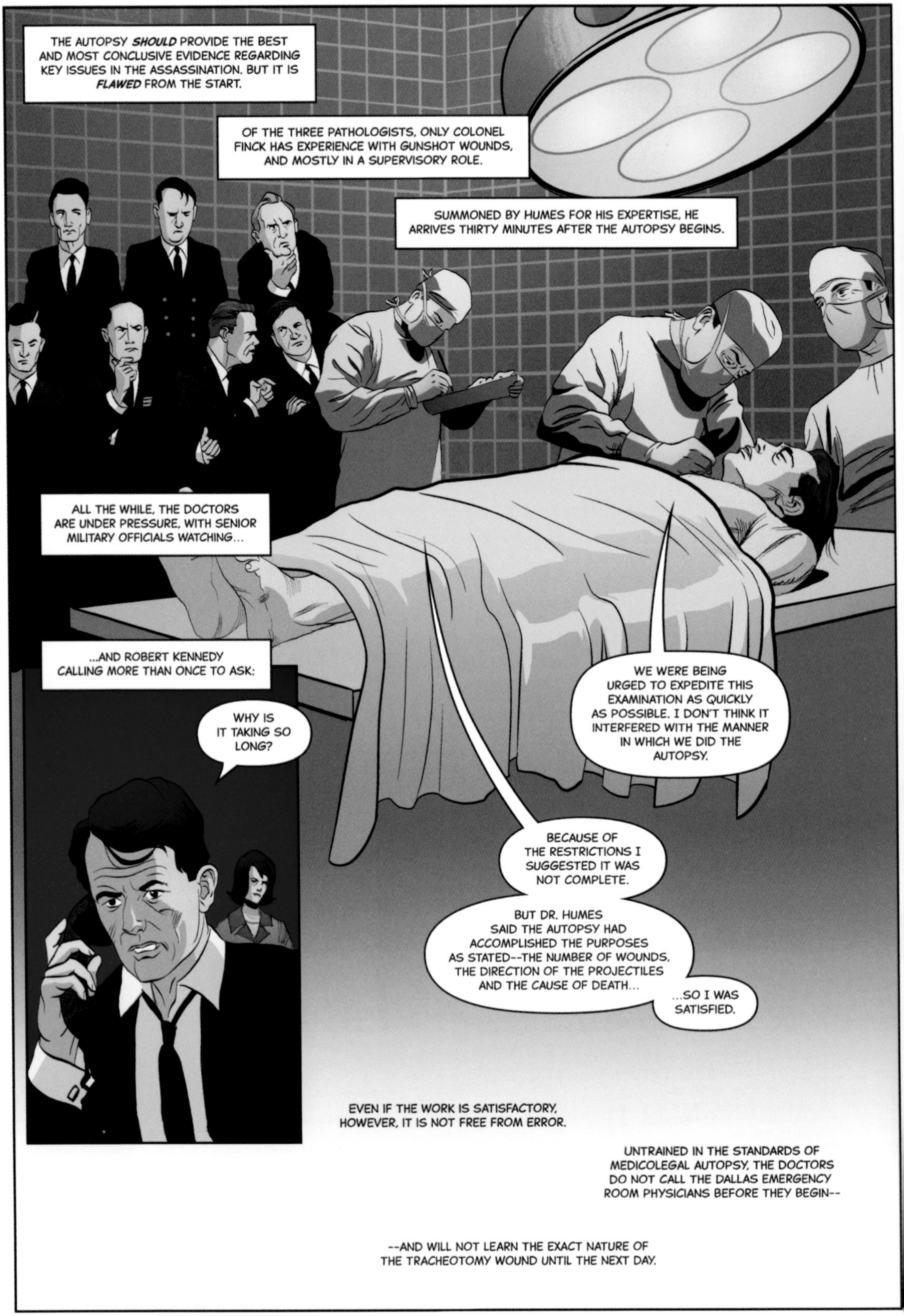
THE AUTOPSY *SHOULD* PROVIDE THE BEST AND MOST CONCLUSIVE EVIDENCE REGARDING KEY ISSUES IN THE ASSASSINATION. BUT IT IS *FLAWED* FROM THE START.
OF THE THREE PATHOLOGISTS, ONLY COLONEL FINCK HAS EXPERIENCE WITH GUNSHOT WOUNDS, AND MOSTLY IN A SUPERVISORY ROLE.
SUMMONED BY HUMES FOR HIS EXPERTISE, HE ARRIVES THIRTY MINUTES AFTER THE AUTOPSY BEGINS.
ALL THE WHILE, THE DOCTORS ARE UNDER PRESSURE, WITH SENIOR MILITARY OFFICIALS WATCHING...
...AND ROBERT KENNEDY CALLING MORE THAN ONCE TO ASK:
WHY IS IT TAKING SO LONG?
WE WERE BEING URGED TO EXPEDITE THIS EXAMINATION AS QUICKLY AS POSSIBLE. I DON'T THINK IT INTERFERED WITH THE MANNER IN WHICH WE DID THE AUTOPSY.
BECAUSE OF THE RESTRICTIONS I SUGGESTED IT WAS NOT COMPLETE.
BUT DR. HUMES SAID THE AUTOPSY HAD ACCOMPLISHED THE PURPOSES AS STATED--THE NUMBER OF WOUNDS, THE DIRECTION OF THE PROJECTILES AND THE CAUSE OF DEATH...
...SO I WAS SATISFIED.
EVEN IF THE WORK IS SATISFACTORY, HOWEVER, IT IS NOT FREE FROM ERROR.
UNTRAINED IN THE STANDARDS OF MEDICOLEGAL AUTOPSY, THE DOCTORS DO NOT CALL THE DALLAS EMERGENCY ROOM PHYSICIANS BEFORE THEY BEGIN--
--AND WILL NOT LEARN THE EXACT NATURE OF THE TRACHEOTOMY WOUND UNTIL THE NEXT DAY.

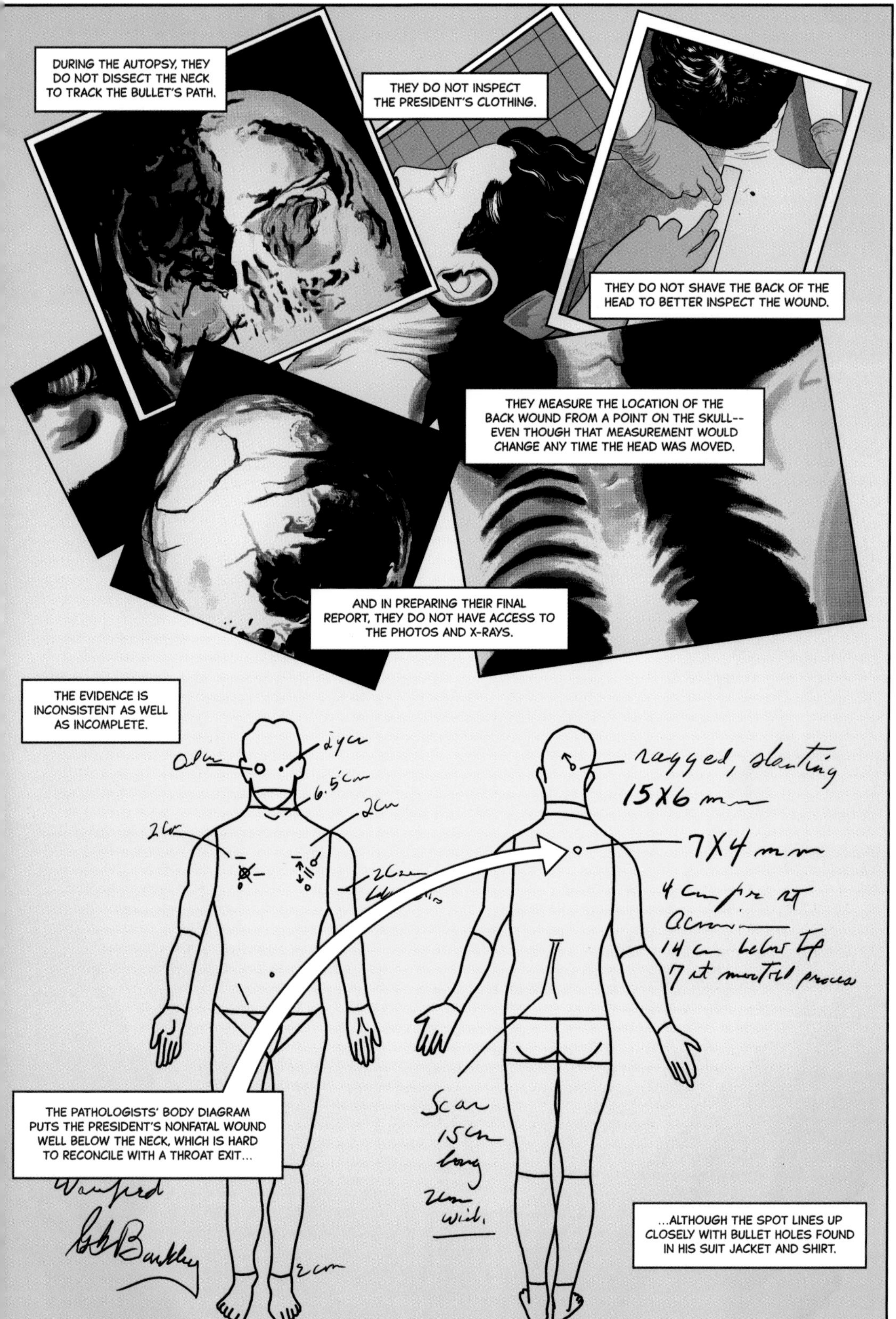
DURING THE AUTOPSY, THEY DO NOT DISSECT THE NECK TO TRACK THE BULLET'S PATH.
THEY DO NOT INSPECT THE PRESIDENT'S CLOTHING.
THEY DO NOT SHAVE THE BACK OF THE HEAD TO BETTER INSPECT THE WOUND.
THEY MEASURE THE LOCATION OF THE BACK WOUND FROM A POINT ON THE SKULL-- EVEN THOUGH THAT MEASUREMENT WOULD CHANGE ANY TIME THE HEAD WAS MOVED.
AND IN PREPARING THEIR FINAL REPORT, THEY DO NOT HAVE ACCESS TO THE PHOTOS AND X-RAYS.
THE EVIDENCE IS INCONSISTENT AS WELL AS INCOMPLETE.
6.5 cm
2 cm
ragged, slanting
15 X 6 mm
7 X 4 mm
Scar
15 cm
long
THE PATHOLOGISTS' BODY DIAGRAM PUTS THE PRESIDENT'S NONFATAL WOUND WELL BELOW THE NECK, WHICH IS HARD TO RECONCILE WITH A THROAT EXIT…
…ALTHOUGH THE SPOT LINES UP CLOSELY WITH BULLET HOLES FOUND IN HIS SUIT JACKET AND SHIRT.

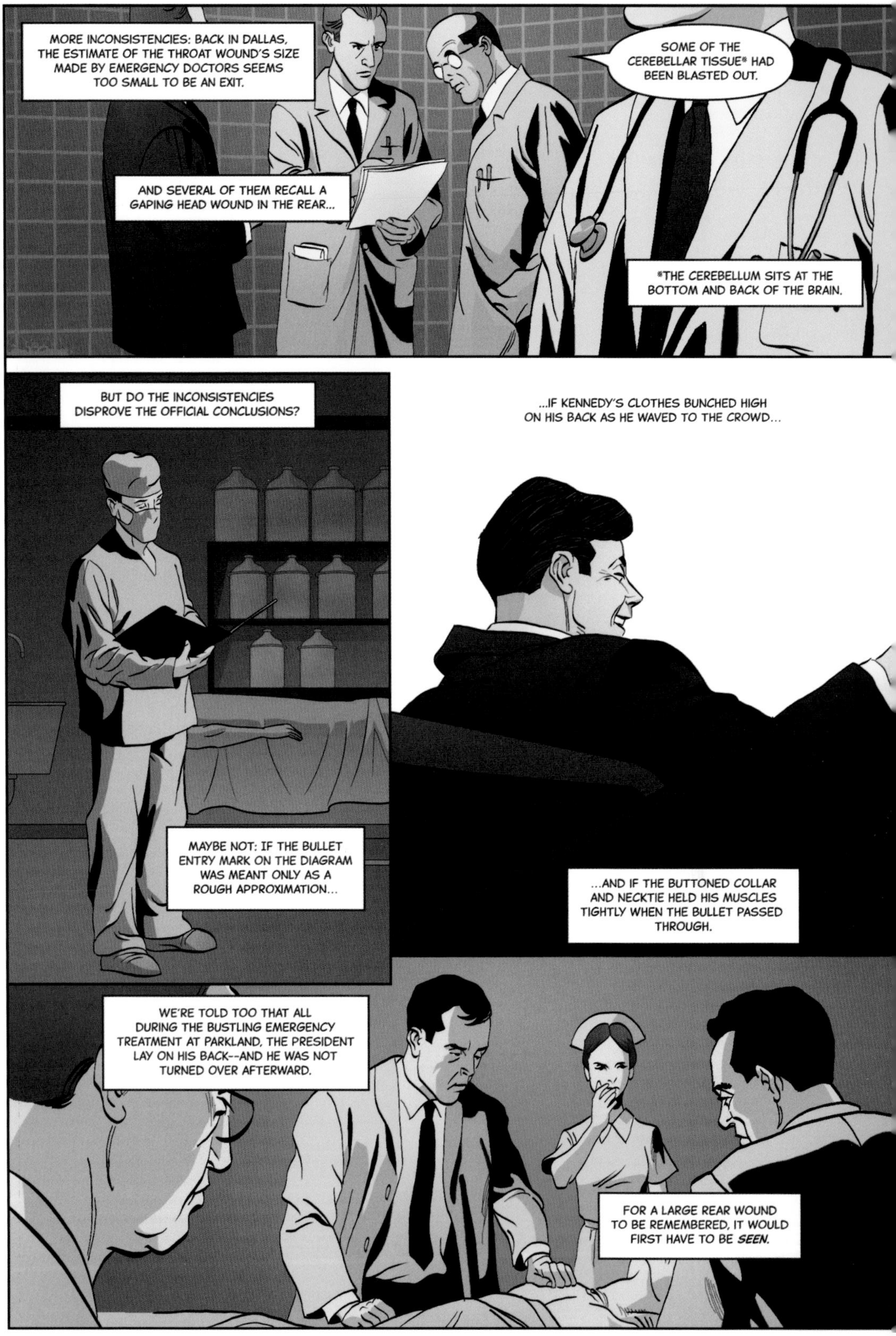
MORE INCONSISTENCIES: BACK IN DALLAS, THE ESTIMATE OF THE THROAT WOUND'S SIZE MADE BY EMERGENCY DOCTORS SEEMS TOO SMALL TO BE AN EXIT.
SOME OF THE CEREBELLAR TISSUE* HAD BEEN BLASTED OUT.
AND SEVERAL OF THEM RECALL A GAPING HEAD WOUND IN THE REAR...
*THE CEREBELLUM SITS AT THE BOTTOM AND BACK OF THE BRAIN.
BUT DO THE INCONSISTENCIES DISPROVE THE OFFICIAL CONCLUSIONS?
MAYBE NOT: IF THE BULLET ENTRY MARK ON THE DIAGRAM WAS MEANT ONLY AS A ROUGH APPROXIMATION...
...IF KENNEDY'S CLOTHES BUNCHED HIGH ON HIS BACK AS HE WAVED TO THE CROWD...
...AND IF THE BUTTONED COLLAR AND NECKTIE HELD HIS MUSCLES TIGHTLY WHEN THE BULLET PASSED THROUGH.
WE'RE TOLD TOO THAT ALL DURING THE BUSTLING EMERGENCY TREATMENT AT PARKLAND, THE PRESIDENT LAY ON HIS BACK--AND HE WAS NOT TURNED OVER AFTERWARD.
FOR A LARGE REAR WOUND TO BE REMEMBERED, IT WOULD FIRST HAVE TO BE *SEEN.*

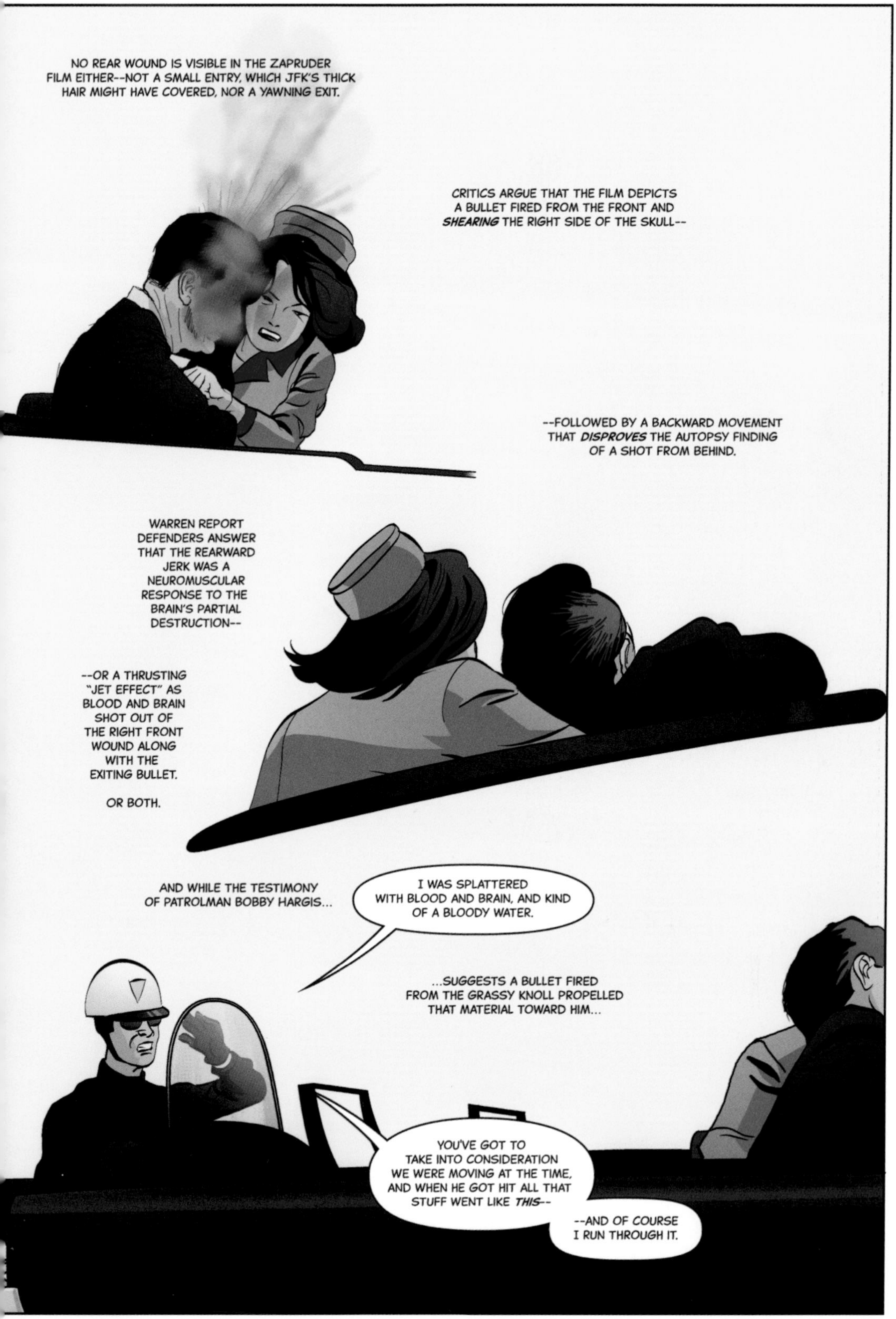
NO REAR WOUND IS VISIBLE IN THE ZAPRUDER FILM EITHER--NOT A SMALL ENTRY, WHICH JFK'S THICK HAIR MIGHT HAVE COVERED, NOR A YAWNING EXIT.
CRITICS ARGUE THAT THE FILM DEPICTS A BULLET FIRED FROM THE FRONT AND *SHEARING* THE RIGHT SIDE OF THE SKULL--
--FOLLOWED BY A BACKWARD MOVEMENT THAT *DISPROVES* THE AUTOPSY FINDING OF A SHOT FROM BEHIND.
WARREN REPORT DEFENDERS ANSWER THAT THE REARWARD JERK WAS A NEUROMUSCULAR RESPONSE TO THE BRAIN'S PARTIAL DESTRUCTION--
--OR A THRUSTING "JET EFFECT" AS BLOOD AND BRAIN SHOT OUT OF THE RIGHT FRONT WOUND ALONG WITH THE EXITING BULLET.
OR BOTH.
AND WHILE THE TESTIMONY OF PATROLMAN BOBBY HARGIS...
I WAS SPLATTERED WITH BLOOD AND BRAIN, AND KIND OF A BLOODY WATER.
...SUGGESTS A BULLET FIRED FROM THE GRASSY KNOLL PROPELLED THAT MATERIAL TOWARD HIM...
YOU'VE GOT TO TAKE INTO CONSIDERATION WE WERE MOVING AT THE TIME, AND WHEN HE GOT HIT ALL THAT STUFF WENT LIKE *THIS*--
--AND OF COURSE I RUN THROUGH IT.

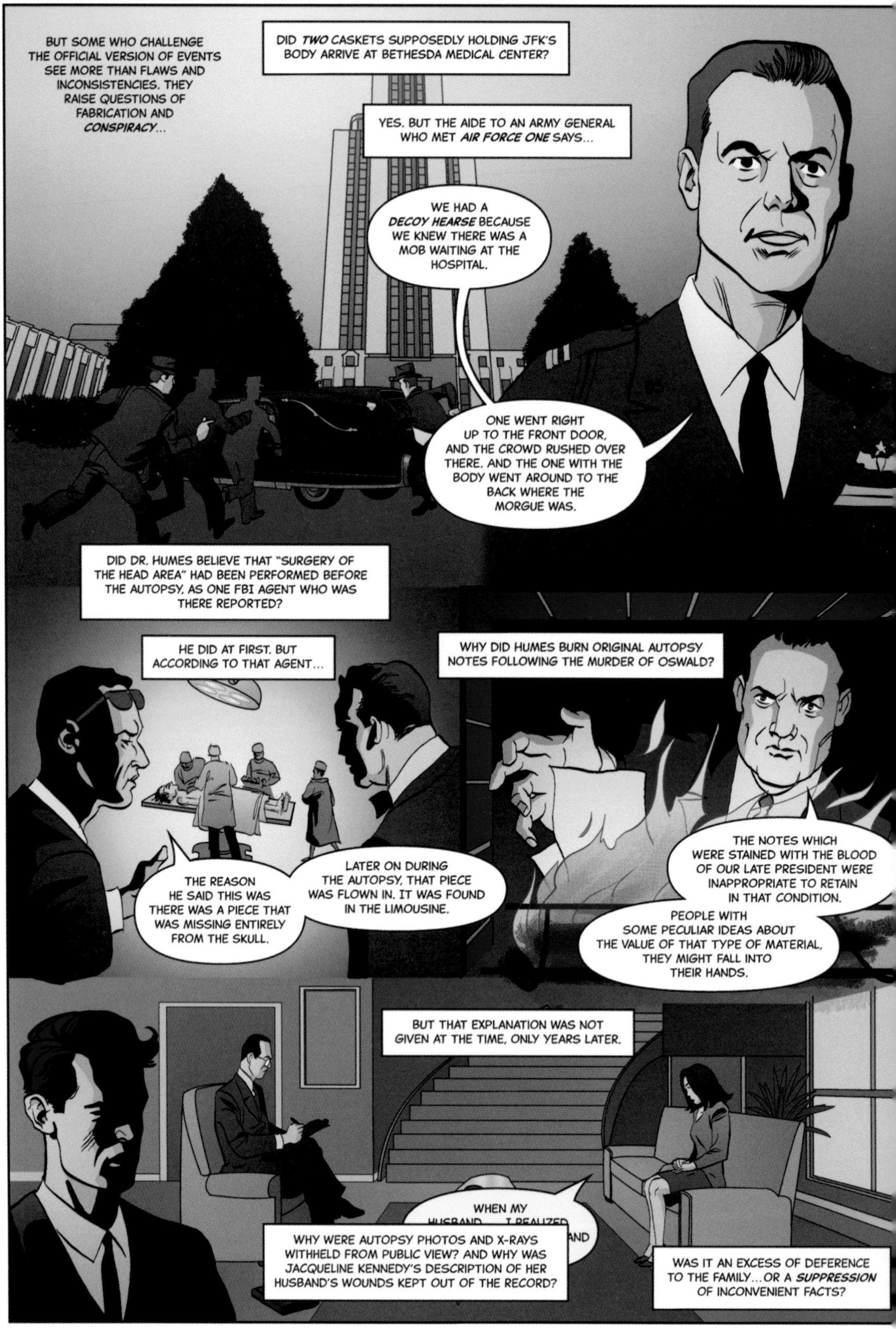
BUT SOME WHO CHALLENGE THE OFFICIAL VERSION OF EVENTS SEE MORE THAN FLAWS AND INCONSISTENCIES. THEY RAISE QUESTIONS OF FABRICATION AND *CONSPIRACY*...
DID *TWO* CASKETS SUPPOSEDLY HOLDING JFK'S BODY ARRIVE AT BETHESDA MEDICAL CENTER?
YES. BUT THE AIDE TO AN ARMY GENERAL WHO MET *AIR FORCE ONE* SAYS...
WE HAD A *DECOY HEARSE* BECAUSE WE KNEW THERE WAS A MOB WAITING AT THE HOSPITAL.
ONE WENT RIGHT UP TO THE FRONT DOOR, AND THE CROWD RUSHED OVER THERE. AND THE ONE WITH THE BODY WENT AROUND TO THE BACK WHERE THE MORGUE WAS.
DID DR. HUMES BELIEVE THAT "SURGERY OF THE HEAD AREA" HAD BEEN PERFORMED BEFORE THE AUTOPSY, AS ONE FBI AGENT WHO WAS THERE REPORTED?
HE DID AT FIRST. BUT ACCORDING TO THAT AGENT...
THE REASON HE SAID THIS WAS THERE WAS A PIECE THAT WAS MISSING ENTIRELY FROM THE SKULL.
LATER ON DURING THE AUTOPSY, THAT PIECE WAS FLOWN IN. IT WAS FOUND IN THE LIMOUSINE.
WHY DID HUMES BURN ORIGINAL AUTOPSY NOTES FOLLOWING THE MURDER OF OSWALD?
THE NOTES WHICH WERE STAINED WITH THE BLOOD OF OUR LATE PRESIDENT WERE INAPPROPRIATE TO RETAIN IN THAT CONDITION.
PEOPLE WITH SOME PECULIAR IDEAS ABOUT THE VALUE OF THAT TYPE OF MATERIAL, THEY MIGHT FALL INTO THEIR HANDS.
BUT THAT EXPLANATION WAS NOT GIVEN AT THE TIME, ONLY YEARS LATER.
WHEN MY
WHY WERE AUTOPSY PHOTOS AND X-RAYS WITHHELD FROM PUBLIC VIEW? AND WHY WAS JACQUELINE KENNEDY'S DESCRIPTION OF HER HUSBAND'S WOUNDS KEPT OUT OF THE RECORD?
WAS IT AN EXCESS OF DEFERENCE TO THE FAMILY...OR A *SUPPRESSION* OF INCONVENIENT FACTS?

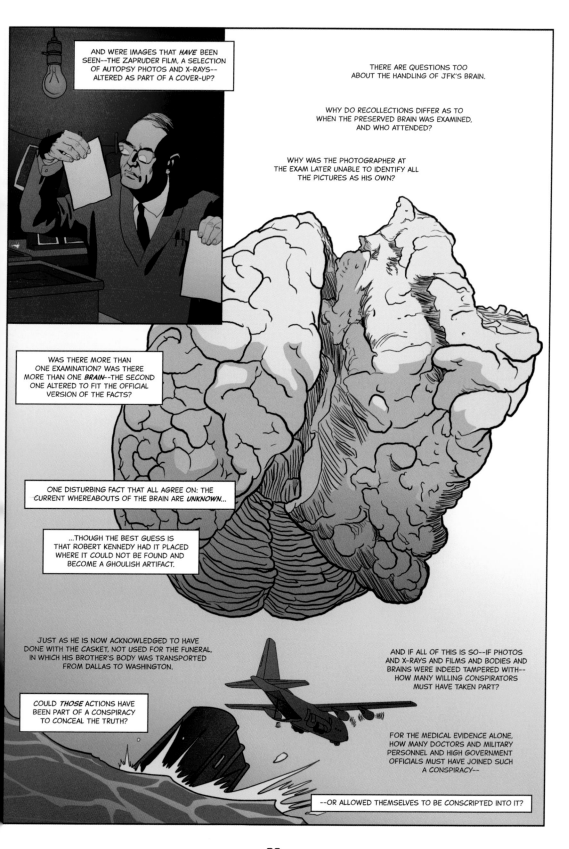

AND WERE IMAGES THAT *HAVE* BEEN SEEN--THE ZAPRUDER FILM, A SELECTION OF AUTOPSY PHOTOS AND X-RAYS-- ALTERED AS PART OF A COVER-UP?

THERE ARE QUESTIONS TOO ABOUT THE HANDLING OF JFK'S BRAIN.

WHY DO RECOLLECTIONS DIFFER AS TO WHEN THE PRESERVED BRAIN WAS EXAMINED, AND WHO ATTENDED?

WHY WAS THE PHOTOGRAPHER AT THE EXAM LATER UNABLE TO IDENTIFY ALL THE PICTURES AS HIS OWN?

WAS THERE MORE THAN ONE EXAMINATION? WAS THERE MORE THAN ONE *BRAIN*--THE SECOND ONE ALTERED TO FIT THE OFFICIAL VERSION OF THE FACTS?

ONE DISTURBING FACT THAT ALL AGREE ON: THE CURRENT WHEREABOUTS OF THE BRAIN ARE *UNKNOWN*...

...THOUGH THE BEST GUESS IS THAT ROBERT KENNEDY HAD IT PLACED WHERE IT COULD NOT BE FOUND AND BECOME A GHOULISH ARTIFACT.

JUST AS HE IS NOW ACKNOWLEDGED TO HAVE DONE WITH THE CASKET, NOT USED FOR THE FUNERAL, IN WHICH HIS BROTHER'S BODY WAS TRANSPORTED FROM DALLAS TO WASHINGTON.

AND IF ALL OF THIS IS SO--IF PHOTOS AND X-RAYS AND FILMS AND BODIES AND BRAINS WERE INDEED TAMPERED WITH-- HOW MANY WILLING CONSPIRATORS MUST HAVE TAKEN PART?

COULD *THOSE* ACTIONS HAVE BEEN PART OF A CONSPIRACY TO CONCEAL THE TRUTH?

FOR THE MEDICAL EVIDENCE ALONE, HOW MANY DOCTORS AND MILITARY PERSONNEL AND HIGH GOVERNMENT OFFICIALS MUST HAVE JOINED SUCH A CONSPIRACY--

--OR ALLOWED THEMSELVES TO BE CONSCRIPTED INTO IT?

BUT *ANY* THEORY OF THE CASE MUST ANSWER QUESTIONS OF PLAUSIBILITY--

THE SINGLE-BULLET THEORY

--INCLUDING WHAT IS PROBABLY THE WARREN COMMISSION'S MOST CONTROVERSIAL CONCLUSION...

IF OSWALD WAS THE SOLE ASSASSIN, THEN FINDING THREE SHELL CASINGS IN HIS SNIPER'S NEST MEANS ONLY THREE BULLETS WERE FIRED.

THUS THE FBI REPORT DELIVERED TO THE WARREN COMMISSION IN DECEMBER DECIDES--

As the ~~motorcade was traveling through downtown~~ Dallas on Elm Street about fifty yards west of the intersection with Houston Street (Exhibit 1), three shots rang out. Two bullets struck President Kennedy, and one wounded Governor Connally. The

AND ACCORDING TO THE CONNALLYS...

IT WAS JUST A FRIGHTENING NOISE. I TURNED AND SAW THE PRESIDENT AS HE HAD BOTH HANDS AT HIS NECK.

THEN VERY SOON THERE WAS A *SECOND SHOT* THAT HIT JOHN.

IT IS *INCONCEIVABLE* TO ME THAT I COULD HAVE BEEN HIT BY THE FIRST BULLET.

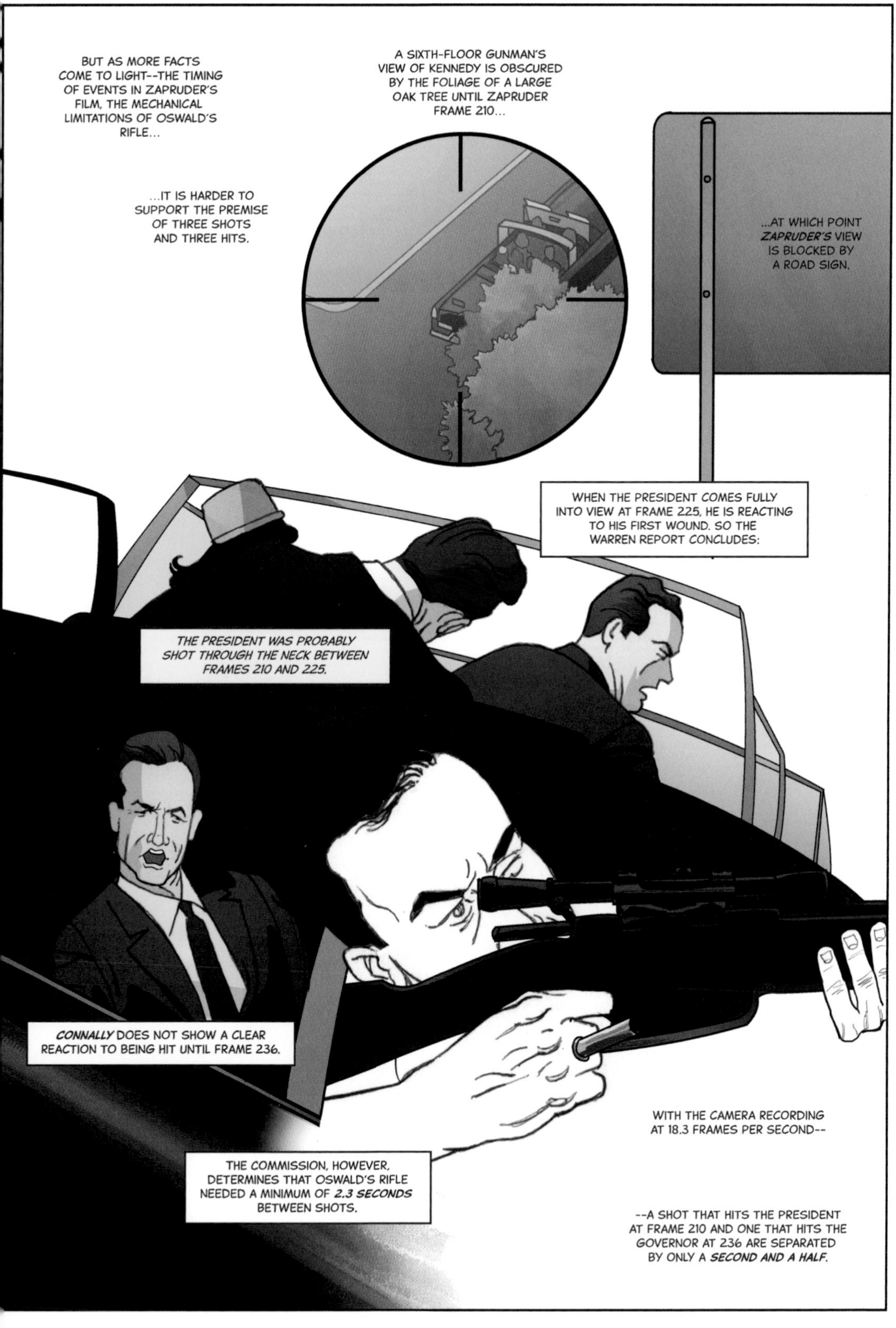

BUT AS MORE FACTS COME TO LIGHT--THE TIMING OF EVENTS IN ZAPRUDER'S FILM, THE MECHANICAL LIMITATIONS OF OSWALD'S RIFLE...
...IT IS HARDER TO SUPPORT THE PREMISE OF THREE SHOTS AND THREE HITS.
A SIXTH-FLOOR GUNMAN'S VIEW OF KENNEDY IS OBSCURED BY THE FOLIAGE OF A LARGE OAK TREE UNTIL ZAPRUDER FRAME 210...
...AT WHICH POINT *ZAPRUDER'S* VIEW IS BLOCKED BY A ROAD SIGN.
WHEN THE PRESIDENT COMES FULLY INTO VIEW AT FRAME 225, HE IS REACTING TO HIS FIRST WOUND. SO THE WARREN REPORT CONCLUDES:
THE PRESIDENT WAS PROBABLY SHOT THROUGH THE NECK BETWEEN FRAMES 210 AND 225.
CONNALLY DOES NOT SHOW A CLEAR REACTION TO BEING HIT UNTIL FRAME 236.
THE *COMMISSION*, HOWEVER, DETERMINES THAT OSWALD'S RIFLE NEEDED A MINIMUM OF ***2.3 SECONDS*** BETWEEN SHOTS.
WITH THE CAMERA RECORDING AT 18.3 FRAMES PER SECOND--
--A SHOT THAT HITS THE PRESIDENT AT FRAME 210 AND ONE THAT HITS THE GOVERNOR AT 236 ARE SEPARATED BY ONLY A ***SECOND AND A HALF.***

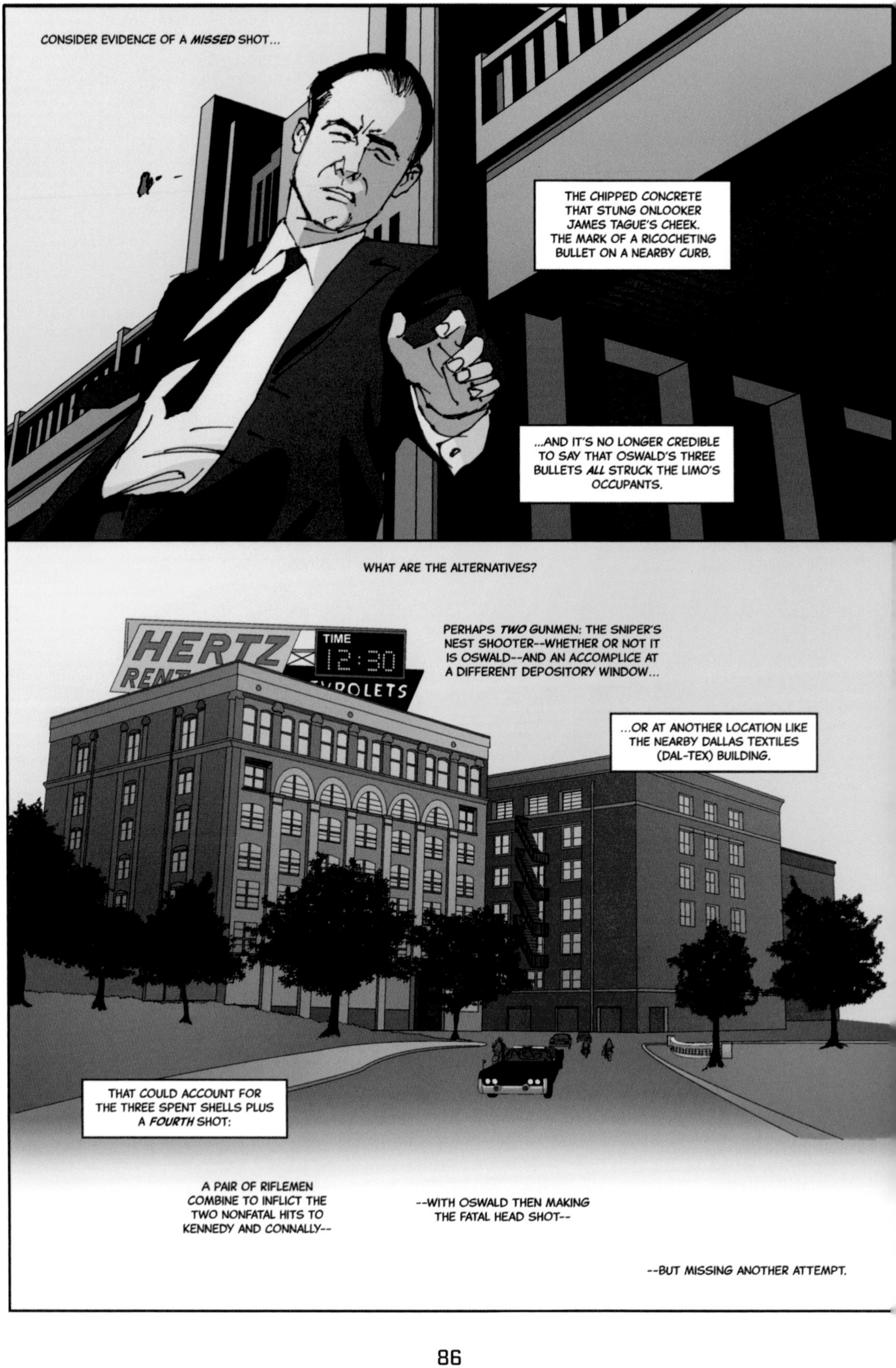
CONSIDER EVIDENCE OF A *MISSED* SHOT...
THE CHIPPED CONCRETE THAT STUNG ONLOOKER JAMES TAGUE'S CHEEK. THE MARK OF A RICOCHETING BULLET ON A NEARBY CURB.
...AND IT'S NO LONGER CREDIBLE TO SAY THAT OSWALD'S THREE BULLETS *ALL* STRUCK THE LIMO'S OCCUPANTS.
WHAT ARE THE ALTERNATIVES?
HERTZ
TIME
12:30
PERHAPS *TWO* GUNMEN: THE SNIPER'S NEST SHOOTER--WHETHER OR NOT IT IS OSWALD--AND AN ACCOMPLICE AT A DIFFERENT DEPOSITORY WINDOW...
...OR AT ANOTHER LOCATION LIKE THE NEARBY DALLAS TEXTILES (DAL-TEX) BUILDING.
THAT COULD ACCOUNT FOR THE THREE SPENT SHELLS PLUS A *FOURTH* SHOT:
A PAIR OF RIFLEMEN COMBINE TO INFLICT THE TWO NONFATAL HITS TO KENNEDY AND CONNALLY--
--WITH OSWALD THEN MAKING THE FATAL HEAD SHOT--
--BUT MISSING ANOTHER ATTEMPT.

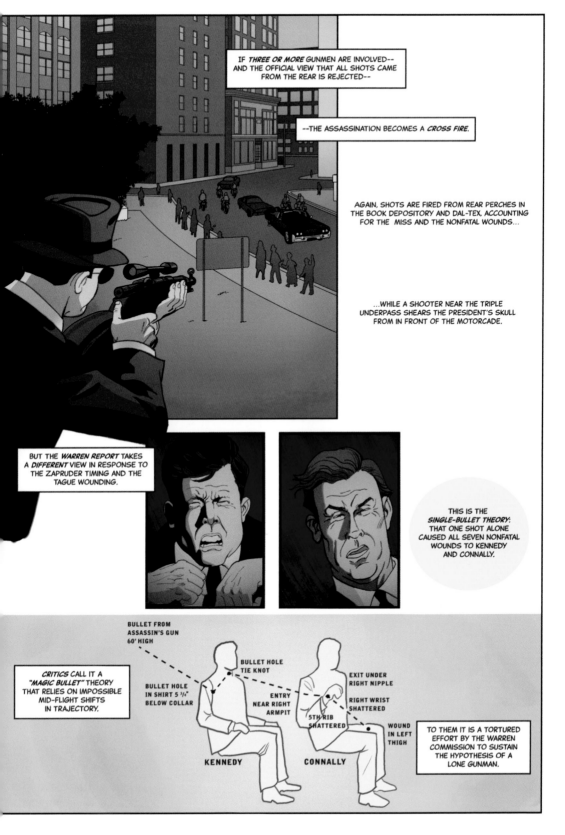

IF *THREE OR MORE* GUNMEN ARE INVOLVED-- AND THE OFFICIAL VIEW THAT ALL SHOTS CAME FROM THE REAR IS REJECTED--

--THE ASSASSINATION BECOMES A *CROSS FIRE.*

AGAIN, SHOTS ARE FIRED FROM REAR PERCHES IN THE BOOK DEPOSITORY AND DAL-TEX, ACCOUNTING FOR THE MISS AND THE NONFATAL WOUNDS...

...WHILE A SHOOTER NEAR THE TRIPLE UNDERPASS SHEARS THE PRESIDENT'S SKULL FROM IN FRONT OF THE MOTORCADE.

BUT THE *WARREN REPORT* TAKES A *DIFFERENT* VIEW IN RESPONSE TO THE ZAPRUDER TIMING AND THE TAGUE WOUNDING.

THIS IS THE *SINGLE-BULLET THEORY:* THAT ONE SHOT ALONE CAUSED ALL SEVEN NONFATAL WOUNDS TO KENNEDY AND CONNALLY.

CRITICS CALL IT A *"MAGIC BULLET"* THEORY THAT RELIES ON IMPOSSIBLE MID-FLIGHT SHIFTS IN TRAJECTORY.

BULLET FROM ASSASSIN'S GUN 60' HIGH

BULLET HOLE TIE KNOT

BULLET HOLE IN SHIRT 5 3/4" BELOW COLLAR

ENTRY NEAR RIGHT ARMPIT

EXIT UNDER RIGHT NIPPLE

RIGHT WRIST SHATTERED

5TH RIB SHATTERED

WOUND IN LEFT THIGH

KENNEDY

CONNALLY

TO THEM IT IS A TORTURED EFFORT BY THE WARREN COMMISSION TO SUSTAIN THE HYPOTHESIS OF A LONE GUNMAN.

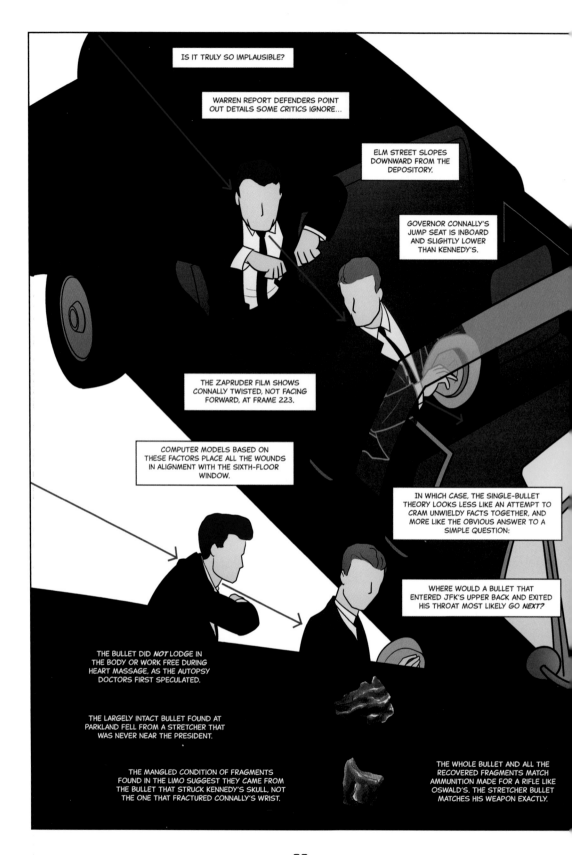

IS IT TRULY SO IMPLAUSIBLE?

WARREN REPORT DEFENDERS POINT OUT DETAILS SOME *CRITICS* IGNORE...

ELM STREET SLOPES DOWNWARD FROM THE DEPOSITORY.

GOVERNOR CONNALLY'S JUMP SEAT IS INBOARD AND SLIGHTLY LOWER THAN KENNEDY'S.

THE ZAPRUDER FILM SHOWS CONNALLY TWISTED, NOT FACING FORWARD, AT FRAME 223.

COMPUTER MODELS BASED ON THESE FACTORS PLACE ALL THE WOUNDS IN ALIGNMENT WITH THE SIXTH-FLOOR WINDOW.

IN WHICH CASE, THE SINGLE-BULLET THEORY LOOKS LESS LIKE AN ATTEMPT TO CRAM UNWIELDY FACTS TOGETHER, AND MORE LIKE THE OBVIOUS ANSWER TO A SIMPLE QUESTION:

WHERE WOULD A BULLET THAT ENTERED JFK'S UPPER BACK AND EXITED HIS THROAT MOST LIKELY GO *NEXT?*

THE BULLET DID *NOT* LODGE IN THE BODY OR WORK FREE DURING HEART MASSAGE, AS THE AUTOPSY DOCTORS FIRST SPECULATED.

THE LARGELY INTACT BULLET FOUND AT PARKLAND FELL FROM A STRETCHER THAT WAS NEVER NEAR THE PRESIDENT.

THE MANGLED CONDITION OF FRAGMENTS FOUND IN THE LIMO SUGGEST THEY CAME FROM THE BULLET THAT STRUCK KENNEDY'S SKULL, NOT THE ONE THAT FRACTURED CONNALLY'S WRIST.

THE WHOLE BULLET AND ALL THE RECOVERED FRAGMENTS MATCH AMMUNITION MADE FOR A RIFLE LIKE OSWALD'S. THE STRETCHER BULLET MATCHES HIS WEAPON EXACTLY.

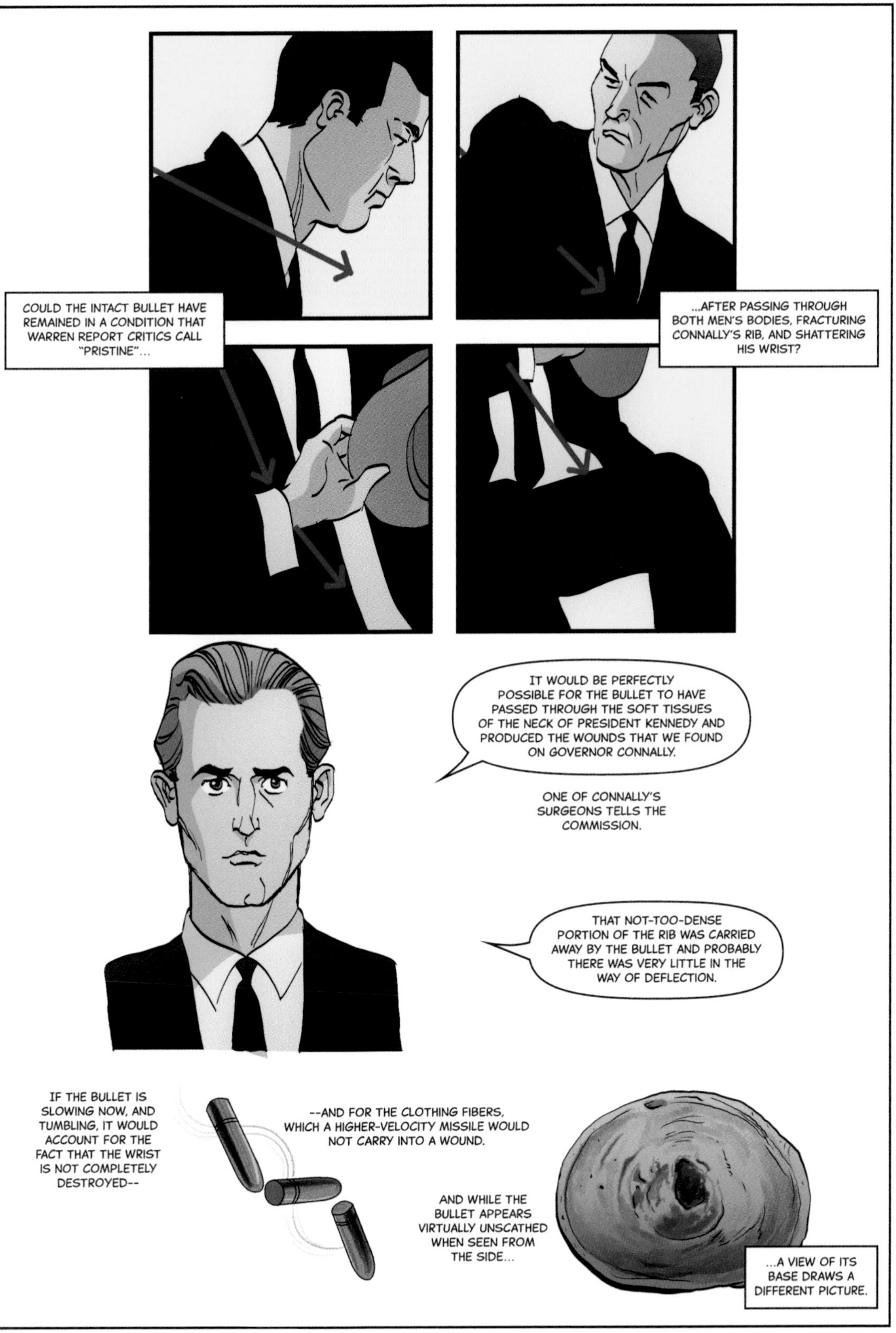
COULD THE INTACT BULLET HAVE REMAINED IN A CONDITION THAT WARREN REPORT CRITICS CALL "PRISTINE"...
...AFTER PASSING THROUGH BOTH MEN'S BODIES, FRACTURING CONNALLY'S RIB, AND SHATTERING HIS WRIST?
IT WOULD BE PERFECTLY POSSIBLE FOR THE BULLET TO HAVE PASSED THROUGH THE SOFT TISSUES OF THE NECK OF PRESIDENT KENNEDY AND PRODUCED THE WOUNDS THAT WE FOUND ON GOVERNOR CONNALLY.
ONE OF CONNALLY'S SURGEONS TELLS THE COMMISSION.
THAT NOT-TOO-DENSE PORTION OF THE RIB WAS CARRIED AWAY BY THE BULLET AND PROBABLY THERE WAS VERY LITTLE IN THE WAY OF DEFLECTION.
IF THE BULLET IS SLOWING NOW, AND TUMBLING, IT WOULD ACCOUNT FOR THE FACT THAT THE WRIST IS NOT COMPLETELY DESTROYED--
--AND FOR THE CLOTHING FIBERS, WHICH A HIGHER-VELOCITY MISSILE WOULD NOT CARRY INTO A WOUND.
AND WHILE THE BULLET APPEARS VIRTUALLY UNSCATHED WHEN SEEN FROM THE SIDE...
...A VIEW OF ITS BASE DRAWS A DIFFERENT PICTURE.

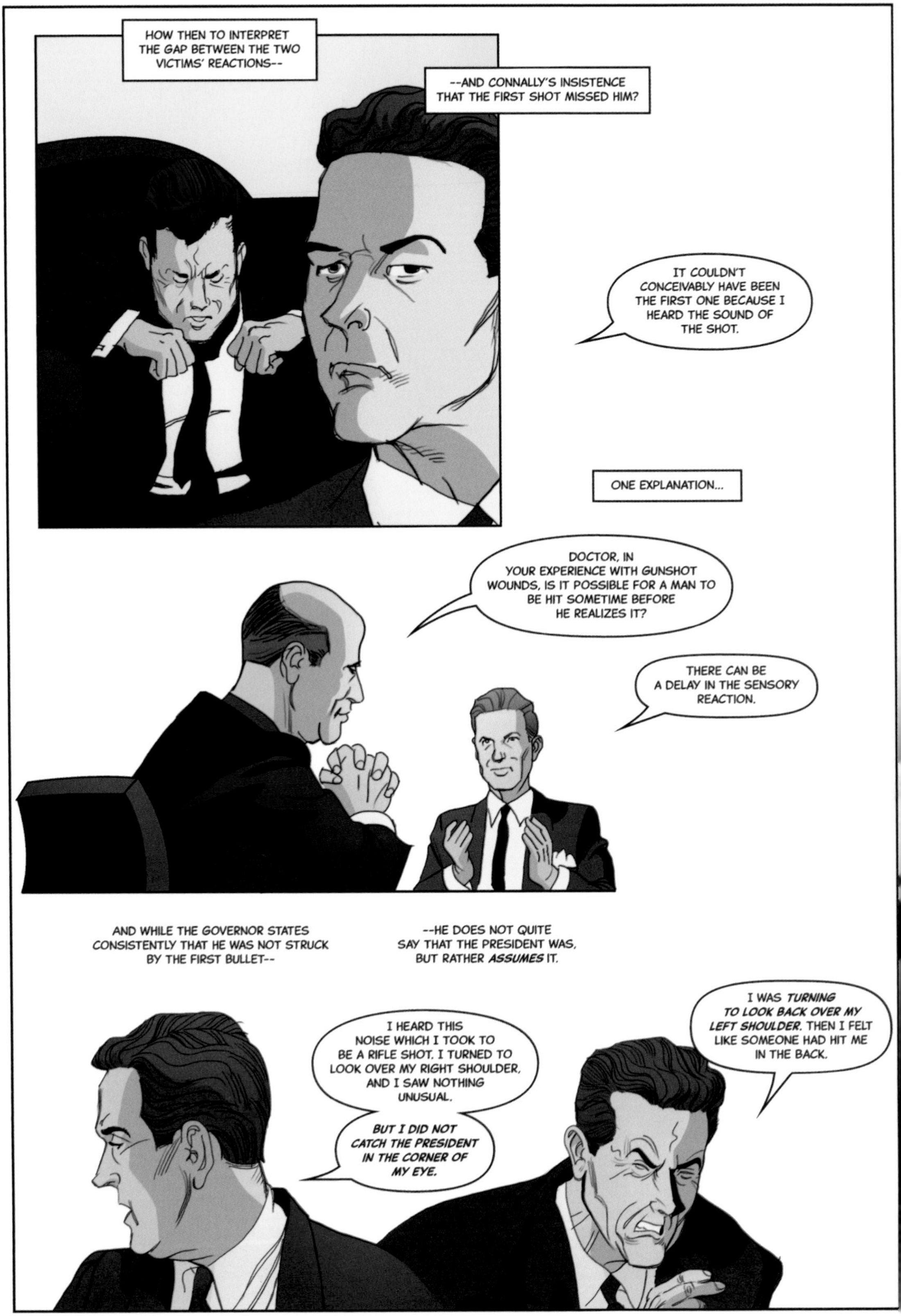
HOW THEN TO INTERPRET THE GAP BETWEEN THE TWO VICTIMS' REACTIONS--
--AND CONNALLY'S INSISTENCE THAT THE FIRST SHOT MISSED HIM?
IT COULDN'T CONCEIVABLY HAVE BEEN THE FIRST ONE BECAUSE I HEARD THE SOUND OF THE SHOT.
ONE EXPLANATION...
DOCTOR, IN YOUR EXPERIENCE WITH GUNSHOT WOUNDS, IS IT POSSIBLE FOR A MAN TO BE HIT SOMETIME BEFORE HE REALIZES IT?
THERE CAN BE A DELAY IN THE SENSORY REACTION.
AND WHILE THE GOVERNOR STATES CONSISTENTLY THAT HE WAS NOT STRUCK BY THE FIRST BULLET--
--HE DOES NOT QUITE SAY THAT THE PRESIDENT WAS, BUT RATHER *ASSUMES* IT.
I HEARD THIS NOISE WHICH I TOOK TO BE A RIFLE SHOT. I TURNED TO LOOK OVER MY RIGHT SHOULDER, AND I SAW NOTHING UNUSUAL.
BUT I DID NOT CATCH THE PRESIDENT IN THE CORNER OF MY EYE.
I WAS *TURNING TO LOOK BACK OVER MY LEFT SHOULDER*. THEN I FELT LIKE SOMEONE HAD HIT ME IN THE BACK.

THE WARREN REPORT DOES
NOT DECLARE WHICH OF THE THREE
DEPOSITORY SHOTS MISSED.

BUT IF IT WAS THE *FIRST*,
DISCREPANCIES OF TIMING CAN
MOSTLY BE EXPLAINED--

--AND CERTAIN EVIDENCE
BEGINS TO MAKE MORE SENSE:

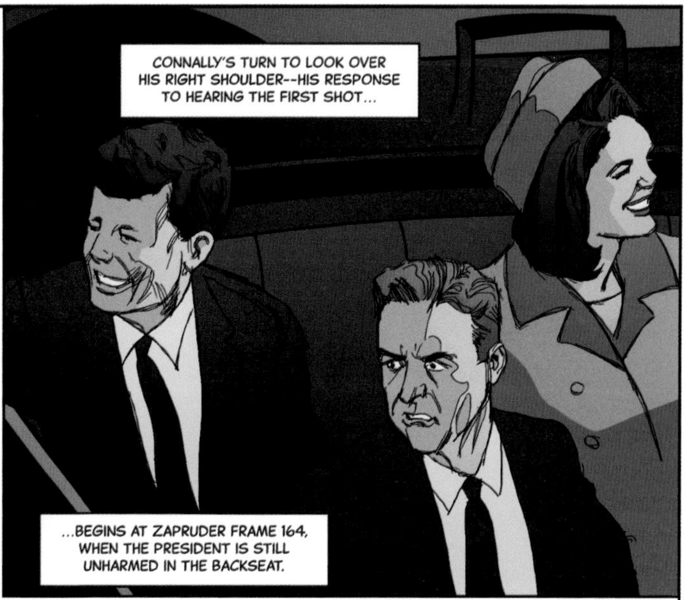
CONNALLY'S TURN TO LOOK OVER HIS RIGHT SHOULDER--HIS RESPONSE TO HEARING THE FIRST SHOT...
...BEGINS AT ZAPRUDER FRAME 164, WHEN THE PRESIDENT IS STILL UNHARMED IN THE BACKSEAT.

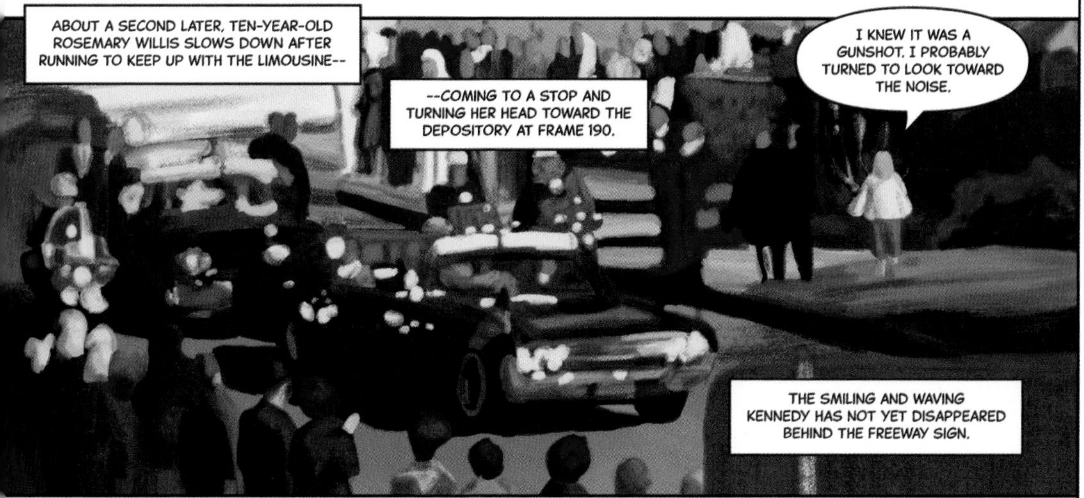
ABOUT A SECOND LATER, TEN-YEAR-OLD ROSEMARY WILLIS SLOWS DOWN AFTER RUNNING TO KEEP UP WITH THE LIMOUSINE--
--COMING TO A STOP AND TURNING HER HEAD TOWARD THE DEPOSITORY AT FRAME 190.
I KNEW IT WAS A GUNSHOT. I PROBABLY TURNED TO LOOK TOWARD THE NOISE.
THE SMILING AND WAVING KENNEDY HAS NOT YET DISAPPEARED BEHIND THE FREEWAY SIGN.

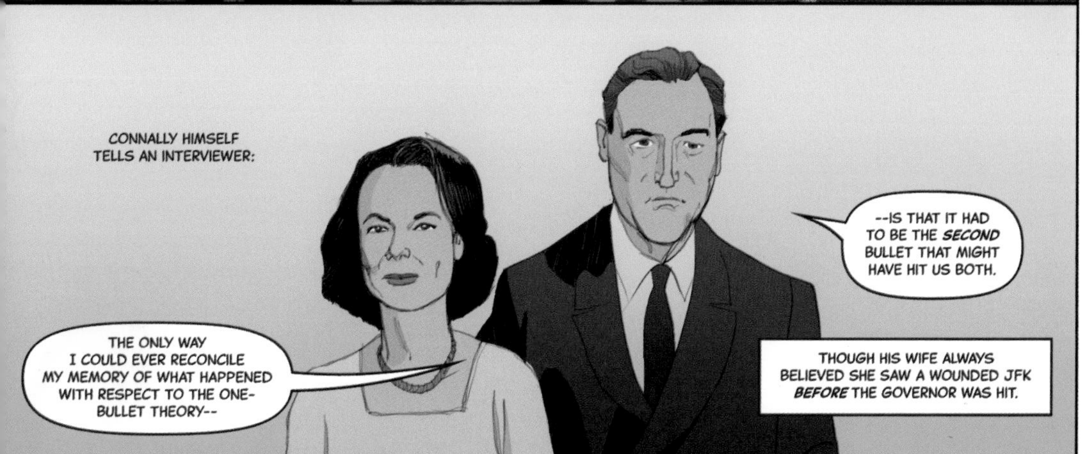
CONNALLY HIMSELF TELLS AN INTERVIEWER:
THE ONLY WAY I COULD EVER RECONCILE MY MEMORY OF WHAT HAPPENED WITH RESPECT TO THE ONE-BULLET THEORY--
--IS THAT IT HAD TO BE THE *SECOND* BULLET THAT MIGHT HAVE HIT US BOTH.
THOUGH HIS WIFE ALWAYS BELIEVED SHE SAW A WOUNDED JFK *BEFORE* THE GOVERNOR WAS HIT.

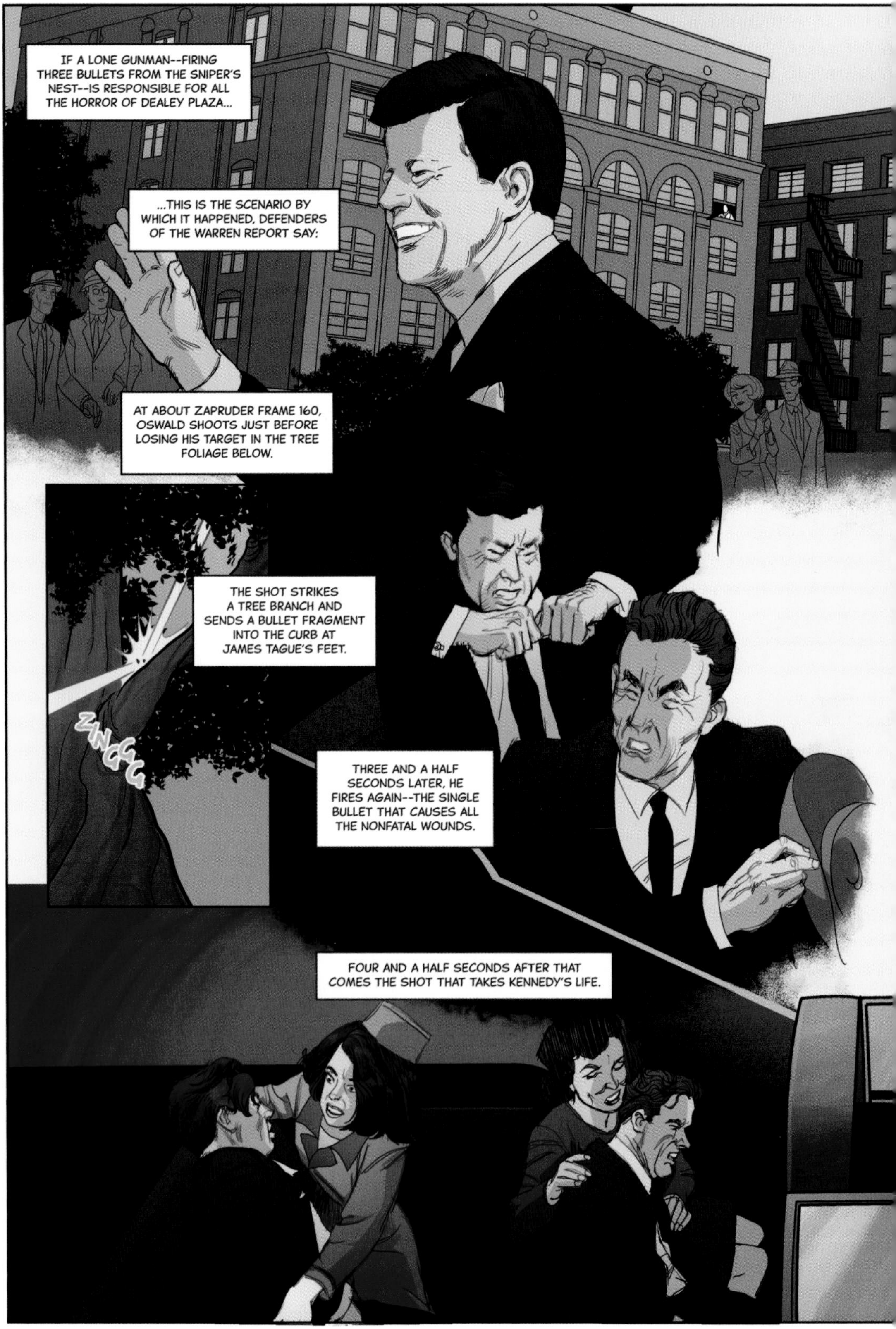
IF A LONE GUNMAN--FIRING THREE BULLETS FROM THE SNIPER'S NEST--IS RESPONSIBLE FOR ALL THE HORROR OF DEALEY PLAZA...
...THIS IS THE SCENARIO BY WHICH IT HAPPENED, DEFENDERS OF THE WARREN REPORT SAY:
AT ABOUT ZAPRUDER FRAME 160, OSWALD SHOOTS JUST BEFORE LOSING HIS TARGET IN THE TREE FOLIAGE BELOW.
THE SHOT STRIKES A TREE BRANCH AND SENDS A BULLET FRAGMENT INTO THE CURB AT JAMES TAGUE'S FEET.
ZINGGG
THREE AND A HALF SECONDS LATER, HE FIRES AGAIN--THE SINGLE BULLET THAT CAUSES ALL THE NONFATAL WOUNDS.
FOUR AND A HALF SECONDS AFTER THAT COMES THE SHOT THAT TAKES KENNEDY'S LIFE.

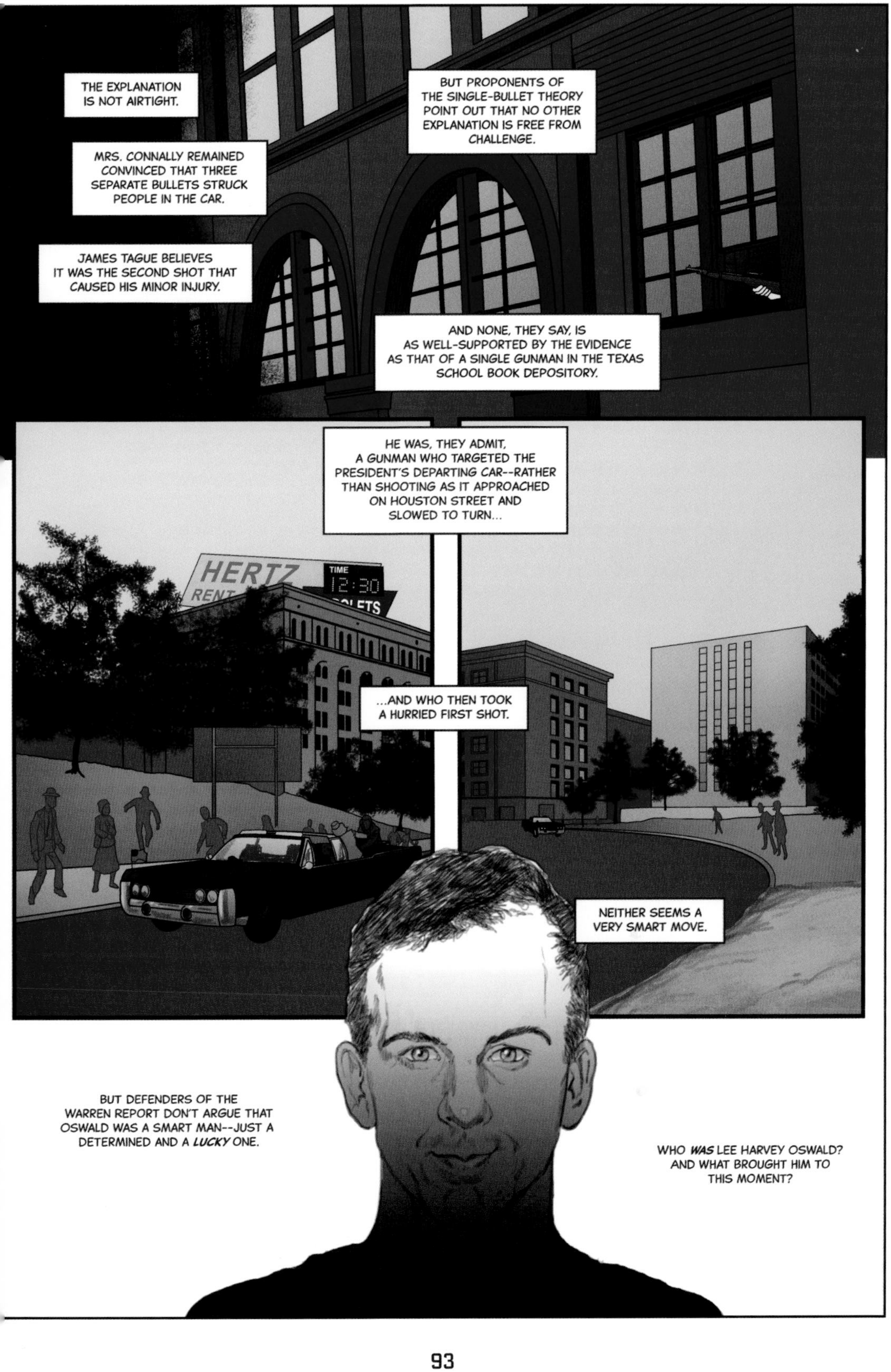
THE EXPLANATION IS NOT AIRTIGHT.
MRS. CONNALLY REMAINED CONVINCED THAT THREE SEPARATE BULLETS STRUCK PEOPLE IN THE CAR.
JAMES TAGUE BELIEVES IT WAS THE SECOND SHOT THAT CAUSED HIS MINOR INJURY.
BUT PROPONENTS OF THE SINGLE-BULLET THEORY POINT OUT THAT NO OTHER EXPLANATION IS FREE FROM CHALLENGE.
AND NONE, THEY SAY, IS AS WELL-SUPPORTED BY THE EVIDENCE AS THAT OF A SINGLE GUNMAN IN THE TEXAS SCHOOL BOOK DEPOSITORY.
HE WAS, THEY ADMIT, A GUNMAN WHO TARGETED THE PRESIDENT'S DEPARTING CAR--RATHER THAN SHOOTING AS IT APPROACHED ON HOUSTON STREET AND SLOWED TO TURN...
HERTZ
RENT
TIME
12:30
...AND WHO THEN TOOK A HURRIED FIRST SHOT.
NEITHER SEEMS A VERY SMART MOVE.
BUT DEFENDERS OF THE WARREN REPORT DON'T ARGUE THAT OSWALD WAS A SMART MAN--JUST A DETERMINED AND A *LUCKY* ONE.
WHO *WAS* LEE HARVEY OSWALD? AND WHAT BROUGHT HIM TO THIS MOMENT?

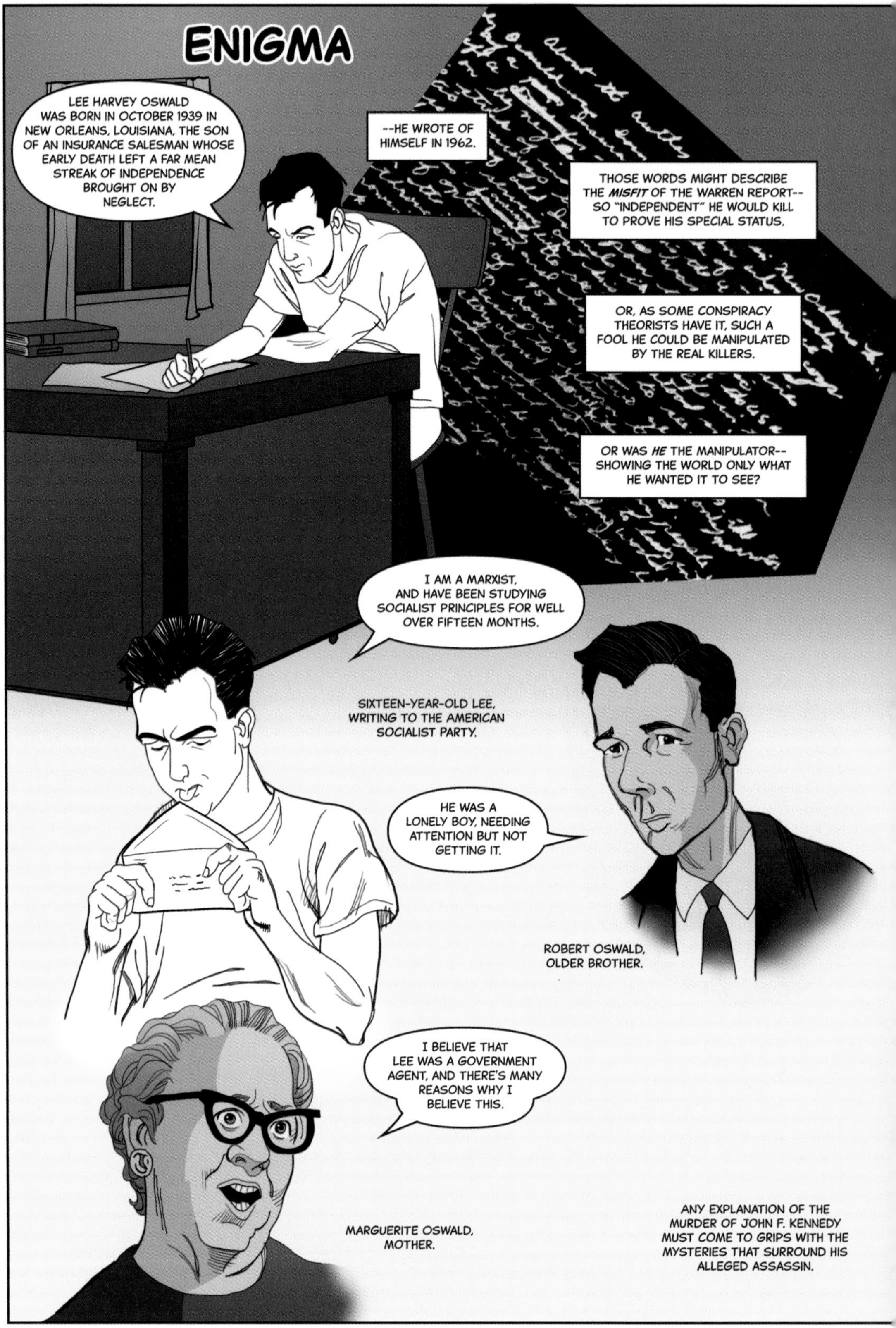
ENIGMA
LEE HARVEY OSWALD WAS BORN IN OCTOBER 1939 IN NEW ORLEANS, LOUISIANA, THE SON OF AN INSURANCE SALESMAN WHOSE EARLY DEATH LEFT A FAR MEAN STREAK OF INDEPENDENCE BROUGHT ON BY NEGLECT.
--HE WROTE OF HIMSELF IN 1962.
THOSE WORDS MIGHT DESCRIBE THE *MISFIT* OF THE WARREN REPORT-- SO "INDEPENDENT" HE WOULD KILL TO PROVE HIS SPECIAL STATUS.
OR, AS SOME CONSPIRACY THEORISTS HAVE IT, SUCH A FOOL HE COULD BE MANIPULATED BY THE REAL KILLERS.
OR WAS *HE* THE MANIPULATOR-- SHOWING THE WORLD ONLY WHAT HE WANTED IT TO SEE?
I AM A MARXIST, AND HAVE BEEN STUDYING SOCIALIST PRINCIPLES FOR WELL OVER FIFTEEN MONTHS.
SIXTEEN-YEAR-OLD LEE, WRITING TO THE AMERICAN SOCIALIST PARTY.
HE WAS A LONELY BOY, NEEDING ATTENTION BUT NOT GETTING IT.
ROBERT OSWALD, OLDER BROTHER.
I BELIEVE THAT LEE WAS A GOVERNMENT AGENT, AND THERE'S MANY REASONS WHY I BELIEVE THIS.
MARGUERITE OSWALD, MOTHER.
ANY EXPLANATION OF THE MURDER OF JOHN F. KENNEDY MUST COME TO GRIPS WITH THE MYSTERIES THAT SURROUND HIS ALLEGED ASSASSIN.

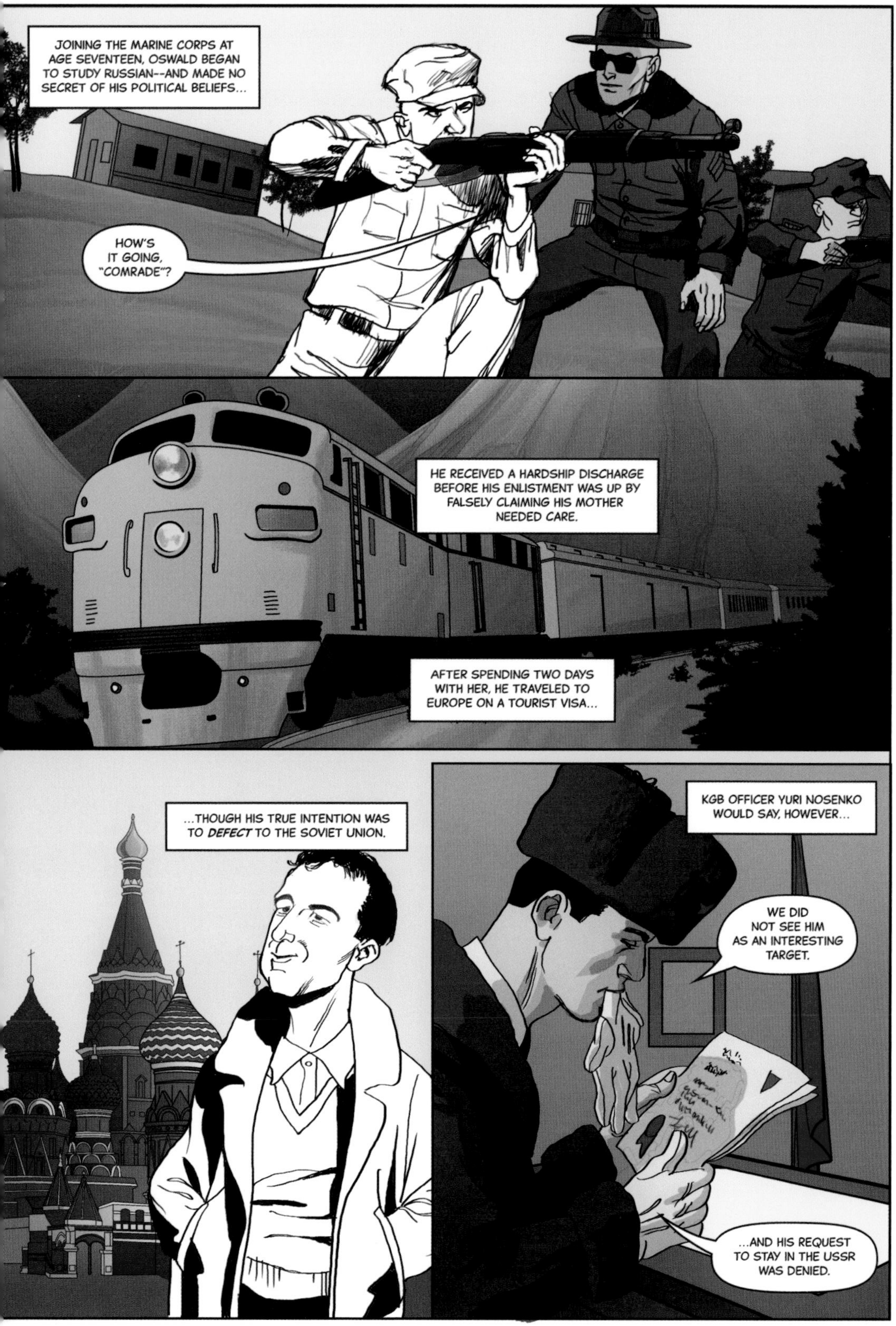
JOINING THE MARINE CORPS AT AGE SEVENTEEN, OSWALD BEGAN TO STUDY RUSSIAN--AND MADE NO SECRET OF HIS POLITICAL BELIEFS...
HOW'S IT GOING, "COMRADE"?
HE RECEIVED A HARDSHIP DISCHARGE BEFORE HIS ENLISTMENT WAS UP BY FALSELY CLAIMING HIS MOTHER NEEDED CARE.
AFTER SPENDING TWO DAYS WITH HER, HE TRAVELED TO EUROPE ON A TOURIST VISA...
...THOUGH HIS TRUE INTENTION WAS TO *DEFECT* TO THE SOVIET UNION.
KGB OFFICER YURI NOSENKO WOULD SAY, HOWEVER...
WE DID NOT SEE HIM AS AN INTERESTING TARGET.
...AND HIS REQUEST TO STAY IN THE USSR WAS DENIED.

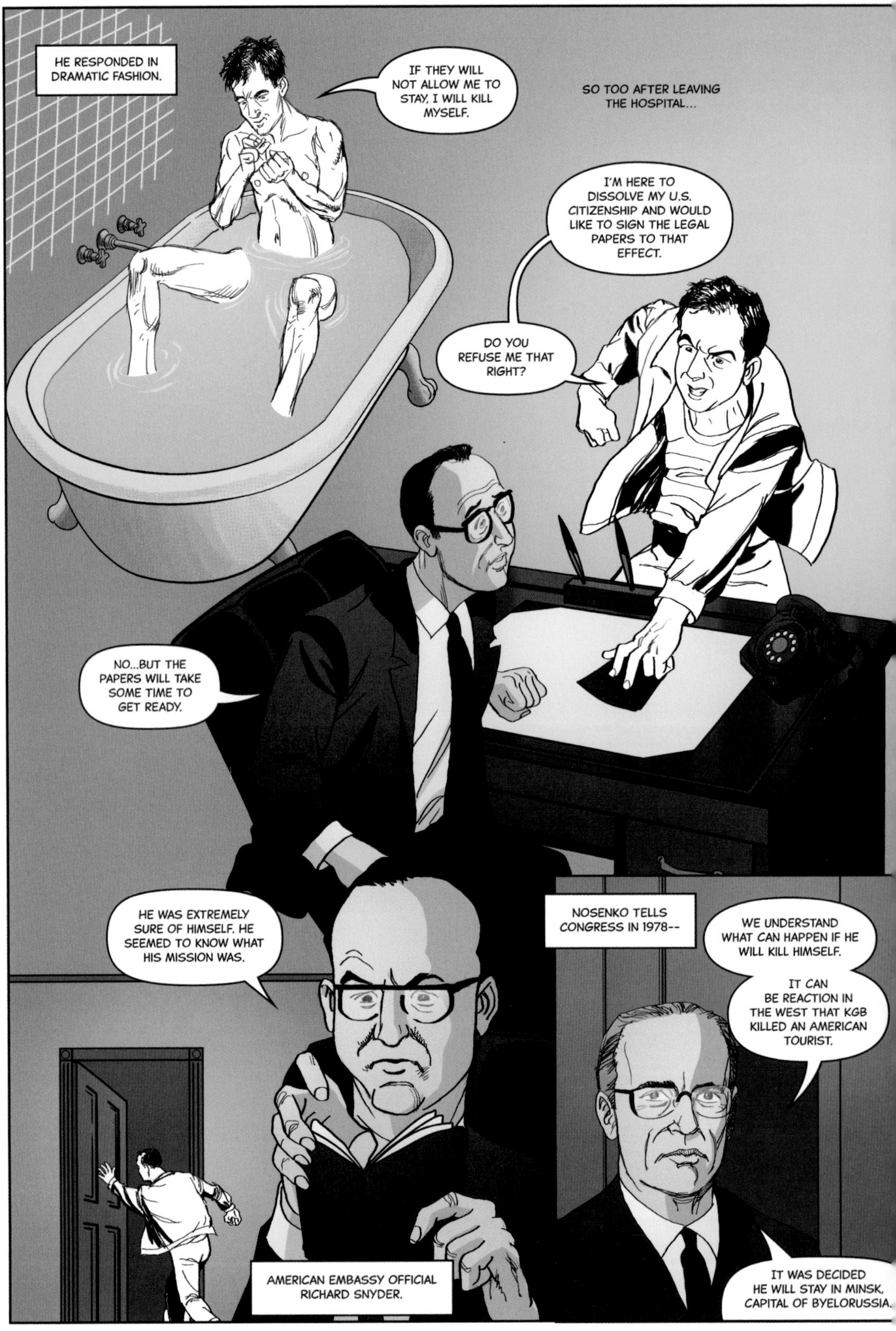
HE RESPONDED IN DRAMATIC FASHION.
IF THEY WILL NOT ALLOW ME TO STAY, I WILL KILL MYSELF.
SO TOO AFTER LEAVING THE HOSPITAL...
I'M HERE TO DISSOLVE MY U.S. CITIZENSHIP AND WOULD LIKE TO SIGN THE LEGAL PAPERS TO THAT EFFECT.
DO YOU REFUSE ME THAT RIGHT?
NO...BUT THE PAPERS WILL TAKE SOME TIME TO GET READY.
HE WAS EXTREMELY SURE OF HIMSELF. HE SEEMED TO KNOW WHAT HIS MISSION WAS.
AMERICAN EMBASSY OFFICIAL RICHARD SNYDER.
NOSENKO TELLS CONGRESS IN 1978--
WE UNDERSTAND WHAT CAN HAPPEN IF HE WILL KILL HIMSELF.
IT CAN BE REACTION IN THE WEST THAT KGB KILLED AN AMERICAN TOURIST.
IT WAS DECIDED HE WILL STAY IN MINSK, CAPITAL OF BYELORUSSIA.

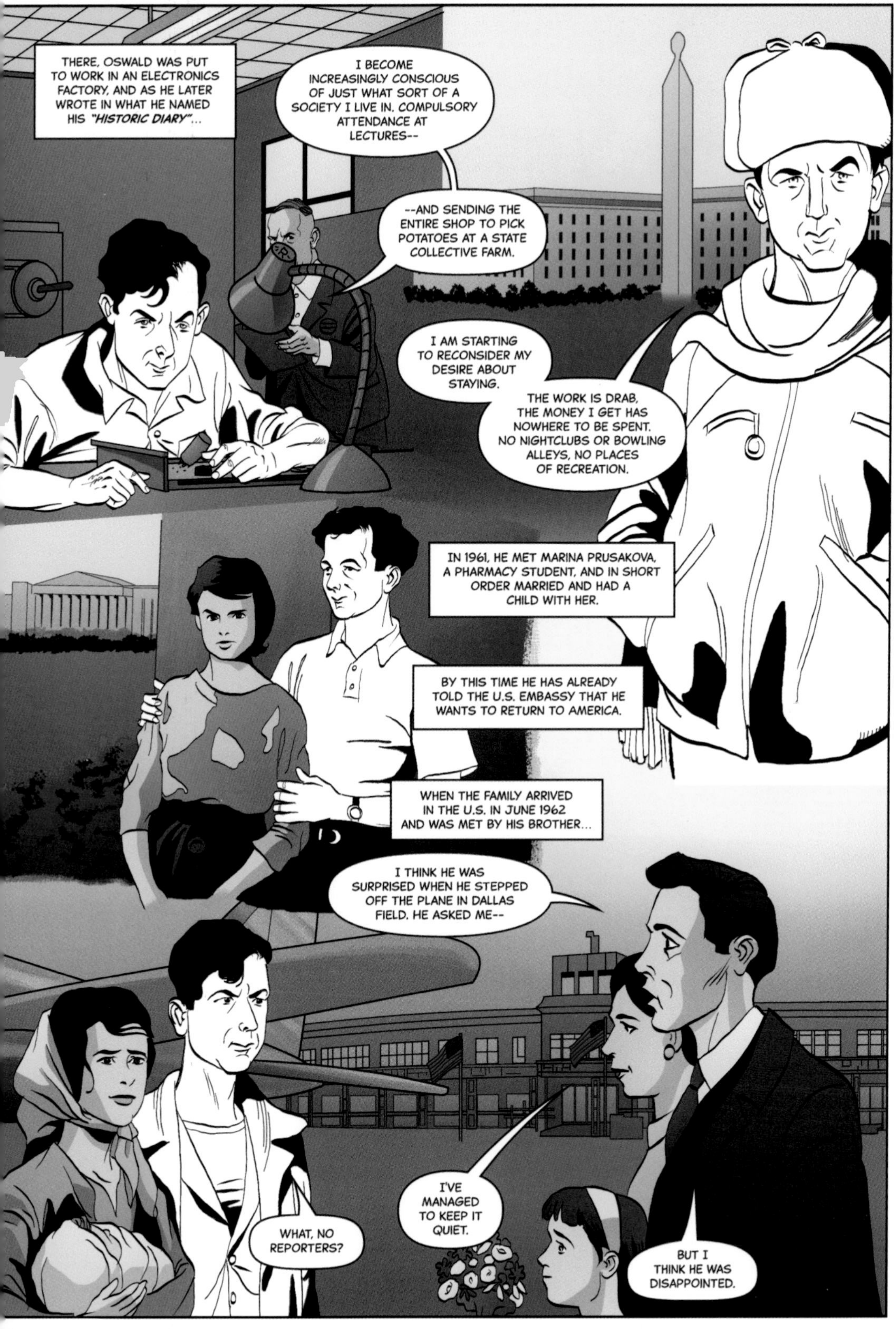
THERE, OSWALD WAS PUT TO WORK IN AN ELECTRONICS FACTORY, AND AS HE LATER WROTE IN WHAT HE NAMED HIS "HISTORIC DIARY"...
I BECOME INCREASINGLY CONSCIOUS OF JUST WHAT SORT OF A SOCIETY I LIVE IN. COMPULSORY ATTENDANCE AT LECTURES--
--AND SENDING THE ENTIRE SHOP TO PICK POTATOES AT A STATE COLLECTIVE FARM.
I AM STARTING TO RECONSIDER MY DESIRE ABOUT STAYING.
THE WORK IS DRAB, THE MONEY I GET HAS NOWHERE TO BE SPENT. NO NIGHTCLUBS OR BOWLING ALLEYS, NO PLACES OF RECREATION.
IN 1961, HE MET MARINA PRUSAKOVA, A PHARMACY STUDENT, AND IN SHORT ORDER MARRIED AND HAD A CHILD WITH HER.
BY THIS TIME HE HAS ALREADY TOLD THE U.S. EMBASSY THAT HE WANTS TO RETURN TO AMERICA.
WHEN THE FAMILY ARRIVED IN THE U.S. IN JUNE 1962 AND WAS MET BY HIS BROTHER...
I THINK HE WAS SURPRISED WHEN HE STEPPED OFF THE PLANE IN DALLAS FIELD. HE ASKED ME--
WHAT, NO REPORTERS?
I'VE MANAGED TO KEEP IT QUIET.
BUT I THINK HE WAS DISAPPOINTED.

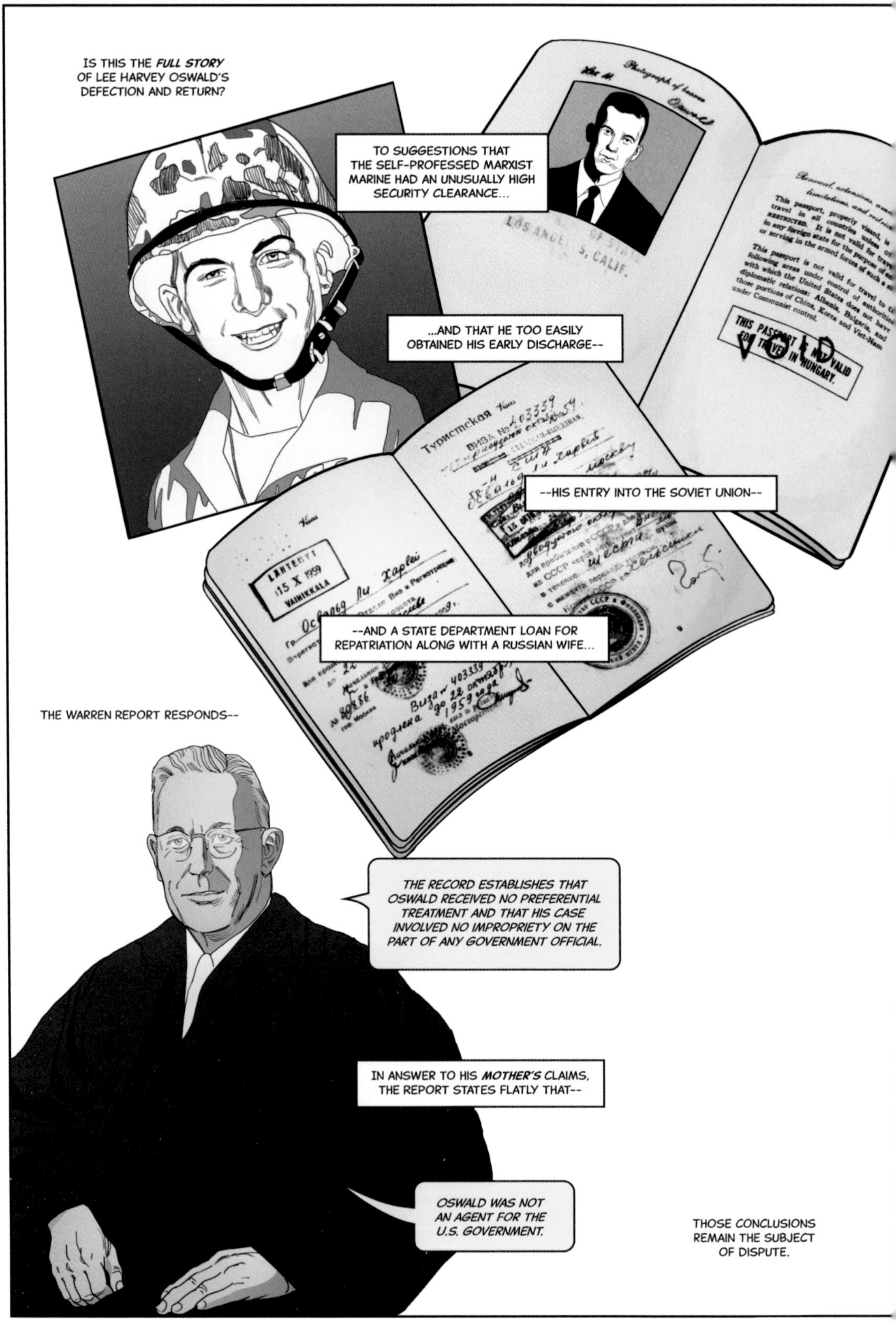
IS THIS THE *FULL STORY* OF LEE HARVEY OSWALD'S DEFECTION AND RETURN?
TO SUGGESTIONS THAT THE SELF-PROFESSED MARXIST MARINE HAD AN UNUSUALLY HIGH SECURITY CLEARANCE...
...AND THAT HE TOO EASILY OBTAINED HIS EARLY DISCHARGE--
--HIS ENTRY INTO THE SOVIET UNION--
--AND A STATE DEPARTMENT LOAN FOR REPATRIATION ALONG WITH A RUSSIAN WIFE...
THE WARREN REPORT RESPONDS--
THE RECORD ESTABLISHES THAT OSWALD RECEIVED NO PREFERENTIAL TREATMENT AND THAT HIS CASE INVOLVED NO IMPROPRIETY ON THE PART OF ANY GOVERNMENT OFFICIAL.
IN ANSWER TO HIS ***MOTHER'S*** CLAIMS, THE REPORT STATES FLATLY THAT--
OSWALD WAS NOT AN AGENT FOR THE U.S. GOVERNMENT.
THOSE CONCLUSIONS REMAIN THE SUBJECT OF DISPUTE.

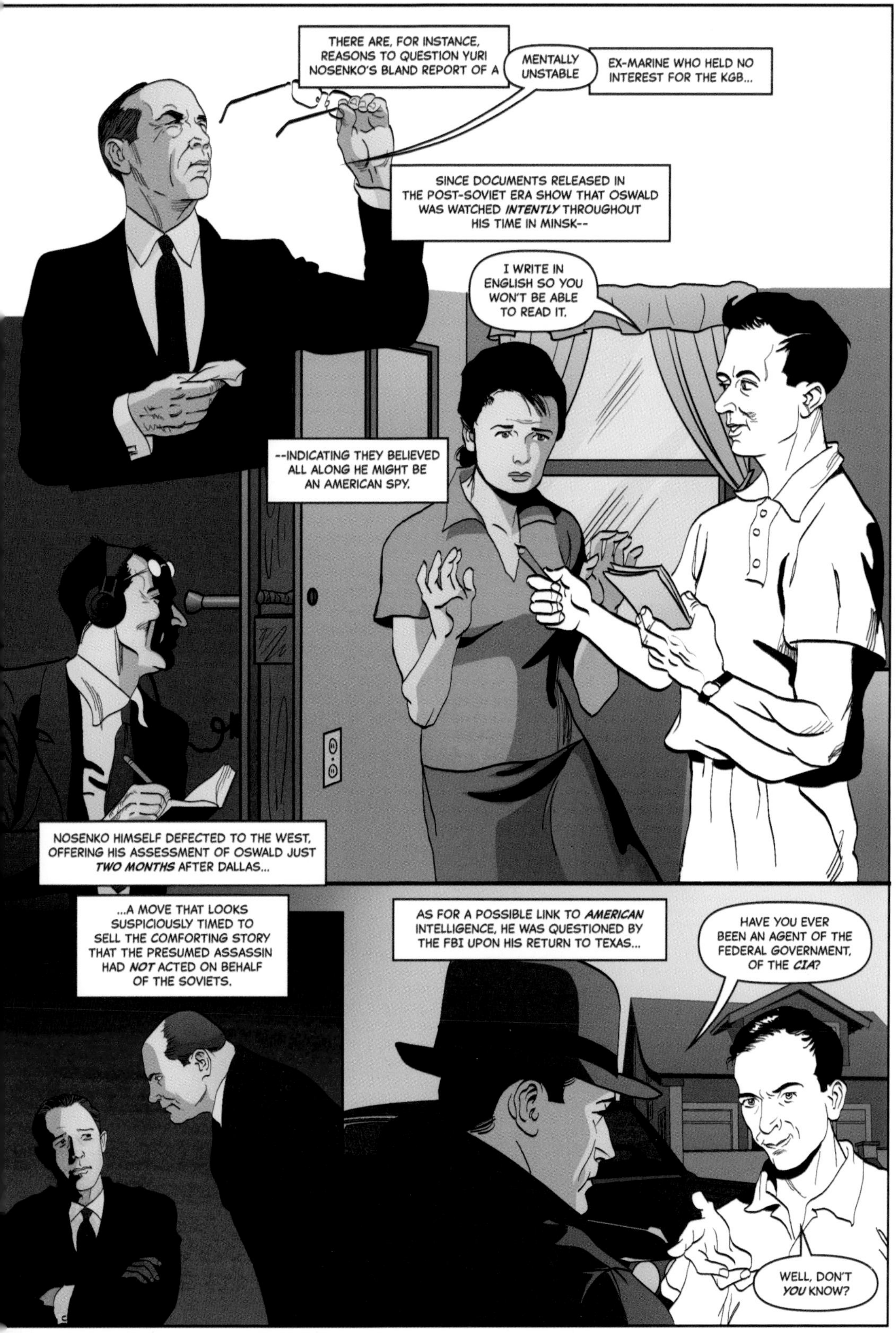
THERE ARE, FOR INSTANCE, REASONS TO QUESTION YURI NOSENKO'S BLAND REPORT OF A
MENTALLY UNSTABLE
EX-MARINE WHO HELD NO INTEREST FOR THE KGB...
SINCE DOCUMENTS RELEASED IN THE POST-SOVIET ERA SHOW THAT OSWALD WAS WATCHED *INTENTLY* THROUGHOUT HIS TIME IN MINSK--
I WRITE IN ENGLISH SO YOU WON'T BE ABLE TO READ IT.
--INDICATING THEY BELIEVED ALL ALONG HE MIGHT BE AN AMERICAN SPY.
NOSENKO HIMSELF DEFECTED TO THE WEST, OFFERING HIS ASSESSMENT OF OSWALD JUST *TWO MONTHS* AFTER DALLAS...
...A MOVE THAT LOOKS SUSPICIOUSLY TIMED TO SELL THE COMFORTING STORY THAT THE PRESUMED ASSASSIN HAD *NOT* ACTED ON BEHALF OF THE SOVIETS.
AS FOR A POSSIBLE LINK TO *AMERICAN* INTELLIGENCE, HE WAS QUESTIONED BY THE FBI UPON HIS RETURN TO TEXAS...
HAVE YOU EVER BEEN AN AGENT OF THE FEDERAL GOVERNMENT, OF THE *CIA*?
WELL, DON'T *YOU* KNOW?

THE FBI CASE ON OSWALD--OPENED AT THE TIME OF HIS DEFECTION--WAS CLOSED FOLLOWING THE INTERVIEWS IN THE SUMMER OF 1962.

UNITED STATES DEPARTMENT OF JUSTICE
FEDERAL BUREAU OF INVESTIGATION

CONFIDENTIAL

ONE REPORT IN THE FILE TELLS OF AN AGENT'S 1960 CONVERSATION WITH HIS MOTHER:

Co... ...s (RM)
...aturalization Service,
Dallas ...)
Report of: JOHN W. FAIN
Date: 8/30/62

Office: DALLAS

Field Office File No...

No...

CONCERNED THAT LETTERS TO LEE WERE BEING RETURNED TO HER, MARGUERITE OSWALD TOLD THE BUREAU--

I'M AFRAID HE MIGHT BE STRANDED AND IN DANGER.

ADDING--

HE TOOK HIS *BIRTH CERTIFICATE* WITH HIM WHEN HE LEFT.

WHICH PROMPTED DIRECTOR HOOVER TO WRITE A MEMO ALERTING THE STATE DEPARTMENT:

THERE IS A POSSIBILITY THAT AN IMPOSTOR IS USING OSWALD'S BIRTH CERTIFICATE.

CONSPIRACY THEORISTS SUGGEST THAT HOOVER DIDN'T JUST FEAR A RUSSIAN AGENT WITH A U.S. BIRTH CERTIFICATE COULD FORGE A COVER IDENTITY AND ELUDE DISCOVERY IN AMERICA.

THEY CLAIM HE MEANT WHAT *THEY* DO WHEN THEY USE THE WORD "IMPOSTOR"...

THAT A *FAKE* OSWALD WAS SENT OUT TO COMMIT ACTS THAT WOULD IMPLICATE THE *REAL* ONE.

A SINGLE OSWALD--THE MARINE, THE MARXIST, THE WOULD-BE TRAITOR, THE RE-DEFECTOR--IS HARD ENOUGH TO READ ACCURATELY.

A SECOND ONE VASTLY COMPLICATES THE QUESTION OF WHAT IS TRUTH AND WHAT IS DISGUISE.

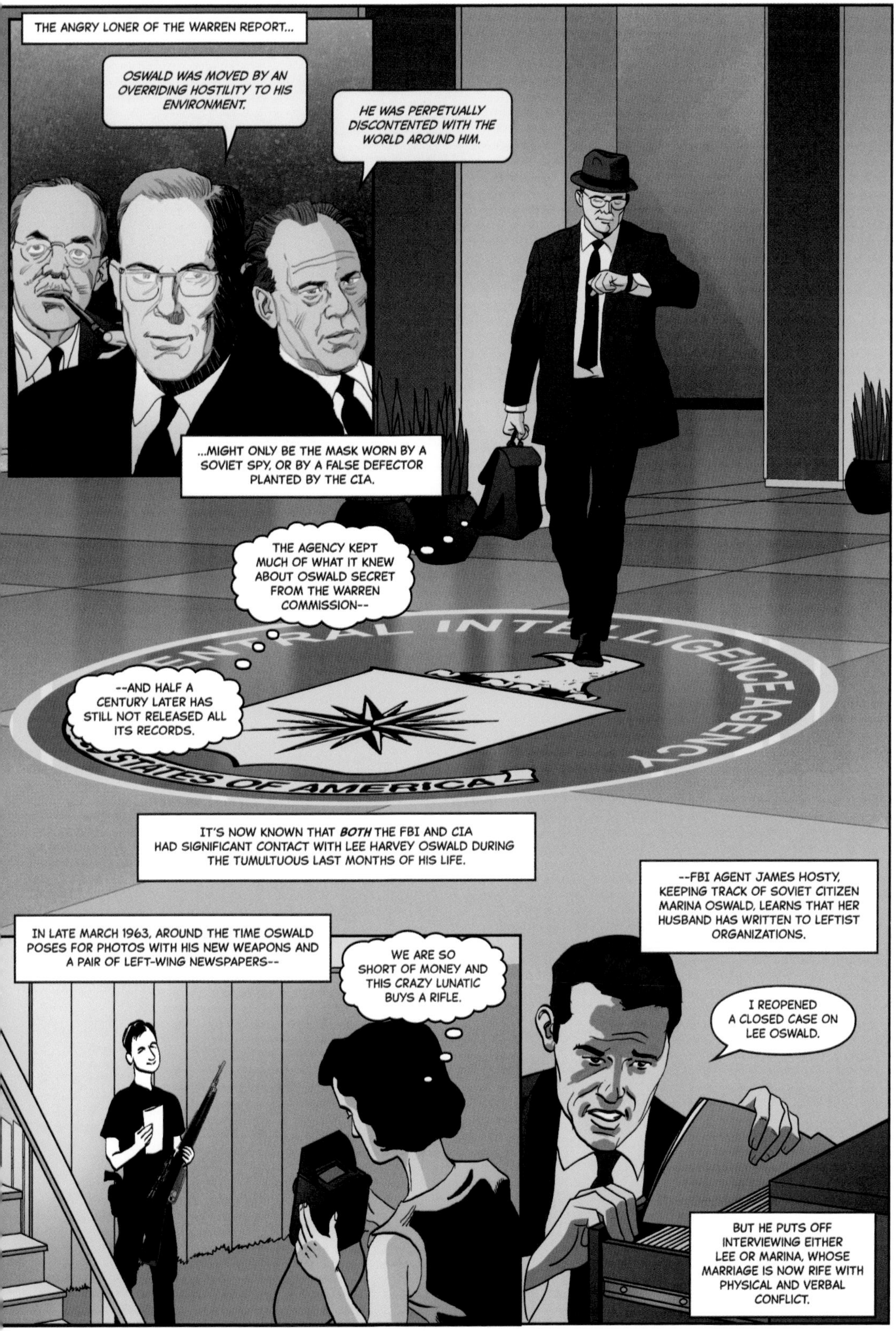
THE ANGRY LONER OF THE WARREN REPORT...
OSWALD WAS MOVED BY AN OVERRIDING HOSTILITY TO HIS ENVIRONMENT.
HE WAS PERPETUALLY DISCONTENTED WITH THE WORLD AROUND HIM.
...MIGHT ONLY BE THE MASK WORN BY A SOVIET SPY, OR BY A FALSE DEFECTOR PLANTED BY THE CIA.
THE AGENCY KEPT MUCH OF WHAT IT KNEW ABOUT OSWALD SECRET FROM THE WARREN COMMISSION--
--AND HALF A CENTURY LATER HAS STILL NOT RELEASED ALL ITS RECORDS.
CENTRAL INTELLIGENCE AGENCY
STATES OF AMERICA
IT'S NOW KNOWN THAT ***BOTH*** THE FBI AND CIA HAD SIGNIFICANT CONTACT WITH LEE HARVEY OSWALD DURING THE TUMULTUOUS LAST MONTHS OF HIS LIFE.
IN LATE MARCH 1963, AROUND THE TIME OSWALD POSES FOR PHOTOS WITH HIS NEW WEAPONS AND A PAIR OF LEFT-WING NEWSPAPERS--
WE ARE SO SHORT OF MONEY AND THIS CRAZY LUNATIC BUYS A RIFLE.
--FBI AGENT JAMES HOSTY, KEEPING TRACK OF SOVIET CITIZEN MARINA OSWALD, LEARNS THAT HER HUSBAND HAS WRITTEN TO LEFTIST ORGANIZATIONS.
I REOPENED A CLOSED CASE ON LEE OSWALD.
BUT HE PUTS OFF INTERVIEWING EITHER LEE OR MARINA, WHOSE MARRIAGE IS NOW RIFE WITH PHYSICAL AND VERBAL CONFLICT.

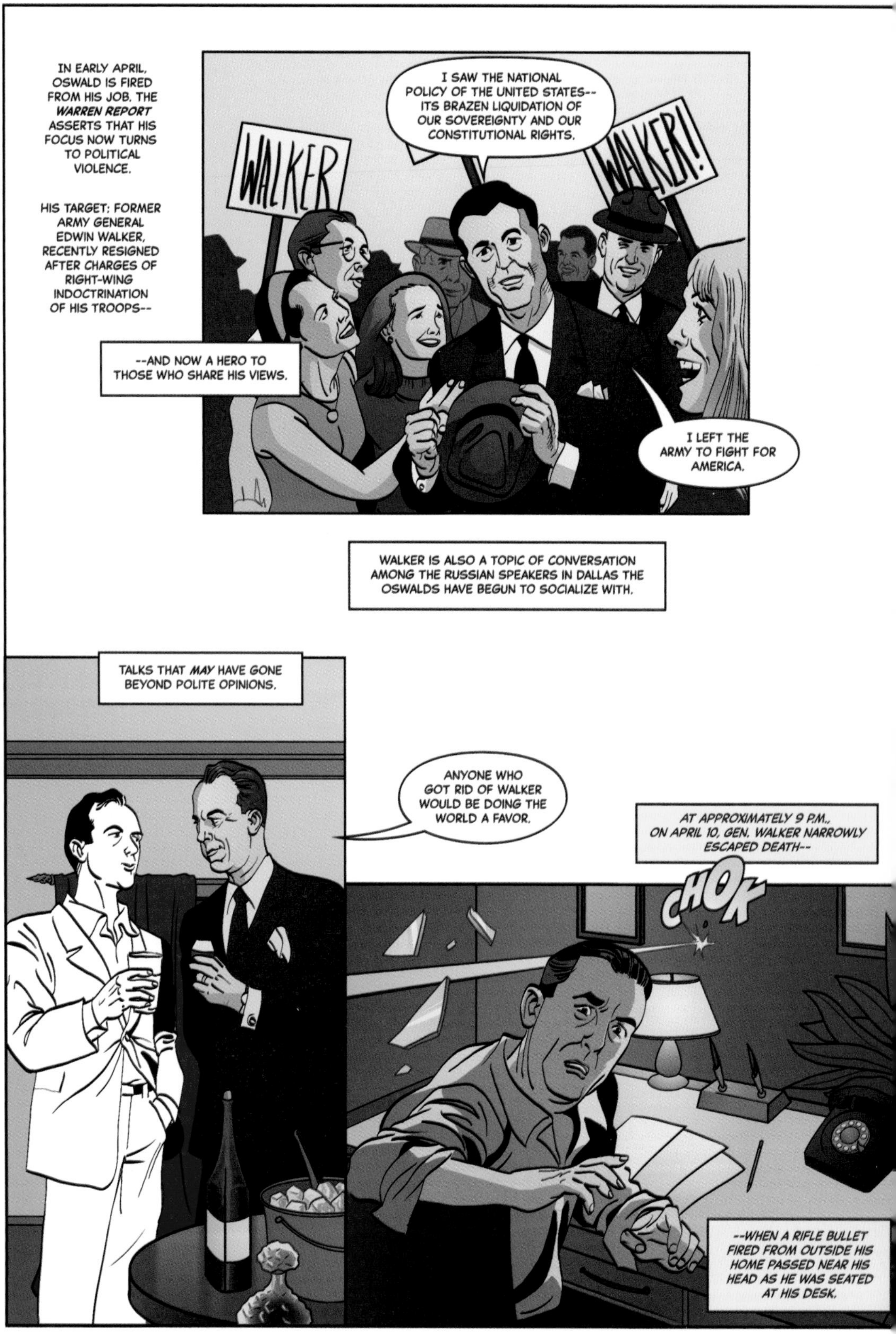
IN EARLY APRIL, OSWALD IS FIRED FROM HIS JOB. THE *WARREN REPORT* ASSERTS THAT HIS FOCUS NOW TURNS TO POLITICAL VIOLENCE.
HIS TARGET: FORMER ARMY GENERAL EDWIN WALKER, RECENTLY RESIGNED AFTER CHARGES OF RIGHT-WING INDOCTRINATION OF HIS TROOPS--
WALKER
I SAW THE NATIONAL POLICY OF THE UNITED STATES--ITS BRAZEN LIQUIDATION OF OUR SOVEREIGNTY AND OUR CONSTITUTIONAL RIGHTS.
WALKER!
--AND NOW A HERO TO THOSE WHO SHARE HIS VIEWS.
I LEFT THE ARMY TO FIGHT FOR AMERICA.
WALKER IS ALSO A TOPIC OF CONVERSATION AMONG THE RUSSIAN SPEAKERS IN DALLAS THE OSWALDS HAVE BEGUN TO SOCIALIZE WITH.
TALKS THAT *MAY* HAVE GONE BEYOND POLITE OPINIONS.
ANYONE WHO GOT RID OF WALKER WOULD BE DOING THE WORLD A FAVOR.
AT APPROXIMATELY 9 P.M., ON APRIL 10, GEN. WALKER NARROWLY ESCAPED DEATH--
CHOK
--WHEN A RIFLE BULLET FIRED FROM OUTSIDE HIS HOME PASSED NEAR HIS HEAD AS HE WAS SEATED AT HIS DESK.

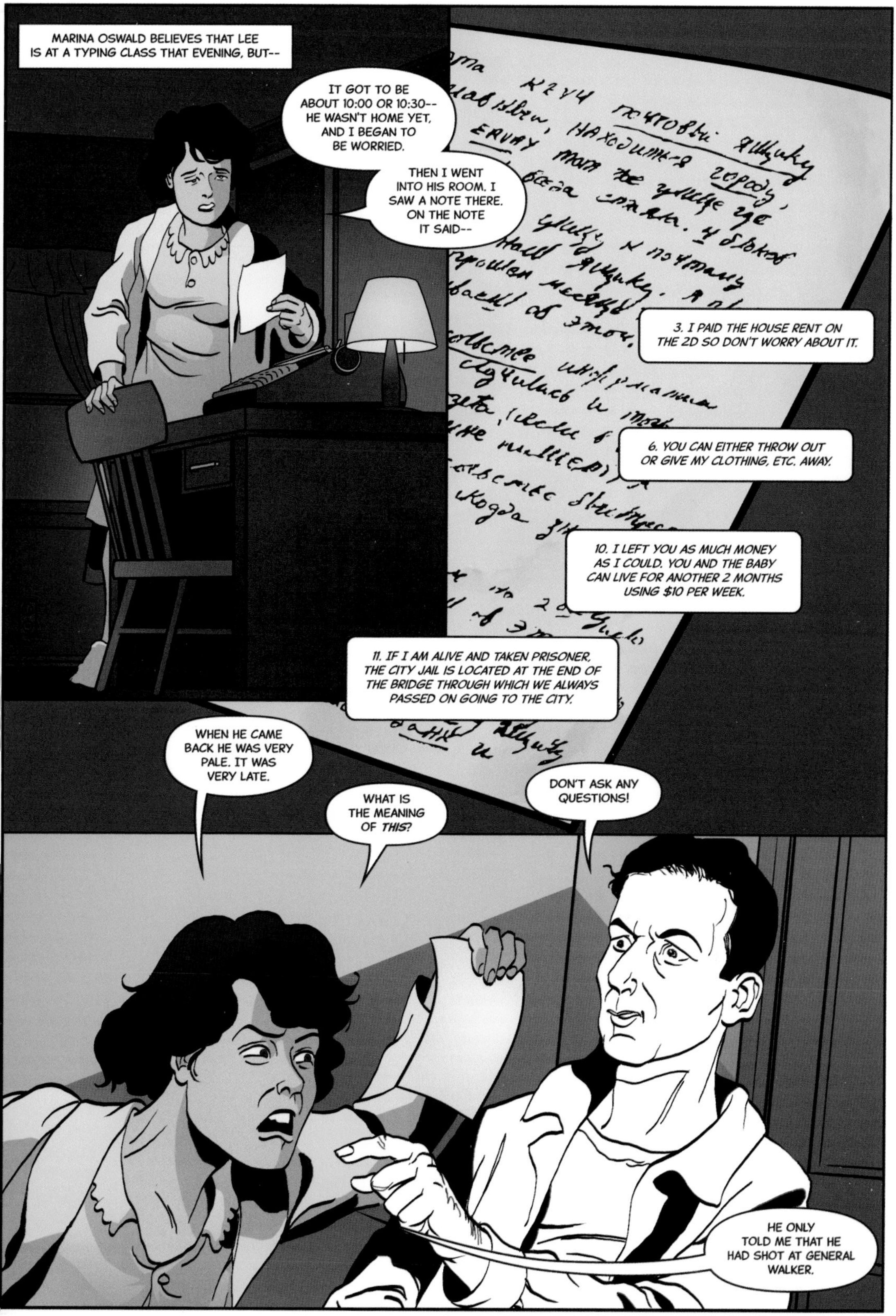
MARINA OSWALD BELIEVES THAT LEE IS AT A TYPING CLASS THAT EVENING, BUT--
IT GOT TO BE ABOUT 10:00 OR 10:30-- HE WASN'T HOME YET, AND I BEGAN TO BE WORRIED.
THEN I WENT INTO HIS ROOM. I SAW A NOTE THERE. ON THE NOTE IT SAID--
3. I PAID THE HOUSE RENT ON THE 2D SO DON'T WORRY ABOUT IT.
6. YOU CAN EITHER THROW OUT OR GIVE MY CLOTHING, ETC. AWAY.
10. I LEFT YOU AS MUCH MONEY AS I COULD. YOU AND THE BABY CAN LIVE FOR ANOTHER 2 MONTHS USING $10 PER WEEK.
11. IF I AM ALIVE AND TAKEN PRISONER, THE CITY JAIL IS LOCATED AT THE END OF THE BRIDGE THROUGH WHICH WE ALWAYS PASSED ON GOING TO THE CITY.
WHEN HE CAME BACK HE WAS VERY PALE. IT WAS VERY LATE.
WHAT IS THE MEANING OF THIS?
DON'T ASK ANY QUESTIONS!
HE ONLY TOLD ME THAT HE HAD SHOT AT GENERAL WALKER.

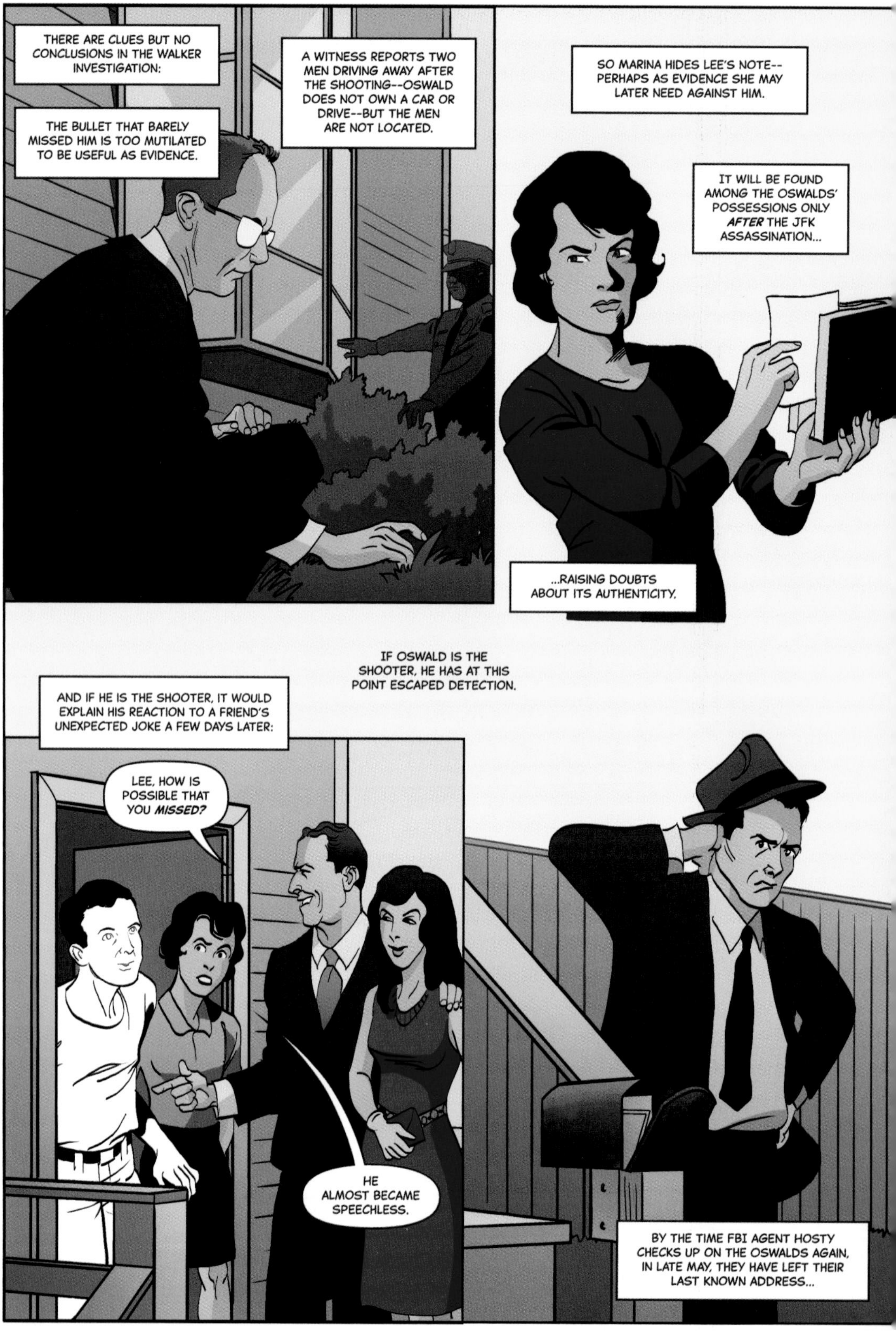
THERE ARE CLUES BUT NO CONCLUSIONS IN THE WALKER INVESTIGATION:
THE BULLET THAT BARELY MISSED HIM IS TOO MUTILATED TO BE USEFUL AS EVIDENCE.
A WITNESS REPORTS TWO MEN DRIVING AWAY AFTER THE SHOOTING--OSWALD DOES NOT OWN A CAR OR DRIVE--BUT THE MEN ARE NOT LOCATED.
SO MARINA HIDES LEE'S NOTE--PERHAPS AS EVIDENCE SHE MAY LATER NEED AGAINST HIM.
IT WILL BE FOUND AMONG THE OSWALDS' POSSESSIONS ONLY *AFTER* THE JFK ASSASSINATION...
...RAISING DOUBTS ABOUT ITS AUTHENTICITY.
IF OSWALD IS THE SHOOTER, HE HAS AT THIS POINT ESCAPED DETECTION.
AND IF HE IS THE SHOOTER, IT WOULD EXPLAIN HIS REACTION TO A FRIEND'S UNEXPECTED JOKE A FEW DAYS LATER:
LEE, HOW IS POSSIBLE THAT YOU *MISSED?*
HE ALMOST BECAME SPEECHLESS.
BY THE TIME FBI AGENT HOSTY CHECKS UP ON THE OSWALDS AGAIN, IN LATE MAY, THEY HAVE LEFT THEIR LAST KNOWN ADDRESS...

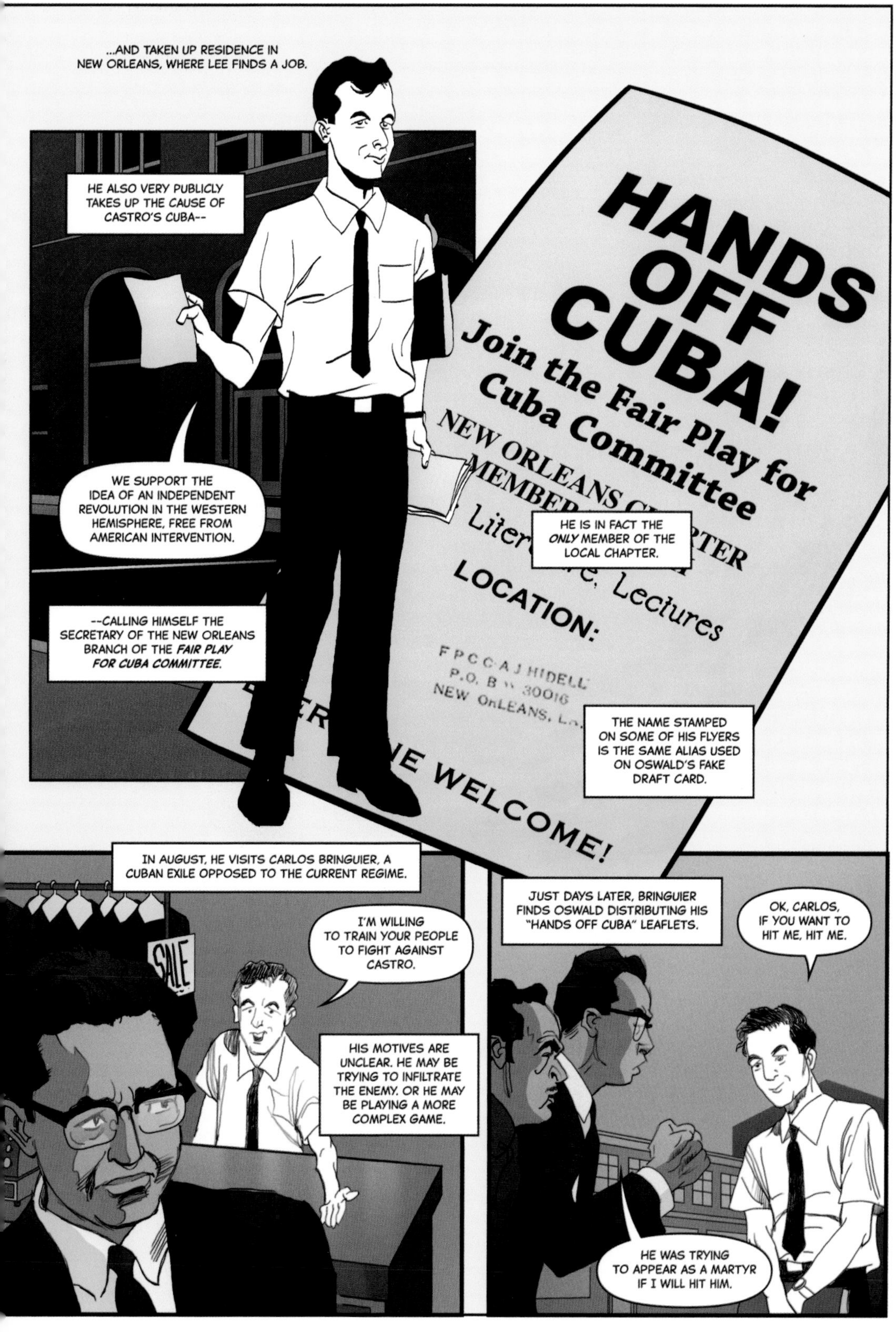
...AND TAKEN UP RESIDENCE IN NEW ORLEANS, WHERE LEE FINDS A JOB.
HE ALSO VERY PUBLICLY TAKES UP THE CAUSE OF CASTRO'S CUBA--
WE SUPPORT THE IDEA OF AN INDEPENDENT REVOLUTION IN THE WESTERN HEMISPHERE, FREE FROM AMERICAN INTERVENTION.
--CALLING HIMSELF THE SECRETARY OF THE NEW ORLEANS BRANCH OF THE *FAIR PLAY FOR CUBA COMMITTEE.*
HANDS OFF CUBA!
Join the Fair Play for Cuba Committee
NEW ORLEANS CHARTER MEMBER
Literature, Lectures
LOCATION:
F P C C-A J HIDELL
P.O. B 30016
NEW OrLEANS, La.
E WELCOME!
HE IS IN FACT THE *ONLY* MEMBER OF THE LOCAL CHAPTER.
THE NAME STAMPED ON SOME OF HIS FLYERS IS THE SAME ALIAS USED ON OSWALD'S FAKE DRAFT CARD.
IN AUGUST, HE VISITS CARLOS BRINGUIER, A CUBAN EXILE OPPOSED TO THE CURRENT REGIME.
SALE
I'M WILLING TO TRAIN YOUR PEOPLE TO FIGHT AGAINST CASTRO.
HIS MOTIVES ARE UNCLEAR. HE MAY BE TRYING TO INFILTRATE THE ENEMY. OR HE MAY BE PLAYING A MORE COMPLEX GAME.
JUST DAYS LATER, BRINGUIER FINDS OSWALD DISTRIBUTING HIS "HANDS OFF CUBA" LEAFLETS.
OK, CARLOS, IF YOU WANT TO HIT ME, HIT ME.
HE WAS TRYING TO APPEAR AS A MARTYR IF I WILL HIT HIM.

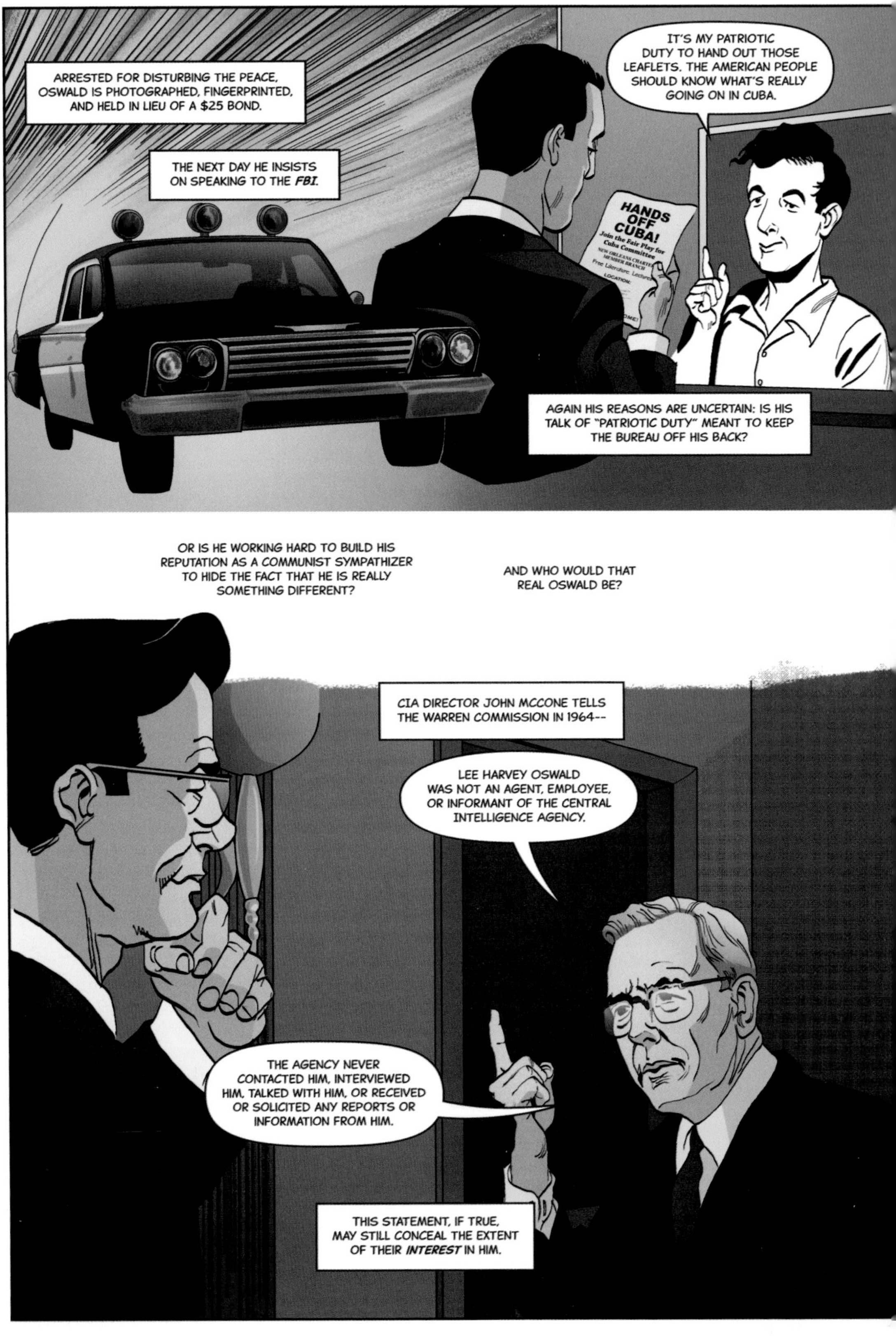
ARRESTED FOR DISTURBING THE PEACE, OSWALD IS PHOTOGRAPHED, FINGERPRINTED, AND HELD IN LIEU OF A $25 BOND.
THE NEXT DAY HE INSISTS ON SPEAKING TO THE *FBI*.
HANDS OFF CUBA!
Join the Fair Play for Cuba Committee
IT'S MY PATRIOTIC DUTY TO HAND OUT THOSE LEAFLETS. THE AMERICAN PEOPLE SHOULD KNOW WHAT'S REALLY GOING ON IN CUBA.
AGAIN HIS REASONS ARE UNCERTAIN: IS HIS TALK OF "PATRIOTIC DUTY" MEANT TO KEEP THE BUREAU OFF HIS BACK?
OR IS HE WORKING HARD TO BUILD HIS REPUTATION AS A COMMUNIST SYMPATHIZER TO HIDE THE FACT THAT HE IS REALLY SOMETHING DIFFERENT?
AND WHO WOULD THAT REAL OSWALD BE?
CIA DIRECTOR JOHN MCCONE TELLS THE WARREN COMMISSION IN 1964--
LEE HARVEY OSWALD WAS NOT AN AGENT, EMPLOYEE, OR INFORMANT OF THE CENTRAL INTELLIGENCE AGENCY.
THE AGENCY NEVER CONTACTED HIM, INTERVIEWED HIM, TALKED WITH HIM, OR RECEIVED OR SOLICITED ANY REPORTS OR INFORMATION FROM HIM.
THIS STATEMENT, IF TRUE, MAY STILL CONCEAL THE EXTENT OF THEIR *INTEREST* IN HIM.

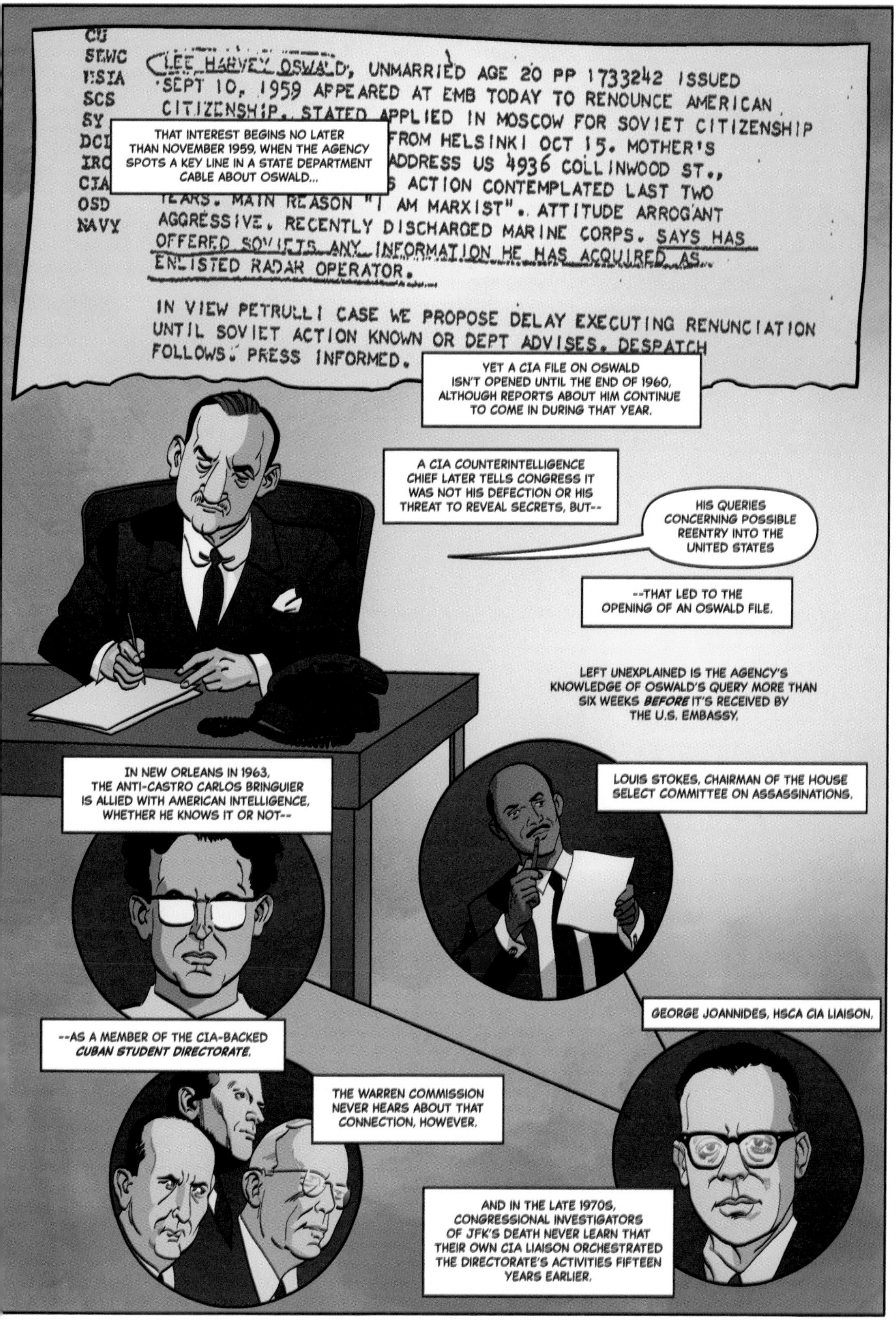

CU
SEWC
USIA
SCS
SY
DCI
IRO
CIA
OSD
NAVY
LEE HARVEY OSWALD, UNMARRIED AGE 20 PP 1733242 ISSUED
SEPT 10, 1959 APPEARED AT EMB TODAY TO RENOUNCE AMERICAN
CITIZENSHIP. STATED APPLIED IN MOSCOW FOR SOVIET CITIZENSHIP
FROM HELSINKI OCT 15. MOTHER'S
ADDRESS US 4936 COLLINWOOD ST.,
S ACTION CONTEMPLATED LAST TWO
YEARS. MAIN REASON "I AM MARXIST". ATTITUDE ARROGANT
AGGRESSIVE. RECENTLY DISCHARGED MARINE CORPS. SAYS HAS
OFFERED SOVIETS ANY INFORMATION HE HAS ACQUIRED AS
ENLISTED RADAR OPERATOR.
IN VIEW PETRULLI CASE WE PROPOSE DELAY EXECUTING RENUNCIATION
UNTIL SOVIET ACTION KNOWN OR DEPT ADVISES. DESPATCH
FOLLOWS. PRESS INFORMED.
THAT INTEREST BEGINS NO LATER THAN NOVEMBER 1959, WHEN THE AGENCY SPOTS A KEY LINE IN A STATE DEPARTMENT CABLE ABOUT OSWALD...
YET A CIA FILE ON OSWALD ISN'T OPENED UNTIL THE END OF 1960, ALTHOUGH REPORTS ABOUT HIM CONTINUE TO COME IN DURING THAT YEAR.
A CIA COUNTERINTELLIGENCE CHIEF LATER TELLS CONGRESS IT WAS NOT HIS DEFECTION OR HIS THREAT TO REVEAL SECRETS, BUT--
HIS QUERIES CONCERNING POSSIBLE REENTRY INTO THE UNITED STATES
--THAT LED TO THE OPENING OF AN OSWALD FILE.
LEFT UNEXPLAINED IS THE AGENCY'S KNOWLEDGE OF OSWALD'S QUERY MORE THAN SIX WEEKS *BEFORE* IT'S RECEIVED BY THE U.S. EMBASSY.
IN NEW ORLEANS IN 1963, THE ANTI-CASTRO CARLOS BRINGUIER IS ALLIED WITH AMERICAN INTELLIGENCE, WHETHER HE KNOWS IT OR NOT--
--AS A MEMBER OF THE CIA-BACKED *CUBAN STUDENT DIRECTORATE.*
THE WARREN COMMISSION NEVER HEARS ABOUT THAT CONNECTION, HOWEVER.
LOUIS STOKES, CHAIRMAN OF THE HOUSE SELECT COMMITTEE ON ASSASSINATIONS.
GEORGE JOANNIDES, HSCA CIA LIAISON.
AND IN THE LATE 1970S, CONGRESSIONAL INVESTIGATORS OF JFK'S DEATH NEVER LEARN THAT THEIR OWN CIA LIAISON ORCHESTRATED THE DIRECTORATE'S ACTIVITIES FIFTEEN YEARS EARLIER.

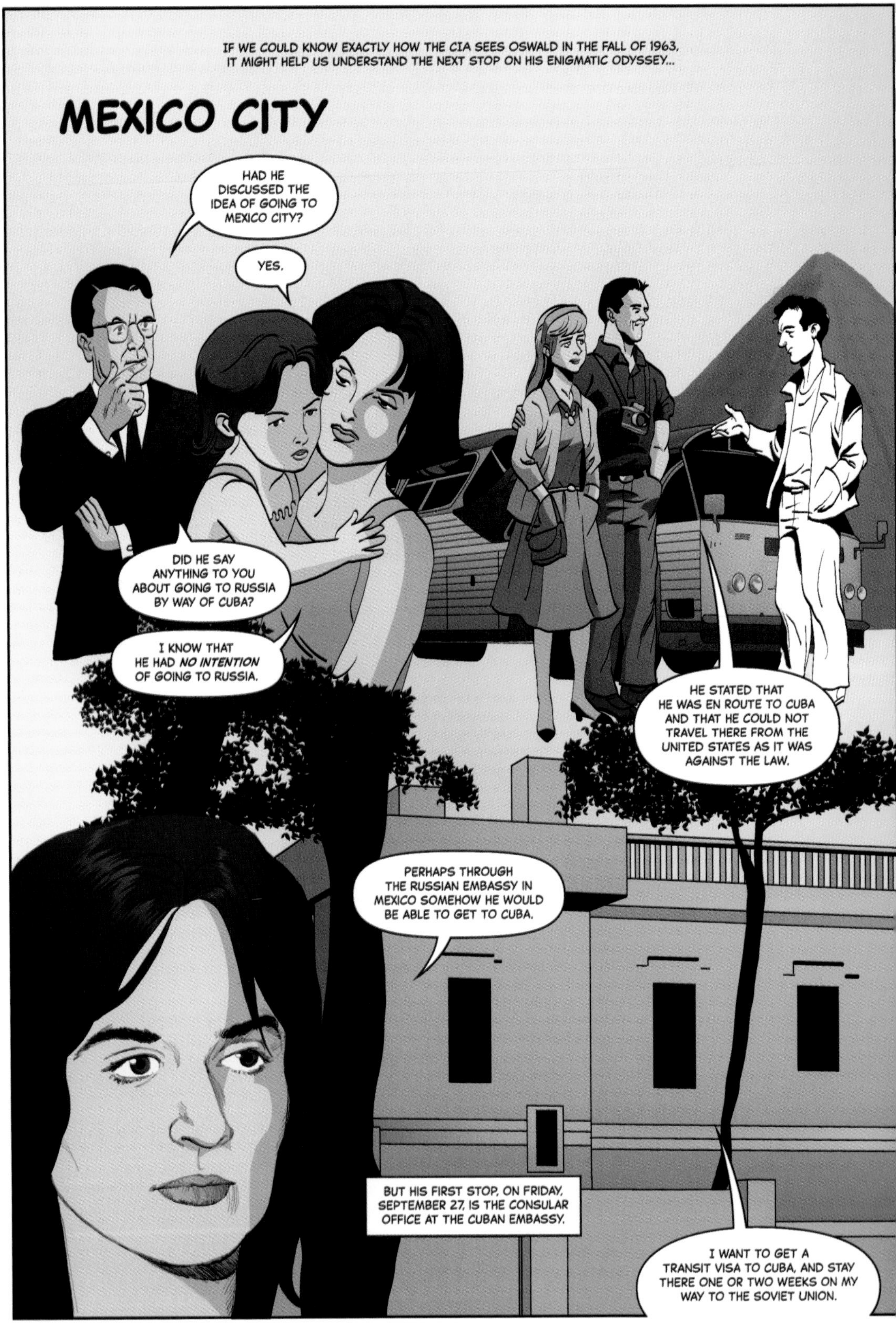
IF WE COULD KNOW EXACTLY HOW THE CIA SEES OSWALD IN THE FALL OF 1963, IT MIGHT HELP US UNDERSTAND THE NEXT STOP ON HIS ENIGMATIC ODYSSEY...
MEXICO CITY
HAD HE DISCUSSED THE IDEA OF GOING TO MEXICO CITY?
YES.
DID HE SAY ANYTHING TO YOU ABOUT GOING TO RUSSIA BY WAY OF CUBA?
I KNOW THAT HE HAD *NO INTENTION* OF GOING TO RUSSIA.
HE STATED THAT HE WAS EN ROUTE TO CUBA AND THAT HE COULD NOT TRAVEL THERE FROM THE UNITED STATES AS IT WAS AGAINST THE LAW.
PERHAPS THROUGH THE RUSSIAN EMBASSY IN MEXICO SOMEHOW HE WOULD BE ABLE TO GET TO CUBA.
BUT HIS FIRST STOP, ON FRIDAY, SEPTEMBER 27, IS THE CONSULAR OFFICE AT THE CUBAN EMBASSY.
I WANT TO GET A TRANSIT VISA TO CUBA, AND STAY THERE ONE OR TWO WEEKS ON MY WAY TO THE SOVIET UNION.

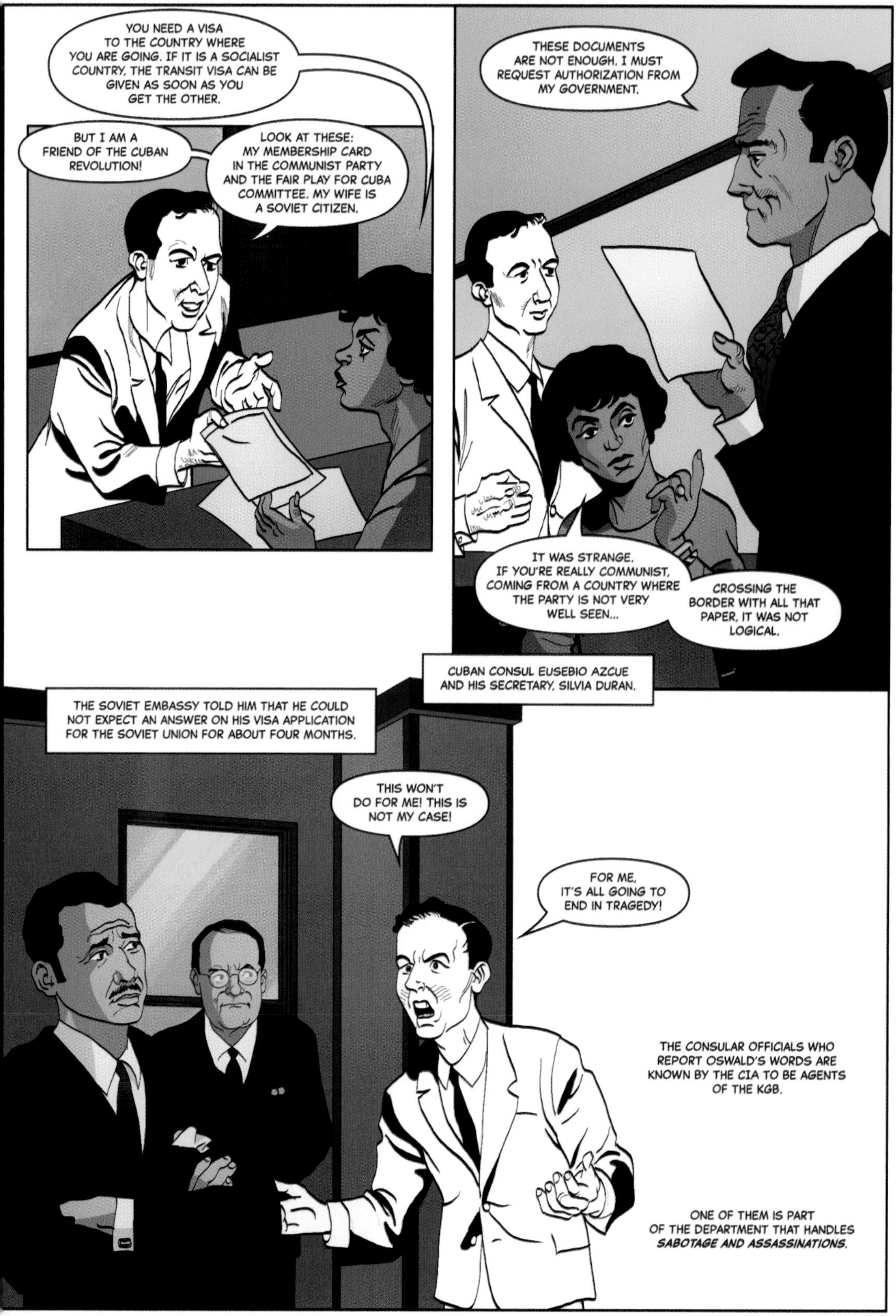
YOU NEED A VISA TO THE COUNTRY WHERE YOU ARE GOING. IF IT IS A SOCIALIST COUNTRY, THE TRANSIT VISA CAN BE GIVEN AS SOON AS YOU GET THE OTHER.
BUT I AM A FRIEND OF THE CUBAN REVOLUTION!
LOOK AT THESE: MY MEMBERSHIP CARD IN THE COMMUNIST PARTY AND THE FAIR PLAY FOR CUBA COMMITTEE. MY WIFE IS A SOVIET CITIZEN.
THESE DOCUMENTS ARE NOT ENOUGH. I MUST REQUEST AUTHORIZATION FROM MY GOVERNMENT.
IT WAS STRANGE. IF YOU'RE REALLY COMMUNIST, COMING FROM A COUNTRY WHERE THE PARTY IS NOT VERY WELL SEEN...
CROSSING THE BORDER WITH ALL THAT PAPER, IT WAS NOT LOGICAL.
CUBAN CONSUL EUSEBIO AZCUE AND HIS SECRETARY, SILVIA DURAN.
THE SOVIET EMBASSY TOLD HIM THAT HE COULD NOT EXPECT AN ANSWER ON HIS VISA APPLICATION FOR THE SOVIET UNION FOR ABOUT FOUR MONTHS.
THIS WON'T DO FOR ME! THIS IS NOT MY CASE!
FOR ME, IT'S ALL GOING TO END IN TRAGEDY!
THE CONSULAR OFFICIALS WHO REPORT OSWALD'S WORDS ARE KNOWN BY THE CIA TO BE AGENTS OF THE KGB.
ONE OF THEM IS PART OF THE DEPARTMENT THAT HANDLES *SABOTAGE AND ASSASSINATIONS.*

HIS VISA APPLICATION COMPLETED AND SENT TO HAVANA, OSWALD'S ATTEMPTS TO HURRY THE BUREAUCRACY ARE REBUFFED--

CONSULADO DE CUBA, MEXICO, D.F.

Solicitud de visa No.: ___779___

Focha: 27 de septiembre de 1963.

Nombre: Lee

Ciadadania norteamericana

a y luga

--AND THE MYSTERIES SURROUNDING HIM GROW.

ON THE DAY HE PREPARES TO LEAVE MEXICO CITY FOR DALLAS, THE SOVIET EMBASSY RECEIVES A PHONE CALL...

THIS IS LEE OSWALD. I WAS AT YOUR PLACE LAST SATURDAY AND SPOKE TO A CONSUL, AND THEY SAID THEY'D SEND A TELEGRAM TO WASHINGTON, SO I WANT TO FIND OUT IF YOU HAVE ANYTHING NEW?

NOTHING HAS BEEN RECEIVED AS YET.

THE CALL IS RECORDED BY A CIA WIRETAP.

A SHORT TIME LATER, A SURVEILLANCE TEAM PHOTOGRAPHS A MAN WHO "APPEARS TO BE AMERICAN" OUTSIDE THE SOVIET EMBASSY.

A CIA CABLE REPORTS ON BOTH THE PHONE CALL AND THE PHOTOS, SEEMING TO CONNECT THE MAN IN THE PICTURES WITH THE MAN WHO CALLED.

BUT THE PHOTO SUBJECT IS DESCRIBED AS "AGE 35, ATHLETIC BUILD, CIRCA 6 FEET," WHILE OSWALD IS 24, SLIGHT, AND SHORTER.

WHAT THE CIA CANNOT PRODUCE IS A SINGLE PHOTOGRAPH OF *OSWALD* ENTERING OR LEAVING THE CUBAN OR SOVIET EMBASSY COMPOUNDS.

WARREN COMMISSION CRITICS HAVE SEIZED ON THIS AS EVIDENCE OF AN OSWALD IMPERSONATOR.

IT IS NOT THE ONLY EVIDENCE THEY FIND.

MYSTERY MEN

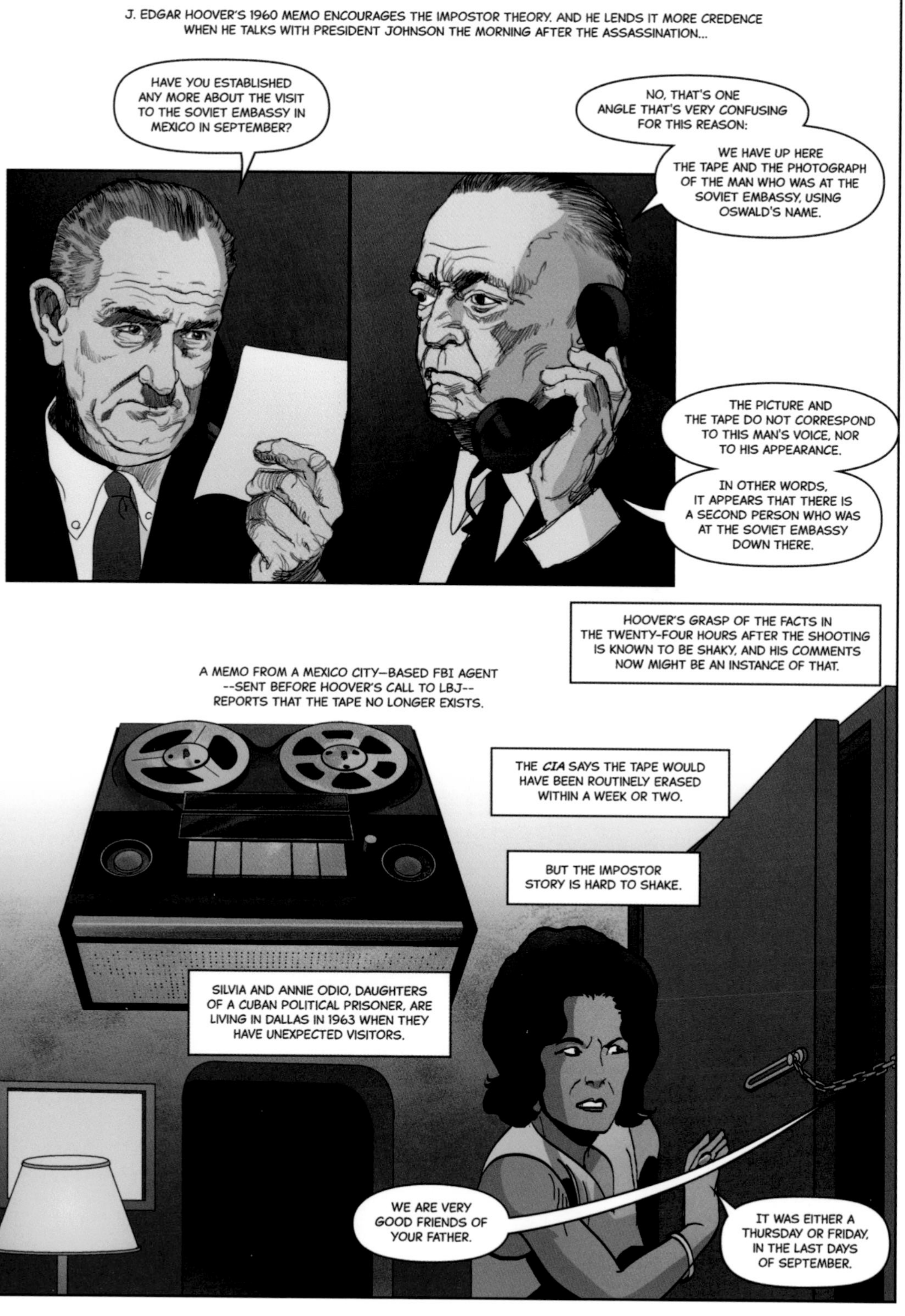

J. EDGAR HOOVER'S 1960 MEMO ENCOURAGES THE IMPOSTOR THEORY. AND HE LENDS IT MORE CREDENCE WHEN HE TALKS WITH PRESIDENT JOHNSON THE MORNING AFTER THE ASSASSINATION...
HAVE YOU ESTABLISHED ANY MORE ABOUT THE VISIT TO THE SOVIET EMBASSY IN MEXICO IN SEPTEMBER?
NO, THAT'S ONE ANGLE THAT'S VERY CONFUSING FOR THIS REASON:
WE HAVE UP HERE THE TAPE AND THE PHOTOGRAPH OF THE MAN WHO WAS AT THE SOVIET EMBASSY, USING OSWALD'S NAME.
THE PICTURE AND THE TAPE DO NOT CORRESPOND TO THIS MAN'S VOICE, NOR TO HIS APPEARANCE.
IN OTHER WORDS, IT APPEARS THAT THERE IS A SECOND PERSON WHO WAS AT THE SOVIET EMBASSY DOWN THERE.
HOOVER'S GRASP OF THE FACTS IN THE TWENTY-FOUR HOURS AFTER THE SHOOTING IS KNOWN TO BE SHAKY, AND HIS COMMENTS NOW MIGHT BE AN INSTANCE OF THAT.
A MEMO FROM A MEXICO CITY–BASED FBI AGENT --SENT BEFORE HOOVER'S CALL TO LBJ-- REPORTS THAT THE TAPE NO LONGER EXISTS.
THE *CIA* SAYS THE TAPE WOULD HAVE BEEN ROUTINELY ERASED WITHIN A WEEK OR TWO.
BUT THE IMPOSTOR STORY IS HARD TO SHAKE.
SILVIA AND ANNIE ODIO, DAUGHTERS OF A CUBAN POLITICAL PRISONER, ARE LIVING IN DALLAS IN 1963 WHEN THEY HAVE UNEXPECTED VISITORS.
WE ARE VERY GOOD FRIENDS OF YOUR FATHER.
IT WAS EITHER A THURSDAY OR FRIDAY, IN THE LAST DAYS OF SEPTEMBER.

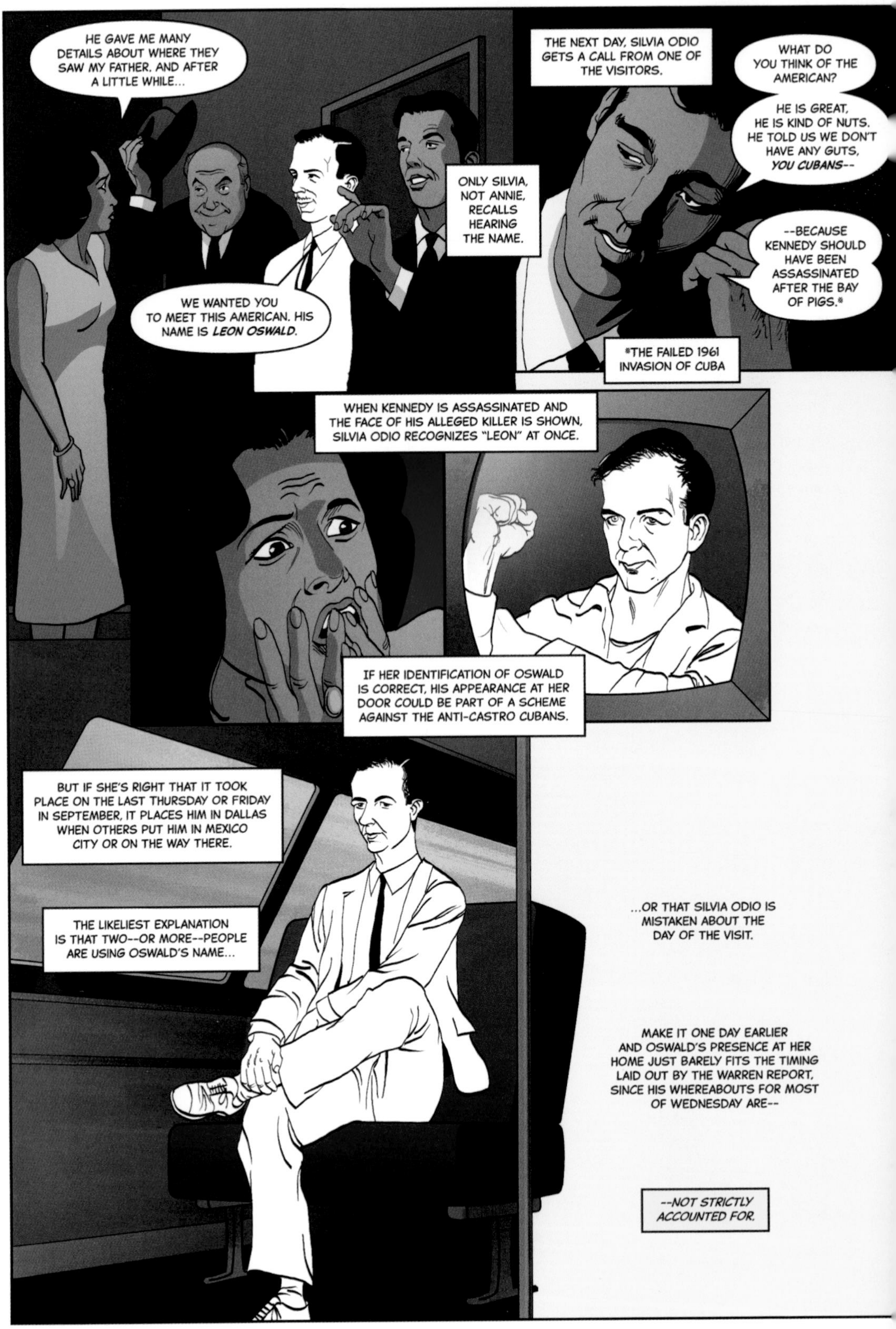

HE GAVE ME MANY DETAILS ABOUT WHERE THEY SAW MY FATHER, AND AFTER A LITTLE WHILE...
WE WANTED YOU TO MEET THIS AMERICAN. HIS NAME IS *LEON OSWALD*.
ONLY SILVIA, NOT ANNIE, RECALLS HEARING THE NAME.
THE NEXT DAY, SILVIA ODIO GETS A CALL FROM ONE OF THE VISITORS.
WHAT DO YOU THINK OF THE AMERICAN?
HE IS GREAT, HE IS KIND OF NUTS. HE TOLD US WE DON'T HAVE ANY GUTS, *YOU CUBANS*--
--BECAUSE KENNEDY SHOULD HAVE BEEN ASSASSINATED AFTER THE BAY OF PIGS.*
*THE FAILED 1961 INVASION OF CUBA
WHEN KENNEDY IS ASSASSINATED AND THE FACE OF HIS ALLEGED KILLER IS SHOWN, SILVIA ODIO RECOGNIZES "LEON" AT ONCE.
IF HER IDENTIFICATION OF OSWALD IS CORRECT, HIS APPEARANCE AT HER DOOR COULD BE PART OF A SCHEME AGAINST THE ANTI-CASTRO CUBANS.
BUT IF SHE'S RIGHT THAT IT TOOK PLACE ON THE LAST THURSDAY OR FRIDAY IN SEPTEMBER, IT PLACES HIM IN DALLAS WHEN OTHERS PUT HIM IN MEXICO CITY OR ON THE WAY THERE.
THE LIKELIEST EXPLANATION IS THAT TWO--OR MORE--PEOPLE ARE USING OSWALD'S NAME...
...OR THAT SILVIA ODIO IS MISTAKEN ABOUT THE DAY OF THE VISIT.
MAKE IT ONE DAY EARLIER AND OSWALD'S PRESENCE AT HER HOME JUST BARELY FITS THE TIMING LAID OUT BY THE WARREN REPORT, SINCE HIS WHEREABOUTS FOR MOST OF WEDNESDAY ARE--
--NOT STRICTLY ACCOUNTED FOR.

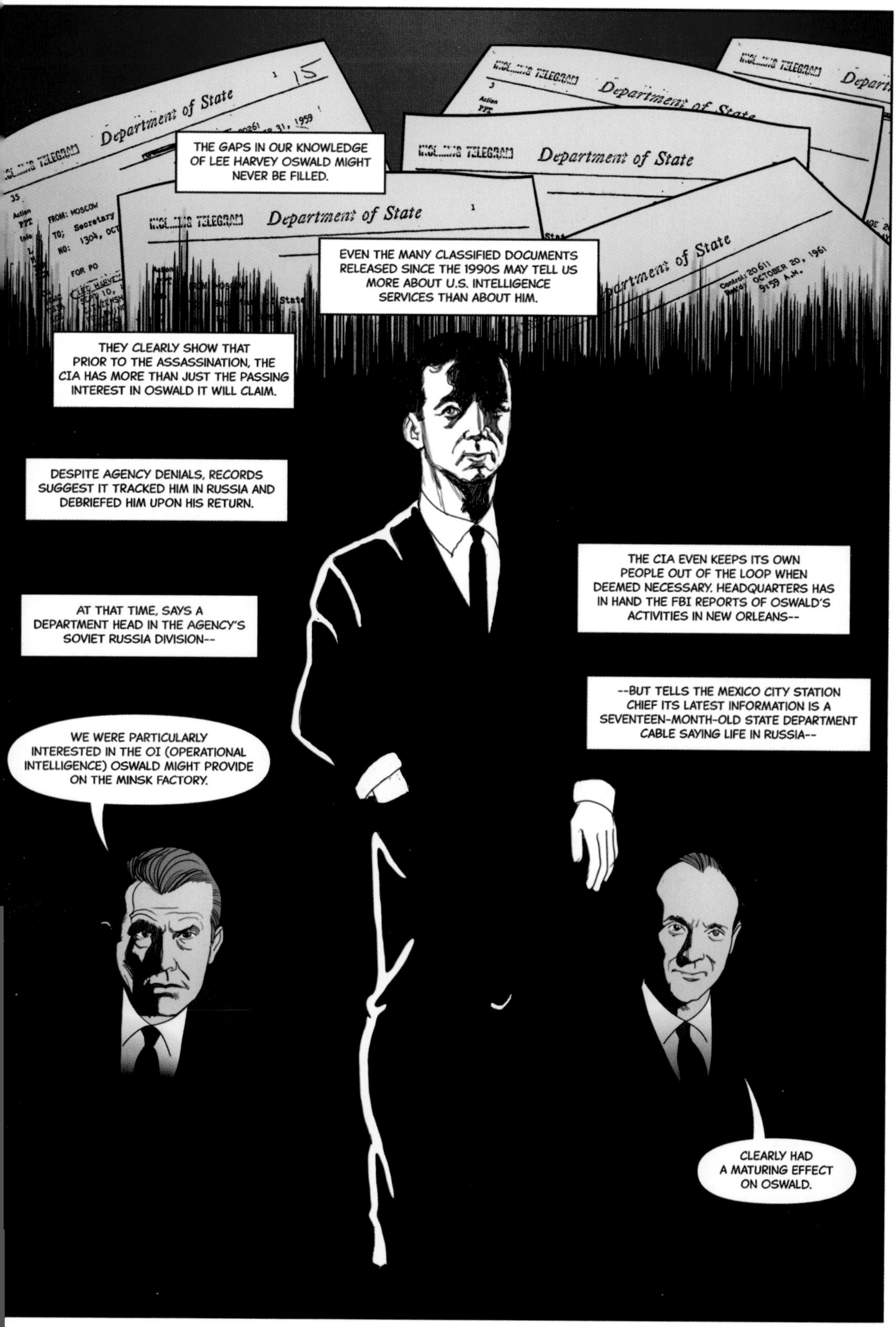
Department of State
THE GAPS IN OUR KNOWLEDGE OF LEE HARVEY OSWALD MIGHT NEVER BE FILLED.
EVEN THE MANY CLASSIFIED DOCUMENTS RELEASED SINCE THE 1990S MAY TELL US MORE ABOUT U.S. INTELLIGENCE SERVICES THAN ABOUT HIM.
THEY CLEARLY SHOW THAT PRIOR TO THE ASSASSINATION, THE CIA HAS MORE THAN JUST THE PASSING INTEREST IN OSWALD IT WILL CLAIM.
DESPITE AGENCY DENIALS, RECORDS SUGGEST IT TRACKED HIM IN RUSSIA AND DEBRIEFED HIM UPON HIS RETURN.
AT THAT TIME, SAYS A DEPARTMENT HEAD IN THE AGENCY'S SOVIET RUSSIA DIVISION--
WE WERE PARTICULARLY INTERESTED IN THE OI (OPERATIONAL INTELLIGENCE) OSWALD MIGHT PROVIDE ON THE MINSK FACTORY.
THE CIA EVEN KEEPS ITS OWN PEOPLE OUT OF THE LOOP WHEN DEEMED NECESSARY. HEADQUARTERS HAS IN HAND THE FBI REPORTS OF OSWALD'S ACTIVITIES IN NEW ORLEANS--
--BUT TELLS THE MEXICO CITY STATION CHIEF ITS LATEST INFORMATION IS A SEVENTEEN-MONTH-OLD STATE DEPARTMENT CABLE SAYING LIFE IN RUSSIA--
CLEARLY HAD A MATURING EFFECT ON OSWALD.

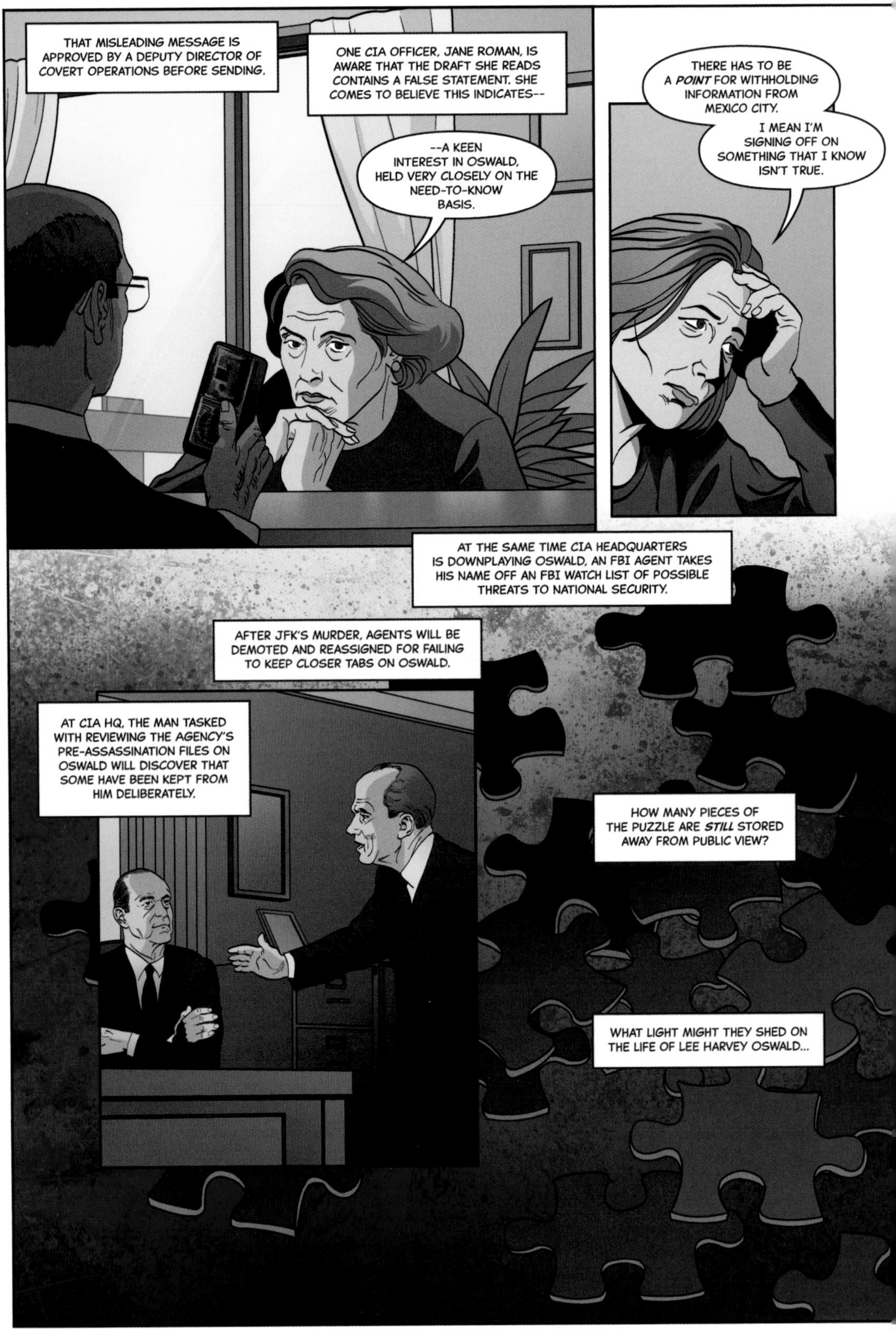
THAT MISLEADING MESSAGE IS APPROVED BY A DEPUTY DIRECTOR OF COVERT OPERATIONS BEFORE SENDING.
ONE CIA OFFICER, JANE ROMAN, IS AWARE THAT THE DRAFT SHE READS CONTAINS A FALSE STATEMENT. SHE COMES TO BELIEVE THIS INDICATES--
--A KEEN INTEREST IN OSWALD, HELD VERY CLOSELY ON THE NEED-TO-KNOW BASIS.
THERE HAS TO BE A *POINT* FOR WITHHOLDING INFORMATION FROM MEXICO CITY.
I MEAN I'M SIGNING OFF ON SOMETHING THAT I KNOW ISN'T TRUE.
AT THE SAME TIME CIA HEADQUARTERS IS DOWNPLAYING OSWALD, AN FBI AGENT TAKES HIS NAME OFF AN FBI WATCH LIST OF POSSIBLE THREATS TO NATIONAL SECURITY.
AFTER JFK'S MURDER, AGENTS WILL BE DEMOTED AND REASSIGNED FOR FAILING TO KEEP CLOSER TABS ON OSWALD.
AT CIA HQ, THE MAN TASKED WITH REVIEWING THE AGENCY'S PRE-ASSASSINATION FILES ON OSWALD WILL DISCOVER THAT SOME HAVE BEEN KEPT FROM HIM DELIBERATELY.
HOW MANY PIECES OF THE PUZZLE ARE *STILL* STORED AWAY FROM PUBLIC VIEW?
WHAT LIGHT MIGHT THEY SHED ON THE LIFE OF LEE HARVEY OSWALD...

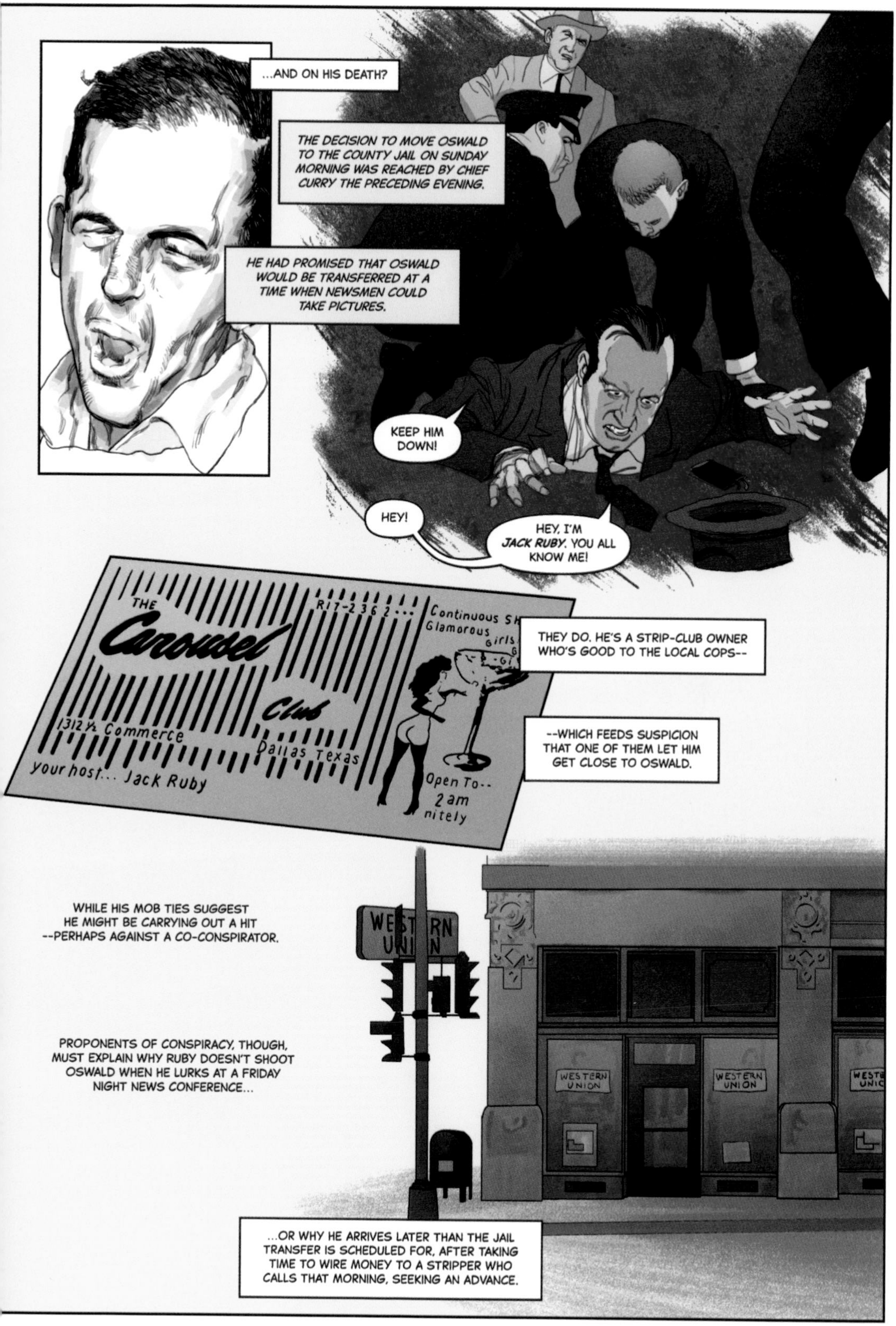
...AND ON HIS DEATH?
THE DECISION TO MOVE OSWALD TO THE COUNTY JAIL ON SUNDAY MORNING WAS REACHED BY CHIEF CURRY THE PRECEDING EVENING.
HE HAD PROMISED THAT OSWALD WOULD BE TRANSFERRED AT A TIME WHEN NEWSMEN COULD TAKE PICTURES.
KEEP HIM DOWN!
HEY!
HEY, I'M JACK RUBY. YOU ALL KNOW ME!
THE Carousel Club
RI7-2362
Continuous
Glamorous
girls
1312½ Commerce
Dallas Texas
your host... Jack Ruby
Open To-- 2am nitely
THEY DO. HE'S A STRIP-CLUB OWNER WHO'S GOOD TO THE LOCAL COPS--
--WHICH FEEDS SUSPICION THAT ONE OF THEM LET HIM GET CLOSE TO OSWALD.
WHILE HIS MOB TIES SUGGEST HE MIGHT BE CARRYING OUT A HIT --PERHAPS AGAINST A CO-CONSPIRATOR.
PROPONENTS OF CONSPIRACY, THOUGH, MUST EXPLAIN WHY RUBY DOESN'T SHOOT OSWALD WHEN HE LURKS AT A FRIDAY NIGHT NEWS CONFERENCE...
WESTERN UNION
WESTERN UNION
WESTERN UNION
...OR WHY HE ARRIVES LATER THAN THE JAIL TRANSFER IS SCHEDULED FOR, AFTER TAKING TIME TO WIRE MONEY TO A STRIPPER WHO CALLS THAT MORNING, SEEKING AN ADVANCE.

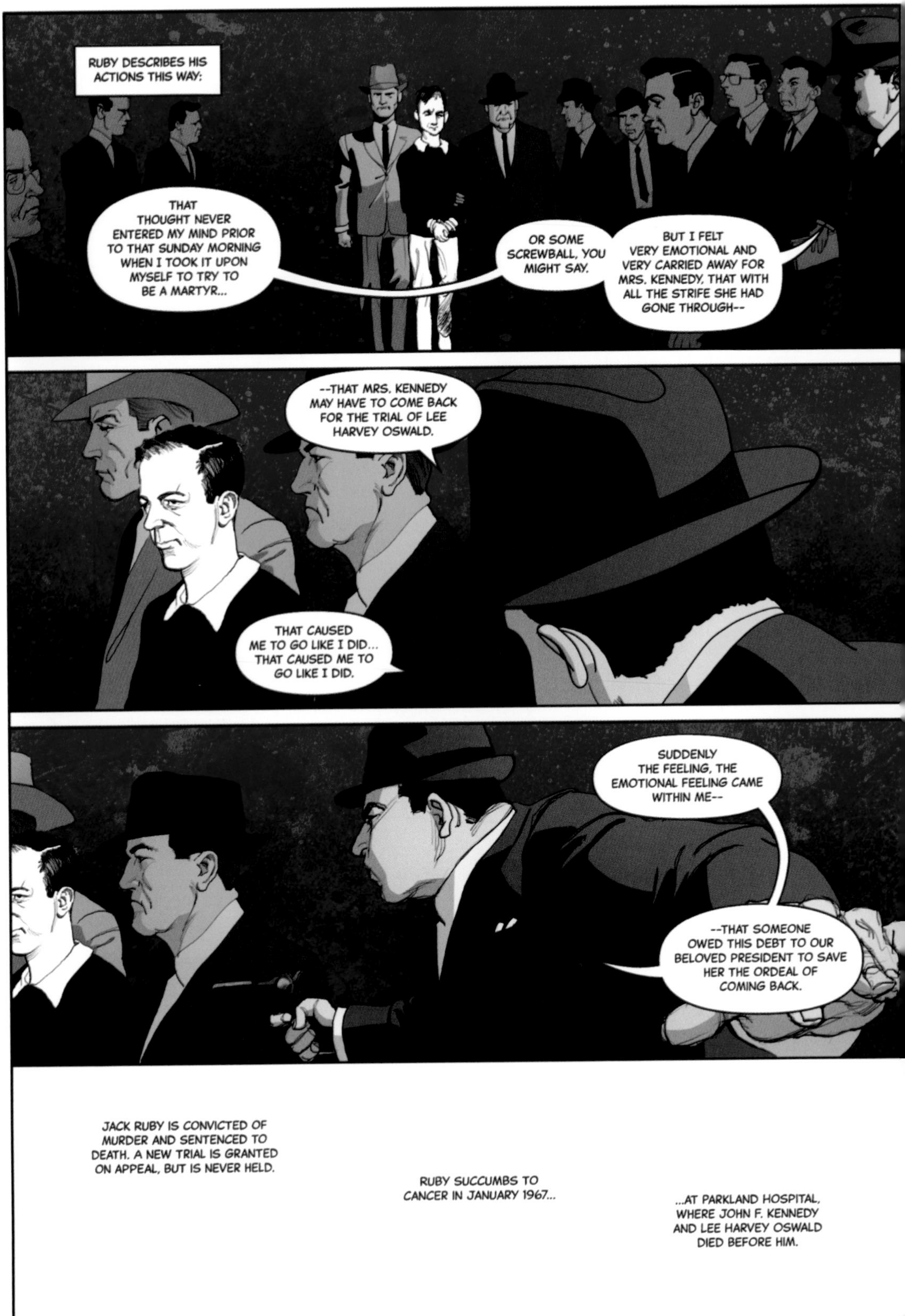
RUBY DESCRIBES HIS ACTIONS THIS WAY:
THAT THOUGHT NEVER ENTERED MY MIND PRIOR TO THAT SUNDAY MORNING WHEN I TOOK IT UPON MYSELF TO TRY TO BE A MARTYR...
OR SOME SCREWBALL, YOU MIGHT SAY.
BUT I FELT VERY EMOTIONAL AND VERY CARRIED AWAY FOR MRS. KENNEDY, THAT WITH ALL THE STRIFE SHE HAD GONE THROUGH--
--THAT MRS. KENNEDY MAY HAVE TO COME BACK FOR THE TRIAL OF LEE HARVEY OSWALD.
THAT CAUSED ME TO GO LIKE I DID... THAT CAUSED ME TO GO LIKE I DID.
SUDDENLY THE FEELING, THE EMOTIONAL FEELING CAME WITHIN ME--
--THAT SOMEONE OWED THIS DEBT TO OUR BELOVED PRESIDENT TO SAVE HER THE ORDEAL OF COMING BACK.
JACK RUBY IS CONVICTED OF MURDER AND SENTENCED TO DEATH. A NEW TRIAL IS GRANTED ON APPEAL, BUT IS NEVER HELD.
RUBY SUCCUMBS TO CANCER IN JANUARY 1967...
...AT PARKLAND HOSPITAL, WHERE JOHN F. KENNEDY AND LEE HARVEY OSWALD DIED BEFORE HIM.

CONSPIRACY AND CHANGE

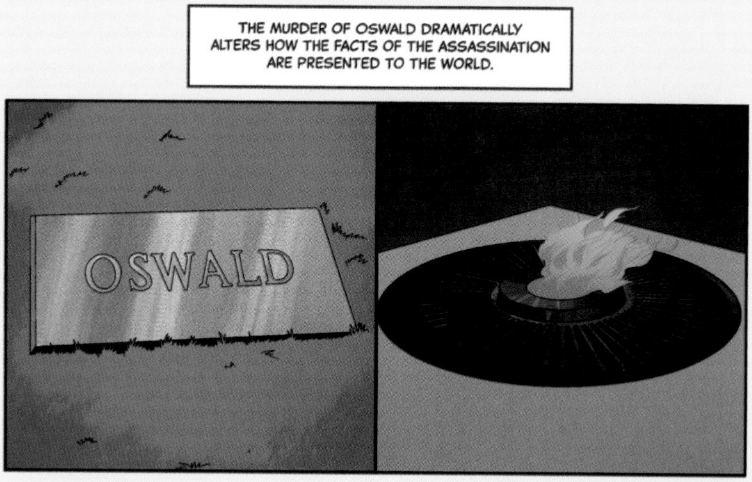
THE MURDER OF OSWALD DRAMATICALLY ALTERS HOW THE FACTS OF THE ASSASSINATION ARE PRESENTED TO THE WORLD.
OSWALD

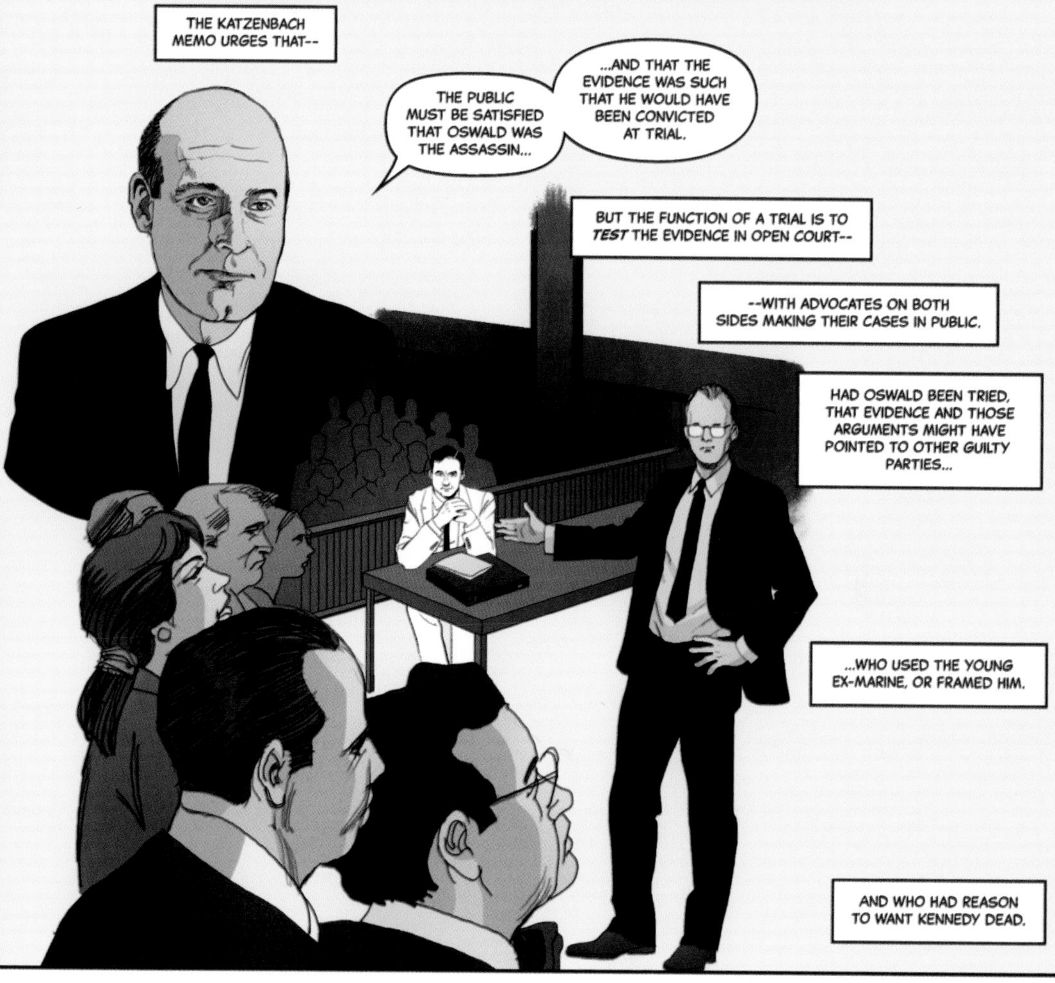
THE KATZENBACH MEMO URGES THAT--
THE PUBLIC MUST BE SATISFIED THAT OSWALD WAS THE ASSASSIN...
...AND THAT THE EVIDENCE WAS SUCH THAT HE WOULD HAVE BEEN CONVICTED AT TRIAL.
BUT THE FUNCTION OF A TRIAL IS TO *TEST* THE EVIDENCE IN OPEN COURT--
--WITH ADVOCATES ON BOTH SIDES MAKING THEIR CASES IN PUBLIC.
HAD OSWALD BEEN TRIED, THAT EVIDENCE AND THOSE ARGUMENTS MIGHT HAVE POINTED TO OTHER GUILTY PARTIES...
...WHO USED THE YOUNG EX-MARINE, OR FRAMED HIM.
AND WHO HAD REASON TO WANT KENNEDY DEAD.

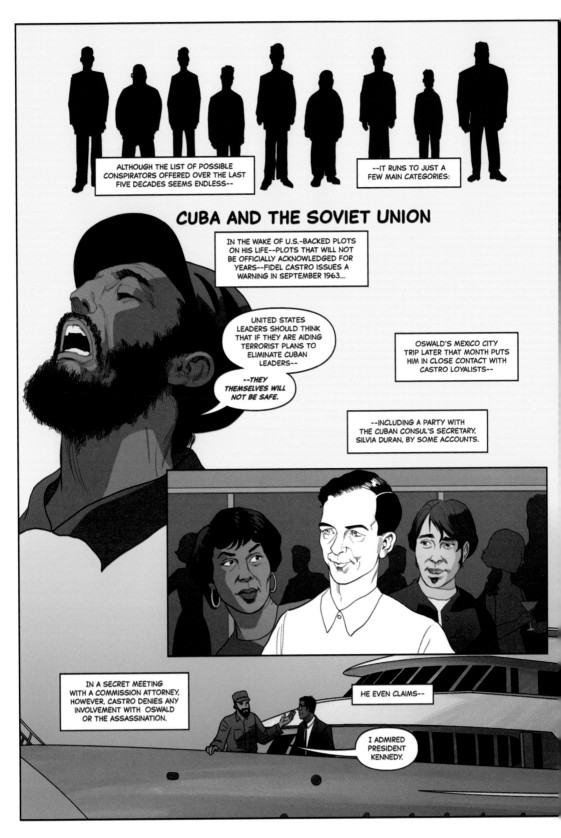

ALTHOUGH THE LIST OF POSSIBLE CONSPIRATORS OFFERED OVER THE LAST FIVE DECADES SEEMS ENDLESS--

--IT RUNS TO JUST A FEW MAIN CATEGORIES:

CUBA AND THE SOVIET UNION

IN THE WAKE OF U.S.-BACKED PLOTS ON HIS LIFE--PLOTS THAT WILL NOT BE OFFICIALLY ACKNOWLEDGED FOR YEARS--FIDEL CASTRO ISSUES A WARNING IN SEPTEMBER 1963...

UNITED STATES LEADERS SHOULD THINK THAT IF THEY ARE AIDING TERRORIST PLANS TO ELIMINATE CUBAN LEADERS--

--THEY THEMSELVES WILL NOT BE SAFE.

OSWALD'S MEXICO CITY TRIP LATER THAT MONTH PUTS HIM IN CLOSE CONTACT WITH CASTRO LOYALISTS--

--INCLUDING A PARTY WITH THE CUBAN CONSUL'S SECRETARY, SILVIA DURAN, BY SOME ACCOUNTS.

IN A SECRET MEETING WITH A COMMISSION ATTORNEY, HOWEVER, CASTRO DENIES ANY INVOLVEMENT WITH OSWALD OR THE ASSASSINATION.

HE EVEN CLAIMS--

I ADMIRED PRESIDENT KENNEDY.

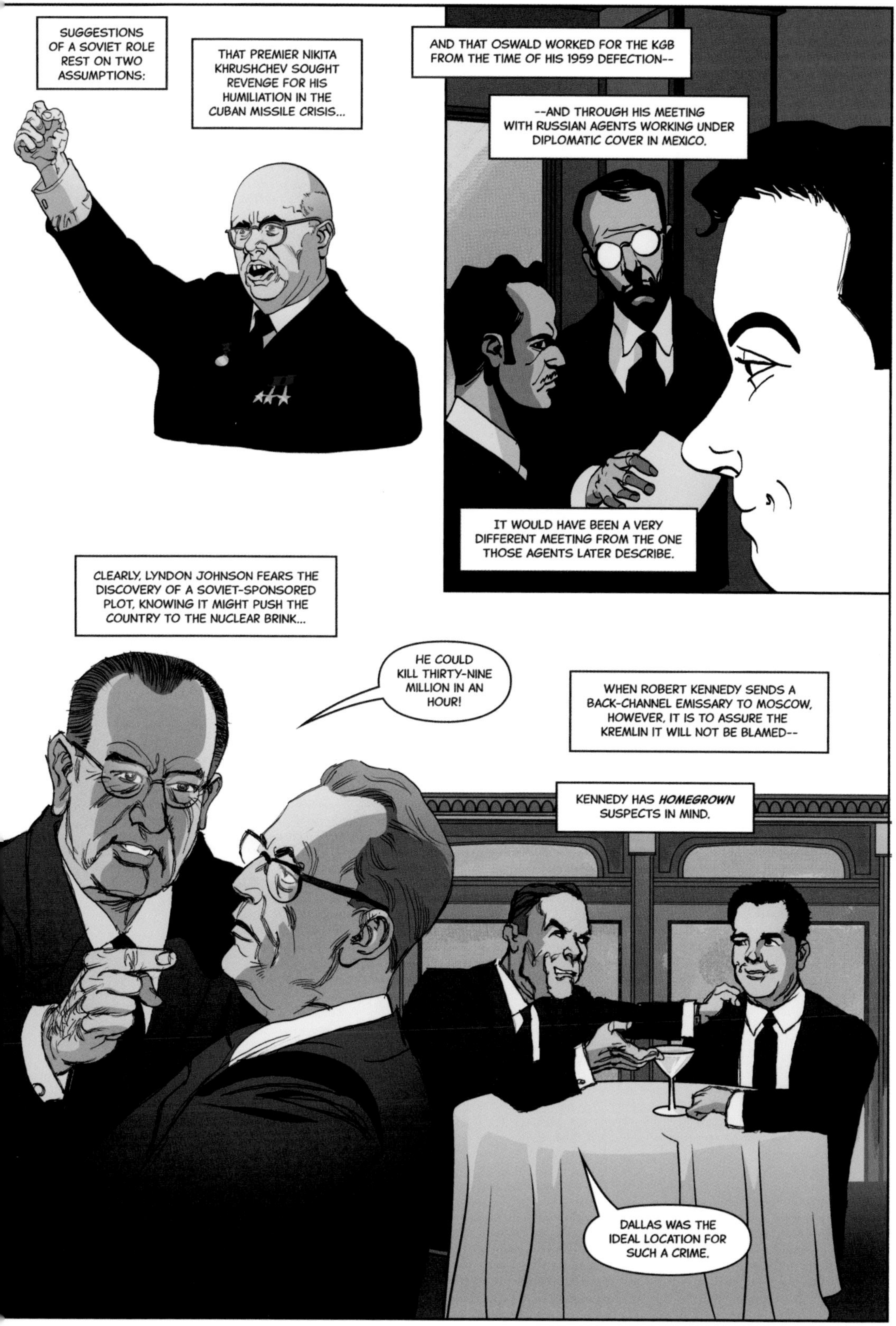
SUGGESTIONS OF A SOVIET ROLE REST ON TWO ASSUMPTIONS:
THAT PREMIER NIKITA KHRUSHCHEV SOUGHT REVENGE FOR HIS HUMILIATION IN THE CUBAN MISSILE CRISIS...
AND THAT OSWALD WORKED FOR THE KGB FROM THE TIME OF HIS 1959 DEFECTION--
--AND THROUGH HIS MEETING WITH RUSSIAN AGENTS WORKING UNDER DIPLOMATIC COVER IN MEXICO.
IT WOULD HAVE BEEN A VERY DIFFERENT MEETING FROM THE ONE THOSE AGENTS LATER DESCRIBE.
CLEARLY, LYNDON JOHNSON FEARS THE DISCOVERY OF A SOVIET-SPONSORED PLOT, KNOWING IT MIGHT PUSH THE COUNTRY TO THE NUCLEAR BRINK...
HE COULD KILL THIRTY-NINE MILLION IN AN HOUR!
WHEN ROBERT KENNEDY SENDS A BACK-CHANNEL EMISSARY TO MOSCOW, HOWEVER, IT IS TO ASSURE THE KREMLIN IT WILL NOT BE BLAMED--
KENNEDY HAS *HOMEGROWN* SUSPECTS IN MIND.
DALLAS WAS THE IDEAL LOCATION FOR SUCH A CRIME.

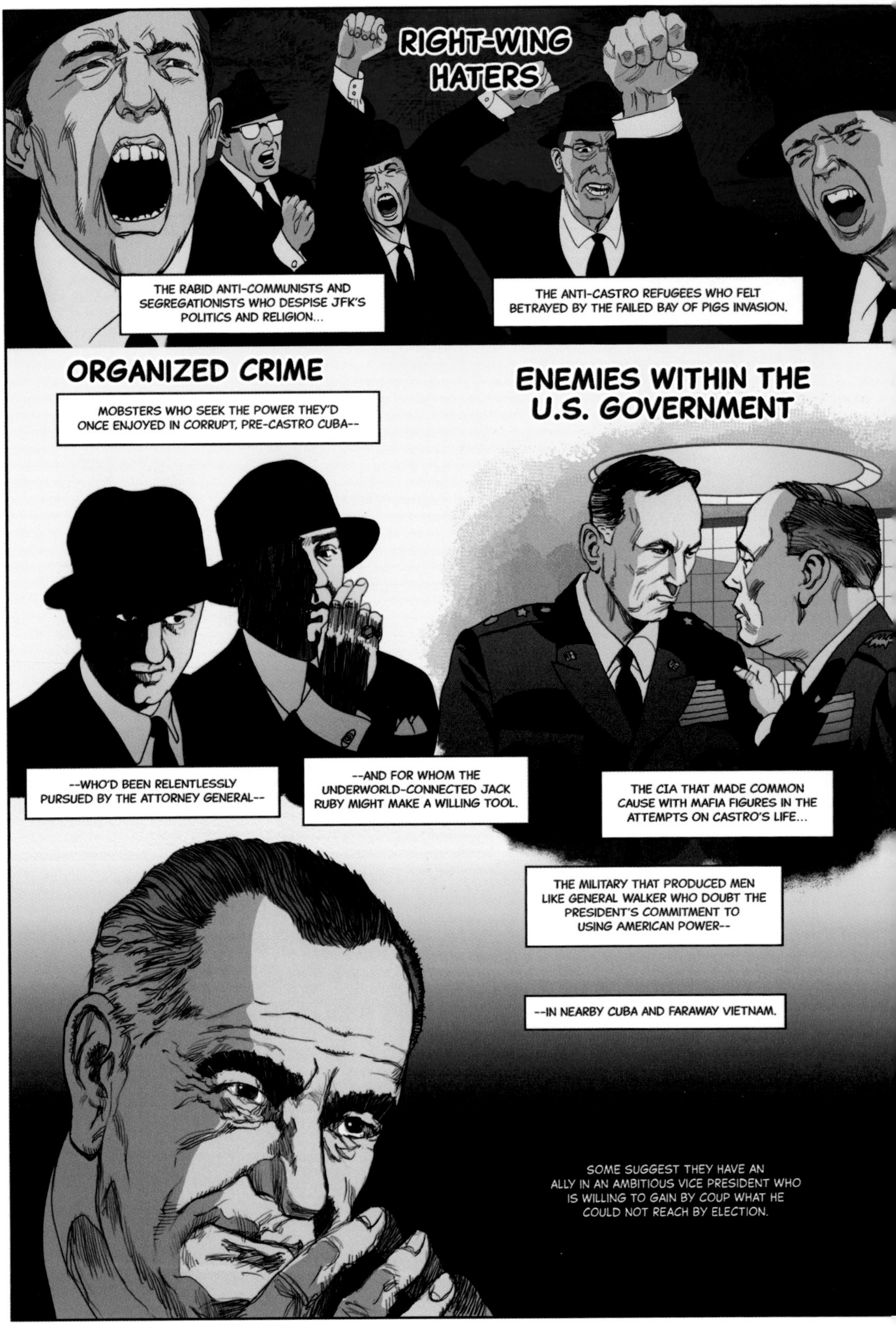
RIGHT-WING HATERS
THE RABID ANTI-COMMUNISTS AND SEGREGATIONISTS WHO DESPISE JFK'S POLITICS AND RELIGION...
THE ANTI-CASTRO REFUGEES WHO FELT BETRAYED BY THE FAILED BAY OF PIGS INVASION.
ORGANIZED CRIME
MOBSTERS WHO SEEK THE POWER THEY'D ONCE ENJOYED IN CORRUPT, PRE-CASTRO CUBA--
--WHO'D BEEN RELENTLESSLY PURSUED BY THE ATTORNEY GENERAL--
--AND FOR WHOM THE UNDERWORLD-CONNECTED JACK RUBY MIGHT MAKE A WILLING TOOL.
ENEMIES WITHIN THE U.S. GOVERNMENT
THE CIA THAT MADE COMMON CAUSE WITH MAFIA FIGURES IN THE ATTEMPTS ON CASTRO'S LIFE...
THE MILITARY THAT PRODUCED MEN LIKE GENERAL WALKER WHO DOUBT THE PRESIDENT'S COMMITMENT TO USING AMERICAN POWER--
--IN NEARBY CUBA AND FARAWAY VIETNAM.
SOME SUGGEST THEY HAVE AN ALLY IN AN AMBITIOUS VICE PRESIDENT WHO IS WILLING TO GAIN BY COUP WHAT HE COULD NOT REACH BY ELECTION.

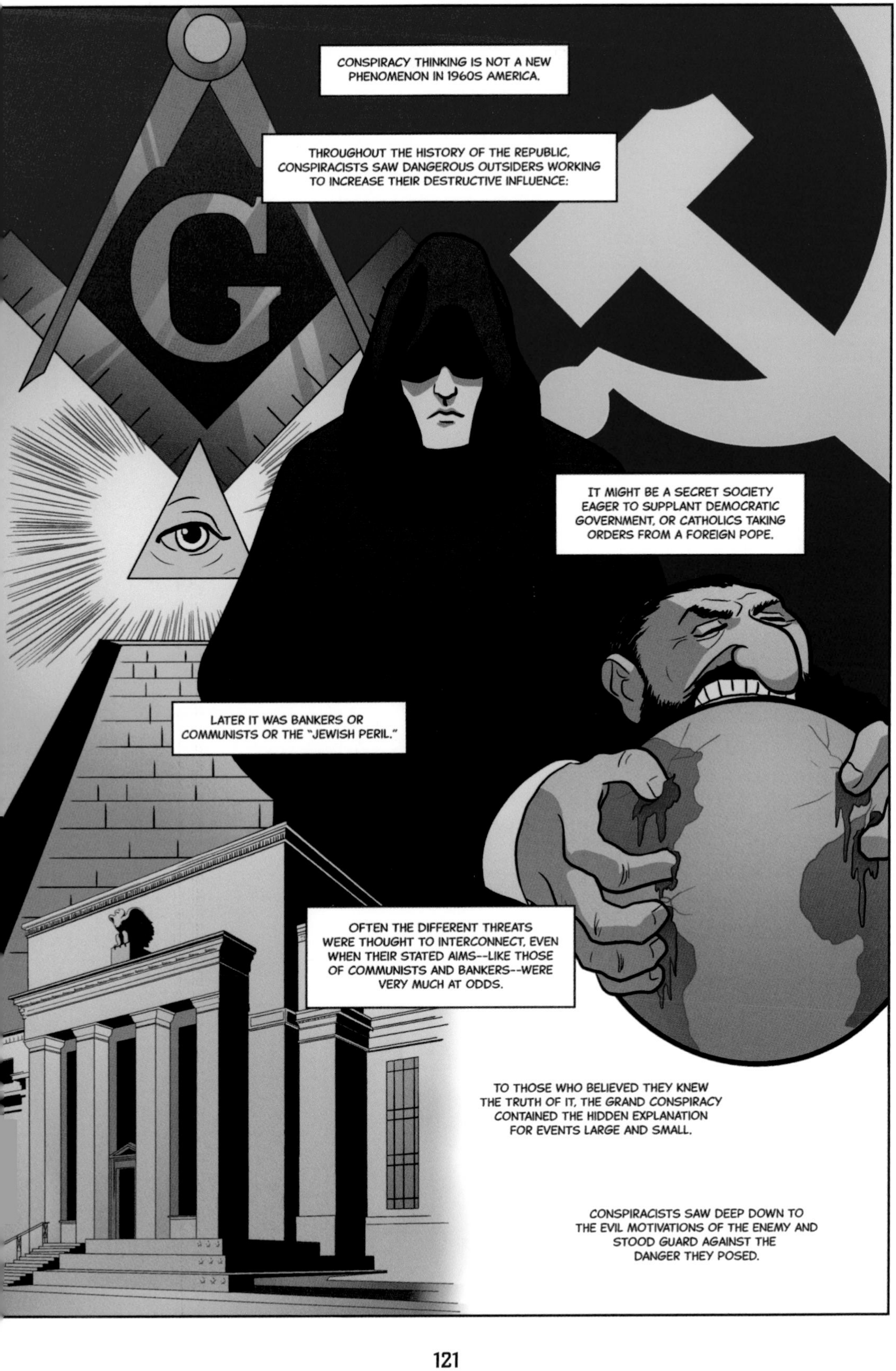
CONSPIRACY THINKING IS NOT A NEW PHENOMENON IN 1960S AMERICA.
THROUGHOUT THE HISTORY OF THE REPUBLIC, CONSPIRACISTS SAW DANGEROUS OUTSIDERS WORKING TO INCREASE THEIR DESTRUCTIVE INFLUENCE:
IT MIGHT BE A SECRET SOCIETY EAGER TO SUPPLANT DEMOCRATIC GOVERNMENT, OR CATHOLICS TAKING ORDERS FROM A FOREIGN POPE.
LATER IT WAS BANKERS OR COMMUNISTS OR THE "JEWISH PERIL."
OFTEN THE DIFFERENT THREATS WERE THOUGHT TO INTERCONNECT, EVEN WHEN THEIR STATED AIMS--LIKE THOSE OF COMMUNISTS AND BANKERS--WERE VERY MUCH AT ODDS.
TO THOSE WHO BELIEVED THEY KNEW THE TRUTH OF IT, THE GRAND CONSPIRACY CONTAINED THE HIDDEN EXPLANATION FOR EVENTS LARGE AND SMALL.
CONSPIRACISTS SAW DEEP DOWN TO THE EVIL MOTIVATIONS OF THE ENEMY AND STOOD GUARD AGAINST THE DANGER THEY POSED.

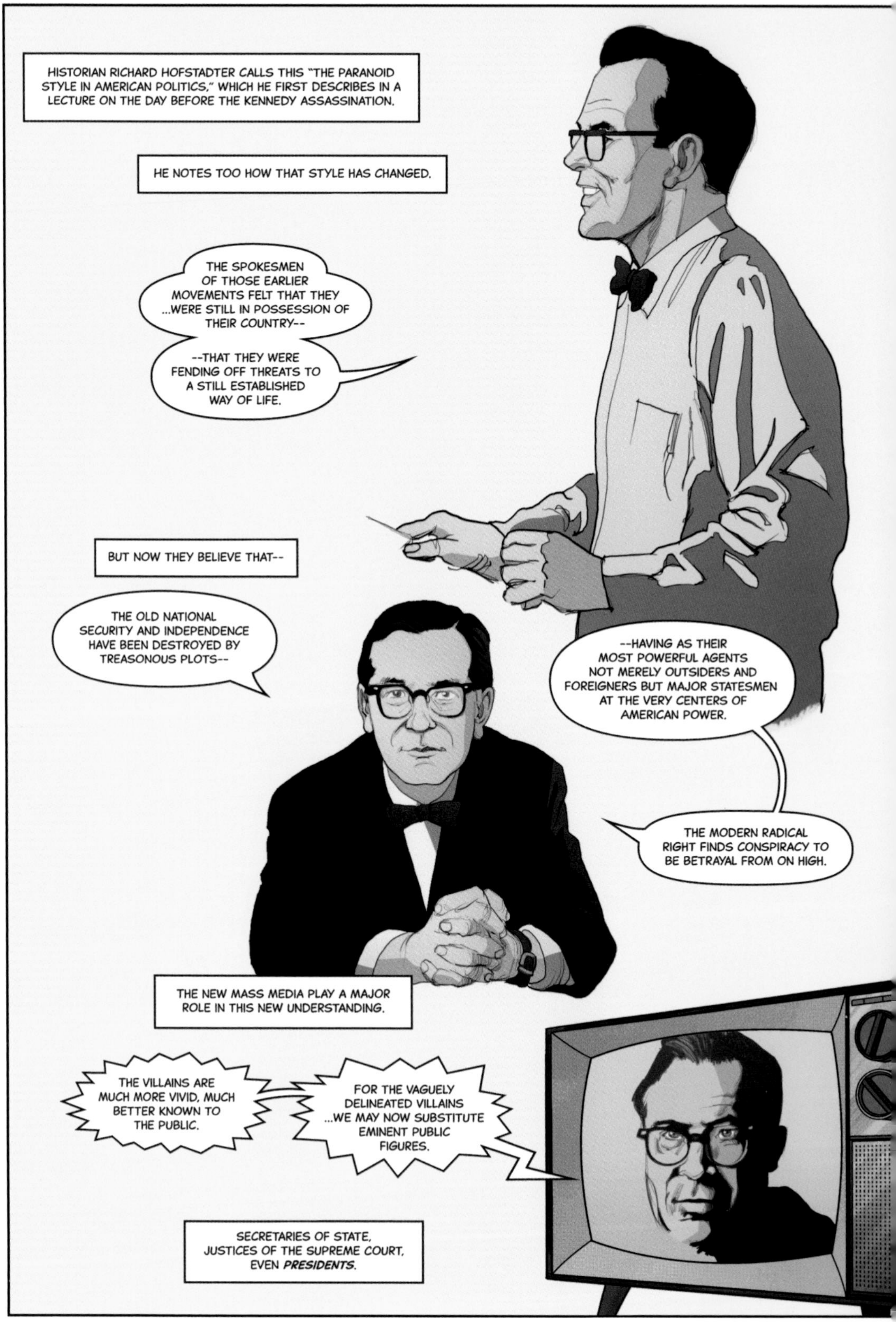
HISTORIAN RICHARD HOFSTADTER CALLS THIS "THE PARANOID STYLE IN AMERICAN POLITICS," WHICH HE FIRST DESCRIBES IN A LECTURE ON THE DAY BEFORE THE KENNEDY ASSASSINATION.
HE NOTES TOO HOW THAT STYLE HAS CHANGED.
THE SPOKESMEN OF THOSE EARLIER MOVEMENTS FELT THAT THEY ...WERE STILL IN POSSESSION OF THEIR COUNTRY--
--THAT THEY WERE FENDING OFF THREATS TO A STILL ESTABLISHED WAY OF LIFE.
BUT NOW THEY BELIEVE THAT--
THE OLD NATIONAL SECURITY AND INDEPENDENCE HAVE BEEN DESTROYED BY TREASONOUS PLOTS--
--HAVING AS THEIR MOST POWERFUL AGENTS NOT MERELY OUTSIDERS AND FOREIGNERS BUT MAJOR STATESMEN AT THE VERY CENTERS OF AMERICAN POWER.
THE MODERN RADICAL RIGHT FINDS CONSPIRACY TO BE BETRAYAL FROM ON HIGH.
THE NEW MASS MEDIA PLAY A MAJOR ROLE IN THIS NEW UNDERSTANDING.
THE VILLAINS ARE MUCH MORE VIVID, MUCH BETTER KNOWN TO THE PUBLIC.
FOR THE VAGUELY DELINEATED VILLAINS ...WE MAY NOW SUBSTITUTE EMINENT PUBLIC FIGURES.
SECRETARIES OF STATE, JUSTICES OF THE SUPREME COURT, EVEN *PRESIDENTS*.

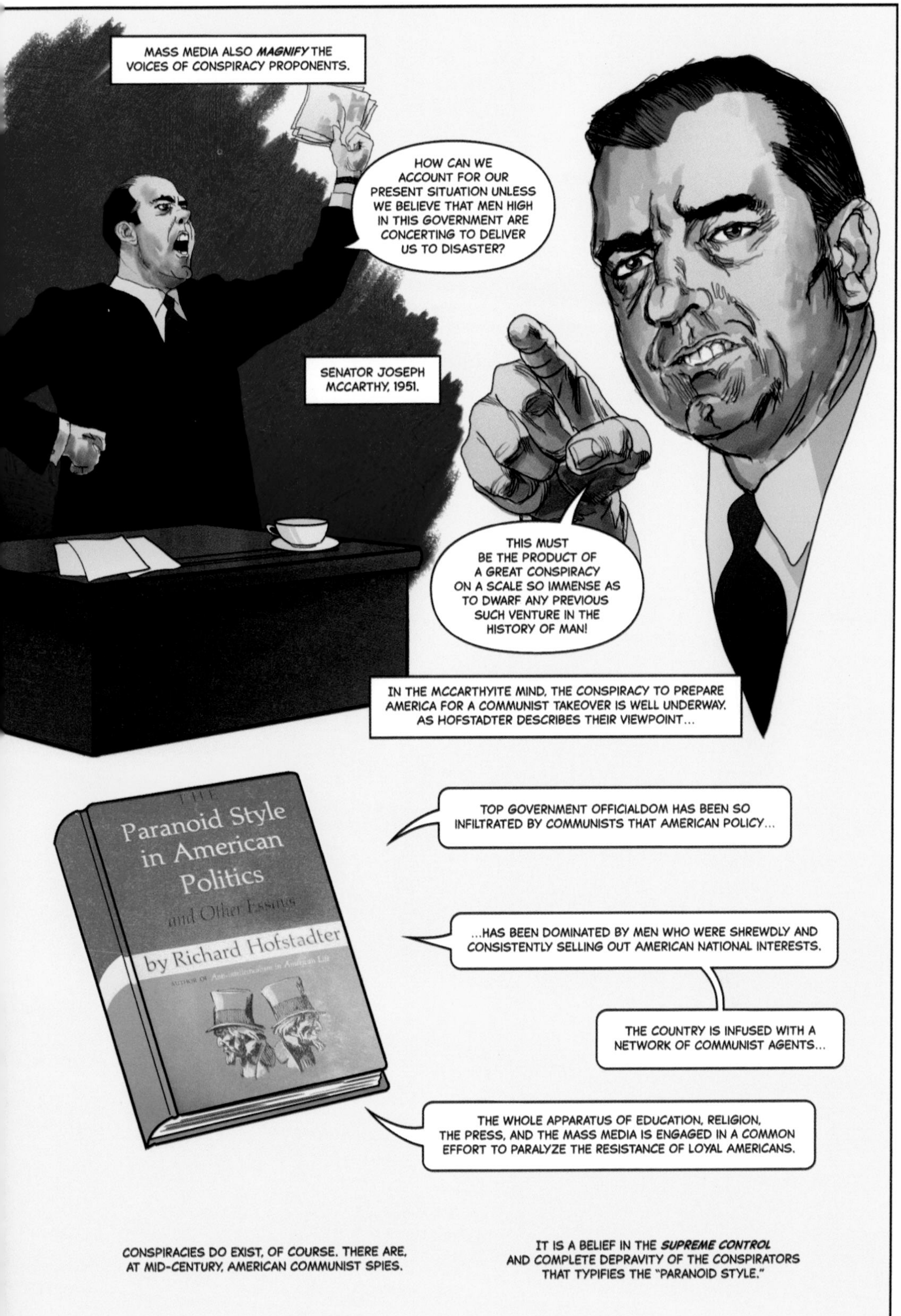
MASS MEDIA ALSO *MAGNIFY* THE VOICES OF CONSPIRACY PROPONENTS.
HOW CAN WE ACCOUNT FOR OUR PRESENT SITUATION UNLESS WE BELIEVE THAT MEN HIGH IN THIS GOVERNMENT ARE CONCERTING TO DELIVER US TO DISASTER?
SENATOR JOSEPH MCCARTHY, 1951.
THIS MUST BE THE PRODUCT OF A GREAT CONSPIRACY ON A SCALE SO IMMENSE AS TO DWARF ANY PREVIOUS SUCH VENTURE IN THE HISTORY OF MAN!
IN THE MCCARTHYITE MIND, THE CONSPIRACY TO PREPARE AMERICA FOR A COMMUNIST TAKEOVER IS WELL UNDERWAY. AS HOFSTADTER DESCRIBES THEIR VIEWPOINT...
THE Paranoid Style in American Politics
and Other Essays
by Richard Hofstadter
TOP GOVERNMENT OFFICIALDOM HAS BEEN SO INFILTRATED BY COMMUNISTS THAT AMERICAN POLICY...
...HAS BEEN DOMINATED BY MEN WHO WERE SHREWDLY AND CONSISTENTLY SELLING OUT AMERICAN NATIONAL INTERESTS.
THE COUNTRY IS INFUSED WITH A NETWORK OF COMMUNIST AGENTS...
THE WHOLE APPARATUS OF EDUCATION, RELIGION, THE PRESS, AND THE MASS MEDIA IS ENGAGED IN A COMMON EFFORT TO PARALYZE THE RESISTANCE OF LOYAL AMERICANS.
CONSPIRACIES DO EXIST, OF COURSE. THERE ARE, AT MID-CENTURY, AMERICAN COMMUNIST SPIES.
IT IS A BELIEF IN THE *SUPREME CONTROL* AND COMPLETE DEPRAVITY OF THE CONSPIRATORS THAT TYPIFIES THE "PARANOID STYLE."

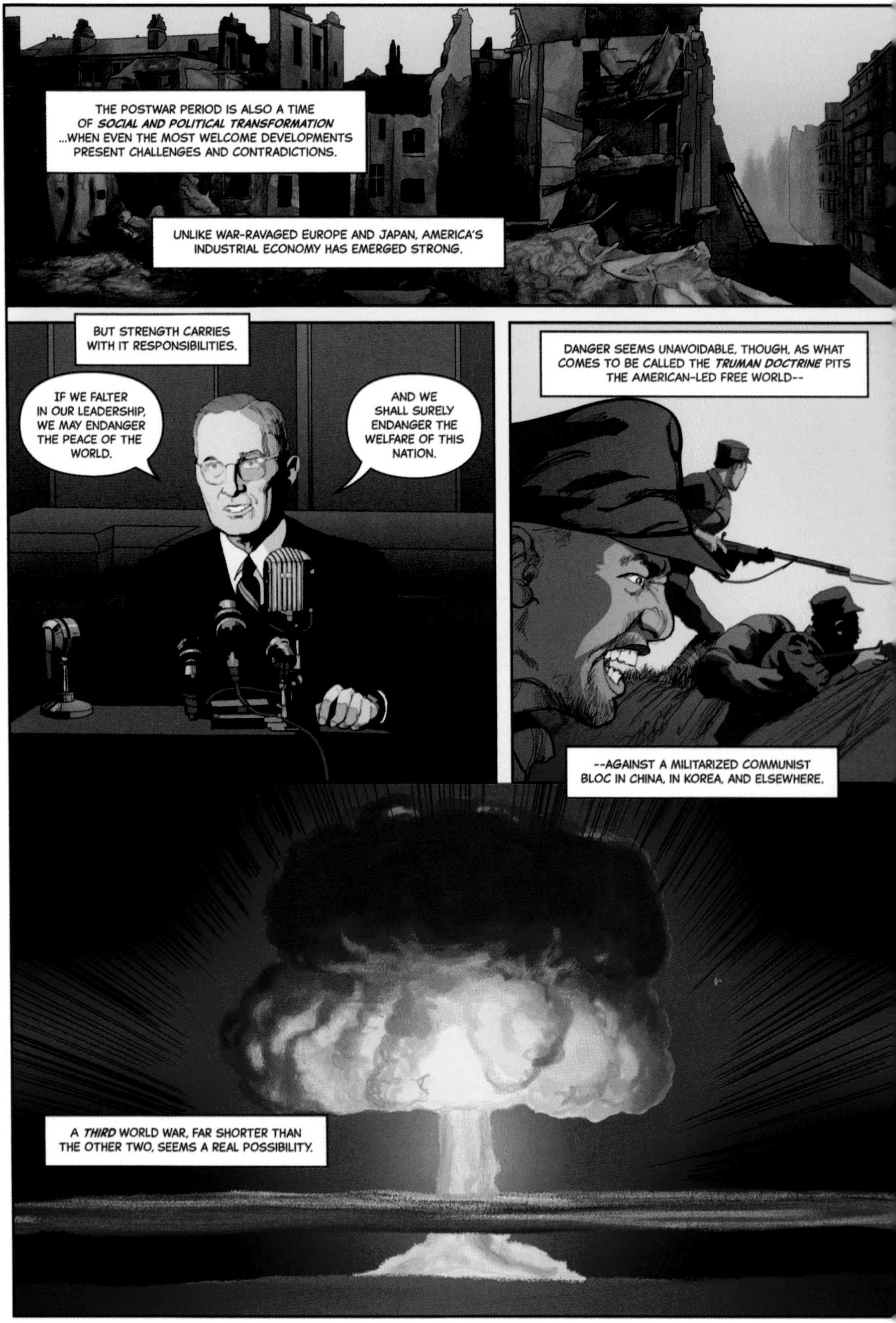
THE POSTWAR PERIOD IS ALSO A TIME OF *SOCIAL AND POLITICAL TRANSFORMATION* ...WHEN EVEN THE MOST WELCOME DEVELOPMENTS PRESENT CHALLENGES AND CONTRADICTIONS.
UNLIKE WAR-RAVAGED EUROPE AND JAPAN, AMERICA'S INDUSTRIAL ECONOMY HAS EMERGED STRONG.
BUT STRENGTH CARRIES WITH IT RESPONSIBILITIES.
IF WE FALTER IN OUR LEADERSHIP, WE MAY ENDANGER THE PEACE OF THE WORLD.
AND WE SHALL SURELY ENDANGER THE WELFARE OF THIS NATION.
DANGER SEEMS UNAVOIDABLE, THOUGH, AS WHAT COMES TO BE CALLED THE *TRUMAN DOCTRINE* PITS THE AMERICAN-LED FREE WORLD--
--AGAINST A MILITARIZED COMMUNIST BLOC IN CHINA, IN KOREA, AND ELSEWHERE.
A *THIRD* WORLD WAR, FAR SHORTER THAN THE OTHER TWO, SEEMS A REAL POSSIBILITY.

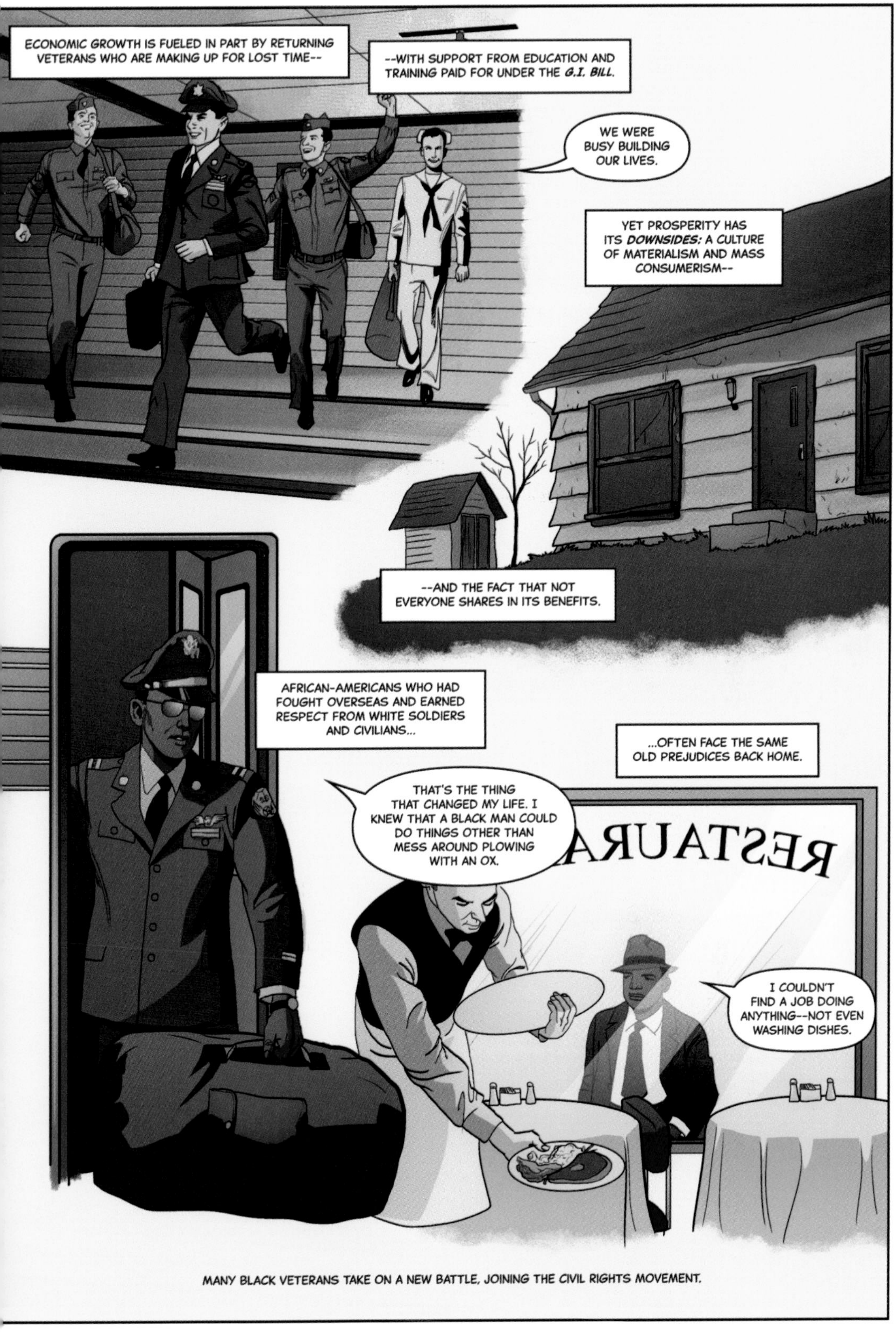
ECONOMIC GROWTH IS FUELED IN PART BY RETURNING VETERANS WHO ARE MAKING UP FOR LOST TIME--
--WITH SUPPORT FROM EDUCATION AND TRAINING PAID FOR UNDER THE *G.I. BILL*.
WE WERE BUSY BUILDING OUR LIVES.
YET PROSPERITY HAS ITS ***DOWNSIDES:*** A CULTURE OF MATERIALISM AND MASS CONSUMERISM--
--AND THE FACT THAT NOT EVERYONE SHARES IN ITS BENEFITS.
AFRICAN-AMERICANS WHO HAD FOUGHT OVERSEAS AND EARNED RESPECT FROM WHITE SOLDIERS AND CIVILIANS...
...OFTEN FACE THE SAME OLD PREJUDICES BACK HOME.
THAT'S THE THING THAT CHANGED MY LIFE. I KNEW THAT A BLACK MAN COULD DO THINGS OTHER THAN MESS AROUND PLOWING WITH AN OX.
RESTAURA
I COULDN'T FIND A JOB DOING ANYTHING--NOT EVEN WASHING DISHES.
MANY BLACK VETERANS TAKE ON A NEW BATTLE, JOINING THE CIVIL RIGHTS MOVEMENT.

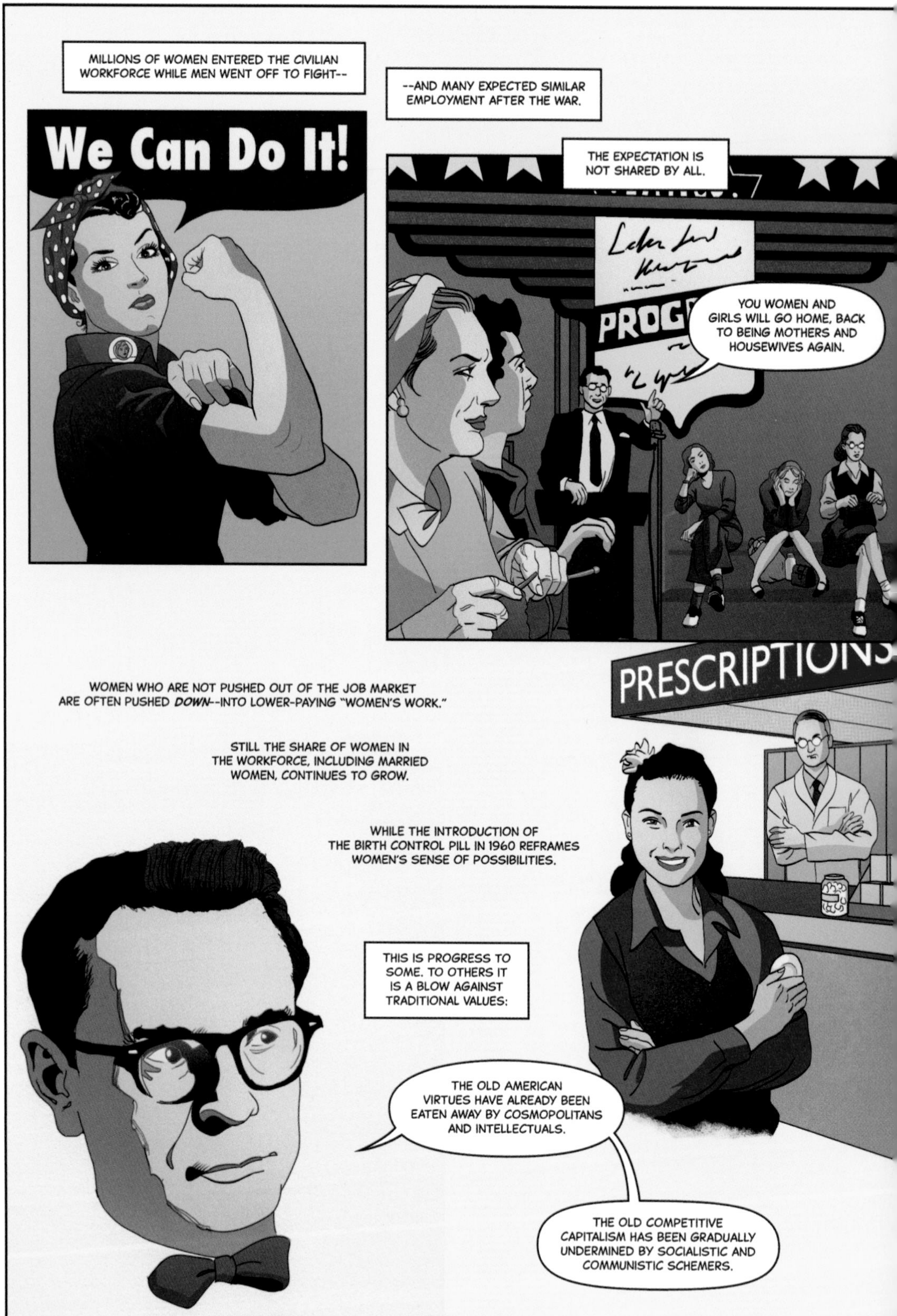
MILLIONS OF WOMEN ENTERED THE CIVILIAN WORKFORCE WHILE MEN WENT OFF TO FIGHT--
We Can Do It!
--AND MANY EXPECTED SIMILAR EMPLOYMENT AFTER THE WAR.
THE EXPECTATION IS NOT SHARED BY ALL.
YOU WOMEN AND GIRLS WILL GO HOME, BACK TO BEING MOTHERS AND HOUSEWIVES AGAIN.
PRESCRIPTIONS
WOMEN WHO ARE NOT PUSHED OUT OF THE JOB MARKET ARE OFTEN PUSHED *DOWN*--INTO LOWER-PAYING "WOMEN'S WORK."
STILL THE SHARE OF WOMEN IN THE WORKFORCE, INCLUDING MARRIED WOMEN, CONTINUES TO GROW.
WHILE THE INTRODUCTION OF THE BIRTH CONTROL PILL IN 1960 REFRAMES WOMEN'S SENSE OF POSSIBILITIES.
THIS IS PROGRESS TO SOME. TO OTHERS IT IS A BLOW AGAINST TRADITIONAL VALUES:
THE OLD AMERICAN VIRTUES HAVE ALREADY BEEN EATEN AWAY BY COSMOPOLITANS AND INTELLECTUALS.
THE OLD COMPETITIVE CAPITALISM HAS BEEN GRADUALLY UNDERMINED BY SOCIALISTIC AND COMMUNISTIC SCHEMERS.

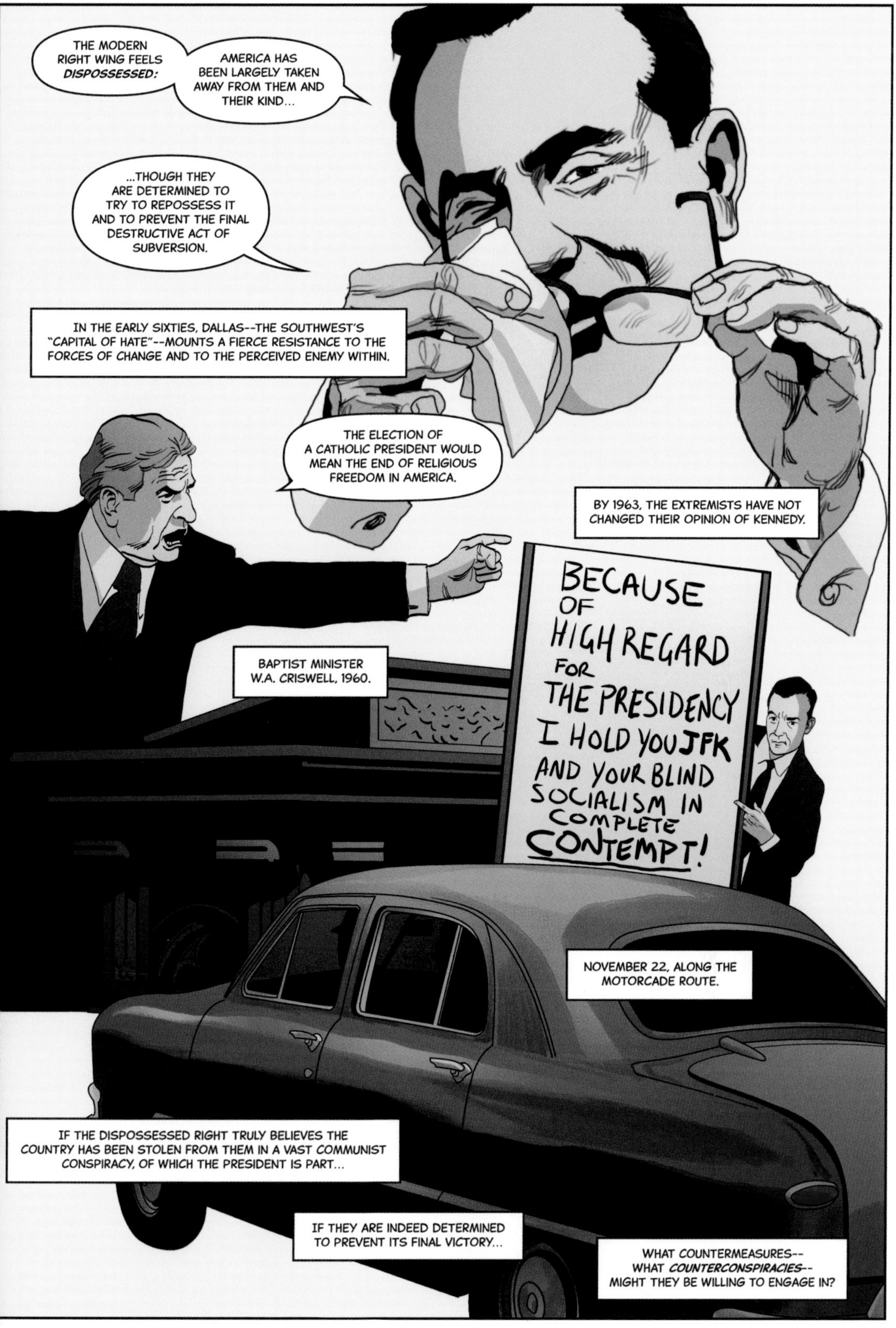
THE MODERN RIGHT WING FEELS *DISPOSSESSED:*
AMERICA HAS BEEN LARGELY TAKEN AWAY FROM THEM AND THEIR KIND...
...THOUGH THEY ARE DETERMINED TO TRY TO REPOSSESS IT AND TO PREVENT THE FINAL DESTRUCTIVE ACT OF SUBVERSION.
IN THE EARLY SIXTIES, DALLAS--THE SOUTHWEST'S "CAPITAL OF HATE"--MOUNTS A FIERCE RESISTANCE TO THE FORCES OF CHANGE AND TO THE PERCEIVED ENEMY WITHIN.
THE ELECTION OF A CATHOLIC PRESIDENT WOULD MEAN THE END OF RELIGIOUS FREEDOM IN AMERICA.
BAPTIST MINISTER W.A. CRISWELL, 1960.
BY 1963, THE EXTREMISTS HAVE NOT CHANGED THEIR OPINION OF KENNEDY.
BECAUSE OF HIGH REGARD FOR THE PRESIDENCY I HOLD YOU JFK AND YOUR BLIND SOCIALISM IN COMPLETE CONTEMPT!
NOVEMBER 22, ALONG THE MOTORCADE ROUTE.
IF THE DISPOSSESSED RIGHT TRULY BELIEVES THE COUNTRY HAS BEEN STOLEN FROM THEM IN A VAST COMMUNIST CONSPIRACY, OF WHICH THE PRESIDENT IS PART...
IF THEY ARE INDEED DETERMINED TO PREVENT ITS FINAL VICTORY...
WHAT COUNTERMEASURES-- WHAT *COUNTERCONSPIRACIES*-- MIGHT THEY BE WILLING TO ENGAGE IN?

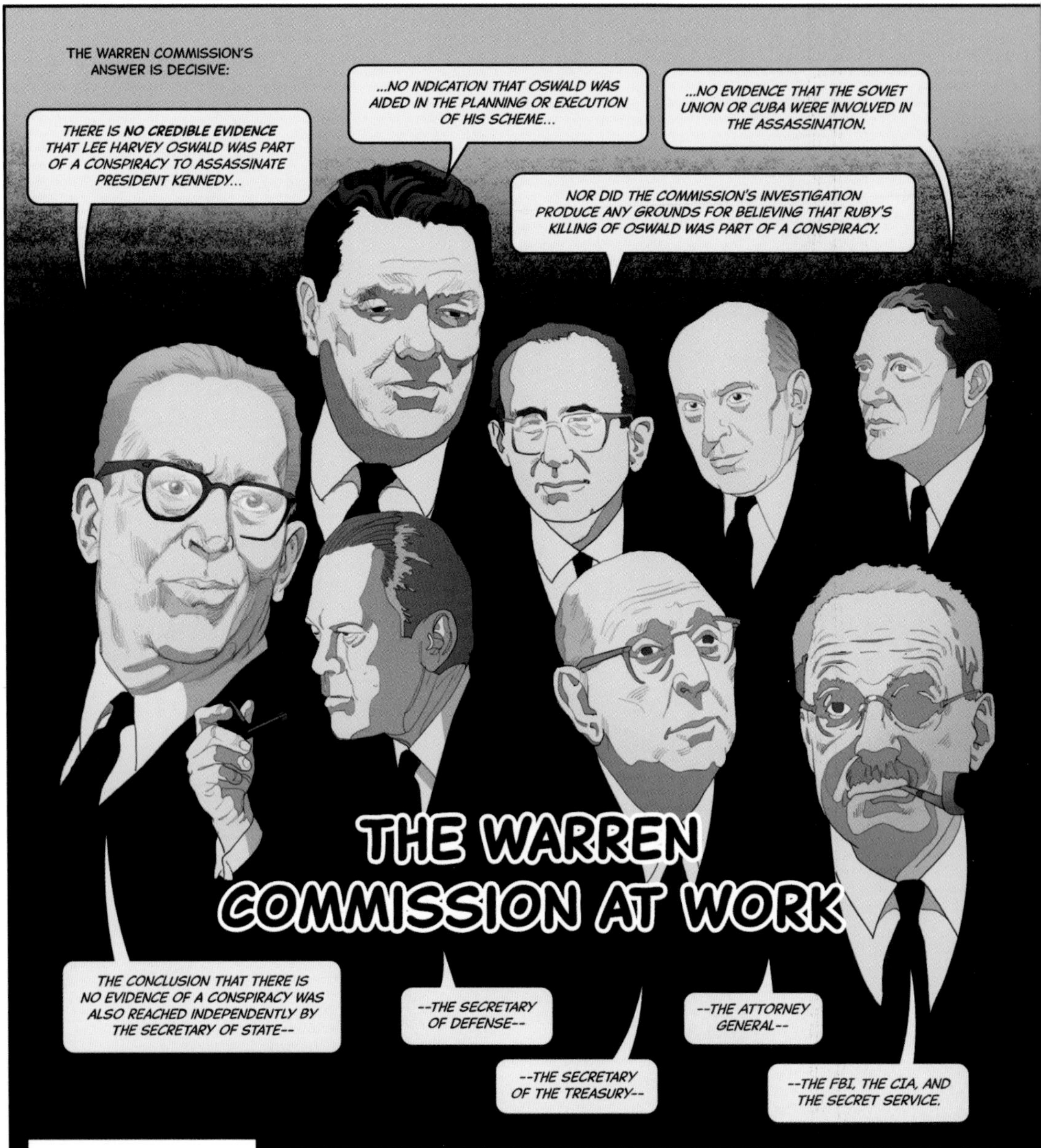
THE WARREN COMMISSION'S ANSWER IS DECISIVE:
THERE IS NO CREDIBLE EVIDENCE THAT LEE HARVEY OSWALD WAS PART OF A CONSPIRACY TO ASSASSINATE PRESIDENT KENNEDY...
...NO INDICATION THAT OSWALD WAS AIDED IN THE PLANNING OR EXECUTION OF HIS SCHEME...
...NO EVIDENCE THAT THE SOVIET UNION OR CUBA WERE INVOLVED IN THE ASSASSINATION.
NOR DID THE COMMISSION'S INVESTIGATION PRODUCE ANY GROUNDS FOR BELIEVING THAT RUBY'S KILLING OF OSWALD WAS PART OF A CONSPIRACY.
THE WARREN COMMISSION AT WORK
THE CONCLUSION THAT THERE IS NO EVIDENCE OF A CONSPIRACY WAS ALSO REACHED INDEPENDENTLY BY THE SECRETARY OF STATE--
--THE SECRETARY OF DEFENSE--
--THE SECRETARY OF THE TREASURY--
--THE ATTORNEY GENERAL--
--THE FBI, THE CIA, AND THE SECRET SERVICE.

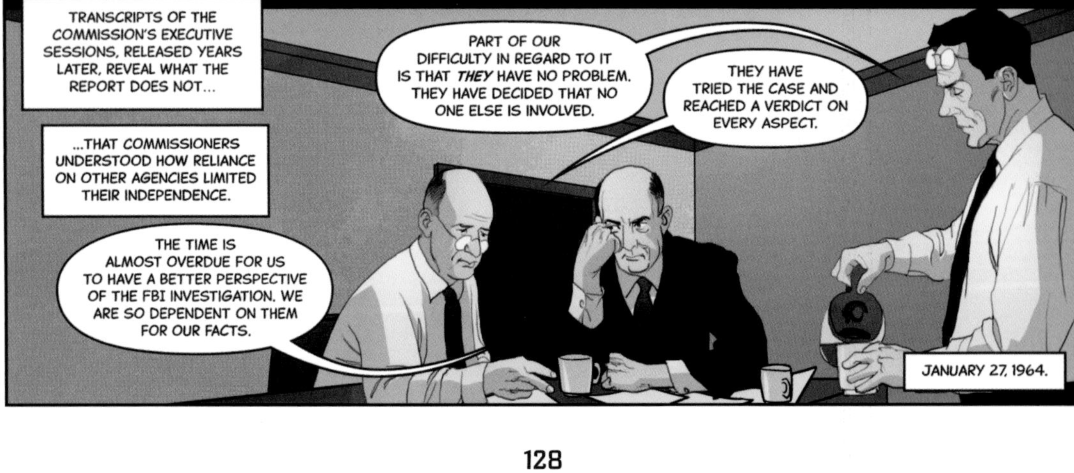
TRANSCRIPTS OF THE COMMISSION'S EXECUTIVE SESSIONS, RELEASED YEARS LATER, REVEAL WHAT THE REPORT DOES NOT...
...THAT COMMISSIONERS UNDERSTOOD HOW RELIANCE ON OTHER AGENCIES LIMITED THEIR INDEPENDENCE.
PART OF OUR DIFFICULTY IN REGARD TO IT IS THAT THEY HAVE NO PROBLEM. THEY HAVE DECIDED THAT NO ONE ELSE IS INVOLVED.
THEY HAVE TRIED THE CASE AND REACHED A VERDICT ON EVERY ASPECT.
THE TIME IS ALMOST OVERDUE FOR US TO HAVE A BETTER PERSPECTIVE OF THE FBI INVESTIGATION. WE ARE SO DEPENDENT ON THEM FOR OUR FACTS.
JANUARY 27, 1964.

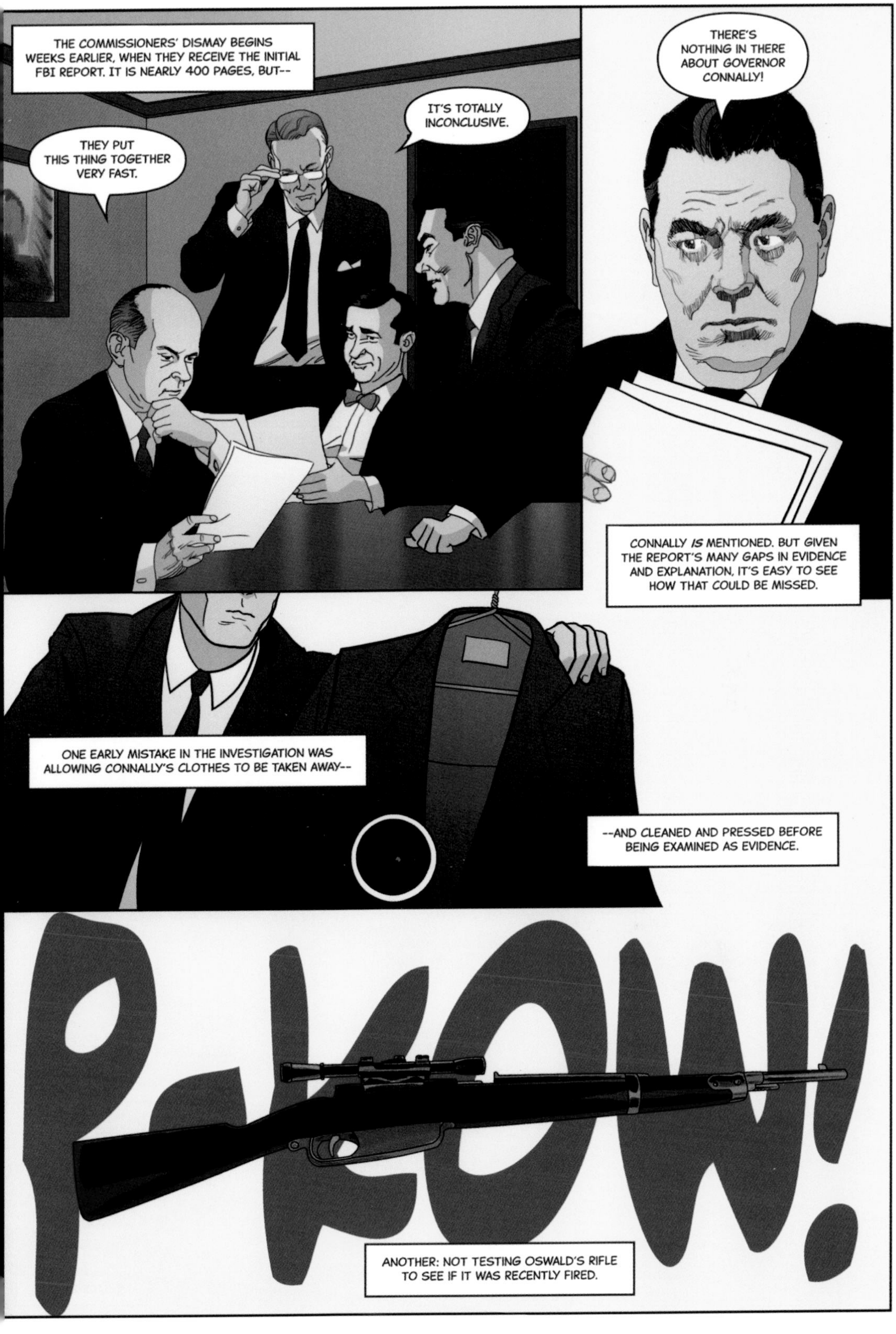
THE COMMISSIONERS' DISMAY BEGINS WEEKS EARLIER, WHEN THEY RECEIVE THE INITIAL FBI REPORT. IT IS NEARLY 400 PAGES, BUT--
THEY PUT THIS THING TOGETHER VERY FAST.
IT'S TOTALLY INCONCLUSIVE.
THERE'S NOTHING IN THERE ABOUT GOVERNOR CONNALLY!
CONNALLY *IS* MENTIONED. BUT GIVEN THE REPORT'S MANY GAPS IN EVIDENCE AND EXPLANATION, IT'S EASY TO SEE HOW THAT COULD BE MISSED.
ONE EARLY MISTAKE IN THE INVESTIGATION WAS ALLOWING CONNALLY'S CLOTHES TO BE TAKEN AWAY--
--AND CLEANED AND PRESSED BEFORE BEING EXAMINED AS EVIDENCE.
P-KOW!
ANOTHER: NOT TESTING OSWALD'S RIFLE TO SEE IF IT WAS RECENTLY FIRED.

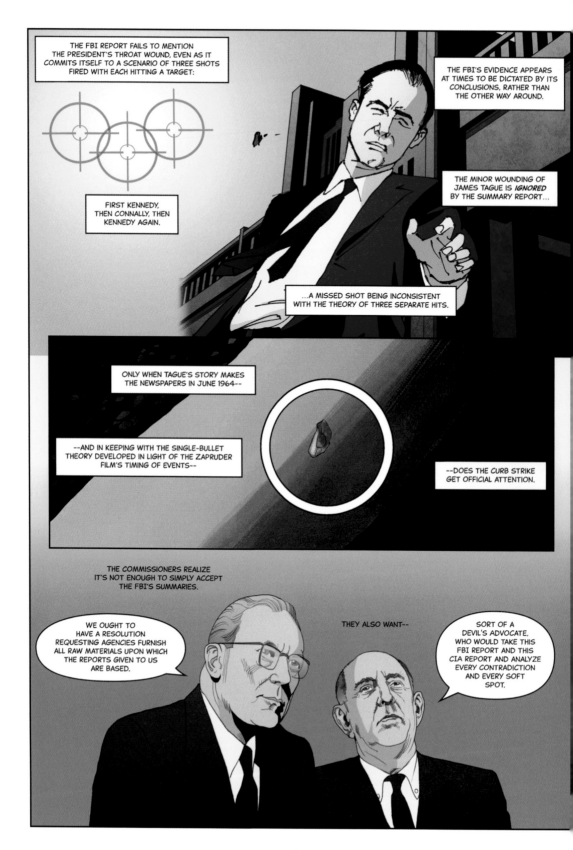

THE FBI REPORT FAILS TO MENTION THE PRESIDENT'S THROAT WOUND, EVEN AS IT COMMITS ITSELF TO A SCENARIO OF THREE SHOTS FIRED WITH EACH HITTING A TARGET:

FIRST KENNEDY, THEN CONNALLY, THEN KENNEDY AGAIN.

THE FBI'S EVIDENCE APPEARS AT TIMES TO BE DICTATED BY ITS CONCLUSIONS, RATHER THAN THE OTHER WAY AROUND.

THE MINOR WOUNDING OF JAMES TAGUE IS *IGNORED* BY THE SUMMARY REPORT...

...A MISSED SHOT BEING INCONSISTENT WITH THE THEORY OF THREE SEPARATE HITS.

ONLY WHEN TAGUE'S STORY MAKES THE NEWSPAPERS IN JUNE 1964--

--AND IN KEEPING WITH THE SINGLE-BULLET THEORY DEVELOPED IN LIGHT OF THE ZAPRUDER FILM'S TIMING OF EVENTS--

--DOES THE CURB STRIKE GET OFFICIAL ATTENTION.

THE COMMISSIONERS REALIZE IT'S NOT ENOUGH TO SIMPLY ACCEPT THE FBI'S SUMMARIES.

WE OUGHT TO HAVE A RESOLUTION REQUESTING AGENCIES FURNISH ALL RAW MATERIALS UPON WHICH THE REPORTS GIVEN TO US ARE BASED.

THEY ALSO WANT--

SORT OF A DEVIL'S ADVOCATE, WHO WOULD TAKE THIS FBI REPORT AND THIS CIA REPORT AND ANALYZE EVERY CONTRADICTION AND EVERY SOFT SPOT.

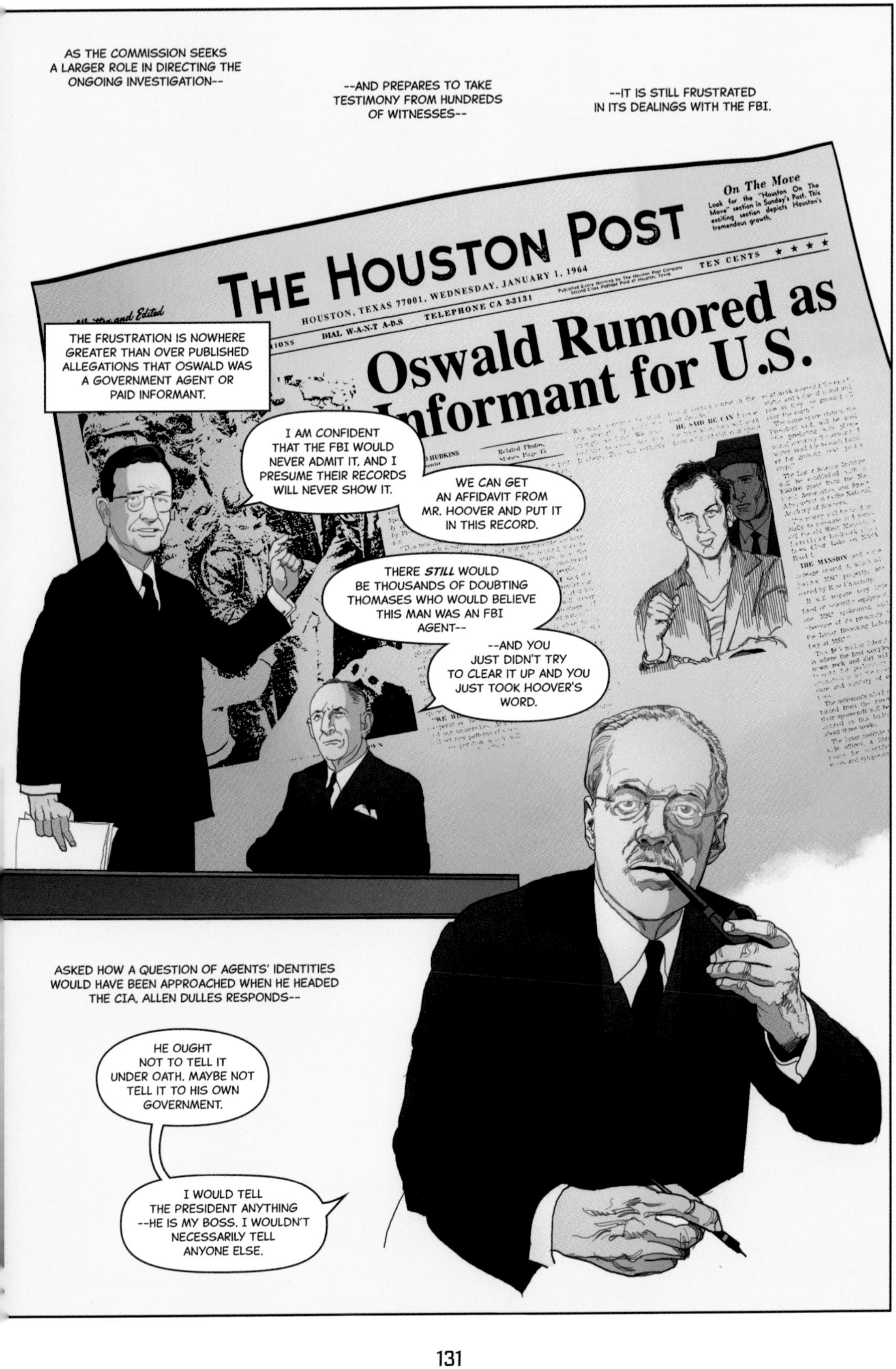

AS THE COMMISSION SEEKS A LARGER ROLE IN DIRECTING THE ONGOING INVESTIGATION--
--AND PREPARES TO TAKE TESTIMONY FROM HUNDREDS OF WITNESSES--
--IT IS STILL FRUSTRATED IN ITS DEALINGS WITH THE FBI.
On The Move
Look for the "Houston On The Move" section in Sunday's Post. This exciting section depicts Houston's tremendous growth.
THE HOUSTON POST
HOUSTON, TEXAS 77001, WEDNESDAY, JANUARY 1, 1964
TEN CENTS
DIAL W-A-N-T A-D-S
TELEPHONE CA 3-3131
Oswald Rumored as Informant for U.S.
THE FRUSTRATION IS NOWHERE GREATER THAN OVER PUBLISHED ALLEGATIONS THAT OSWALD WAS A GOVERNMENT AGENT OR PAID INFORMANT.
I AM CONFIDENT THAT THE FBI WOULD NEVER ADMIT IT, AND I PRESUME THEIR RECORDS WILL NEVER SHOW IT.
WE CAN GET AN AFFIDAVIT FROM MR. HOOVER AND PUT IT IN THIS RECORD.
THERE *STILL* WOULD BE THOUSANDS OF DOUBTING THOMASES WHO WOULD BELIEVE THIS MAN WAS AN FBI AGENT--
--AND YOU JUST DIDN'T TRY TO CLEAR IT UP AND YOU JUST TOOK HOOVER'S WORD.
ASKED HOW A QUESTION OF AGENTS' IDENTITIES WOULD HAVE BEEN APPROACHED WHEN HE HEADED THE CIA, ALLEN DULLES RESPONDS--
HE OUGHT NOT TO TELL IT UNDER OATH. MAYBE NOT TELL IT TO HIS OWN GOVERNMENT.
I WOULD TELL THE PRESIDENT ANYTHING --HE IS MY BOSS. I WOULDN'T NECESSARILY TELL ANYONE ELSE.

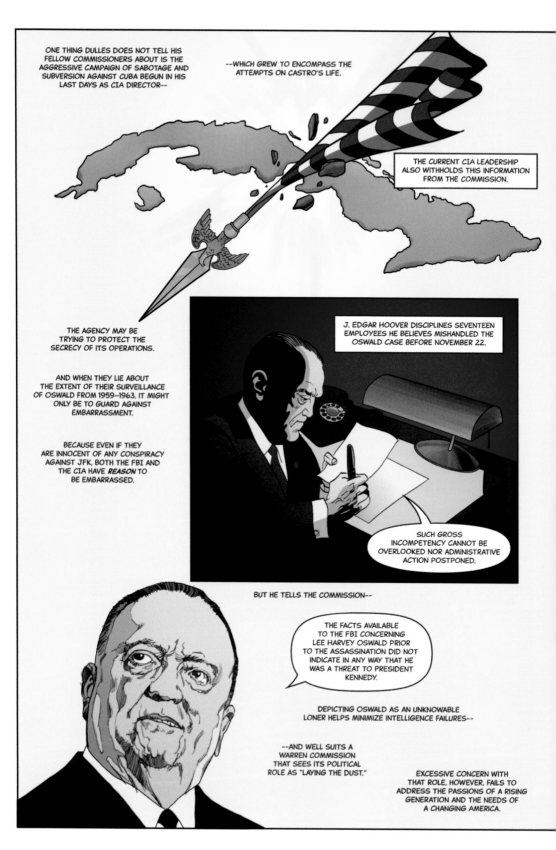

ONE THING DULLES DOES NOT TELL HIS FELLOW COMMISSIONERS ABOUT IS THE AGGRESSIVE CAMPAIGN OF SABOTAGE AND SUBVERSION AGAINST CUBA BEGUN IN HIS LAST DAYS AS CIA DIRECTOR--

--WHICH GREW TO ENCOMPASS THE ATTEMPTS ON CASTRO'S LIFE.

THE CURRENT CIA LEADERSHIP ALSO WITHHOLDS THIS INFORMATION FROM THE COMMISSION.

THE AGENCY MAY BE TRYING TO PROTECT THE SECRECY OF ITS OPERATIONS.

AND WHEN THEY LIE ABOUT THE EXTENT OF THEIR SURVEILLANCE OF OSWALD FROM 1959–1963, IT MIGHT ONLY BE TO GUARD AGAINST EMBARRASSMENT.

BECAUSE EVEN IF THEY ARE INNOCENT OF ANY CONSPIRACY AGAINST JFK, BOTH THE FBI AND THE CIA HAVE *REASON* TO BE EMBARRASSED.

J. EDGAR HOOVER DISCIPLINES SEVENTEEN EMPLOYEES HE BELIEVES MISHANDLED THE OSWALD CASE BEFORE NOVEMBER 22.

SUCH GROSS INCOMPETENCY CANNOT BE OVERLOOKED NOR ADMINISTRATIVE ACTION POSTPONED.

BUT HE TELLS THE COMMISSION--

THE FACTS AVAILABLE TO THE FBI CONCERNING LEE HARVEY OSWALD PRIOR TO THE ASSASSINATION DID NOT INDICATE IN ANY WAY THAT HE WAS A THREAT TO PRESIDENT KENNEDY.

DEPICTING OSWALD AS AN UNKNOWABLE LONER HELPS MINIMIZE INTELLIGENCE FAILURES--

--AND WELL SUITS A WARREN COMMISSION THAT SEES ITS POLITICAL ROLE AS "LAYING THE DUST."

EXCESSIVE CONCERN WITH THAT ROLE, HOWEVER, FAILS TO ADDRESS THE PASSIONS OF A RISING GENERATION AND THE NEEDS OF A CHANGING AMERICA.

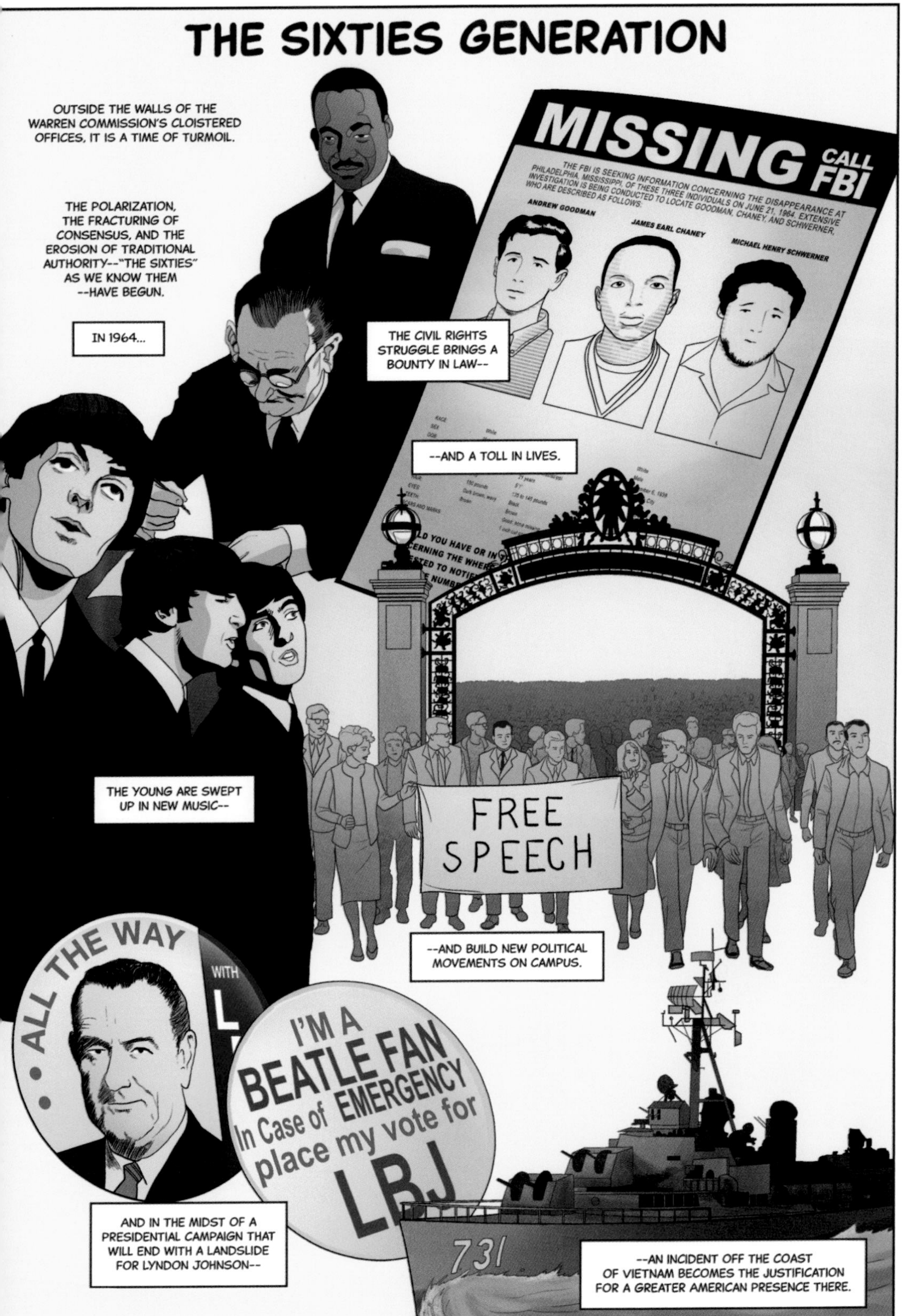
THE SIXTIES GENERATION
OUTSIDE THE WALLS OF THE WARREN COMMISSION'S CLOISTERED OFFICES, IT IS A TIME OF TURMOIL.
THE POLARIZATION, THE FRACTURING OF CONSENSUS, AND THE EROSION OF TRADITIONAL AUTHORITY--"THE SIXTIES" AS WE KNOW THEM --HAVE BEGUN.
IN 1964...
MISSING CALL FBI
THE FBI IS SEEKING INFORMATION CONCERNING THE DISAPPEARANCE AT PHILADELPHIA, MISSISSIPPI, OF THESE THREE INDIVIDUALS ON JUNE 21, 1964. EXTENSIVE INVESTIGATION IS BEING CONDUCTED TO LOCATE GOODMAN, CHANEY, AND SCHWERNER, WHO ARE DESCRIBED AS FOLLOWS:
ANDREW GOODMAN
JAMES EARL CHANEY
MICHAEL HENRY SCHWERNER
THE CIVIL RIGHTS STRUGGLE BRINGS A BOUNTY IN LAW--
--AND A TOLL IN LIVES.
THE YOUNG ARE SWEPT UP IN NEW MUSIC--
FREE SPEECH
--AND BUILD NEW POLITICAL MOVEMENTS ON CAMPUS.
ALL THE WAY WITH L
I'M A BEATLE FAN In Case of EMERGENCY place my vote for LBJ
AND IN THE MIDST OF A PRESIDENTIAL CAMPAIGN THAT WILL END WITH A LANDSLIDE FOR LYNDON JOHNSON--
731
--AN INCIDENT OFF THE COAST OF VIETNAM BECOMES THE JUSTIFICATION FOR A GREATER AMERICAN PRESENCE THERE.

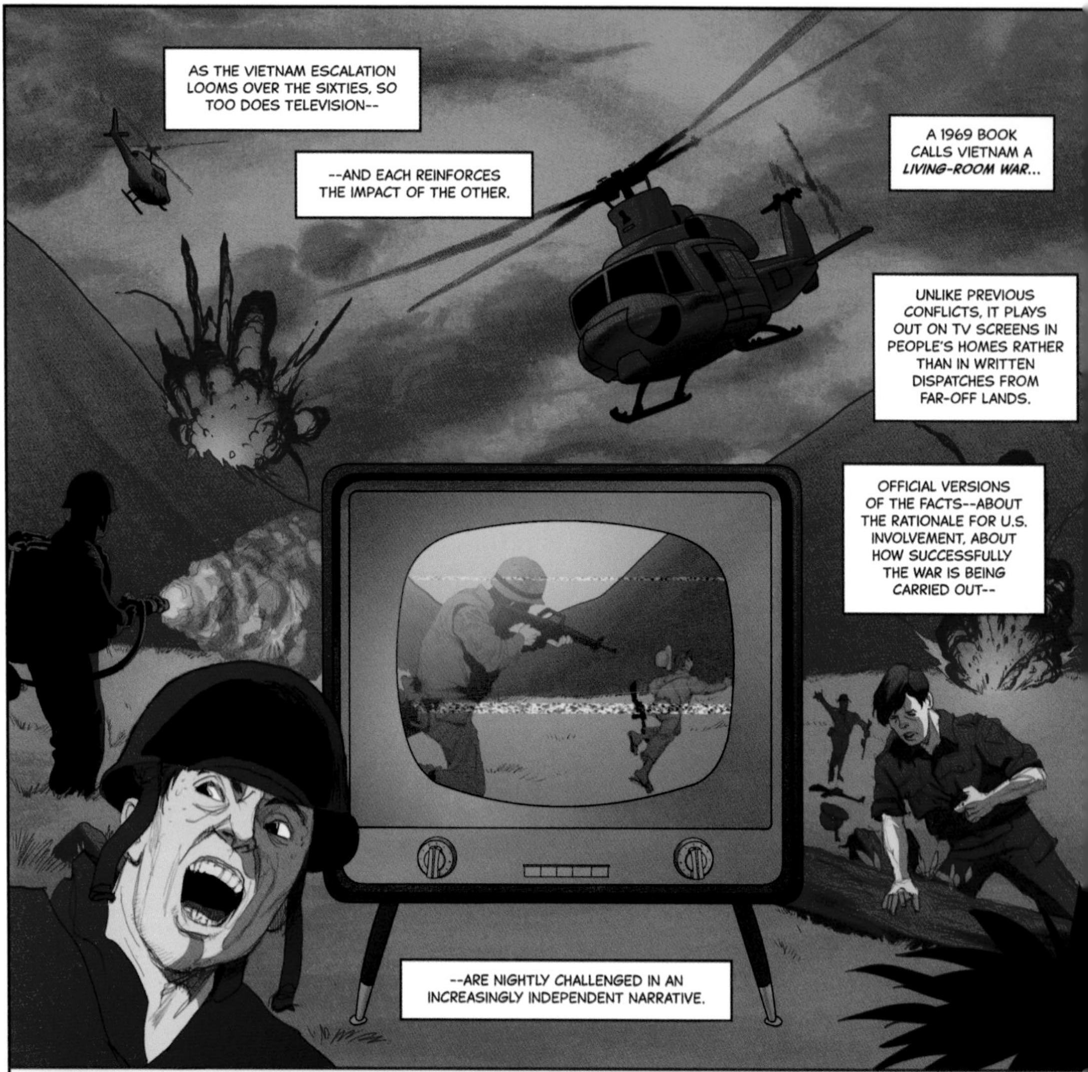
AS THE VIETNAM ESCALATION LOOMS OVER THE SIXTIES, SO TOO DOES TELEVISION--
--AND EACH REINFORCES THE IMPACT OF THE OTHER.
A 1969 BOOK CALLS VIETNAM A *LIVING-ROOM WAR*...
UNLIKE PREVIOUS CONFLICTS, IT PLAYS OUT ON TV SCREENS IN PEOPLE'S HOMES RATHER THAN IN WRITTEN DISPATCHES FROM FAR-OFF LANDS.
OFFICIAL VERSIONS OF THE FACTS--ABOUT THE RATIONALE FOR U.S. INVOLVEMENT, ABOUT HOW SUCCESSFULLY THE WAR IS BEING CARRIED OUT--
--ARE NIGHTLY CHALLENGED IN AN INCREASINGLY INDEPENDENT NARRATIVE.

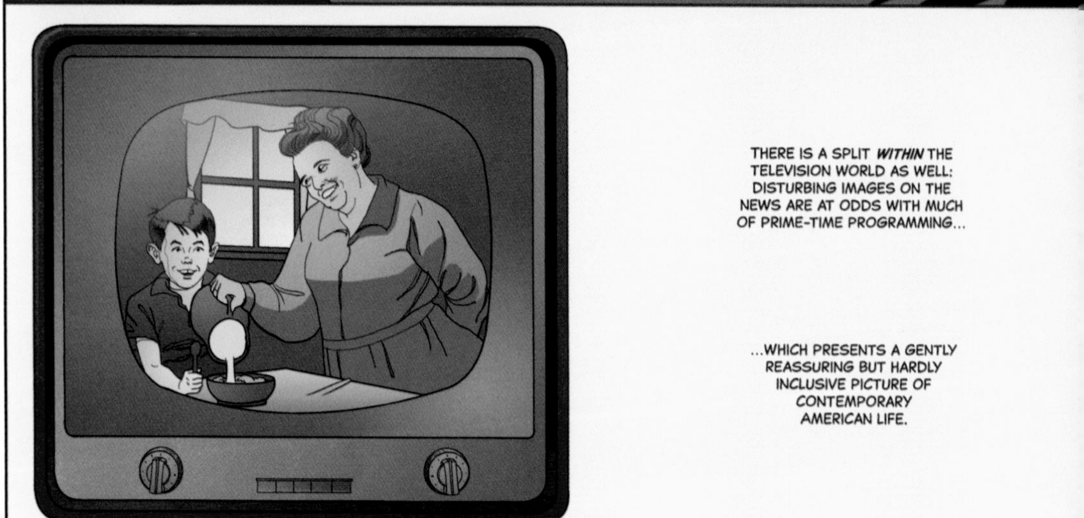
THERE IS A SPLIT *WITHIN* THE TELEVISION WORLD AS WELL: DISTURBING IMAGES ON THE NEWS ARE AT ODDS WITH MUCH OF PRIME-TIME PROGRAMMING...
...WHICH PRESENTS A GENTLY REASSURING BUT HARDLY INCLUSIVE PICTURE OF CONTEMPORARY AMERICAN LIFE.

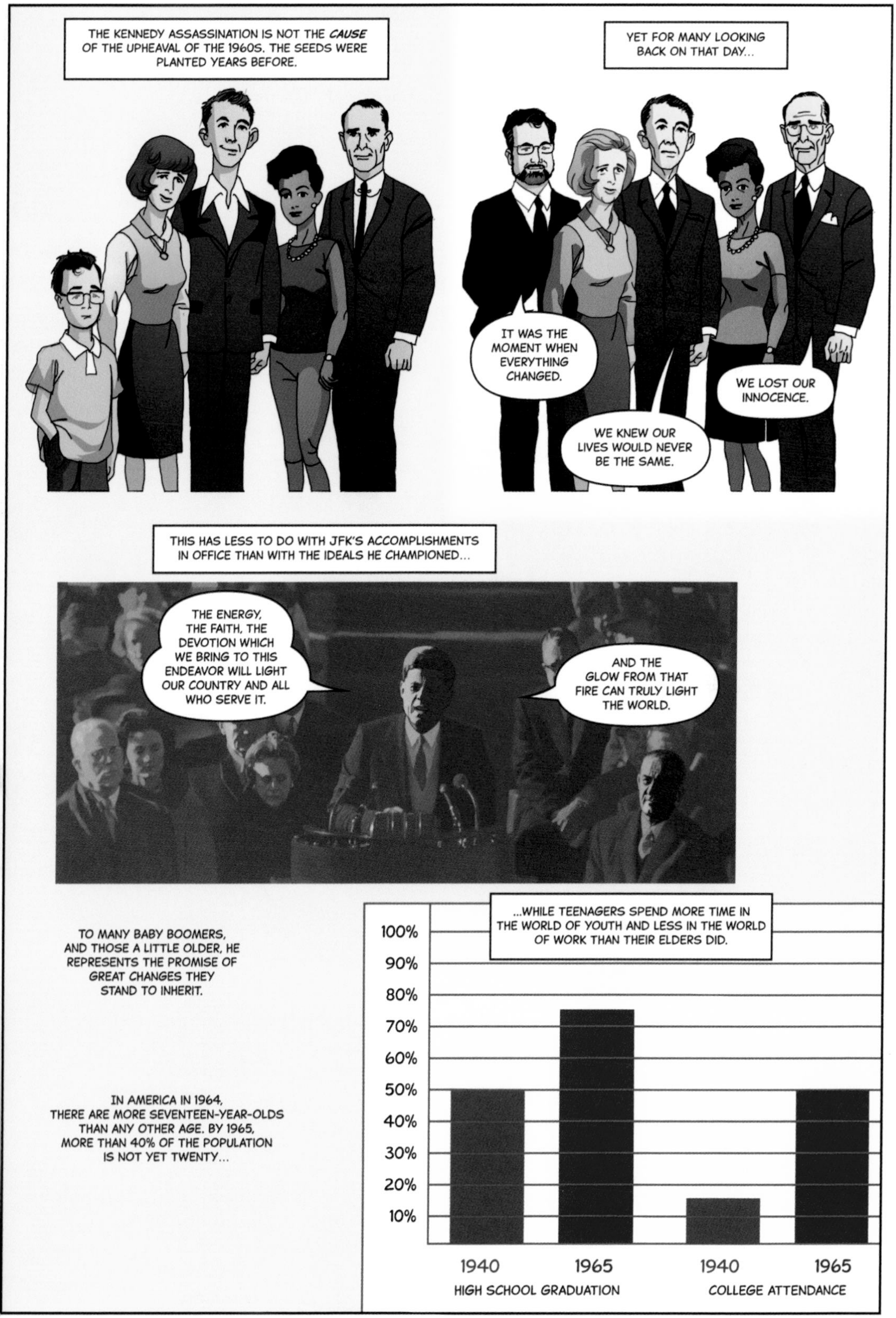
THE KENNEDY ASSASSINATION IS NOT THE *CAUSE* OF THE UPHEAVAL OF THE 1960S. THE SEEDS WERE PLANTED YEARS BEFORE.
YET FOR MANY LOOKING BACK ON THAT DAY...
IT WAS THE MOMENT WHEN EVERYTHING CHANGED.
WE KNEW OUR LIVES WOULD NEVER BE THE SAME.
WE LOST OUR INNOCENCE.
THIS HAS LESS TO DO WITH JFK'S ACCOMPLISHMENTS IN OFFICE THAN WITH THE IDEALS HE CHAMPIONED...
THE ENERGY, THE FAITH, THE DEVOTION WHICH WE BRING TO THIS ENDEAVOR WILL LIGHT OUR COUNTRY AND ALL WHO SERVE IT.
AND THE GLOW FROM THAT FIRE CAN TRULY LIGHT THE WORLD.
TO MANY BABY BOOMERS, AND THOSE A LITTLE OLDER, HE REPRESENTS THE PROMISE OF GREAT CHANGES THEY STAND TO INHERIT.
IN AMERICA IN 1964, THERE ARE MORE SEVENTEEN-YEAR-OLDS THAN ANY OTHER AGE. BY 1965, MORE THAN 40% OF THE POPULATION IS NOT YET TWENTY...
...WHILE TEENAGERS SPEND MORE TIME IN THE WORLD OF YOUTH AND LESS IN THE WORLD OF WORK THAN THEIR ELDERS DID.
100%
90%
80%
70%
60%
50%
40%
30%
20%
10%
1940
1965
1940
1965
HIGH SCHOOL GRADUATION
COLLEGE ATTENDANCE

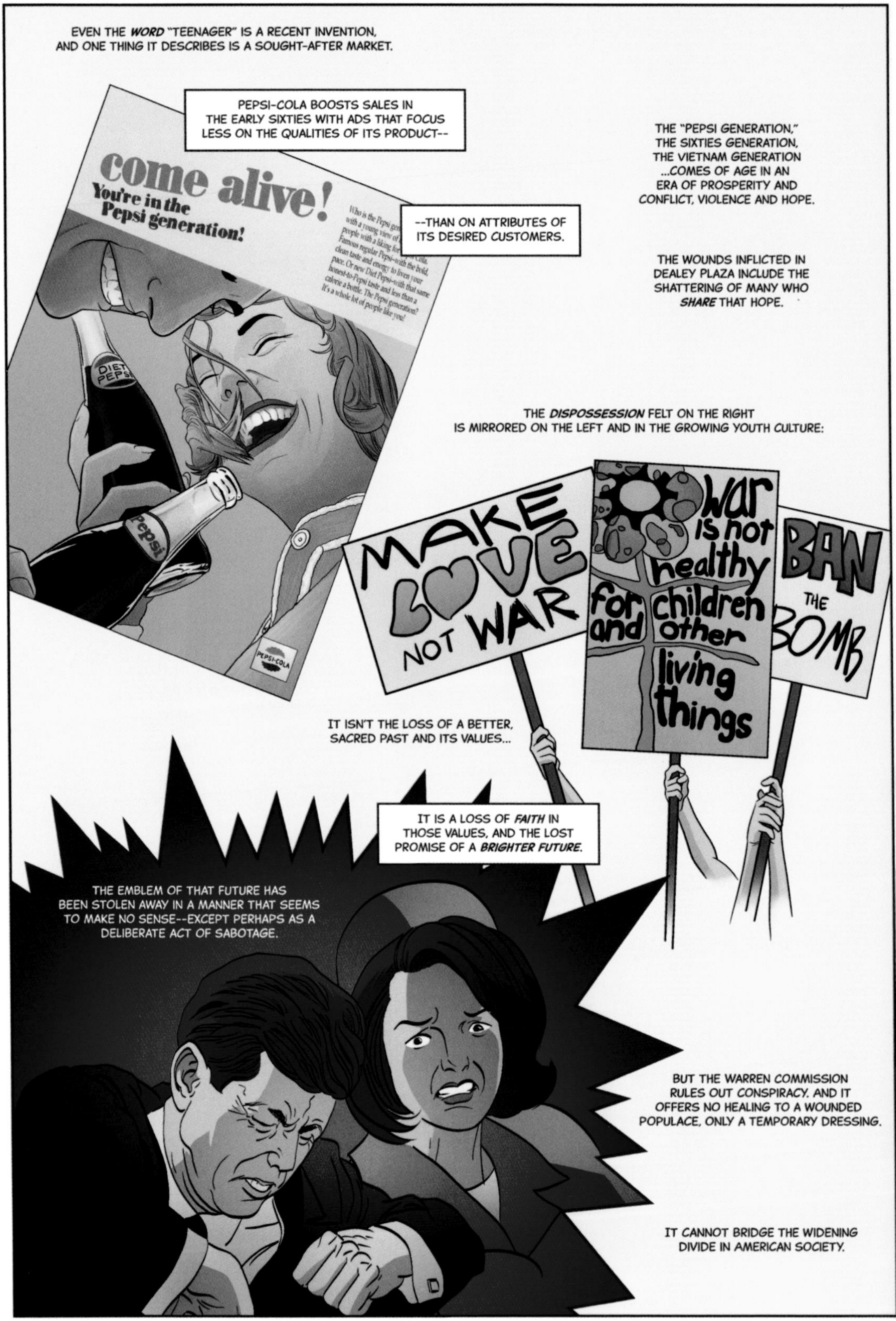
EVEN THE *WORD* "TEENAGER" IS A RECENT INVENTION, AND ONE THING IT DESCRIBES IS A SOUGHT-AFTER MARKET.
PEPSI-COLA BOOSTS SALES IN THE EARLY SIXTIES WITH ADS THAT FOCUS LESS ON THE QUALITIES OF ITS PRODUCT--
come alive!
You're in the Pepsi generation!
--THAN ON ATTRIBUTES OF ITS DESIRED CUSTOMERS.
DIET PEPSI
Pepsi
PEPSI-COLA
THE "PEPSI GENERATION," THE SIXTIES GENERATION, THE VIETNAM GENERATION ...COMES OF AGE IN AN ERA OF PROSPERITY AND CONFLICT, VIOLENCE AND HOPE.
THE WOUNDS INFLICTED IN DEALEY PLAZA INCLUDE THE SHATTERING OF MANY WHO *SHARE* THAT HOPE.
THE *DISPOSSESSION* FELT ON THE RIGHT IS MIRRORED ON THE LEFT AND IN THE GROWING YOUTH CULTURE:
MAKE LOVE NOT WAR
WAR is not healthy for children and other living things
BAN THE BOMB
IT ISN'T THE LOSS OF A BETTER, SACRED PAST AND ITS VALUES...
IT IS A LOSS OF *FAITH* IN THOSE VALUES, AND THE LOST PROMISE OF A *BRIGHTER FUTURE*.
THE EMBLEM OF THAT FUTURE HAS BEEN STOLEN AWAY IN A MANNER THAT SEEMS TO MAKE NO SENSE--EXCEPT PERHAPS AS A DELIBERATE ACT OF SABOTAGE.
BUT THE WARREN COMMISSION RULES OUT CONSPIRACY. AND IT OFFERS NO HEALING TO A WOUNDED POPULACE, ONLY A TEMPORARY DRESSING.
IT CANNOT BRIDGE THE WIDENING DIVIDE IN AMERICAN SOCIETY.

COVER-UP?

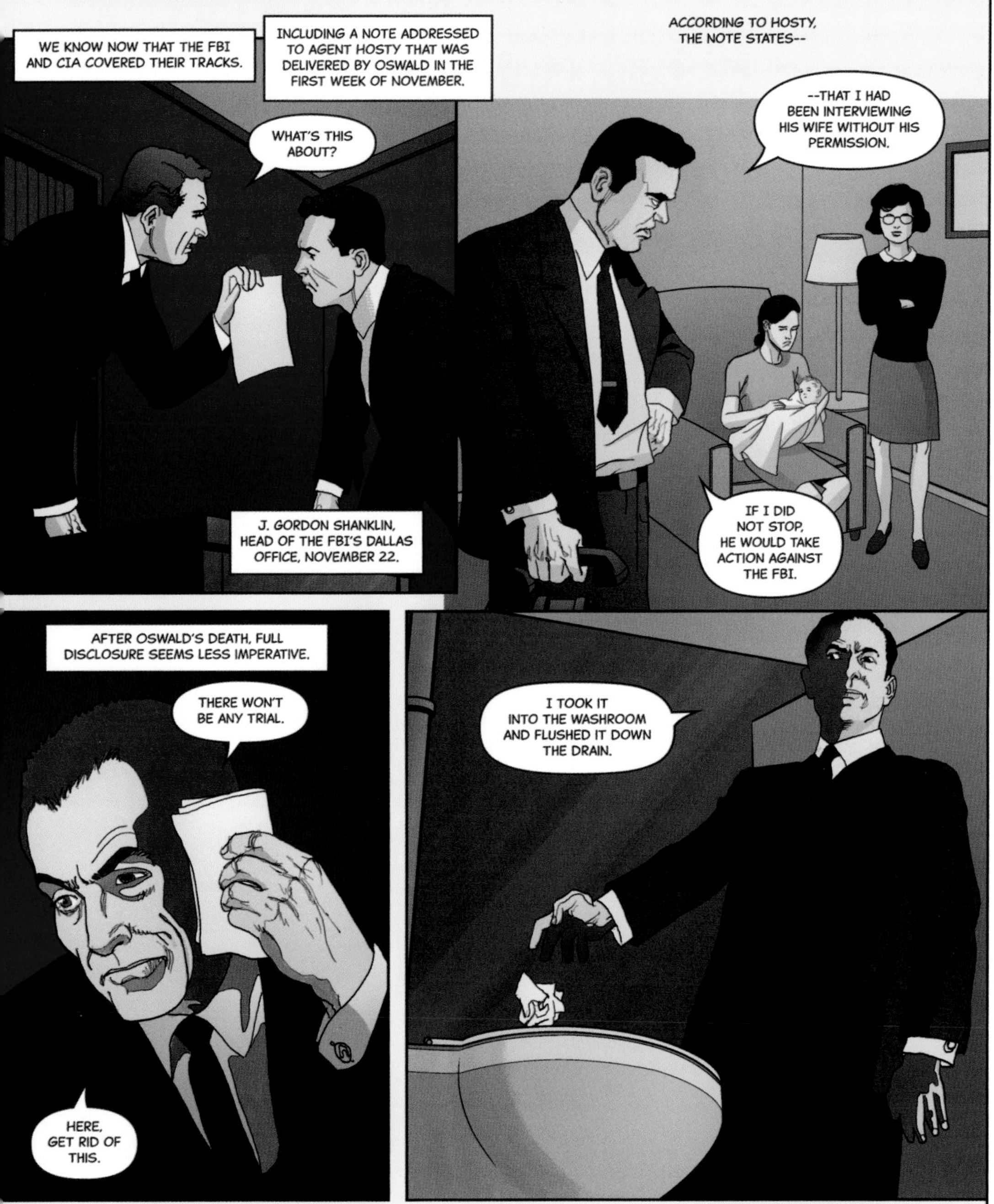
WE KNOW NOW THAT THE FBI AND CIA COVERED THEIR TRACKS.
INCLUDING A NOTE ADDRESSED TO AGENT HOSTY THAT WAS DELIVERED BY OSWALD IN THE FIRST WEEK OF NOVEMBER.
WHAT'S THIS ABOUT?
J. GORDON SHANKLIN, HEAD OF THE FBI'S DALLAS OFFICE, NOVEMBER 22.
ACCORDING TO HOSTY, THE NOTE STATES--
--THAT I HAD BEEN INTERVIEWING HIS WIFE WITHOUT HIS PERMISSION.
IF I DID NOT STOP, HE WOULD TAKE ACTION AGAINST THE FBI.
AFTER OSWALD'S DEATH, FULL DISCLOSURE SEEMS LESS IMPERATIVE.
THERE WON'T BE ANY TRIAL.
HERE, GET RID OF THIS.
I TOOK IT INTO THE WASHROOM AND FLUSHED IT DOWN THE DRAIN.

IT IS SUNDAY, NOVEMBER 24, THE SAME DAY DR. HUMES BURNS HIS ORIGINAL AUTOPSY NOTES.

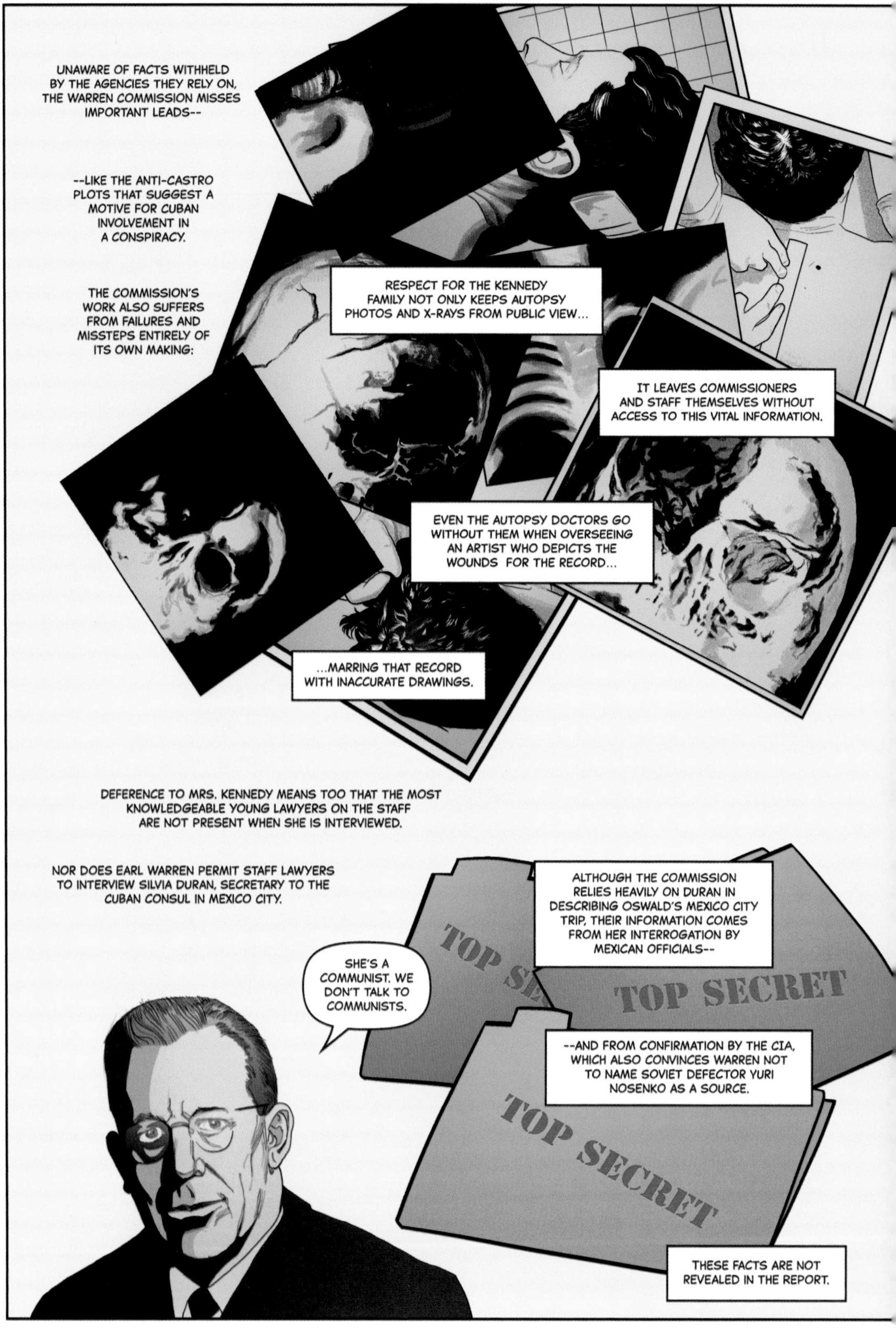
UNAWARE OF FACTS WITHHELD BY THE AGENCIES THEY RELY ON, THE WARREN COMMISSION MISSES IMPORTANT LEADS--
--LIKE THE ANTI-CASTRO PLOTS THAT SUGGEST A MOTIVE FOR CUBAN INVOLVEMENT IN A CONSPIRACY.
THE COMMISSION'S WORK ALSO SUFFERS FROM FAILURES AND MISSTEPS ENTIRELY OF ITS OWN MAKING:
RESPECT FOR THE KENNEDY FAMILY NOT ONLY KEEPS AUTOPSY PHOTOS AND X-RAYS FROM PUBLIC VIEW...
IT LEAVES COMMISSIONERS AND STAFF THEMSELVES WITHOUT ACCESS TO THIS VITAL INFORMATION.
EVEN THE AUTOPSY DOCTORS GO WITHOUT THEM WHEN OVERSEEING AN ARTIST WHO DEPICTS THE WOUNDS FOR THE RECORD...
...MARRING THAT RECORD WITH INACCURATE DRAWINGS.
DEFERENCE TO MRS. KENNEDY MEANS TOO THAT THE MOST KNOWLEDGEABLE YOUNG LAWYERS ON THE STAFF ARE NOT PRESENT WHEN SHE IS INTERVIEWED.
NOR DOES EARL WARREN PERMIT STAFF LAWYERS TO INTERVIEW SILVIA DURAN, SECRETARY TO THE CUBAN CONSUL IN MEXICO CITY.
ALTHOUGH THE COMMISSION RELIES HEAVILY ON DURAN IN DESCRIBING OSWALD'S MEXICO CITY TRIP, THEIR INFORMATION COMES FROM HER INTERROGATION BY MEXICAN OFFICIALS--
SHE'S A COMMUNIST. WE DON'T TALK TO COMMUNISTS.
TOP SECRET
TOP SECRET
--AND FROM CONFIRMATION BY THE CIA, WHICH ALSO CONVINCES WARREN NOT TO NAME SOVIET DEFECTOR YURI NOSENKO AS A SOURCE.
TOP SECRET
THESE FACTS ARE NOT REVEALED IN THE REPORT.

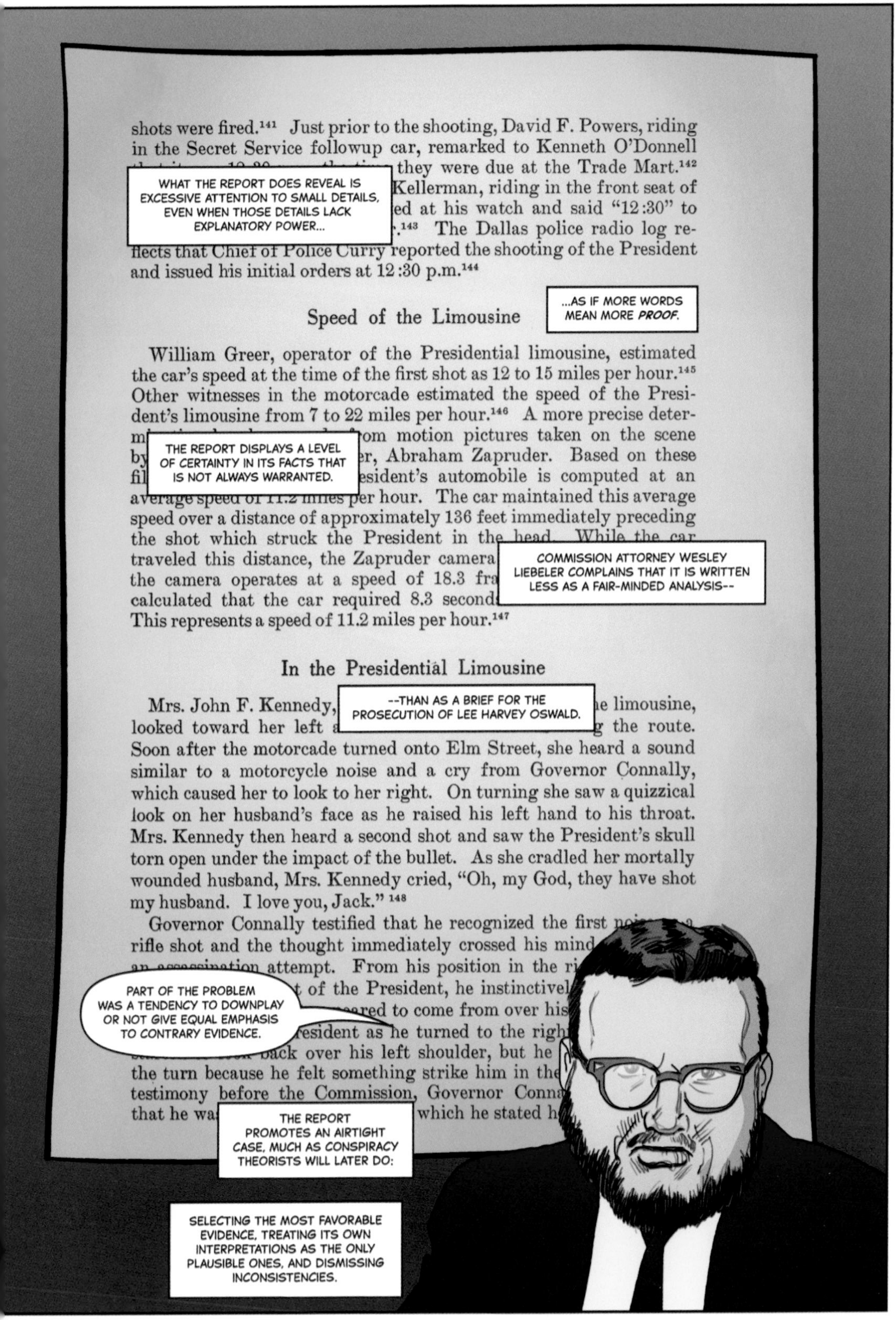

shots were fired.[141]   Just prior to the shooting, David F. Powers, riding in the Secret Service followup car, remarked to Kenneth O'Donnell

that it [was] 12:30 . . . the time they were due at the Trade Mart.[142]

WHAT THE REPORT DOES REVEAL IS EXCESSIVE ATTENTION TO SMALL DETAILS, EVEN WHEN THOSE DETAILS LACK EXPLANATORY POWER...

[...] Kellerman, riding in the front seat of [the limousine, look]ed at his watch and said "12:30" to [...].[143]   The Dallas police radio log reflects that Chief of Police Curry reported the shooting of the President and issued his initial orders at 12:30 p.m.[144]

Speed of the Limousine

...AS IF MORE WORDS MEAN MORE *PROOF.*

William Greer, operator of the Presidential limousine, estimated the car's speed at the time of the first shot as 12 to 15 miles per hour.[145] Other witnesses in the motorcade estimated the speed of the President's limousine from 7 to 22 miles per hour.[146]   A more precise deter-

THE REPORT DISPLAYS A LEVEL OF CERTAINTY IN ITS FACTS THAT IS NOT ALWAYS WARRANTED.

mination has been made from motion pictures taken on the scene by [an amateur photograph]er, Abraham Zapruder.   Based on these fil[ms, the speed of the Pr]esident's automobile is computed at an average speed of 11.2 miles per hour.   The car maintained this average speed over a distance of approximately 136 feet immediately preceding the shot which struck the President in the head.   While the car traveled this distance, the Zapruder camera [...]

COMMISSION ATTORNEY WESLEY LIEBELER *COMPLAINS* THAT IT IS WRITTEN LESS AS A FAIR-MINDED ANALYSIS--

the camera operates at a speed of 18.3 fra[mes ...] calculated that the car required 8.3 second[s ...] This represents a speed of 11.2 miles per hour.[147]

In the Presidential Limousine

Mrs. John F. Kennedy, [...in th]e limousine,

--THAN AS A BRIEF FOR THE PROSECUTION OF LEE HARVEY OSWALD.

looked toward her left a[...] the route. Soon after the motorcade turned onto Elm Street, she heard a sound similar to a motorcycle noise and a cry from Governor Connally, which caused her to look to her right.   On turning she saw a quizzical look on her husband's face as he raised his left hand to his throat. Mrs. Kennedy then heard a second shot and saw the President's skull torn open under the impact of the bullet.   As she cradled her mortally wounded husband, Mrs. Kennedy cried, "Oh, my God, they have shot my husband.   I love you, Jack." [148]

Governor Connally testified that he recognized the first no[ise as a] rifle shot and the thought immediately crossed his mind [...] an assassination attempt.   From his position in the ri[ght ...]

PART OF THE PROBLEM WAS A TENDENCY TO DOWNPLAY OR NOT GIVE EQUAL EMPHASIS TO CONTRARY EVIDENCE.

[...] of the President, he instinctivel[y ...] [app]eared to come from over his [...] [the Pr]esident as he turned to the righ[t ...] [...] back over his left shoulder, but he [...] the turn because he felt something strike him in the [...] testimony before the Commission, Governor Conna[lly ...] that he wa[s ...] which he stated h[e ...]

THE REPORT PROMOTES AN AIRTIGHT CASE, MUCH AS CONSPIRACY THEORISTS WILL LATER DO:

SELECTING THE MOST FAVORABLE EVIDENCE, TREATING ITS OWN INTERPRETATIONS AS THE ONLY PLAUSIBLE ONES, AND DISMISSING INCONSISTENCIES.

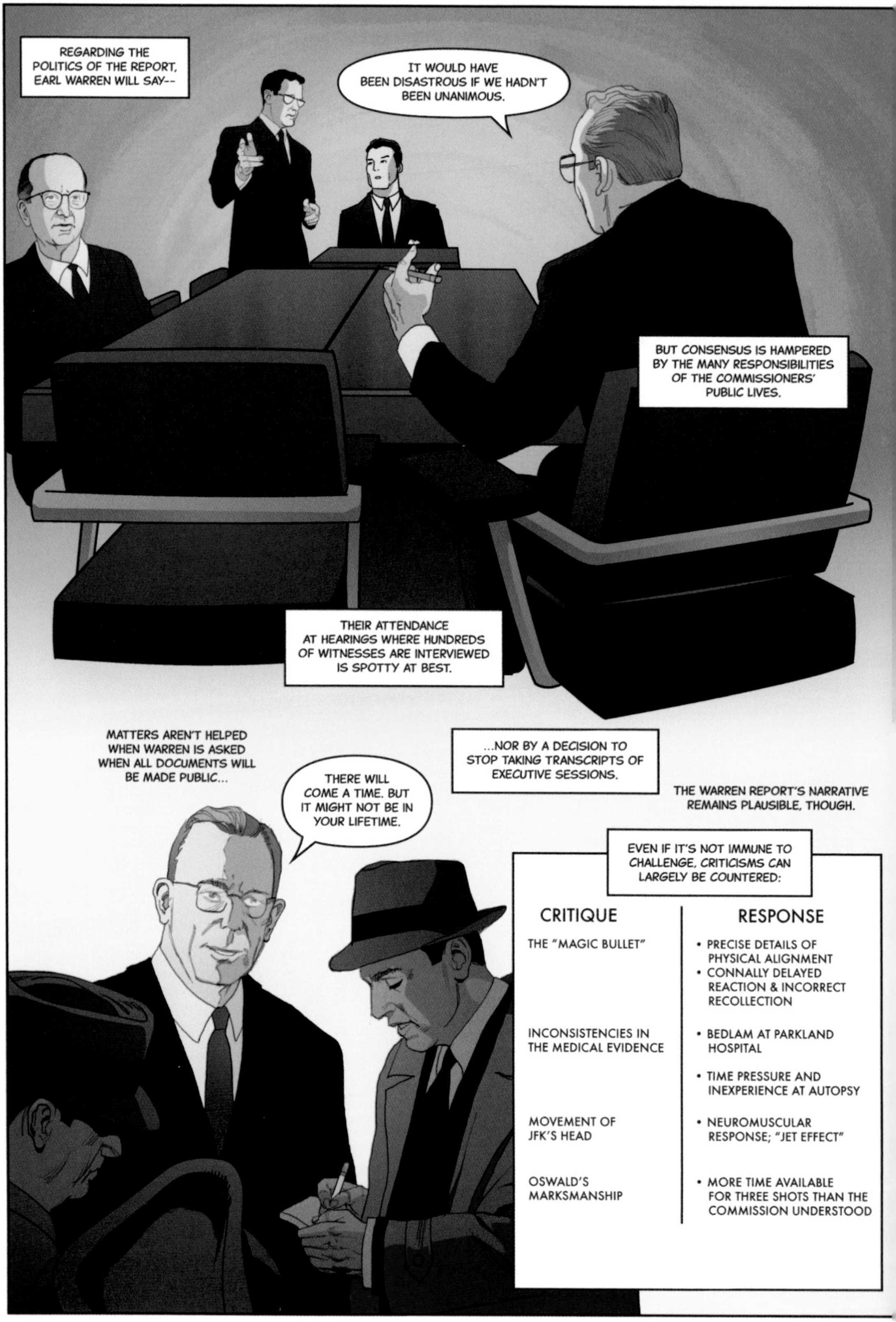
REGARDING THE POLITICS OF THE REPORT, EARL WARREN WILL SAY--
IT WOULD HAVE BEEN DISASTROUS IF WE HADN'T BEEN UNANIMOUS.
BUT CONSENSUS IS HAMPERED BY THE MANY RESPONSIBILITIES OF THE COMMISSIONERS' PUBLIC LIVES.
THEIR ATTENDANCE AT HEARINGS WHERE HUNDREDS OF WITNESSES ARE INTERVIEWED IS SPOTTY AT BEST.
MATTERS AREN'T HELPED WHEN WARREN IS ASKED WHEN ALL DOCUMENTS WILL BE MADE PUBLIC...
THERE WILL COME A TIME. BUT IT MIGHT NOT BE IN YOUR LIFETIME.
...NOR BY A DECISION TO STOP TAKING TRANSCRIPTS OF EXECUTIVE SESSIONS.
THE WARREN REPORT'S NARRATIVE REMAINS PLAUSIBLE, THOUGH.
EVEN IF IT'S NOT IMMUNE TO CHALLENGE, CRITICISMS CAN LARGELY BE COUNTERED:
CRITIQUE
RESPONSE
THE "MAGIC BULLET"
• PRECISE DETAILS OF PHYSICAL ALIGNMENT
• CONNALLY DELAYED REACTION & INCORRECT RECOLLECTION
INCONSISTENCIES IN THE MEDICAL EVIDENCE
• BEDLAM AT PARKLAND HOSPITAL
• TIME PRESSURE AND INEXPERIENCE AT AUTOPSY
MOVEMENT OF JFK'S HEAD
• NEUROMUSCULAR RESPONSE; "JET EFFECT"
OSWALD'S MARKSMANSHIP
• MORE TIME AVAILABLE FOR THREE SHOTS THAN THE COMMISSION UNDERSTOOD

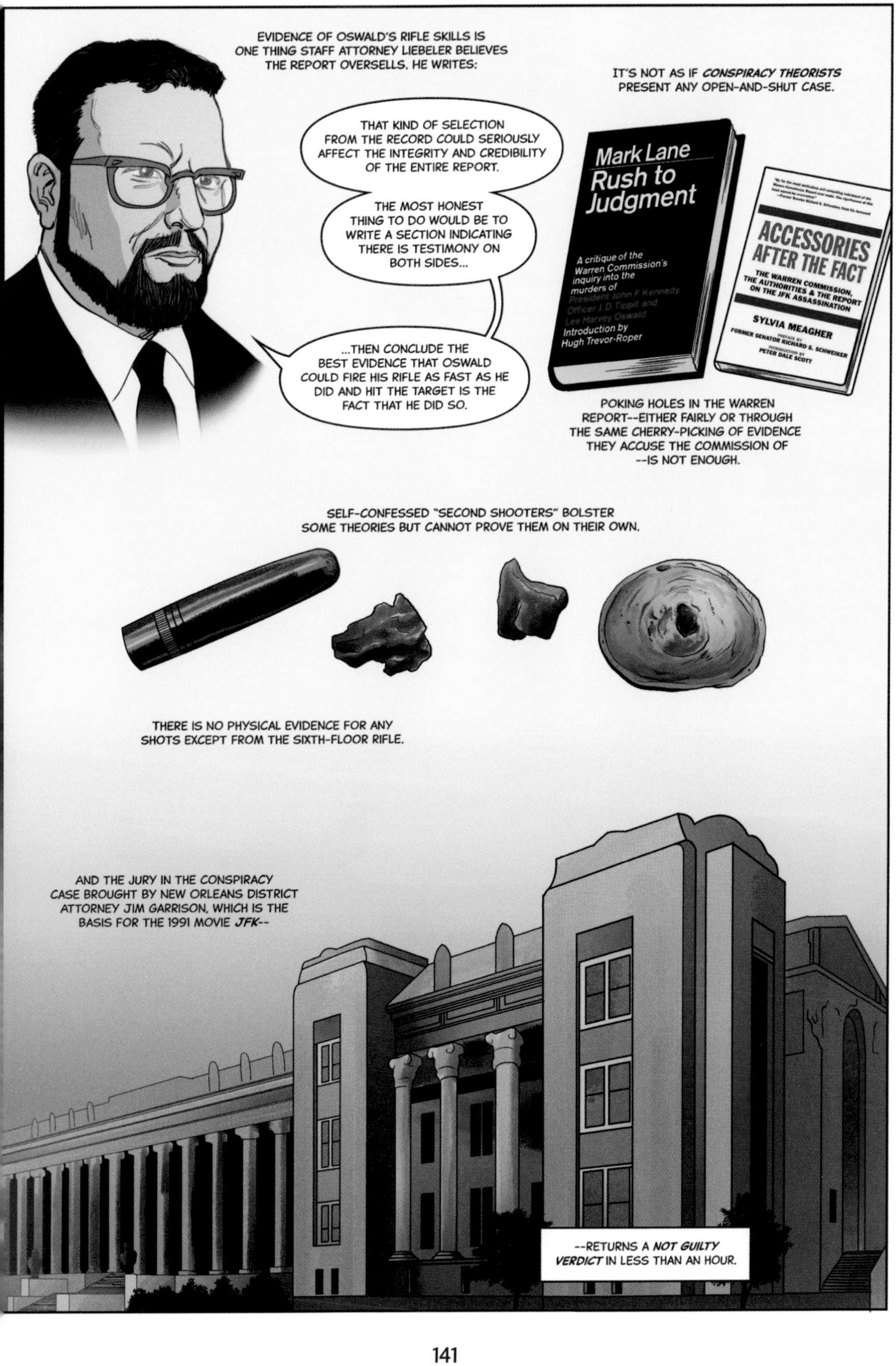
EVIDENCE OF OSWALD'S RIFLE SKILLS IS ONE THING STAFF ATTORNEY LIEBELER BELIEVES THE REPORT OVERSELLS. HE WRITES:
THAT KIND OF SELECTION FROM THE RECORD COULD SERIOUSLY AFFECT THE INTEGRITY AND CREDIBILITY OF THE ENTIRE REPORT.
THE MOST HONEST THING TO DO WOULD BE TO WRITE A SECTION INDICATING THERE IS TESTIMONY ON BOTH SIDES...
...THEN CONCLUDE THE BEST EVIDENCE THAT OSWALD COULD FIRE HIS RIFLE AS FAST AS HE DID AND HIT THE TARGET IS THE FACT THAT HE DID SO.
IT'S NOT AS IF *CONSPIRACY THEORISTS* PRESENT ANY OPEN-AND-SHUT CASE.
Mark Lane
Rush to Judgment
A critique of the Warren Commission's inquiry into the murders of President John F Kennedy, Officer J. D Tippit and Lee Harvey Oswald
Introduction by Hugh Trevor-Roper
ACCESSORIES AFTER THE FACT
THE WARREN COMMISSION, THE AUTHORITIES & THE REPORT ON THE JFK ASSASSINATION
SYLVIA MEAGHER
PREFACE BY FORMER SENATOR RICHARD S. SCHWEIKER
INTRODUCTION BY PETER DALE SCOTT
POKING HOLES IN THE WARREN REPORT--EITHER FAIRLY OR THROUGH THE SAME CHERRY-PICKING OF EVIDENCE THEY ACCUSE THE COMMISSION OF --IS NOT ENOUGH.
SELF-CONFESSED "SECOND SHOOTERS" BOLSTER SOME THEORIES BUT CANNOT PROVE THEM ON THEIR OWN.
THERE IS NO PHYSICAL EVIDENCE FOR ANY SHOTS EXCEPT FROM THE SIXTH-FLOOR RIFLE.
AND THE JURY IN THE CONSPIRACY CASE BROUGHT BY NEW ORLEANS DISTRICT ATTORNEY JIM GARRISON, WHICH IS THE BASIS FOR THE 1991 MOVIE *JFK*--
--RETURNS A *NOT GUILTY VERDICT* IN LESS THAN AN HOUR.

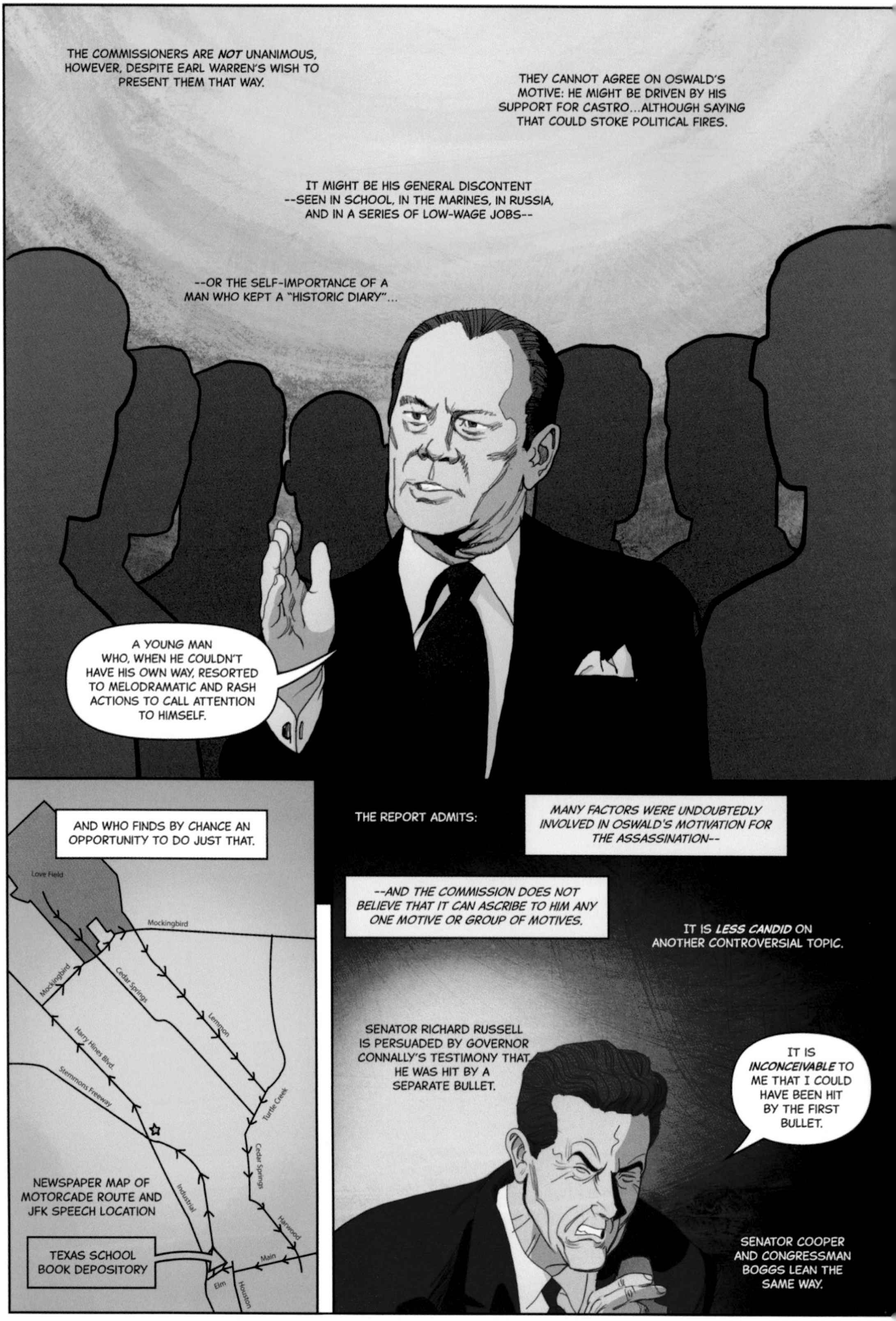
THE COMMISSIONERS ARE *NOT* UNANIMOUS, HOWEVER, DESPITE EARL WARREN'S WISH TO PRESENT THEM THAT WAY.
THEY CANNOT AGREE ON OSWALD'S MOTIVE: HE MIGHT BE DRIVEN BY HIS SUPPORT FOR CASTRO...ALTHOUGH SAYING THAT COULD STOKE POLITICAL FIRES.
IT MIGHT BE HIS GENERAL DISCONTENT --SEEN IN SCHOOL, IN THE MARINES, IN RUSSIA, AND IN A SERIES OF LOW-WAGE JOBS--
--OR THE SELF-IMPORTANCE OF A MAN WHO KEPT A "HISTORIC DIARY"...
A YOUNG MAN WHO, WHEN HE COULDN'T HAVE HIS OWN WAY, RESORTED TO MELODRAMATIC AND RASH ACTIONS TO CALL ATTENTION TO HIMSELF.
AND WHO FINDS BY CHANCE AN OPPORTUNITY TO DO JUST THAT.
Love Field
Mockingbird
Mockingbird
Cedar Springs
Lemmon
Harry Hines Blvd
Stemmons Freeway
Turtle Creek
Cedar Springs
Industrial
Harwood
Main
Elm
Houston
NEWSPAPER MAP OF MOTORCADE ROUTE AND JFK SPEECH LOCATION
TEXAS SCHOOL BOOK DEPOSITORY
THE REPORT ADMITS:
MANY FACTORS WERE UNDOUBTEDLY INVOLVED IN OSWALD'S MOTIVATION FOR THE ASSASSINATION--
--AND THE COMMISSION DOES NOT BELIEVE THAT IT CAN ASCRIBE TO HIM ANY ONE MOTIVE OR GROUP OF MOTIVES.
IT IS ***LESS CANDID*** ON ANOTHER CONTROVERSIAL TOPIC.
SENATOR RICHARD RUSSELL IS PERSUADED BY GOVERNOR CONNALLY'S TESTIMONY THAT HE WAS HIT BY A SEPARATE BULLET.
IT IS ***INCONCEIVABLE*** TO ME THAT I COULD HAVE BEEN HIT BY THE FIRST BULLET.
SENATOR COOPER AND CONGRESSMAN BOGGS LEAN THE SAME WAY.

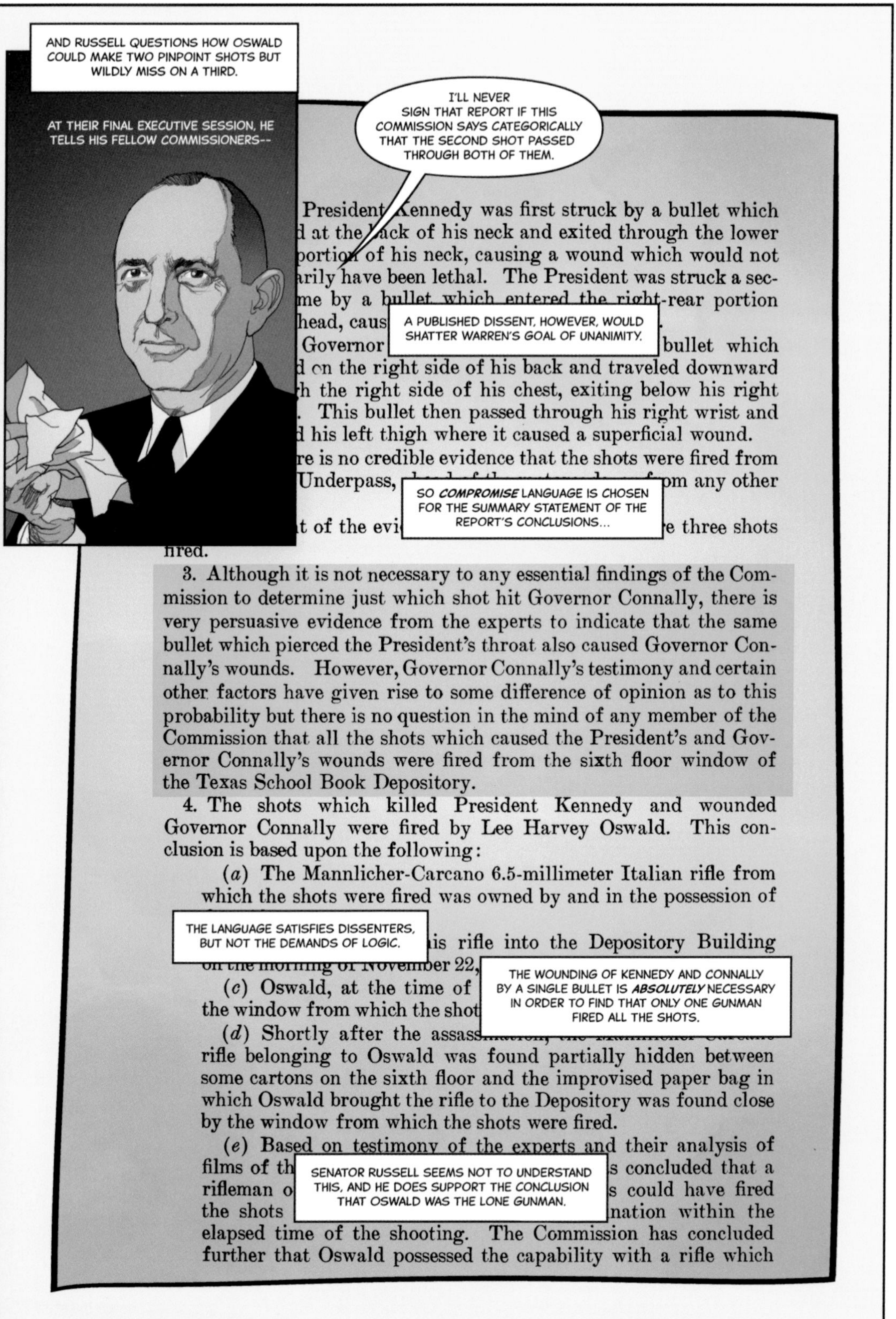
AND RUSSELL QUESTIONS HOW OSWALD COULD MAKE TWO PINPOINT SHOTS BUT WILDLY MISS ON A THIRD.
AT THEIR FINAL EXECUTIVE SESSION, HE TELLS HIS FELLOW COMMISSIONERS--
I'LL NEVER SIGN THAT REPORT IF THIS COMMISSION SAYS CATEGORICALLY THAT THE SECOND SHOT PASSED THROUGH BOTH OF THEM.
President Kennedy was first struck by a bullet which
d at the back of his neck and exited through the lower
portion of his neck, causing a wound which would not
arily have been lethal. The President was struck a sec-
me by a
-rear portion
head, caus
A PUBLISHED DISSENT, HOWEVER, WOULD SHATTER WARREN'S GOAL OF UNANIMITY.
Governor
bullet which
d on the right side of his back and traveled downward
h the right side of his chest, exiting below his right
. This bullet then passed through his right wrist and
d his left thigh where it caused a superficial wound.
re is no credible evidence that the shots were fired from
Underpass,
om any other
SO COMPROMISE LANGUAGE IS CHOSEN FOR THE SUMMARY STATEMENT OF THE REPORT'S CONCLUSIONS...
t of the evi
e three shots
fired.
3. Although it is not necessary to any essential findings of the Commission to determine just which shot hit Governor Connally, there is very persuasive evidence from the experts to indicate that the same bullet which pierced the President's throat also caused Governor Connally's wounds. However, Governor Connally's testimony and certain other factors have given rise to some difference of opinion as to this probability but there is no question in the mind of any member of the Commission that all the shots which caused the President's and Governor Connally's wounds were fired from the sixth floor window of the Texas School Book Depository.
4. The shots which killed President Kennedy and wounded Governor Connally were fired by Lee Harvey Oswald. This conclusion is based upon the following:
(a) The Mannlicher-Carcano 6.5-millimeter Italian rifle from which the shots were fired was owned by and in the possession of
THE LANGUAGE SATISFIES DISSENTERS, BUT NOT THE DEMANDS OF LOGIC.
is rifle into the Depository Building
ber 22,
(c) Oswald, at the time of
the window from which the shot
THE WOUNDING OF KENNEDY AND CONNALLY BY A SINGLE BULLET IS ABSOLUTELY NECESSARY IN ORDER TO FIND THAT ONLY ONE GUNMAN FIRED ALL THE SHOTS.
(d) Shortly after the assass
rifle belonging to Oswald was found partially hidden between some cartons on the sixth floor and the improvised paper bag in which Oswald brought the rifle to the Depository was found close by the window from which the shots were fired.
(e) Based on testimony of the experts and their analysis of
films of th
s concluded that a
rifleman o
s could have fired
the shots
nation within the
SENATOR RUSSELL SEEMS NOT TO UNDERSTAND THIS, AND HE DOES SUPPORT THE CONCLUSION THAT OSWALD WAS THE LONE GUNMAN.
elapsed time of the shooting. The Commission has concluded further that Oswald possessed the capability with a rifle which

THE WARREN REPORT MIGHT BE CORRECT IN ITS OVERALL CONCLUSIONS, AND IN MOST OF ITS FACTS.

BUT IN OVERSTATING ITS CONFIDENCE AND DISMISSING UNCERTAINTY--

--IN ITS WELL-INTENDED EFFORT TO QUIET FEARS--

--AND IN ITS LACK OF TRANSPARENCY...

THE COMMISSION ACTS IN WAYS THAT ARE HARD TO DISTINGUISH FROM A COVER-UP.

AS PREDICTED BY STAFF, THE REPORT PLANTS--

SEEDS OF DOUBT

--THAT WILL GROW TO PLAGUE ITS ACCEPTANCE.

IT IS AN ERA OF GROWING SKEPTICISM AND CHALLENGE TO AUTHORITY...

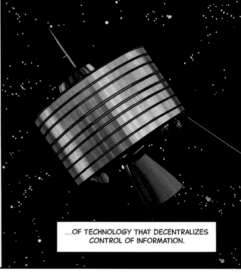

...OF TECHNOLOGY THAT DECENTRALIZES CONTROL OF INFORMATION.

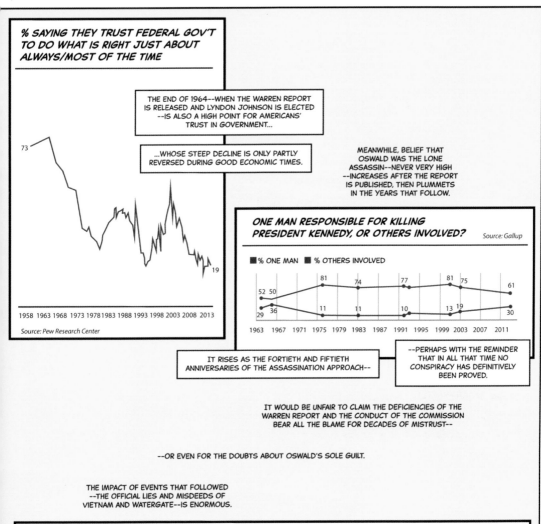

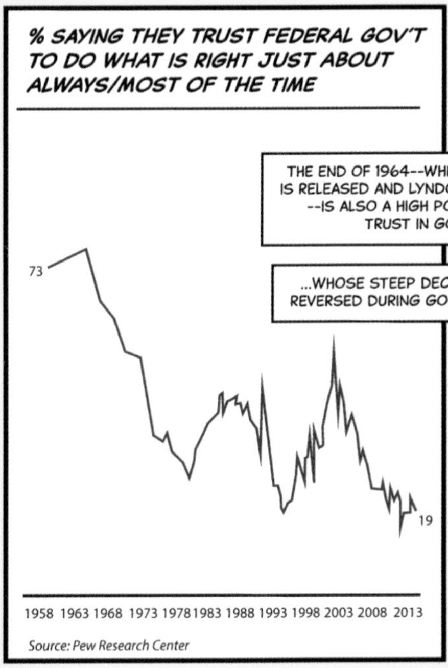
% SAYING THEY TRUST FEDERAL GOV'T TO DO WHAT IS RIGHT JUST ABOUT ALWAYS/MOST OF THE TIME
73
19
1958 1963 1968 1973 1978 1983 1988 1993 1998 2003 2008 2013
Source: Pew Research Center

THE END OF 1964--WHEN THE WARREN REPORT IS RELEASED AND LYNDON JOHNSON IS ELECTED --IS ALSO A HIGH POINT FOR AMERICANS' TRUST IN GOVERNMENT...

...WHOSE STEEP DECLINE IS ONLY PARTLY REVERSED DURING GOOD ECONOMIC TIMES.

MEANWHILE, BELIEF THAT OSWALD WAS THE LONE ASSASSIN--NEVER VERY HIGH --INCREASES AFTER THE REPORT IS PUBLISHED, THEN PLUMMETS IN THE YEARS THAT FOLLOW.

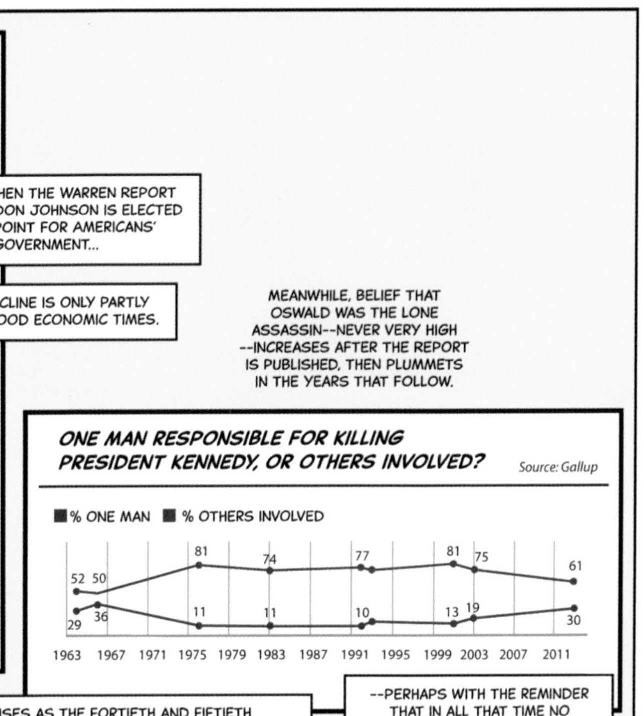
ONE MAN RESPONSIBLE FOR KILLING PRESIDENT KENNEDY, OR OTHERS INVOLVED?
Source: Gallup
% ONE MAN
% OTHERS INVOLVED
52 50 81 74 77 81 75 61
29 36 11 11 10 13 19 30
1963 1967 1971 1975 1979 1983 1987 1991 1995 1999 2003 2007 2011

IT RISES AS THE FORTIETH AND FIFTIETH ANNIVERSARIES OF THE ASSASSINATION APPROACH--

--PERHAPS WITH THE REMINDER THAT IN ALL THAT TIME NO CONSPIRACY HAS DEFINITIVELY BEEN PROVED.

IT WOULD BE UNFAIR TO CLAIM THE DEFICIENCIES OF THE WARREN REPORT AND THE CONDUCT OF THE COMMISSION BEAR ALL THE BLAME FOR DECADES OF MISTRUST--

--OR EVEN FOR THE DOUBTS ABOUT OSWALD'S SOLE GUILT.

THE IMPACT OF EVENTS THAT FOLLOWED --THE OFFICIAL LIES AND MISDEEDS OF VIETNAM AND WATERGATE--IS ENORMOUS.

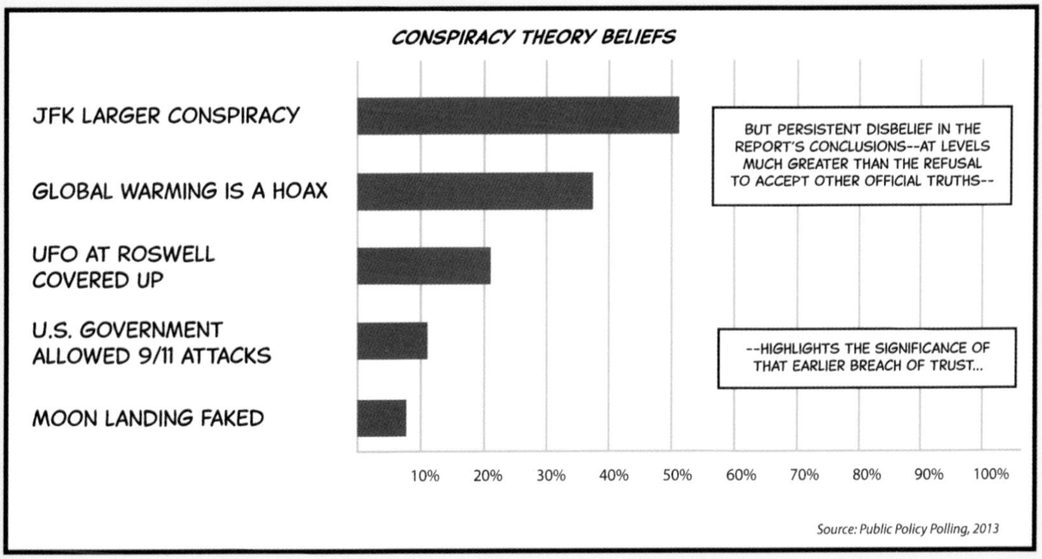
CONSPIRACY THEORY BELIEFS
JFK LARGER CONSPIRACY
GLOBAL WARMING IS A HOAX
UFO AT ROSWELL COVERED UP
U.S. GOVERNMENT ALLOWED 9/11 ATTACKS
MOON LANDING FAKED
10% 20% 30% 40% 50% 60% 70% 80% 90% 100%
Source: Public Policy Polling, 2013

BUT PERSISTENT DISBELIEF IN THE REPORT'S CONCLUSIONS--AT LEVELS MUCH GREATER THAN THE REFUSAL TO ACCEPT OTHER OFFICIAL TRUTHS--

--HIGHLIGHTS THE SIGNIFICANCE OF THAT EARLIER BREACH OF TRUST...

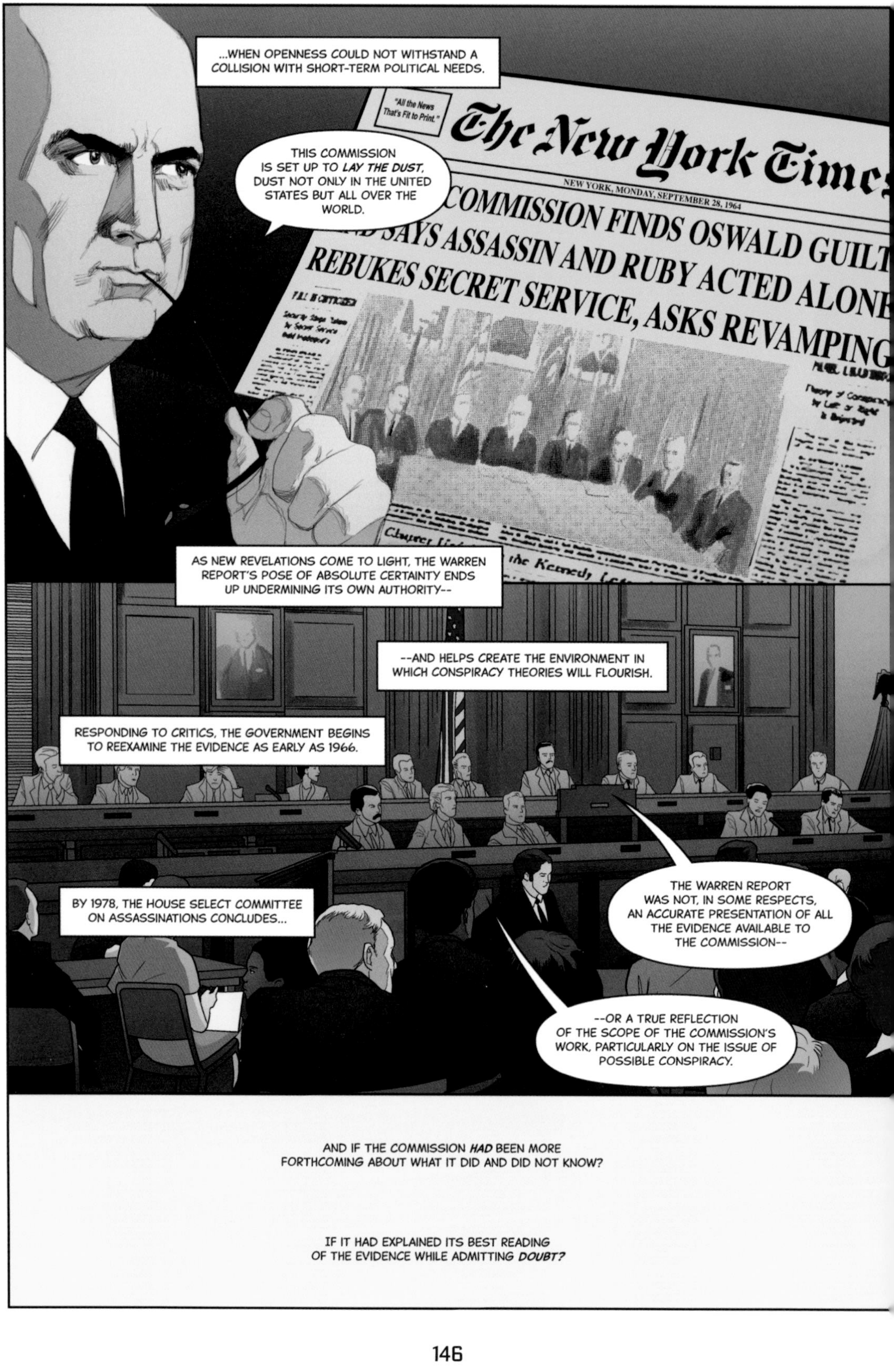
...WHEN OPENNESS COULD NOT WITHSTAND A COLLISION WITH SHORT-TERM POLITICAL NEEDS.
"All the News That's Fit to Print."
NEW YORK, MONDAY, SEPTEMBER 28, 1964
COMMISSION FINDS OSWALD
SAYS ASSASSIN AND RUBY ACTED
REBUKES SECRET SERVICE, ASKS
THIS COMMISSION IS SET UP TO *LAY THE DUST*, DUST NOT ONLY IN THE UNITED STATES BUT ALL OVER THE WORLD.
AS NEW REVELATIONS COME TO LIGHT, THE WARREN REPORT'S POSE OF ABSOLUTE CERTAINTY ENDS UP UNDERMINING ITS OWN AUTHORITY--
--AND HELPS CREATE THE ENVIRONMENT IN WHICH CONSPIRACY THEORIES WILL FLOURISH.
RESPONDING TO CRITICS, THE GOVERNMENT BEGINS TO REEXAMINE THE EVIDENCE AS EARLY AS 1966.
BY 1978, THE HOUSE SELECT COMMITTEE ON ASSASSINATIONS CONCLUDES...
THE WARREN REPORT WAS NOT, IN SOME RESPECTS, AN ACCURATE PRESENTATION OF ALL THE EVIDENCE AVAILABLE TO THE COMMISSION--
--OR A TRUE REFLECTION OF THE SCOPE OF THE COMMISSION'S WORK, PARTICULARLY ON THE ISSUE OF POSSIBLE CONSPIRACY.
AND IF THE COMMISSION *HAD* BEEN MORE FORTHCOMING ABOUT WHAT IT DID AND DID NOT KNOW?
IF IT HAD EXPLAINED ITS BEST READING OF THE EVIDENCE WHILE ADMITTING *DOUBT?*

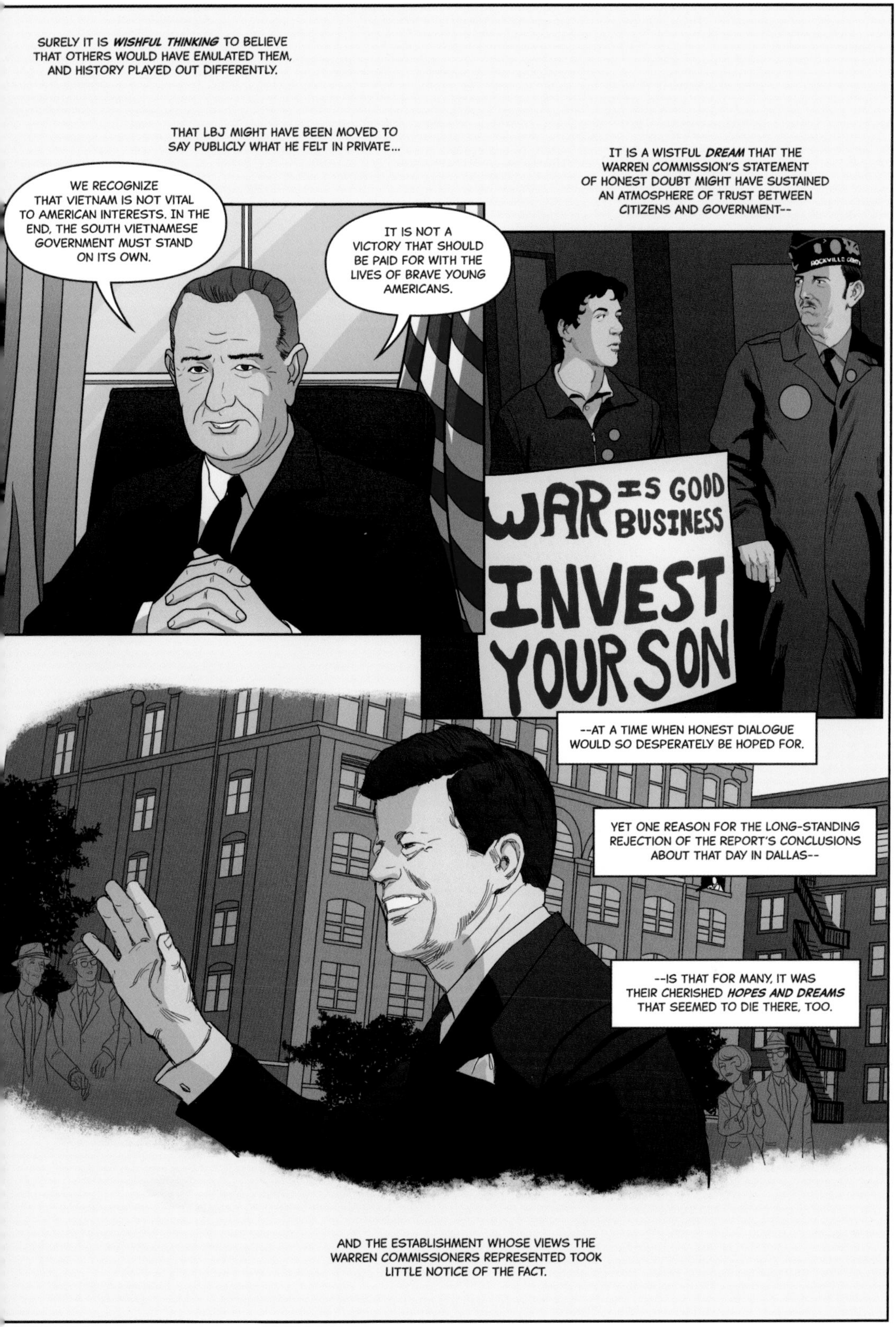
SURELY IT IS ***WISHFUL THINKING*** TO BELIEVE THAT OTHERS WOULD HAVE EMULATED THEM, AND HISTORY PLAYED OUT DIFFERENTLY.
THAT LBJ MIGHT HAVE BEEN MOVED TO SAY PUBLICLY WHAT HE FELT IN PRIVATE...
WE RECOGNIZE THAT VIETNAM IS NOT VITAL TO AMERICAN INTERESTS. IN THE END, THE SOUTH VIETNAMESE GOVERNMENT MUST STAND ON ITS OWN.
IT IS NOT A VICTORY THAT SHOULD BE PAID FOR WITH THE LIVES OF BRAVE YOUNG AMERICANS.
IT IS A WISTFUL ***DREAM*** THAT THE WARREN COMMISSION'S STATEMENT OF HONEST DOUBT MIGHT HAVE SUSTAINED AN ATMOSPHERE OF TRUST BETWEEN CITIZENS AND GOVERNMENT--
WAR IS GOOD BUSINESS
INVEST YOUR SON
--AT A TIME WHEN HONEST DIALOGUE WOULD SO DESPERATELY BE HOPED FOR.
YET ONE REASON FOR THE LONG-STANDING REJECTION OF THE REPORT'S CONCLUSIONS ABOUT THAT DAY IN DALLAS--
--IS THAT FOR MANY, IT WAS THEIR CHERISHED ***HOPES AND DREAMS*** THAT SEEMED TO DIE THERE, TOO.
AND THE ESTABLISHMENT WHOSE VIEWS THE WARREN COMMISSIONERS REPRESENTED TOOK LITTLE NOTICE OF THE FACT.

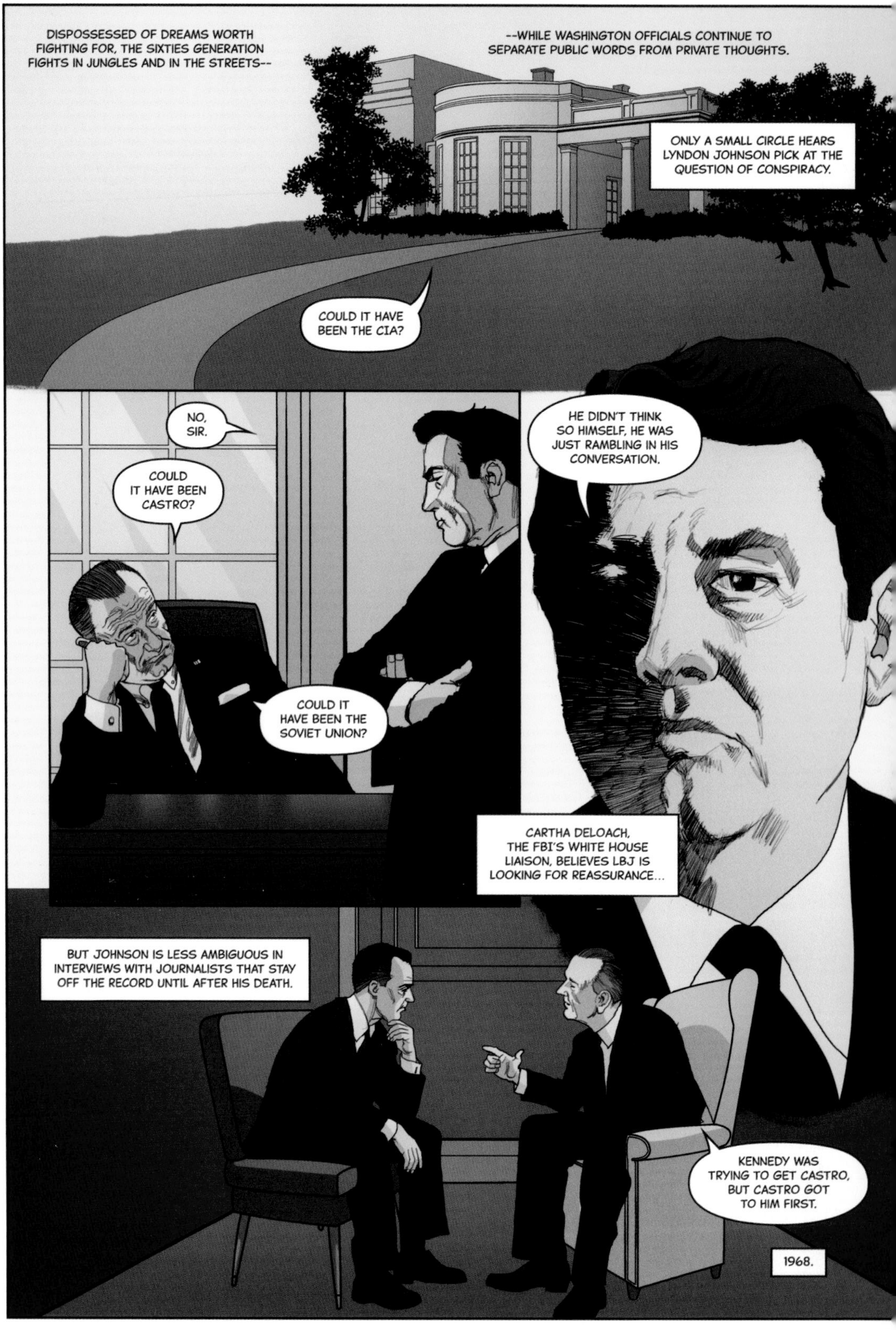
DISPOSSESSED OF DREAMS WORTH FIGHTING FOR, THE SIXTIES GENERATION FIGHTS IN JUNGLES AND IN THE STREETS--
--WHILE WASHINGTON OFFICIALS CONTINUE TO SEPARATE PUBLIC WORDS FROM PRIVATE THOUGHTS.
ONLY A SMALL CIRCLE HEARS LYNDON JOHNSON PICK AT THE QUESTION OF CONSPIRACY.
COULD IT HAVE BEEN THE CIA?
NO, SIR.
COULD IT HAVE BEEN CASTRO?
COULD IT HAVE BEEN THE SOVIET UNION?
HE DIDN'T THINK SO HIMSELF, HE WAS JUST RAMBLING IN HIS CONVERSATION.
CARTHA DELOACH, THE FBI'S WHITE HOUSE LIAISON, BELIEVES LBJ IS LOOKING FOR REASSURANCE...
BUT JOHNSON IS LESS AMBIGUOUS IN INTERVIEWS WITH JOURNALISTS THAT STAY OFF THE RECORD UNTIL AFTER HIS DEATH.
KENNEDY WAS TRYING TO GET CASTRO, BUT CASTRO GOT TO HIM FIRST.
1968.

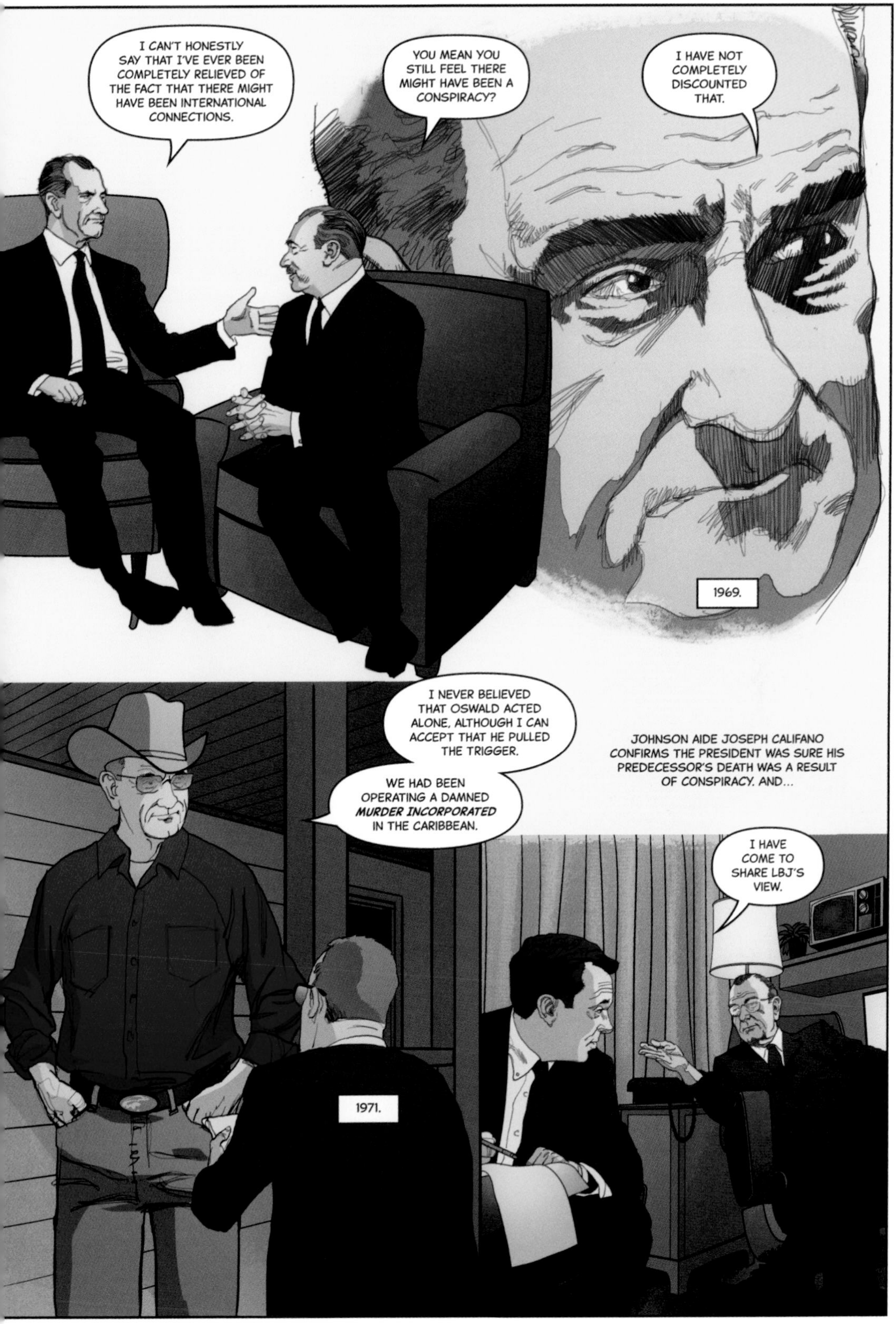
I CAN'T HONESTLY SAY THAT I'VE EVER BEEN COMPLETELY RELIEVED OF THE FACT THAT THERE MIGHT HAVE BEEN INTERNATIONAL CONNECTIONS.
YOU MEAN YOU STILL FEEL THERE MIGHT HAVE BEEN A CONSPIRACY?
I HAVE NOT COMPLETELY DISCOUNTED THAT.
1969.
I NEVER BELIEVED THAT OSWALD ACTED ALONE, ALTHOUGH I CAN ACCEPT THAT HE PULLED THE TRIGGER.
WE HAD BEEN OPERATING A DAMNED ***MURDER INCORPORATED*** IN THE CARIBBEAN.
1971.
JOHNSON AIDE JOSEPH CALIFANO CONFIRMS THE PRESIDENT WAS SURE HIS PREDECESSOR'S DEATH WAS A RESULT OF CONSPIRACY. AND...
I HAVE COME TO SHARE LBJ'S VIEW.

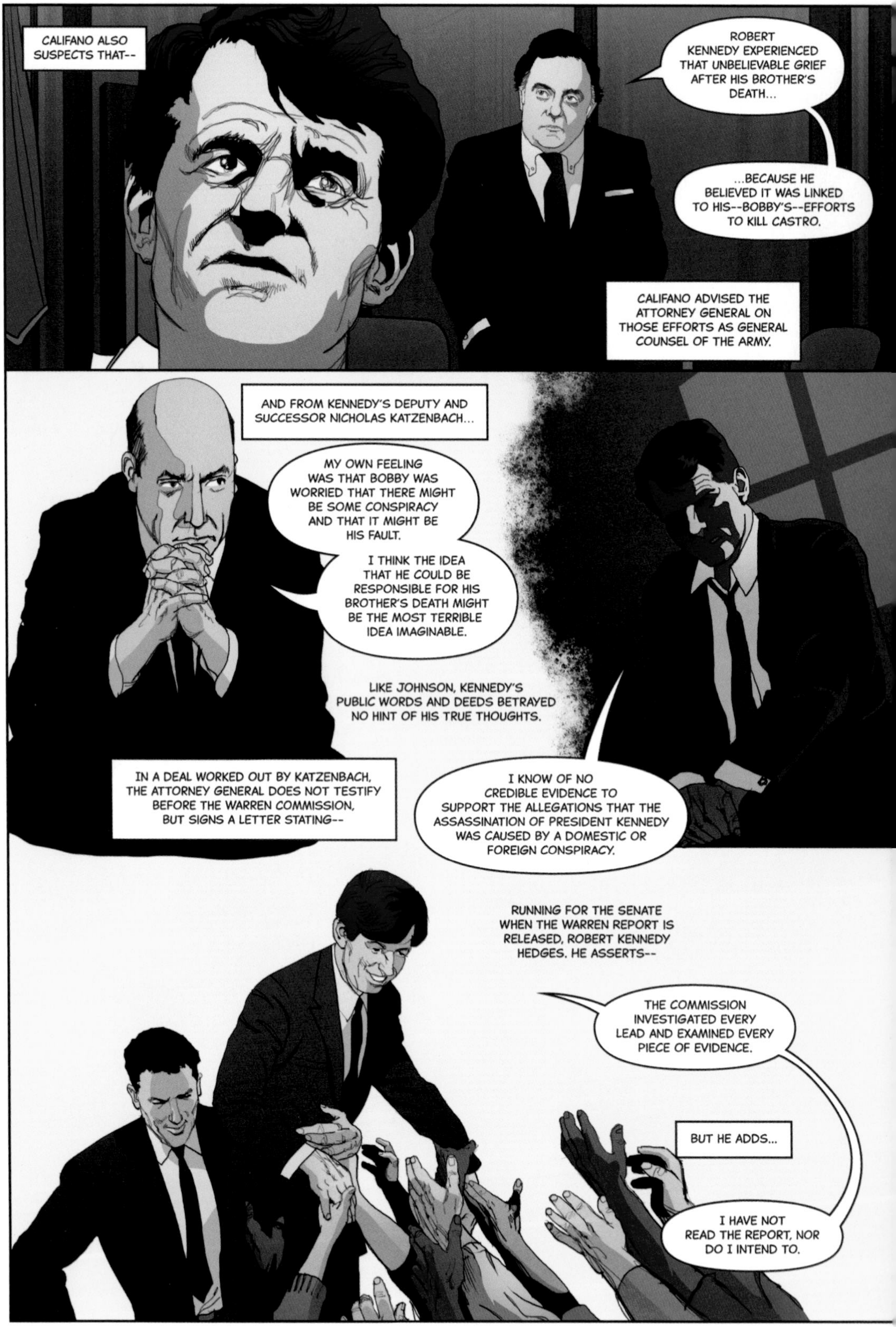

CALIFANO ALSO SUSPECTS THAT--
ROBERT KENNEDY EXPERIENCED THAT UNBELIEVABLE GRIEF AFTER HIS BROTHER'S DEATH...
...BECAUSE HE BELIEVED IT WAS LINKED TO HIS--BOBBY'S--EFFORTS TO KILL CASTRO.
CALIFANO ADVISED THE ATTORNEY GENERAL ON THOSE EFFORTS AS GENERAL COUNSEL OF THE ARMY.
AND FROM KENNEDY'S DEPUTY AND SUCCESSOR NICHOLAS KATZENBACH...
MY OWN FEELING WAS THAT BOBBY WAS WORRIED THAT THERE MIGHT BE SOME CONSPIRACY AND THAT IT MIGHT BE HIS FAULT.
I THINK THE IDEA THAT HE COULD BE RESPONSIBLE FOR HIS BROTHER'S DEATH MIGHT BE THE MOST TERRIBLE IDEA IMAGINABLE.
LIKE JOHNSON, KENNEDY'S PUBLIC WORDS AND DEEDS BETRAYED NO HINT OF HIS TRUE THOUGHTS.
IN A DEAL WORKED OUT BY KATZENBACH, THE ATTORNEY GENERAL DOES NOT TESTIFY BEFORE THE WARREN COMMISSION, BUT SIGNS A LETTER STATING--
I KNOW OF NO CREDIBLE EVIDENCE TO SUPPORT THE ALLEGATIONS THAT THE ASSASSINATION OF PRESIDENT KENNEDY WAS CAUSED BY A DOMESTIC OR FOREIGN CONSPIRACY.
RUNNING FOR THE SENATE WHEN THE WARREN REPORT IS RELEASED, ROBERT KENNEDY HEDGES. HE ASSERTS--
THE COMMISSION INVESTIGATED EVERY LEAD AND EXAMINED EVERY PIECE OF EVIDENCE.
BUT HE ADDS...
I HAVE NOT READ THE REPORT, NOR DO I INTEND TO.

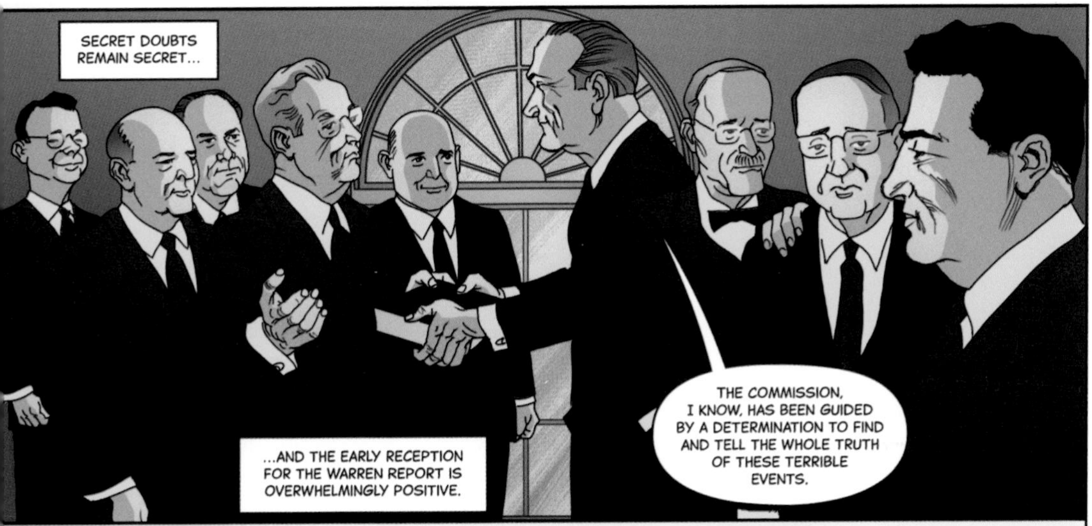
SECRET DOUBTS REMAIN SECRET...
...AND THE EARLY RECEPTION FOR THE WARREN REPORT IS OVERWHELMINGLY POSITIVE.
THE COMMISSION, I KNOW, HAS BEEN GUIDED BY A DETERMINATION TO FIND AND TELL THE WHOLE TRUTH OF THESE TERRIBLE EVENTS.

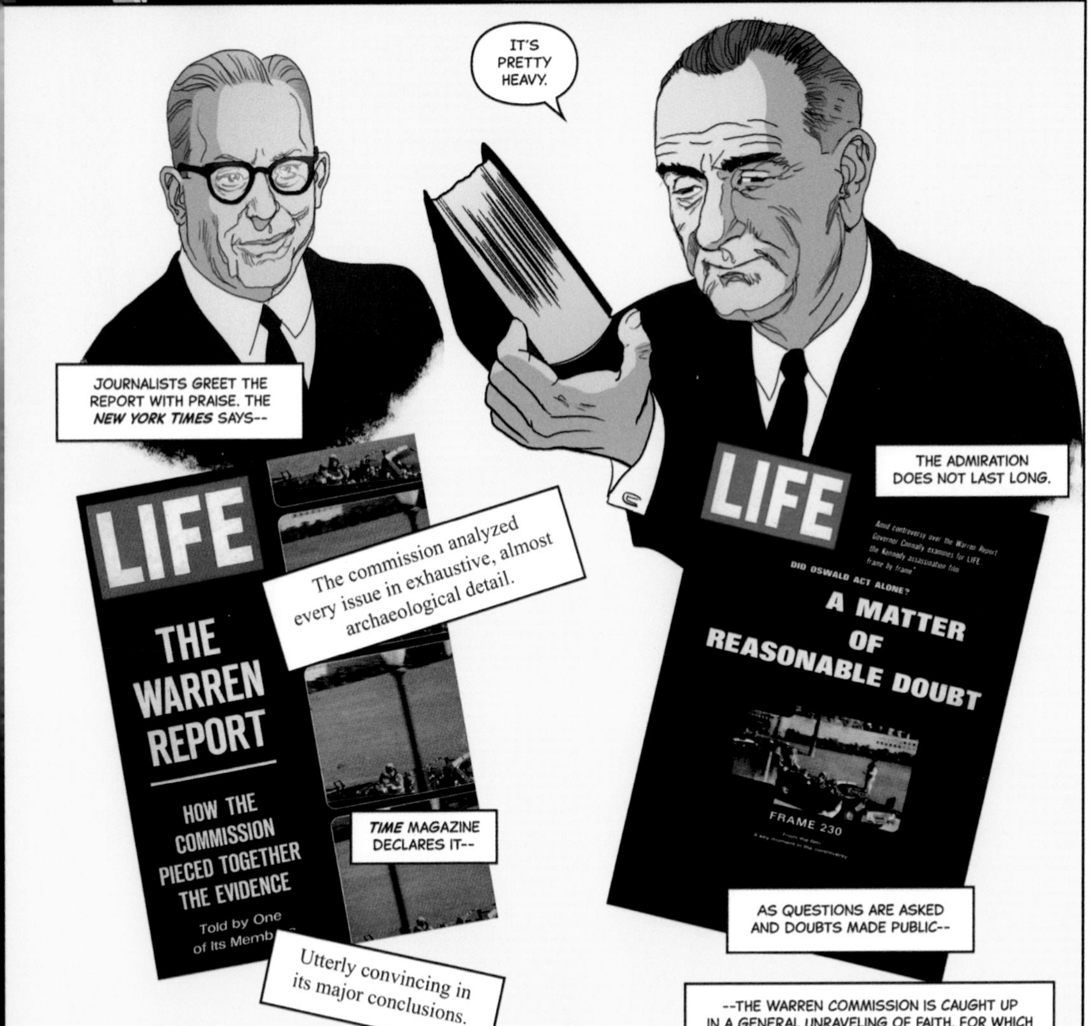
IT'S PRETTY HEAVY.
JOURNALISTS GREET THE REPORT WITH PRAISE. THE *NEW YORK TIMES* SAYS--
LIFE
THE WARREN REPORT
HOW THE COMMISSION PIECED TOGETHER THE EVIDENCE
Told by One of Its Memb
The commission analyzed every issue in exhaustive, almost archaeological detail.
TIME MAGAZINE DECLARES IT--
Utterly convincing in its major conclusions.
THE ADMIRATION DOES NOT LAST LONG.
LIFE
Amid controversy over the Warren Report Governor Connally examines for LIFE the Kennedy assassination film frame by frame
DID OSWALD ACT ALONE?
A MATTER OF REASONABLE DOUBT
FRAME 230
AS QUESTIONS ARE ASKED AND DOUBTS MADE PUBLIC--
--THE WARREN COMMISSION IS CAUGHT UP IN A GENERAL UNRAVELING OF FAITH, FOR WHICH IT BEARS AT LEAST PARTIAL RESPONSIBILITY.

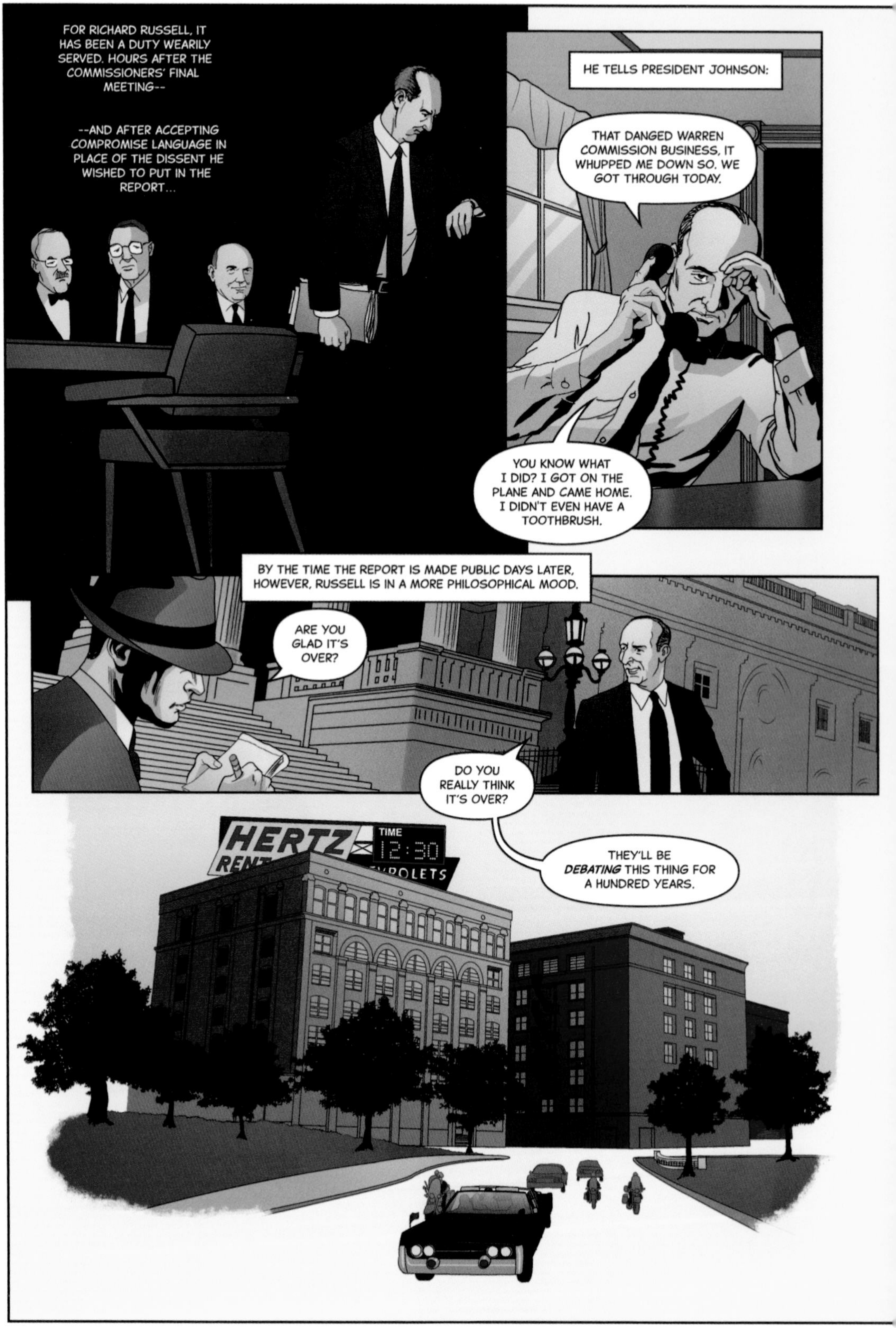

FOR RICHARD RUSSELL, IT HAS BEEN A DUTY WEARILY SERVED. HOURS AFTER THE COMMISSIONERS' FINAL MEETING--
--AND AFTER ACCEPTING COMPROMISE LANGUAGE IN PLACE OF THE DISSENT HE WISHED TO PUT IN THE REPORT...
HE TELLS PRESIDENT JOHNSON:
THAT DANGED WARREN COMMISSION BUSINESS, IT WHUPPED ME DOWN SO. WE GOT THROUGH TODAY.
YOU KNOW WHAT I DID? I GOT ON THE PLANE AND CAME HOME. I DIDN'T EVEN HAVE A TOOTHBRUSH.
BY THE TIME THE REPORT IS MADE PUBLIC DAYS LATER, HOWEVER, RUSSELL IS IN A MORE PHILOSOPHICAL MOOD.
ARE YOU GLAD IT'S OVER?
DO YOU REALLY THINK IT'S OVER?
HERTZ
TIME 12:30
THEY'LL BE *DEBATING* THIS THING FOR A HUNDRED YEARS.

AFTERWORD FROM THE AUTHOR

I was ten years old in 1963, when John F. Kennedy was murdered. That summer, I'd seen the movie *PT 109,* recounting the future president's exploits as a naval officer, and in the fall I checked a book out of the library on the same subject. I hadn't yet finished the book on November 22, when I was playing Frisbee with my best friend on our suburban street—we were home from school for parent-teacher conferences—and my little brother came out of the house with the horrifying news.

I share a version of that scene in the early pages of this volume. Not because my personal story is important in itself, but because it stands, at least in part, for a larger one: the story of a changing America in the post–World War II era. It also illustrates that this was one of those moments in history that, for many who live through them, utterly divide experience and memory into "before" and "after."

And while my experience is not the subject of this book, it has slowly dawned on me that it *is* the reason I wrote it.

I came to this project not as a historian or a journalist—I'm neither of those—but as a product of my times, a child of the baby boom and of the booming suburbs. The grandson of an immigrant bus driver and the son of a lawyer, on a family journey toward the dream of American prosperity that began to come true for many in those times. My own dreams were more inspired by the comic books and science-fiction novels I devoured, in the rocket launches from Cape Canaveral—in tales of courage and of unimpeded progress in technology, and of less certain strides toward social justice.

I don't recall assassinations being plot points in those stories. They didn't turn on some blink-of-an-eye upending of a whole worldview. Even the discovery of alien civilizations, or Godzilla rising from the sea, came off as only temporary interruptions of a settled way of life. The heroes triumphed in the end, and order was safely restored. But the Warren Report restored order only in the most superficial way, its conclusions bringing neither triumph nor a happy ending.

I can't remember clearly what happened after we went into the house that day and heard the news confirmed on the radio. I must have been too stunned to process anything else just then. In a way, I'm still stunned.

What I was surprised to learn as I began to research and write this graphic novel was that I never really got over Kennedy's assassination. When books appeared that challenged the findings of the Warren Commission—particularly Mark Lane's *Rush to Judgment,* which I read with the same enthusiasm I brought to comics and outer-space adventures—I could be counted among the many Americans who doubted the official story. I believed there was a hidden truth that might still be discovered . . . that maybe, with some diligence, I might be the one to discover it.

But diligence wasn't my strong suit back then, and soon my anguish over JFK's death receded—or at least I avoided it—before the more immediate concerns of schoolwork and girls and further assassinations and an escalating foreign war that I might one day be sent to fight in. I realize now, though, that the anguish was more present than I knew. That grief, not politics, was the reason I wore a campaign-style button emblazoned with a drawing of Lyndon Johnson and the words, "Where is Lee Harvey Oswald now that we really need him?"

If I'd been called out on my reasons, I would have pretended otherwise. In college in the early seventies I was cynically amused by a satire that imagined away the assassinations of recent years and made Robert Kennedy his brother's successor . . . but found the nation just as bogged down in Southeast Asia and just as divided. I laughed at the joke that goes, "Aside from that, Mrs. Lincoln, how did you enjoy the play?" And when a friend who must have disagreed with Mark Twain's quip that humor is tragedy plus time—or had not yet learned to fake a cool detachment from the events that shaped our lives—asked if I thought it would be just as funny to say, "Aside from that, Mrs. Kennedy, how did you enjoy the trip to Dallas?" I told her that I thought it was hilarious, lying to us both.

As time went on, I made my way through the world the tumultuous sixties had left us. I married, raised a family, became a writer of the kinds of stories that had sustained me in childhood. I didn't much follow the trickle of revelations or the continuing arguments about Kennedy's murder, didn't go to see Oliver Stone's film *JFK.*

When the fiftieth anniversary approached, the idea of writing about the Warren Report sprang to mind. Not as a way to revisit my earlier obsession, but to reunite with my friend and former collaborator Ernie Colón, whose graphic adaptation of the 9/11 Report is a great example of the way comics can clarify a complex subject. My goal would be neither to parrot the conclusions of the Warren Commission nor to "solve" the mystery of the assassination; it would be to demonstrate just how much mystery still remains despite the Commission's efforts to deny it.

And then I began my research. "OK," I told myself as I read the Summary and Conclusions chapter that opens the Warren Report, "this really is a lot more open-and-shut than I remember and that the critics give the Commission credit for." But it doesn't take very long to see how much nuance is left out by the Report's peremptory prose, or to grow angry at being told in effect not to question the wisdom of those in authority. I'm quick to recall that the "Establishment's" clinging to the prerogatives of power didn't work out so well for those of us who lived through the disastrous foreign policy of the ensuing decade.

The old and buried feelings truly come rushing to the surface, though, as I review the evidence, and especially the images, from that long-ago day in Dallas. There is of course the horror of Zapruder frame 313, with its violent spray of blood and brain from the president's head, and the pictures of the lifeless body (whether autopsy photos or drawings meticulously copied from them, and whether authenticated or not). Yet while the gore could be sickening, that was not what most disturbed me. My strongest reaction was to the images from *before* the shooting began. And it was not so much about what those images depict as what they fail to show.

It's painful to watch the vigorous young president arriving at Love Field and the cheering crowds along the motorcade route, when I know what is to come. Knowing that the world as I understood it then is about to fall apart. And that this is only the beginning.

Preparing to write about the sequence of shots in Dealey Plaza, I turn again to the Zapruder film and to the three or four seconds—fifty or sixty some odd frames—before Kennedy reacts to being hit. This is meant to be research, to pin down what facts I can. I'm looking for signs that it was the first shot from the Book Depository that missed its target, not a later one. And signs are there: Governor Connally turning to the right, as he said he did upon hearing the rifle's crack; Rosemary Willis in her red skirt, ten years old (*my age*), skipping to keep pace with the limo and then slowing, stopping, turning.

But signs are not certainties. And as I play and replay the frames on my computer screen—forward, backward, slowly, at speed—I'm unexpectedly struck by a wave of anxiety. What is *that* about?

Once I calm myself down, I know: It's not just anticipating the awful instants that await, not just my wish that I might stop them from actually happening as easily as I freeze the image. It's not the lingering unknowns about the missed shot. It's that I'm *looking* for something. A person, a movement, an answer—the tiny thing that no one else has noticed before but that once seen, at last, explains it all.

I don't believe that such a thing exists, desperate though I may still be to see it. Not in those moments before the president disappears behind the Stemmons Freeway sign; not, I think, in the violent movements of his head; and not in the shapes that some find lurking in other photographs of that afternoon. To see those shapes, I think one must first will them to be there. I tried to will into existence, at the side of a skipping little girl, the answer to all my questions.

Look the right way at a grainy snapshot of the grassy knoll and you can see the figure of the so-called "badge man" ("shown" on page 58 of this book). And if I say that those who make him out are also in a fashion making him *up,* I don't mean to call anyone a liar. The human brain evolved to recognize patterns, after all. We seek them out—both in images and in sets of facts—and we're prone to find them even when they aren't really there. When we're powerless and hopeless in the face of tragedy, the impulse to hunt for some explanatory order must be even more compelling. To make sense of senselessness: what a comfort that offers.

On all sides of the assassination debate—conspiracy theorists and lone-gunman theorists, those who would challenge authority and those who wish to lay the dust—I think there is at least a little bit of this longing for the final, all-encompassing explanation, the desire to know what can't be known for sure. I can't count how many comments I've read on assassination websites that contain the words, "It's obvious that . . ." and then I've scrolled down the page with a sigh. If it really were that obvious, I don't believe the debates would still be quite so loud and unruly.

I wanted so much to see that thing that wasn't there—to find my answers in the fading, flickering light of fifty years ago—that it left me breathless. And feeling nearly as bereft as my ten-year-old self.

New answers and new evidence may in fact be out there, in CIA records or in still-secret archives. But I think it's time now for me to accept uncertainty and learn to live with it. I only wish the Warren Commission had tried to do the same.

To be too certain carries dangers of its own.

—Dan Mishkin

SELECTED BIBLIOGRAPHY

The number of books, articles, and websites devoted to the assassination of John F. Kennedy is almost uncountable. It's possible to read and research for months on end and still leave a mountain of material untouched.

For those who want to learn more about the events leading up to November 22, 1963, and about the investigations that followed, these books and websites provided valuable information and points of view in the preparation of this volume. They cover a range of opinions, from support of the Warren Commission's findings to suggestions of conspiracy against the president in the very heart of government. The references cited here are generally even-tempered, no matter what perspective they bring; that's something that cannot be said of a large percentage of the writing on the subject.

BOOKS

Bugliosi, Vincent. *Reclaiming History: The Assassination of President John F. Kennedy.* New York: W. W. Norton & Company, 2007.

Chambers, G. Paul. *Head Shot: The Science behind the JFK Assassination.* Amherst, NY: Prometheus Books, 2010.

Kurtz, Michael R. *The JFK Assassination Debates: Lone Gunman versus Conspiracy.* Lawrence, KS: University Press of Kansas, 2006.

McKnight, Gerald D. *Breach of Trust: How the Warren Commission Failed the Nation and Why.* Lawrence, KS: University Press of Kansas, 2005.

Manchester, William. *The Death of a President: November 20–November 25, 1963.* New York: Back Bay Books, 2013.

Newman, John. *Oswald and the CIA: The Documented Truth about the Unknown Relationship between the U.S. Government and the Alleged Killer of JFK.* New York: Skyhorse Publishing, 2008.

Posner, Gerald. *Case Closed: Lee Harvey Oswald and the Assassination of JFK.* New York: Random House, 1993.

Shenon, Philip. *A Cruel and Shocking Act: The Secret History of the Kennedy Assassination.* New York: Henry Holt and Co., 2013.

The Warren Commission. *Report of the President's Commission on the Assassination of President John F. Kennedy.* Washington, DC: U.S. Government Printing Office, 1964. The entire thing can be a slog, but it's worth reading at least the opening chapter of the Warren Report to get the essence of the Commission's case. It's available in book form and online at www.archives.gov/research/jfk/warren-commission-report. The website also has a link to a PDF of the original published Report.

A pair of recent novels turned out to be useful in illuminating issues surrounding the assassination—about the deeper truths of human nature that underlie the superficial facts, and about the fascinating world of ballistics—as well as being enjoyable reads:

King, Stephen. *11/22/63.* New York: Scribner, 2011.

Hunter, Stephen. *The Third Bullet.* New York: Simon & Schuster, 2013.

WEBSITES

The Assassination of President John F. Kennedy: A Lone-Gunman Point of View: www.davidvonpein.blogspot.com

The Kennedy Assassination: mcadams.posc.mu.edu/home.htm

JFK Lancer: www.jfklancer.com

Secrets of a Homicide: JFK Assassination: www.jfkfiles.com

JFK Facts: jfkfacts.org

JFKcountercoup: www.jfkcountercoup.blogspot.com

Mary Ferrell Foundation: www.maryferrell.org

ACKNOWLEDGMENTS

Thanks to the many people who helped make this book possible, beginning with our families, who patiently accommodated the long hours spent working on the project and put up with unending discourses on conspiracy theories, the unreliability of information found online, and the traditional complaints of comic book writers about artists and artists about writers.

Special thanks to our agent, Charlie Olsen, for his encouragement and for guiding the original concept toward a workable reality, and for lots of handholding along the way; and to Carol Burrell and Charles Kochman at Abrams ComicArts for their insights and support, along with their challenging questions that resulted in a more effective finished product. We owe big buckets of gratitude as well to the rest of the dedicated team at Abrams: book designers Katie Fitch and Meagan Bennett, managing editor Jen Graham, plus Melissa Esner from the Marketing department and Maya Bradford from Publicity.

Dan Mishkin would like to thank Ed Rosenbaum, who took the photograph that is reproduced in panel 2 on page 147 and originally appeared in our high school yearbook, and Ira Luft, our classmate shown in the photo. He'd also like to thank friends from the South Side High School (Rockville Centre, New York) class of 1970, who shared their own recollections of November 22, 1963.

Additional thanks must go to the many writers who have carefully reviewed the evidence in the assassination of John F. Kennedy and drawn conclusions that, in conflicting with one another, describe the nature of the historical problem. Of particular value was the late Richard Hofstadter's essay "The Paranoid Style in American Politics." Although Professor Hofstadter did not write about the assassination, he provided a way of understanding the conditions in which that event occurred and the casts of mind through which it was experienced.

Finally, Jerzy Drozd would like to thank his color production assistant, Rachel Polk, without whose efforts the completion of the art would have been impossible.

ABOUT THE AUTHORS

DAN MISHKIN is a comic book writer with more than thirty years' experience, including work for DC, Marvel, and Image Comics, and on Superman, Wonder Woman, Batman, and Star Trek adaptions. With Ernie Colón, he is co-creator of the fantasy series Amethyst, Princess of Gemworld, and is also the co-founder of Kids Read Comics, a nonprofit that promotes lifelong literacy and creative expression for children and teens. Dan Mishkin grew up on Long Island, New York, and spent most of his adulthood in East Lansing, Michigan. He and his wife, a physician, currently reside again in East Lansing.

ERNIE COLÓN has illustrated comics for more than five decades. His distinguished nonfiction track record includes the *New York Times* bestseller *The 9/11 Report: A Graphic Adaptation,* praised for the expert translation to illustration of its politically charged subject. He has worked at Harvey, Marvel, and DC Comics, and created Amethyst, Princess of Gemworld with author Dan Mishkin. He and his wife live in Huntington, New York.

JERZY DROZD has worked on Antarctic Press's *Ninja High School* as well as projects for Marvel Comics and others. He shares his passion for comics by teaching workshops in libraries and schools and is co-founder of the annual Kids Read Comics festival. He lives in Ann Arbor, Michigan, with his wife and two cats.